I0759388

AMERICAN GRAMMAR

Also by Jarvis R. Givens

School Clothes
Fugitive Pedagogy

AMERICAN GRAMMAR

Race, Education, *and the* Building of a Nation

JARVIS R. GIVENS

HARPER
An Imprint of HarperCollins*Publishers*

hc.com

FIRST EDITION

Designed by Bonni Leon-Berman

Library of Congress Cataloging-in-Publication Data has been applied for.

ISBN 978-0-06-325915-7

25 26 27 28 29 LBC 5 4 3 2 1

To Annabelle Davis Singleton and Clementine Davis Martin—
thank you for the gift of your stories all those years ago;
they helped me see the traces.

CONTENTS

AMERICAN GRAMMAR

INTRODUCTION: SUSAN'S MARK
ACCOUNTING FOR THE BLACK AND NATIVE PRESENCE IN AMERICAN EDUCATION

> Invisible things are not necessarily "not there." . . .
> Certain absences are so stressed, so ornate, so
> planned, they call attention to themselves. . . .
>
> —Toni Morrison, "Unspeakable Things Unspoken" (1988)

Susan McCoy arrived at the "Old Goodland" school, located in present-day Oklahoma, on May 11, 1899. The forty-seven-year-old Afro-native woman's purpose was not to attend class at this school in the Choctaw nation, but instead to appear before the Commission to the Five Civilized Tribes, also known as the Dawes Commission, to have her name placed on the tribal rolls.[1] In these final years of the nineteenth century, the United States government began forcing the Choctaw nation to break up and distribute its communally stewarded lands among individual citizens and families within the tribe. Enrollment was a first step in the process. Beginning in 1898, both native and black citizens of the Choctaw nation journeyed to enrollment stations like Goodland to be registered.

When speaking to the enrollment clerk at Goodland, Susan described being born in 1852 to an enslaved black mother named Polly who was owned by a Choctaw man named Sam Colbert, and she described living in the Choctaw nation all her life. Susan recalled that like her mother, she was also the property of "Old man Colbert." However, her father was a man named Martin Guess. When describing her father, she explained, he "was a Choctaw man, come here with the Indians from old Mississippi, lived there with them, and died here."[2]

Following the Indian Removal Act of 1830, the US government violently compelled many tribes, including the Choctaw, to leave their ancestral homelands in the Southeast and settle in new territories west of the Mississippi River. Martin Guess, Susan's father, was a slave owner of European ancestry who moved with the Choctaw nation during this time and who was adopted by the tribe. It is very likely that Susan's mother also traveled with her enslaver, Sam Colbert, during this traumatic journey, commonly referred to as the Trail of Tears.

During her enrollment process with the Dawes Commission, Susan shared some additional details: She had five children with her late husband of thirty-three years, a Choctaw man named Oliver "Boss" McCoy, whom she married shortly after the Civil War; he passed away in 1896. Susan stressed to the Dawes Commission clerk that although she and her children were all "colored," they were also of known Choctaw ancestry. Susan was clear about this last detail because such genealogical information had direct implications on how Choctaw land would be allotted to her. It is worth noting that such details regarding Susan and her children's citizenship status and blood ties were previously substantiated by the Choctaw census rolls of 1885.

Susan's personal history is important, and so too is the story of the school, Old Goodland. This was an enrollment site with a complicated history, as the institution persisted through many transformations within the Choctaw nation. The roots of this boarding school date back to 1835, when the school grounds first received its name from a Choctaw phrase—"Yakni Achukma"—meaning "good land." It emerged amid the period of native removal under President Andrew Jackson, as the Choctaw nation worked to rebuild itself in Indian Territory. Before Goodland became a boarding school during the antebellum period, it was a mission station established in 1835 by missionary Cyrus Kingsbury. This was one year before the Choctaw adopted an anti-literacy law criminalizing education for enslaved people like Susan. As established in 1836 by the constitution and laws of the Choctaw nation, the code read: "Teaching slaves how to read, to write or to sing in meeting-houses or schools or in any open place, without the consent of the owner, or allowing them to sit at a table with him shall be sufficient ground to convict persons of favoring the principles and notions of abolitionism."[3] The punishment for violating such laws ranged from whippings and fines to banishment from the Choctaw nation altogether.

This proscription among the Choctaw nation derived from the racial grammars of education law and policy in the United States. For indeed, the earliest anti-literacy law in North America dates back to 1740, when the colonial legislature of South Carolina passed an act prohibiting the teaching of enslaved people how to write in response to the Stono Slave Rebellion, as the white colonists suspected that these people who were their property used the written word to coordinate and execute their plot.[4] Anti-literacy laws were a key mechanism of social control for African-descendant people as a subjugated population within the Choctaw nation, as it was in the broader context of the United States. Importantly, the Choctaw law criminalized black education at a time when the US government and missionaries worked to expand native schooling in service of "civilizing" indigenous peoples, and as many Choctaw leaders advocated for a centralized national education system to prove their capacity for civilization. The Choctaw elite appropriated settler schooling as a defense mechanism: By performing Western notions of civilization, through schooling, homesteading, and even through racial slavery, tribal leaders hoped to fend off continued US settler encroachment and assert Choctaw sovereignty on new terms. In this context, the Choctaw nation—like most Southern states in antebellum America—criminalized the education of African-descendant people as an effort to suppress the spread of the antislavery movement in Indian Territory. There was a direct relationship between the political economy of race and schooling in the United States and that which formed in the Choctaw nation, as well as other indigenous tribes.

Goodland was not the first mission established by Cyrus Kingsbury. The missionary had also founded Brainerd in 1816 among the Cherokee nation, a mission school that was effectively the first federally funded native boarding school. I understand Brainerd as such because Kingsbury founded the school with funding from the US Department of War while also receiving strong endorsements from Presidents Madison and Jefferson. The latter endorsement is particularly important given

Jefferson's widely recognized role as a founding father of public education in the United States.

Brainerd and Goodland were alike in many ways: Both were white-run boarding schools for native students and, furthermore, both were built and maintained, in part, by enslaved black people. Regarding the white missionaries' reliance on enslaved labor, Kingsbury wrote: "There was no avoiding all contact with it," referring to slavery within the Choctaw nation. "The large boarding school establishments, and other multiplied and constant labors, in a hot and sickly climate, *then* as well as *now*, made the employment of considerable slave labor indispensable."[5] This dependence on enslaved black labor at Goodland ended only after the Choctaw nation was forced to emancipate enslaved people by the Reconstruction Treaty of 1866.

However, before freedom arrived for black people in Indian Territory, Goodland was a military camp for the Confederate army. During the Civil War, Choctaw soldiers set up tents near the school's well while fighting on the opposing side of the Union.[6] It was common to use school sites as barracks and political stations among the Cherokee, Chickasaw, Choctaw, Creek, and Seminole nations—commonly referred to by white settlers in the past as the Five "Civilized" Tribes—and the practice was also common among US government officials working in Indian Territory. Schools were some of the most well-built physical structures within these nations. These political sites also accrued great symbolic value among the Choctaw as the nation worked to redefine itself after being forced to remove from their homelands; and as formal Western education became a key instrument in nation building, mirroring relations between race, power, and schooling in the broader US context.

It is as though Goodland's history as a school site anticipated the function it would serve by the end of the nineteenth century, when Susan McCoy arrived to register and assert her Choctaw identity. How appropriate that the Dawes Commission set up its enrollment station at a settler-colonial school site, given that the commission's aims were so explicitly pedagogical. Indeed, tribal enrollment and land allotment were extensions of long-standing aims of US education policies toward native people. In 1887, Congress passed the General Allotment Act—

better known as the Dawes Act—and while the legislation was framed as an effort to help native people assimilate into American society, by partitioning lands previously held in common into individual plots to encourage homesteading and self-sufficiency, this was only a partial truth. As Lakota historian Nick Estes writes, this act fundamentally "aimed to sever Native tribes and families onto separate, individual plots of acreage without concern for traditional community life by breaking up communal land."[7] At stake for the US government and American citizens was the fact that allotment also opened more territory to be privatized and available for immediate settler expansion.

Enrollment and allotment were about teaching native people to be in a new kind of relationship with land. It was an intentional disruption of tribal relations and identities—a heritage that was fundamentally based on collective kinship, not just among people, but also to land (and waters). Allotment was a pedagogical lesson meant to teach native people to see land, not as a living thing, but only as property to be individually owned—fenced in, borders drawn, cultivated for personal consumption and commercial purposes, both natural resource and raw capital to be used for predatory forms of wealth accumulation.[8]

The Cherokee, Chickasaw, Choctaw, Creek, and Seminole nations were initially excluded from the Dawes Act's forced allotment process—that is, until Congress passed the Curtis Act of 1893, which assembled the Dawes Commission to negotiate with the Five Tribes and extend allotment into these nations as well. Despite their model-minority status as "more civilized" than other indigenous nations, the United States worked to dissolve their tribal governments as it previously did with others. In 1897 the United States government established the Atoka Agreement with the Chickasaw and Choctaw nations, and it outlined the process of land allotment for two distinct categories of citizens: those who were citizens "by blood" and those who were "freedmen." Such legal designations would have great implications for people like Susan and her children.

Freedmen was a legal term for black citizens within the Five Tribes (presumably without any known native ancestry), most of whom were formerly enslaved or descendants of formerly enslaved people within the tribe. Citizens "by blood" was a category applied to individuals deemed natural, or biological, descendants of indigenous members within the tribe.[9] Such categories were fraught, and they were heavily contested. Yet, based on these faulty divisions, the Atoka Agreement established that land allotments for Chickasaw and Choctaw freedmen would be distributed in the amount of forty acres, and allotments for citizens "by blood" should amount to 320 acres.[10]

The inequitable distribution of land between freedmen and citizens by blood reflected deep-seated racial politics within Indian Territory. This also served an explicitly educational function. The allotment process administered at Old Goodland reinforced anti-indigenous and antiblack ideas long taught and rehearsed through protocols of schooling within the American social order, and such lessons were endemic to "the white man's world of paper." As explained by Estes, this "rational world of the white man—as personified in paper relations and transactions—was transposed onto the world of Indigenous relations, typically enacted through kinship and relation to the land."[11] Tribal enrollment and land allotment were prime examples of how the white man's world of paper intruded on indigenous ways of being. What's more, the racial politics of this world of paper extended far beyond the bureaucratic processes of the Dawes Commission; it extended from interactions between literacy, formal education, and social hierarchies of power informed by racial ideas in the United States. Indeed, this world of paper was structured by race, and it formed the foundation of formal education and knowledge production. This broader educational world was literally and symbolically represented by Old Goodland; it was also expressed through the very mandate of the enrollment station assembled at this school by the Dawes Commission.

This relationship between race, power, and schooling is also sharply reflected in Susan McCoy's personal enrollment story, as this unschooled woman set out to register herself and her children as citizens in the Choctaw nation entitled to equal rights and opportunity. Though Susan provided testimony and evidence of her and her children's known Choctaw heritage, this Afro-native woman experienced a kind of erasure and dispossession that was, unfortunately, a perpetual reality for black and native people.

When Susan arrived at Goodland, she faced a bureaucratic process run by the Dawes Commission that was extremely difficult for tribal communities. The enrollment process was even further complicated for Afro-native citizens, as white commission clerks engaged in actions that reflected antiblack sentiments that long existed in the American social order, and that ultimately conditioned race relations among the Five Tribes as well. As explained by genealogical scholar and descendant of Choctaw freedmen Terry Ligon, "many of those who would apply were illiterate, making the application process difficult." This difficulty was intensified by the fact that instructions for enrollment often reached freedmen communities late. These delayed notices forced formerly enslaved people and their children "to gather documents and witnesses to testify on their behalf" on short notice, at times having to travel to enrollment locations that were considerable "miles away from their homes at great expense."[12] For individuals like Susan, who could not read and write, illiteracy exacerbated an already cumbersome process because it forced them to rely on government officials who had proven themselves unworthy of such trust. During the enrollment process, commission clerks abused their authority by making assessments about native and Afro-native peoples' identities based on racially motivated value judgments concerning who they deemed worthy of certain rights and privileges.

The enrollment station at Goodland itself was also racially segregated. Susan explained, when she appeared before the commission: "Indians [enrolled] at one table and colored people at one table."[13] Despite being forced to enroll at the table for freedmen—again, a legal term for black Choctaw citizens without any known native ancestry—Susan explained to the enrollment clerk that both she and her children were also Choctaw. Susan had always understood herself to be a black woman who was Indian as well. Therefore, for her and her children, the idea of being either Choctaw "freedmen" or Choctaw "by blood" simply did not apply. Readers may find it interesting, or perhaps unsurprising, that no parallel category existed for those of European ancestry, and that individuals with white mothers had no issue being enrolled as citizens by blood. Such restrictions were enforced only on black women, and the children of black women.

As one freedman working for the commission later testified, the Dawes clerks informally enacted a policy "that those applicants who were born to slave mothers or to negro women who were descended of slaves, were freedmen, and would be enrolled as such only." He recalled commission officials instructing enrollment staff "to discontinue hearing the statement of applicants as to their Indian blood, as in no case would they be enrolled as Indian citizens."[14] Despite the commission's de facto policy behind the scene, Susan insisted on the classification that guaranteed her and her children the full rights to which they were entitled based on rules and policies imposed upon the Choctaw nation by the United States. Again, it is important to point out that Susan's negotiations of this complex terrain would have taken place within the white man's world of paper, an extremely complicated process for Susan as a woman who had been systematically barred from formal educational opportunities, having lived the first two decades of her life under the Choctaw nation's anti-literacy law which explicitly criminalized black education.

Susan later described what happened to her at the enrollment station, when she was written out of her rights by white clerks working for the Dawes Commission; white officials who, to be clear, colluded with Choctaw elites to systematically reduce citizens with African ancestry to a permanent underclass of people within the tribe. By her testimony, the enrollment clerk assured Susan that her family would not be enrolled as freedmen. She explained, when "they enrolled us, that is all my children . . . They said that my children ought not to come on the colored roll at all, ought to be on the Indian roll." It was not until someone asked Susan's daughter, Mary Jane, "how she come to be down on the colored roll and asked her, why aint you on the roll with your daddy," that Susan learned she and her family had been willfully misclassified by the Dawes Commission.[15]

White and native officials would assert that if a mistake took place during enrollment, it was Susan's own fault. The Choctaw nation's attorney later asked Susan, "If you were an Indian and claimed Indian rights why did you not go where the Indians were [at the enrollment station]?" Susan's response was simple: "Well, they would have pushed me away." Her appearance as a black woman—though of a light complexion—meant that she and her children were relegated to the black side of the color line in Indian Territory.

Like many native and Afro-native people, the McCoys were enrolled by Dawes Commission clerks working on behalf of the US Department of the Interior. If illiterate, these individuals were forced to blindly trust that information they provided was accurately written down and submitted. Susan's inability to read or write made the McCoys susceptible to what one Afro-native man referred to as a *pencil genocide* enacted by US government officials during the procedures of tribal enrollment and land allotment. Through these processes, native and Afro-native people fell through the cracks of bureaucratic procedure. They were written out of tribal citizenship and therefore denied land and formal recognition of who they were. Such pencil genocide also foreclosed untold names from written history, effectively erasing ancestors and future generations.[16] By intentionally misrepresenting on paper the identities of people like Susan and the McCoy children, enrollment clerks contributed to a violent purging experienced by countless native and Afro-native people.

The white man's world of paper had long been riddled by distortion, erasure, and appropriations of the written word for the exploitation of some and to the benefit of others. Such conquest authorized and enacted by pen and pencil stretched far and wide. Indeed, the world of paper did not begin or end with tribal enrollment or land allotment. Given my own expertise in education, I know paper to also be a metonym for laws and treaties, as well as the archival transcript that informs histories about the United States' past; it also alludes to written scripts of knowledge that narratively condemn black and native people.[17] This world of paper is a synecdoche for education in the modern world. It implies schoolbooks, religious instruction, and various other literary channels through which dominant ideologies are expressed and imposed upon the social context of human life.

There is a submerged history reflected in the clash between Susan's sense of self-definition and the ideas about her symbolized by the very structure of Old Goodland and the enrollment process that ensued at this school site. Though an illiterate woman, she went on to initiate a legal process to contest the actions of the Dawes Commission in 1906, petitioning the US government to transfer the names of her and her children to the rolls for Choctaw citizens by blood. It is only because of such action on the part of this formerly enslaved and unlettered Afro-native woman that I am able to tell her story; because in seeking justice, Susan McCoy left her mark within the settler-colonial archive.

It was like kismet. I first learned of Susan McCoy—my great-great-great grandmother—while conducting research for *American Grammar.* I was poking around the history of black education in Indian Territory, tracking how racial politics of education in the United States influenced similar developments among the Five Tribes, and I stumbled upon Susan because of her second surname, Brashears (from her second marriage). This name was shared by Richard Brashears, a Choctaw freedman who was arrested for planning a Colored Convention in Indian Territory in 1869. While pursuing more information about this political organizer and the story of black people's advocacy for education and citizenship across the Five Tribes, I encountered an excerpt of Susan's 1906 petition contesting her enrollment as a Choctaw freedman. I quickly recognized her first surname—McCoy—and the names of her first husband and children, which were listed in the excerpt. Susan McCoy Brashears was the mother of Mary Jane McCoy, the mother of my great-grandmother, Jewel McCoy Givens, and "Mama Jewel," as I knew her, was the mother of my grandfather, Jarvis Ray Givens, after whom my father and I were both named.

I sought out the original file for my ancestor's petition; and as I learned more about her story, I became increasingly sensitive to its connections to my intellectual concerns as a historian of education. I was in near disbelief when I learned that Old Goodland was Susan's enrollment site. However, the connection became most pronounced when I noticed that Susan McCoy signed her petition by mark. And it was this—her mark—that stuck with me the most.[18]

When I refer to *Susan's mark*, I mean this in a literal sense: that in place of a handwritten signature, Susan McCoy signed her 1906 petition by affixing an X to this legal document used to contest the actions of the Dawes Commission. Signing by mark was common for illiterate people negotiating the power-laden terrain of the white man's world of paper, and it was "considered legally valid when properly witnessed" by some designated officiant or notary.[19] Susan signed by mark because she was an illiterate woman, having been legally denied educational opportunities; yet Susan sought legal recourse as best she could. Though her petition did not end in her civic recognition being restored, the mark of this illiterate woman provides an important standpoint from when and where we might enter a more rigorous study of the educational past. For indeed, "the traces enslaved people [and their progeny] inserted into the archive ...defied the distortions built into the papers of slaveholders" as well as those left by powerful state actors working toward oppressive ends. Their traces "refuse silence" and provide intellectual resources for reading against the grain of imperfect historical sources, allowing for more expansive understandings of our world; understandings that account for the critical perspectives of the most vulnerable among us.[20]

Susan's mark emboldened me to tell a truer story of American

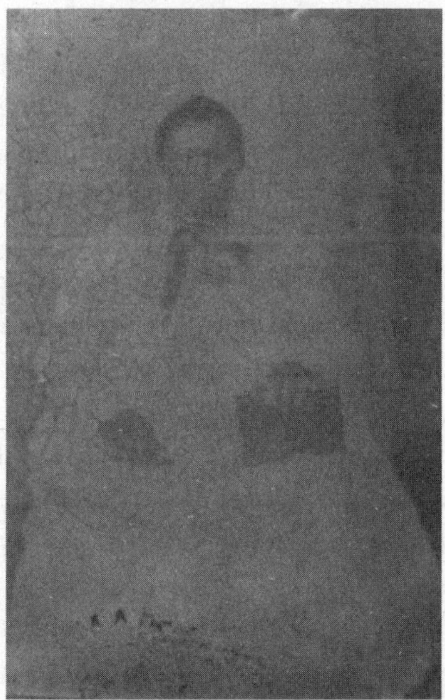

Portrait of Susan McCoy (1852–1927), courtesy of Jarita Givens.

educational beginnings. More specifically, it has challenged me to take seriously the intimate ties between schooling in the United States and the structural legacies of chattel slavery and native land dispossession. Furthermore, the fact that Susan was illiterate and unschooled invited me to think more expansively about the story of race, power, and education in American society and to recognize that a more holistic portrayal demands an accounting of both the administering of education as well as its intentional withholding. Thus I choose to situate the story of educational development in America as one that is always, simultaneously, a story about educational underdevelopment. On one hand, education in America has been a positive project, one focused on the creation of educational opportunities; on the other hand, it has also been about negation, where withholding and criminalizing education for certain people, as well as the suppression of certain kinds of knowledge, has also transpired. Such social realities in the foundation of education in the United States, I argue, have always been structured by the political and economic realities of race—particularly antiblackness and anti-indigeneity and their intimate relation within the racial order of white supremacy in the United States.

The story lurking underneath Susan's mark is a long, complicated history of education as a racial project in the American social order, and I insist that this history includes how forceful US Indian policy shaped the trajectory of formal education within native tribes through the nineteenth century.[21] In this work, I argue that despite the segregated nature of such racially specific educational developments for native, white, and black Americans, these distinct racial projects were all inextricably linked to one another. They were all part of broader developments of race and schooling within the United States. The links between such distinct institutional developments demonstrate how race has been relationally formed in US society, where the racialization of one group has always been defined over and against the racialization experienced by others.[22]

As white government officials expanded American education as a democratic project for white citizens, these same political actors were motivated to use distinct strategies of domination when it came to matters of black and native schooling.[23] For instance, education was violently imposed on native people as an effort to disappear indigenous ways of life, particularly indigenous relations to land, as white American political leaders sought to clear paths for continued US expansion and settler accumulation. At the same time, education was forcefully withheld from black people, particularly during slavery, when literacy became linked with black rebellion and abolition. By suppressing black education, white (and some native) political leaders sought to contain African Americans as an exploitable group of enslaved workers, and then as vulnerable free-wage laborers to be continuously exploited (or disposed of, in the case of the Five Tribes) after slavery was abolished. The former educational strategy, aimed at disappearing indigeneity, mirrored economically driven logics that informed rigid blood-quantum rules meant to shrink native populations. Conversely, the latter efforts to block African Americans' access to education mirrored distinct logics of the one-drop rule, which suggested that any trace of African ancestry, no matter how much or how little, determined one's racial status as black or nonblack; such an all-encompassing conception of black identity was linked to economic motivations, namely the expansion of property holdings for slave owners, and then containing blackness as a social position for those to be superexploited as laborers and for other extractive purposes in the racial regimes that emerged after the Civil War.

•••

I began this book about the history of US education with the story of a formerly enslaved woman of black and Choctaw heritage who could not read and write because her life exposes a deep-seated structural relationship at the center of the story, between the histories of native land dispossession, chattel slavery, and the social foundations of schooling in America. Indeed, to read Susan's story for its deeper conceptual lessons requires a proper literacy; it demands a decoding that accounts for the structural realities of antiblackness and anti-indigeneity in the American social order, and its distinct expression within the habitus of American education.

This concern about the structural context of race and education through the nineteenth century—the foundational century of the United States—is what led me to title this book *American Grammar.* Like all grammar books, this work is a resource for studying the structure of a thing; and in this case, I am concerned with the language of schooling that conditions our collective lives in the United States. Grammar, in a linguistic sense, is fundamentally about syntax and semantics, the technical structure of a statement in written or spoken form, and what it means that such ideas are expressed in the way that they are. This book aims to help us gain a deeper understanding of the structure of schooling—its syntax—as well as its meaning as derived from the distinct forms it came to take on in the foundational years of the United States—its semantics. I argue that education in the United States was arranged by a set of political-economic formations—namely chattel slavery and settler colonialism—that governed how different groups of people were to fit (or not fit) together based on their relationship to the nation's mode of production.

This book refuses national narratives pertaining to the country's development—especially those pertaining to the construction of US education—that fail to account for the enduring presence of black and native people. I refuse such narratives because I know black and native people are always already present in the story, despite their studious omission and marginality in the historical literature and public memory. I also refuse these narratives because I know they are built upon racialized silences that pose threats to any future for educational justice. For indeed, when we look under the hood, we find their lives and their dispossession to be integral parts of the engine moving the thing forward. The exploitation of their labor and land having been used in service of making the wheels turn in the interest of national expansion, and the building of American empire. This is the story at the heart of the matter when it comes to American school beginnings. Yet, until now, it is a story that has yet to be told.

Quiet as it's kept, silences can do as much, if not more, damage than loud racist caricatures and derogatory language. These latter forms of aggression are easy to identify and critique. Things rendered invisible, however, can often go unnamed and form a haunting presence. Silences play a vital role in racial domination, and particularly so in education. However, as the African American writer and theorist Toni Morrison noted, "invisible things are not necessarily 'not there.'" In fact, some "absences are so stressed, so ornate, so planned, they call attention to themselves." The absence of historical analyses attending to chattel slavery and settler colonialism in the stories told and retold about the origins of education in the United States are prime examples of unspoken details screaming out for scholarly attention—demanding to be noticed, accounted for, and allowed to aid in the collective quest for more freedom and justice, and for expanding our educational imaginations.[24]

In calling attention to such silences, one logically arrives at an important set of questions: How might we account for this collective amnesia in histories of American education? What led to our unseeing of such blatant truths hiding in plain sight? Stated more explicitly: How did the black and native presence become sculpted out of the origin stories told and retold about the political and economic development of schooling in early American society, even as their lives were so deeply intertwined with white Americans?

Part of this silence is certainly the result of studious omissions—intentional absences resulting from value judgments made by past scholars about whose stories are and are not important, the way silences have long been manufactured through processes of historical production.[25] However, such omissions can also be attributed to some notable conceptual missteps that are not intentionally deployed to erase the black and native presence. The latter being, perhaps, a less nefarious contributor to the silencing *American Grammar* sets out to correct—and again, I say, "perhaps."

A major lesson learned in writing this book is that we (both scholars and the American public) have struggled to see the relationality between histories of race and education, in part, because a language of exclusion has been the primary frame used to narrate the story of educational injustice in early US history. The language of exclusion has overwhelmingly framed histories of American education, and it distorts our understanding of how central racial domination was to the formation of American society and the institutions that maintain its coherence.[26] For these reasons, I turned to a language of domination as a more appropriate framing for conceptually situating this story. This distinction is about much more than a small pedantic point of clarification. For indeed, exclusion is not reducible to domination. To borrow from political theorist Danielle Allen, exclusion is an instrument of domination. While exclusion is preoccupied with the idea that certain groups are not included in some realm of the political order—in this case, American schools as sites of citizenship formation—domination is concerned with *how* they are inscribed in the political order, presuming that they are always already included and present in some way.[27] Allen clarifies that "exclusion is one of the methods used to effect domination and typically pinpoints the role of legal structures in that process." Furthermore, domination indexes the hierarchical nature of injustice in our political order ("on top" and "below") while exclusion functions along relatively horizontal lines ("inside" and "outside")—here, readers may imagine the image of a student being excluded from sitting at a lunch table with a more popular group of peers. Domination is always structural, whereas exclusion is more specific to interpersonal interactions, though it may express differential relations to power within a given structural context.

So, why is this distinction important for our reflections on the educational past? I argue that this distinction is critical because when we understand exclusion as the root of injustice, we rely on the faulty assumption that the political order and its institutions—such as American education—are sound and ideal on the inside. It can imply that such institutions are purely virtuous, despite evidence of vice all around them. Under such circumstances, some are led to believe that opening doors and "including" those previously excluded can achieve justice and correct past wrongs. Domination, on the other hand, makes clear that native and black Americans have always been within the political sphere, even during periods of their systematic exclusion from equal opportunity in US education, because America's political and economic development was built on their very subjection.

My turn to the intimate realities of domination as the overarching frame for interpreting power in US education, rather than exclusion, helps reveal essential truths: Early architects of American schooling were highly race-conscious when it came to education, and their interactions with (and awareness of) racialized others played a crucial role in determining the future of schooling in the nation. Indigenous, African, and European Americans were intimately bound up in the national project of schooling, though they had different relationships to power and opportunity within this educational landscape. While black and native people experienced educational domination, at times through their exclusion from educational opportunities altogether, we also know these groups were subjected to racial domination through their confinement to certain kinds of education (that is, segregated schools, boarding schools, industrial education, etc.) at other historical junctures. In this way, the native American boarding school and the materially inferior black segregated school were not anomalies in American education; like the white common school of the nineteenth century, they were indeed structural features of an ever-expanding *schooling apparatus of the United States* that always included the *founding racial triad*—a national educational landscape conditioned by distinct education aims (whether it be positive or subtractive forms of schooling) for native, white, and black people.[28]

Through the nineteenth century, a distinct racial grammar formed as the United States became explicitly defined as a white possession through the subjugation of black and native people.[29] If we can agree—and I hope we can—that chattel slavery and native land dispossession conditioned structural arrangements within the American social order, then there should also be agreement that these same structural arrangements informed how education developed as a vital expression of this very social world. Building from such widely documented facts, *American Grammar* sets out to explain how the structural realities of race shaped the conventions and customs of a national educational landscape created to express, govern, and maintain that social order. In the pages to come, I retrace how distinct parts of American education—as distinct racial projects of schooling—formed relationally.

To tell this history, I summon a wide-ranging cast of characters. Readers will meet white missionaries, like Cyrus Kingsbury from New Hampshire, who built a school for native students in 1817 with support from two US presidents and the secretary of war, while also relying on enslaved labor for the construction and maintenance of his boarding school. They will encounter James McDonald, a Choctaw boy from a slaveholding family in Mississippi Territory. McDonald was informally adopted by Thomas McKenney, a Maryland-based government official who led the charge to establish the Civilization Fund Act (CFA) of 1819—a historic, yet underappreciated piece of educational legislation. Readers will also encounter the story of white property owners like Alexander Dickson of Duplin County, North Carolina, whose will, in 1814, instructed that a portion of his slaves "be sold separate to the highest bidder" and that the proceeds go toward the county school fund. Educators like Margaret Douglass will appear, a white woman who was arrested in the 1850s for teaching black students to read in Virginia. They will also encounter a young James Garfield—future president of the United States—as a teenage student in antebellum Ohio, as he debated political issues of the day with his classmates. These scenes recorded in Garfield's diary reveal educational discussions on a range of topics, from the need to displace native people after the discovery of gold in California to whether black people were mentally inferior to whites. School curricula also take on the role of characters themselves, demonstrating how processes of racial formation transpired through written words on the page, providing scripts for human behavior in the social world. I will tell the story of an unnamed Afro-native girl shipped home from the Carlisle Indian Industrial School, a boarding school founded for native Americans in 1879, after her African ancestry was detected. Familiar figures like black educator and school founder Booker T. Washington and Yankton-Sioux writer, teacher, and activist Zitkala-Ša will also appear. I rely on their individual journeys, which intersect in unexpected ways, as windows into the deeply entrenched structural relationship between black, native, and white education within a rapidly expanding schooling apparatus of the United States. These narratives, together, tell a new story of American school beginnings, one where the founding racial triad is always present and accounted for.

American Grammar is organized into four distinct yet interrelated parts. Each part chronicles some piece of the larger story across multiple chapters, and the four sections intentionally overlap chronologically at times, thus reflecting how the stories, ideas, and events overlapped as history unfolded. Part I charts early developments in the racial project of American education, assessing various mechanisms of law and policy conditioning the national educational landscape for native, white, and black people through the first half of the nineteenth century while demonstrating their relationship to one another. Part II frames white settlers' development of native schooling as an expression of the American Indian Wars, and it also charts strategies employed by native people to resist racial domination in education. Part III turns to the unfamiliar story of black education in Indian Territory, and it underscores how schooling among the Five Tribes was always informed by both internal tribal dynamics as well as broader interactions with developments of race, power, and schooling in the United States. In Part IV, I center the familiar life of former slave and school founder Booker T. Washington only to then read his story in an unfamiliar way, exposing the structural relations between native, white, and black education reflected in the institutions, people, and ideas Washington encountered through the late nineteenth century.

In the telling of this history, I also hope to underscore how this grammar continues to structure our collective lives. For it is an inescapable truth that we have all been initiated into society through education in some intimate way. Applying a conscious awareness of this fact, I have chosen to pull along ghosts from my own past that offer important insights or that help guide me to new questions urgently in need of answering. By ghosts, I am referring to lessons and details from people and places I have encountered while writing this book, as well as educational and life experiences that primed me for the stories to be told—whether they be experiences from my own educational journey or pieces of family history, like the story of Susan McCoy recalled above. Some of these ghosts carry a haunting presence, while others offer a guiding light, helping to achieve more clarity and nuance amid deeply complex and tense encounters.

Historian Robin Mitchell, a black woman writing about black women in Francophone history, once asked, "What kind of history can we tell if we bring all of ourselves along with us in our work that we reveal to the public, all shiny and new? What happens if we do not hide ourselves or the mechanics of what we do?" Heeding the sage advice embedded in this scholar's question, I choose to analyze historical records from the archive while also bringing myself along in the rendering of this new interpretation of American education. I do this, in part, because I also want to make clear that this is a living history—it is at once about the dead as well as a deep concern for those yet alive.[30] A wise scholar once put it beautifully in stating that "history is how the secular world attends to the dead."[31] This claim certainly rings true for me. I see this book as a quest to be in right relationship with a complicated past; indeed, a past that continues to fill the present with literal and figurative ghosts, reminding us that history is rarely as distant as it seems on paper.

Bringing myself along in the writing of this narrative is my way of modeling an active engagement with history. I do this in hopes that readers will choose to do the same in their own lives. We can all benefit from cultivating a deeper and more mature historical consciousness, especially when it comes to our nation's educational past. American schools do so little to teach this history, despite the fact that all students are inheritors of an educational legacy shaped by it. We have all been socialized through educational processes meant to initiate individuals into some "common" experience, even as schooling continues to be a key site for stratifying our social world along various categories of difference—especially along the lines of race.

The rules that order our collective educational experiences are easy to overlook, given their deeply immersive quality, and having so long been taken for granted. They are only recognizable when we actively wonder about our role as objects within this field of learning shaped by language—indeed, always by language and stories and narratives of history. For this is an integral part of our collective humanity. Yet studying grammar is necessary if we desire to be more astute objects of said education, as is the case with language more broadly. This is particularly important when we consider that all of us, as objects of education, are acted upon by figures and subjects that have the power to determine the direction of our lives, the ordering of our communities, and the future of the planet, all within a larger social statement. Recognizing education to be a grammatical phenomenon—by which I mean structural and deeply contextual—I have set out to tell a history of education that treats it as such.

American Grammar has an ambitious aim: to reorganize our collective thinking on a subject that is intimately connected to every citizen. My pursuit of a more mature historical consciousness stems from a hope that one day such honest assessments might activate ideas and action toward more justice-oriented repairs. I know history to be a weapon. It is often used toward nefarious ends, but it can also be used for good. Hopefully, this new origin story of US education, as a more honest reckoning with race, power, and schooling in our society, might bolster efforts to reimagine what healing can look like in a world so deeply stratified by education. For indeed, to pursue healing requires that we trace our finger to the source of harm. Only then can we outline its form to be more direct in our targeting, and most explicit in naming the injustice we seek to correct.

PART I

A NEW ORIGIN STORY OF AMERICAN SCHOOLING

1

1819: A CROSSROADS IN EARLY US EDUCATION

Airports are stressful places, so I usually rush to get out of them. This time was no different. I pulled my carry-on—which I stuffed to avoid checking luggage—through Terminal E at Boston Logan International Airport in May 2023, having just returned from the Native American and Indigenous Studies Association (NAISA) Conference in Toronto. The battery in my Bluetooth headphones had died on the plane, so I could not tune out the noise from everyone scurrying about, as I usually do. I briskly rolled down the moving walkway, heading to the rideshare pickup location, only to be stopped dead in my tracks by the prerecorded voice of Massachusetts Governor Maura Healey projecting over the loudspeaker. With a typical mid-Atlantic accent and pleasant tone, she welcomed visitors to the city and shared important facts about the commonwealth. "Thank you for choosing Boston Logan International Airport, our gateway to our incredible state," said Governor Healey. She then boasted of several accolades that proudly distinguishes the state of Massachusetts, declaring: "We are home to America's first public school, library, park, and transit system, and even the first basketball team." She went on to list more noteworthy offerings of the state, including its top-rate universities. My antennae as a historian of education immediately raised as that presumably innocent statement echoed in my head: "*home to America's first public school.*"

I had just returned from NAISA, where my presentation focused on the economic relationship between native land dispossession and the roots of public school funding across the United States. The practice of selling "public" or "federal" lands to establish state school and literary funds was patterned off early methods in colonial New England, and

Massachusetts in particular, before the American Revolution. While most historians writing about education funding in the earliest decades of the United States identify land as raw capital contributing to the development of schools, rarely is such land contextualized by the history of native land dispossession that preceded such designations as "federal" and "public" lands. Healey's message echoed these sanitized narratives in historical scholarship. I never noticed the governor's prerecorded message before this moment, but it was yet another reminder of how the history of race and American education is so deeply integrated into our lives and the national identity. The conundrum between me and my colleagues' NAISA panel on "Crosscurrents in Indigenous and Black Educational History" and the flattened memory of Massachusetts being "home to America's first public school" reflects the kind of gaps in public memory, and historical scholarship, about education that led me to write *American Grammar.* Whitewashed origin narratives of American education, like the one offered by Healey, contribute to widespread misperceptions held by many about a nonpolitical past of education, where schools were neutral social institutions at the heart of US democracy. Nothing could be further from the truth.

In this book, I will offer a more honest history of chattel slavery, native land dispossession, and education in the United States through the nineteenth century, rendering the story of American schooling as one of nation-building and empire. A story where the laws, policies, and funding streams that conditioned the schooling apparatus of the nation were steeped in antiblack and anti-indigenous violence—not just in the educational contexts of native and black people, but also in the context of white schooling. To offer this more truthful account of American education as a racial project, Part I looks at specific laws and policies, teachers and their students, as well as racist systems of domination and the brave many who resisted them, while focusing primarily on the first half of the nineteenth century. I use documents, student voices, and the American soil itself to tell a story spanning thousands of miles and a wide range of time. However, to begin, we start with two days in March 1819.

March 1819 marks a watershed moment in the history of United

States education law and policy. In the span of two days—March 2 and 3—one state law and one federal policy, respectively, codified long-standing relationships between the infrastructure of United States schooling and the two racially dominated groups in the North American territory: African-descendant people and indigenous nations. Through an anti-literacy law passed by the Virginia legislature and the Civilization Fund Act passed by the US Congress, white government actors criminalized education among African-descendant people, drawing on a practice of antiblack exclusion in education dating back to colonial America, while simultaneously imposing Western education on indigenous people in warlike fashion, also a colonizing practice that began prior to American independence.

Though rarely thought of in conversation with one another, I argue that these two educational phenomena went hand in hand. Such educational policies were integral to an evolving process of racial formation, where racial categories of one group of people developed over and against racial ideas associated with others. In a context where native, white, and black people were evaluated in the American social order always in relation to one another, education laws and policies became social instruments used to organize an increasingly complex social world of the United States; a fledgling republic working to simultaneously expand and define itself, over and against its past of British colonization.

On March 2, Governor Thomas Mann Randolph of Virginia signed a law banning education among enslaved people, who at the time represented 40 percent of the state's population.[1] Governor Randolph, a man who owned dozens of enslaved people, was the son-in-law of the third US president, Thomas Jefferson. President Jefferson was a key architect of American public education—both because of his writing of the Land Ordinance of 1785, which directly connected Northwestern lands with future education funding, as passed under the Articles of Confederation, even as such lands were inhabited by native nations, and also because of his early bills for tax supported education in Virginia.[2] The familial relationship of the two men seems to me a metaphor for the intimacy between the laws they helped to construct. The

Virginia law was an "Act reducing into one, the several acts concerning Slaves, Free Negroes and Mulattoes": a black code resulting from three years of legislative efforts.[3] Thus the anti-literacy law signed by Randolph made it illegal for enslaved people to read and write, and it was part of a comprehensive set of regulations and punishments outlined for the racially specific form of governance designated for black people in the "Old Dominion."

The 1819 law criminalized "meetings or assemblages of slaves . . . at any school or schools for teaching them reading or writing, either in the day or night."[4] It was an amended version of a previous act, originally passed in 1804, targeting religious assemblies.[5] Importantly, anti-assembly laws were closely aligned with anti-literacy laws like the one Randolph signed in 1819. The early law preventing black people from assembling without white oversight was an explicit effort to disrupt the educational function of black social life among the enslaved. Arguing that slaves' "common practice" of gathering in "meeting-houses, and places of religious worship, in the night" could "be productive of considerable evil to the community," the law sought to disrupt environments where black people shared information, relied on literate slaves as leaders, and, sometimes, conspired to manifest their dreams of freedom.[6] While the early anti-assembly law did not specifically criminalize reading and writing, it was fundamentally about disrupting community education among black people, particularly when one takes a more expansive view of education beyond rigid notions of formal schooling. With this context in mind, one might read the 1819 anti-literacy law as a refining of long-standing practices of educational surveillance experienced by black people in the United States.

Virginia's 1819 anti-literacy statute reflected mechanisms of law and policy based on an understanding of education as an instrument that could be used toward both liberatory and oppressive ends. Indeed, it was the threat of the former that led to the creation of such laws that policed and suppressed educational opportunities among black people. This criminalizing of educational opportunity for African Americans, while not focused on the creation and administering of educational opportunity, still constituted explicit educational activity. Such laws were an intimate and integral part of the schooling apparatus of the United States as it was yet emerging. Laws like this one passed in Virginia on March 2, 1819, by the son-in-law of Thomas Jefferson interacted with a more intricate web of educational infrastructure in the state, and the broader sociopolitical context of the developing nation.

The idea of literacy among black populations became widely interpreted as a threat among the white governing population. As warned by the colonial South Carolina legislature in 1740, such literacy as a source of liberation in the hands of enslaved people "may be attended with great inconveniences." Typically, we understand solely the creation and administering of educational opportunity as the primary goal of educational law and policy. But this legal suppression of black education helped condition the context in which educational policies in the state would function, placing limits on what could and could not be done. Such laws—including Colonial Era anti-literacy laws like South Carolina's, antebellum laws like Virginia's, as well as local codes meant to exclude black students in the North, like Connecticut's 1833 Black Law—became structural features of a broader schooling apparatus of the United States, particularly as it emerged through the nineteenth century. Thomas Mann Randolph's actions and his familial tie to Jefferson clarifies how intricately the web of educational infrastructure was woven in the state and it signaled trends in the national culture.

On March 3, one day after Governor Randolph's action, the Fifteenth United States Congress passed the Civilization Fund Act of 1819. This was "An Act making provisions for the civilization of the Indian tribes adjoining the frontier settlements." The CFA apportioned $10,000 annually for grants to Christian missionary societies building and leading schools along the American frontier.[7] In this instance, government agents formalized partnerships with private agencies working to "civilize" indigenous peoples, recognizing such efforts as a worthy enterprise, necessary for the public good of the nation. According to the CFA, missionary schools among indigenous peoples would "provid[e] against the further decline and final extinction of the Indian tribes, and for introducing to them the habits of civilization."[8] Despite such rhetorical flourishes, introducing "habits of civilization" was less about preserving native nations and more about alienating native people from indigenous ways of life—particularly by disrupting their relations to land—helping to clear a path for ongoing American expansion. Like the anti-literacy law passed in Virginia one day before, this act by Congress was also motivated by a very explicit rationale endemic to the political economy of race in the United States. Such early forms of education policy were an expression of overlapping and interrelated racial projects at the heart of American schooling.

Government leaders' concern with civilizing native people through schooling was not merely about introducing education or saving souls by spreading Christianity. For indeed, indigenous people had their own models of education and ways of socializing learners into their established ways of knowing and being.[9] Instead, policies like the CFA program were just as much about subtractive schooling as they were about introducing a new model of education.[10] The CFA was explicitly about eliminating traditions of education internal to native peoples—diminishing indigenous ways of life, undermining their claims to the land, and replacing them through schooling protocols that aligned with a US project of expansion fundamentally at odds with indigenous survivance.[11] These two pieces of education legislation created parameters for subtractive schools policies: one functioning to disappear indigenous ways of being in service of facilitating continued seizure of native lands, while the other sought to isolate black populations as an exploitable group of captive laborers forced to cultivate the land. Value was perpetually accrued by white citizens through stolen land and stolen bodies; and theft, to be clear, was a precondition for the establishment of both as property.

Education has always been the underside of US empire. The story of the CFA, like the story of anti-literacy laws in Virginia and beyond, point to this inescapable fact. As future chapters of this book will detail, such value extracted from seized native land, as well as from slave labor and slave capital, not only increased the wealth of individual white citizens but were also central to the economic development of schooling as a public good for white Americans.

Alongside the two racialized educational trajectories expressed by Virginia's anti-literacy law and the CFA of 1819 was an expanding crusade for universal education for white students in the broader public sphere. Though typically understood as separate phenomena, I see these events as relational. White students, the beneficiaries of such policies and laws, were expected to inherit and preserve the American republic. Racialized policies targeting black and native communities were informed by, and were reinforcements of, racial ideologies that place white students at the top of the social hierarchy, a stratification mirrored by the national educational landscape as it was yet forming. The aftermath of such law and policy certainly bears this out.

In 1820, one year after signing Virginia's revised anti-literacy bill into law, Governor Randolph used his annual address to the legislature to emphasize the importance of expanding white education in the state. He outlined plans to make poor white families less ashamed to accept state subsidies for their children's tuition for fear of being seen as "a list of paupers."[12] In effect, Randolph was pushing the government to play a more active role in providing education to white families, fostering solidarity among white citizens through the project of schooling. Common education had long been a growing concern for leaders in Virginia. The state's General Assembly established a Literary Fund in 1811, with the purpose of building schools and providing education for the poor, seeing as wealthy white citizens typically funded their own education through private means. The act establishing the Literary Fund declared "that all escheats, confiscations, fines, penalties and forfeitures, and all rights in personal property accruing to the Commonwealth, as derelict, and having no rightful proprietor, be, and the same are hereby appropriated to the encouragement of learning. That the aforesaid fund shall be appropriated to the sole benefit of a school or schools, to be kept in each and every county within this Commonwealth."[13]

The property used to grow the fund had direct ties to native land dispossession. However, it also included enslaved people as property. What's more, Virginia eventually included money collected from the sale of fugitive slaves as part of the state's Literary Fund.[14]

Virginia's growing strategy around education as a public good was not an isolated phenomenon; it was national in scope. Almost universally, American leaders viewed education as a way of constructing a more coherent national identity among white citizens—a site for initiating white students into a common experience as (white) Americans, where they might put the symbolics and interests of the nation above any distinctions that existed among them as a heterogeneous group.[15] Indeed, schools were used as a key instrument in forging a unified white national identity in the early republic. This national identity was defined as white, English-speaking, and Protestant, and it was carved out of the ethnic, linguistic, gender, and class diversity among the Euro-American population in the United States.

The contrast between Governor Randolph's actions in 1819 and 1820 provide a stark depiction of American education as a racial project: The governor sought to break down financial barriers for white scholars, viewing them as "promising germs of intellect" to develop; meanwhile, the education of black scholars "may be productive of considerable evil to the community."[16] It is also worth noting that Randolph governed from a state that was home to the longest continuous occupation of indigenous lands by Anglo-Americans, and where the first college in the state (and second in the nation)—the College of William and Mary—was created with the objective of civilizing native people as part of its Colonial Era charter in 1693. Such developments in the social world were always intimately related, though they are often thought of as separate in public memory and historical scholarship. The history of native dispossession and federal campaigns for boarding schools have typically been isolated to scholarship in Indigenous Studies just as the history of anti-literacy laws have mostly been interpreted as part of the history of slavery, thus implying that the two have little to no bearing on the nation's conceptualization of education and its political function in the social world. Again, we can look to the words of Randolph to see how ideas between these racial projects in education were bound up with one another, not only when we think about the economic underpinnings of these projects, but also in how they were conceptualized in the minds of powerful white elites.

Scolding the legislature against overturning the state's Literary Fund act of 1811, Randolph proclaimed: "While all minds rejoice at the liberality of the provision made to facilitate transportation, that all parts of the territory susceptible of cultivation may receive it, and that no part of the fruits of the earth may be unprofitably consumed where they grow, certainly none could be pleased at a change which would again leave so many promising germs of capable intellect, ever as abundant in the cottages of the poor as in the mansions of the wealthy, to remain undeveloped and to perish unknown."[17] In telling fashion, Randolph likened the education of poor whites to cultivation of the earth. His concern with "unprofitable" consumption resonates with the arguments of white settlers who promoted Western education focused on land privatization and agriculture. Indeed, native peoples' perceived lack of agricultural development had long been used as justification to displace them and as reason to coerce them into ethnocidal educational settings.

The implications of these early laws and policies went in multiple directions, as the fates of the three races occupying the North American territory had now become so structurally intertwined. Virginia's anti-literacy law helped to preserve white settlement of native lands by maintaining rigid racial distinctions that ensured black people were kept uneducated, helping to reinforce their status as a slave race whose labor could be exploited. Relatedly, the Civilization Fund Act helped to clear a path for more land to be accumulated and ultimately worked by black enslaved laborers. While the former was directly antiblack, it also had implications for the ongoing procedures of settler colonialism; the latter, which had direct and devasting consequences for native people, was also connected to the suppression of black life. Such mechanisms of law and policy which conditioned a growing national educational landscape were mutually constituted.

The relationships between black, white, and native peoples' distinct schooling experiences reflected the political economy of race in the building of the nation. It is a story whereby the allocation and withholding of educational resources and opportunities was motivated by racial ideologies, and where economic motivations pertaining to indigenous land and black captive bodies shaped the political underpinnings of educational policy and practice. Considering such clear historical relations, I insist that contrary to popular historical interpretations, black and native peoples were not excluded from the citizenship project of American schooling.[18] The citizenship project of American schooling was defined, funded, and expanded through the domination of these two subjugated races. This is to say, black and native people were always included in the development of the schooling apparatus of the United States by and through their subjection. Antiblack and anti-indigenous domination fueled the economic development of the national education landscape as well as the westward expansion of the United States. The former was part and parcel of the latter, as education emerged as a key instrument in the building of the nation.

Education has long been understood as a tool for civic empowerment and democracy in America, having been conceptualized by men like Thomas Jefferson, Benjamin Rush, Noah Webster, John Adams, and Horace Mann as an essential tool for internal development of the newly united states. Yet education, as a key societal institution, has also been a tool of racial domination. State officials in Virginia aimed to suppress the formal literacy and self-directed community education practices of enslaved people. Greater governance over black people's minds and movement was their goal, in service of continuing the violent extraction of value and labor from the captive bodies of enslaved African people. From the nation's capital, Congress endeavored to root out indigenous knowledge systems among native nations, who continued to maintain their own ways of knowing and being, which posed a threat to the demands of settler colonialism and westward expansion. Schooling in this context was an act of war—not merely an effort to add "civilization" to the lives of native people, but a violent protocol of subtraction, erasure, and alienation. Through the schooling apparatus of the state, federal officials sought to coerce and compel indigenous peoples to accept alienation from their natal communities and traditional ways of life, insisting that through settler schooling, native people were "learning to do better on less land," as President Thomas Jefferson wrote in 1803.[19] The goal of schooling for native people, as constructed by white settlers, was to shrink native settlements, disrupt long-standing processes of socialization embedded in native cultures, and ultimately facilitate the dispossession of indigenous lands.

Virginia's anti-literacy law and the Civilization Fund established by Congress are two cases in which white government officials imposed a distinctive schooling regime on a non-European group of people, based on political-economic group relations resulting from slavery and settler colonialism, as well as ideas of racial difference that were yet evolving. Such schooling policies and practices helped solidify racial categories, making the grammars of race even more endemic in the American social order. Both educational projects had clear connections to the ongoing structuring phenomena that were foundational to the building of US empire—settler colonialism and chattel slavery—as did Virginia's 1811 act establishing its Literary Fund for building white schools and allocating funding for white students from poor backgrounds.

When we take seriously the material realities of chattel slavery and settler colonialism in the development of the nation, we are forced to confront how landmark policies and laws that facilitated the expansion of public schooling in the United States were conditioned by the political economy of race. What's more, while state and federal policies criminalizing black education and expanding the nation's civilizing mission among indigenous people through education have historically been confined to their role in the stories of slavery and settler colonialism, the remaining pages of Part I will continue to unsettle such prosthetic boundaries.

American Grammar recognizes mechanisms such as Virginia's anti-literacy law and Congress's Civilization Fund Act as direct extensions of *the schooling apparatus of the United States*. Applying this more capacious view, the subsequent chapters detail how the national educational landscape became comprised of a diverse set of educational institutions created in service of the American republic as envisioned by the nation's most powerful elite. They analyze levers of law, policy, and civil society that operated at the margins of the United States, as well as in the mainstream context of white schooling, identifying how they were all involved in the administering *and* the withholding of education, paying particular attention to the experiences of racial domination as an integral part of the story. For as the story of anti-literacy laws and the CFA demonstrate, education policy was not only about the expanding of educational access and opportunity. It could also be a mechanism used for the taking away and curtailing of rights of some to the benefit of others, as we have seen repeated throughout history. The racial life of schooling in the early American republic is an illuminating example of this perpetual social problem in modern human experience.

2

FEDERAL FUNDING FOR NATIVE SCHOOLING IN THE EARLY NINETEENTH CENTURY

The story of the Civilization Fund Act begins at least three years prior to its adoption in 1819. In its origin story is the confluence of education and settler colonialism, a narrative of how each required the other, where settler schooling for native students was an expression of US wars with native peoples. In February 1816, Rev. Cyrus Kingsbury visited the United States Secretary of War William Crawford in Washington with a proposal for a school. The missionary sought federal funds by way of the US military to support a new educational endeavor with native peoples.[1] During this same trip, Kingsbury also visited former President Thomas Jefferson. This architect of American democracy and US education encouraged Kingsbury's settler fantasy of spreading civilization among the tribes through schooling. Kingsbury was raised in New England, a graduate of Brown University, and the first missionary to work for the American Board of Commissioners for Foreign Missions (ABCFM)—the largest and most influential American missionary organization throughout the nineteenth century.[2] More than a story to be confined to native educational history, Kingsbury's school would emerge to be a key extension of a pedagogical project at the heart of the ever-expanding settler nation, especially because it was articulated as a remedy for costly wars with native people.

The development of native education as an integral part of the schooling apparatus of the United States cannot be understood apart from questions of war. When Kingsbury visited former President Jefferson and Secretary Crawford, the United States had been at relative peace for less than a year with native nations along its western border—which traced the Five Tribes (Cherokee, Choctaw, Creek, Chickasaw, and Seminole) in the south, the Plains tribes (Cheyenne, Kiowa, Osage, Pawnee) in the center, and the Lakes tribes (Ojibwa, Potawatomi, et al.) to the northwest. However, as Secretary Crawford contemplated Kingsbury's proposal, the memory of bloody warfare with native nations loomed large in his mind. Costly wars with native nations—including, for instance, the War of 1812, which lasted until 1815—were part of very recent history, and given the United States' commitment to continued expansion, Crawford anticipated more on the horizon.

Leading into 1808, the Shawnee chief Tecumseh facilitated major alliances among western indigenous tribes—the Shawnee, Potawatomi, Piankeshaw, Lakota, Mdewakantonwan Dakota, Yankton Sioux, Omaha, Kickapoo, Osage, Fox, and Iowa nations—to thwart US efforts to claim lands west of the Ohio Valley. Tecumseh's alliance waged outright war in the Northwest. As a means of stopping American westward expansion, this allied force of native warriors also fought alongside the British in the War of 1812.[3]

It was not uncommon for wars to break out across multiple fronts. During the War of 1812, for instance, the Creek "Red Sticks" raided along the southern borders.[4] Such forceful and coordinated resistance from native nations was seen as a great threat to the United States, especially—though not exclusively—because such resistance was encouraged by Great Britain, which was invested in limiting the growing influence of the new republic born out of its former colonies. As the war reached its end, the US government signed peace treaties with more than a dozen indigenous nations between July and October 1815.[5]

Though active combat ended by early 1815, peace between the US government and native peoples was elusive in the following years. The periphery of the American frontier was volatile; accord was tenuous and spotty, especially as settlers acted on aggressive fantasies of westward expansion, predicated on a phased yet continuous process of native elimination and land dispossession. Seminole warriors banded with black fugitive slaves and continued waging defensive guerrilla warfare in northern Florida.[6] Six months after Kingsbury's visit to Washington in February 1816, US forces attacked Negro Fort, launching General Andrew Jackson's attempted conquest of Florida, and thus the Seminole Wars—a war that had an explicit goal of decimating this particular native nation.[7] America faced protracted war with the Seminoles, and indigenous peoples' resistance to settler expansion persisted along the western frontier.[8] It was on the heels of such bloody wars that Kingsbury approached the war secretary with his proposal for a school.

REV. KINGSBURY'S PROPOSAL TO THE SECRETARY OF WAR

Details of Kingsbury's meeting with Secretary Crawford in February 1816 are recovered from their written correspondences, where they allude to a desire for entering a time of peace with the native tribes. Kingsbury understood the federal government's desperation for an end to costly wars. Writing in May, Kingsbury assured the secretary that educating the native peoples was the best path forward. He asserted, "Probably no other means could be so successfully employed to prevent the recurrence of expensive and bloody Indian wars, and to give permanent security to our frontier settlements."[9] Kingsbury proposed building a school that would impart Western ideals in keeping with social norms among settlers; this included standard gender roles, and Christianity, as well as agricultural skills for farming and other practices deemed necessary for maintaining a nuclear family structure. This idea would eventually come to fruition in the form of Brainerd Mission, a boarding school built on land in present-day Tennessee, focused on agricultural training and Christian conversion. Brainerd, which enrolled Cherokee children from early to late adolescent ages, was effectively the first federally owned school in United States history that was not a military academy—though the school was funded by the military arm of the state and coalesced with the aims of the American Indian Wars.

A revelatory precedent indeed. While national leaders encouraged white schooling for citizenship training, yet relegated its provision and oversight to local efforts, and as black education became overwhelmingly suppressed, as an expression of their subjugated position as enslaved laborers, native education emerged as a matter of national security and development—a nation-building project motivated by military aims and settler dreams of boundless expansion.

Kingsbury's request was specific: He wanted federal support to build a school and secure necessary equipment for students. Civilizing indigenous people was "a duty binding on individuals as well as on the Government," Rev. Kingsbury argued.[10] Appealing directly to the purported civilizing mission embedded in America's ongoing wars with indigenous peoples, which fell under Crawford's purview as secretary of war, the ambitious missionary declared, "the exertions which the Government are making to civilize the Indians could not be better aided than by establishing schools."[11] Thanks to such missionary zeal, no support was needed for Kingsbury's salary or any other school officials; the American Board of Commissioners for Foreign Missions vowed to cover such expenses. In this way, a civilian-run charitable organization, based on private funding and interests, could help advance a project that was in the best interest of the settler nation and what it perceived to be in the interest of public good. Kingsbury proposed a partnership between the federal government and this missionary association as a private entity to execute this educational project.

This public-private partnership between a missionary association—the American Board of Commissioners for Foreign Missions—and the federal government reflected an alliance that lasted through most of the nineteenth century. Indeed, the goals of the church and the state had long been mutually constituted, even as they (at times) operated separately. However, as Kingsbury's example makes clear, missionaries' work in early native education was carried out with the blessing and urging of government actors. Such privately orchestrated actions among native communities were widely understood as serving the interests of the white American public.

Education, Kingsbury preached, could solve the nation's ongoing conflicts with indigenous peoples. To study war no more, Kingsbury proposed schools. Education could be an alternative to, or perhaps an expression of, the battlefield. It was a strategy that, he hoped, might bring about more lasting results.

Kingsbury's proposal was persuasive. It received approval from Secretary Crawford, who then discussed the matter with the fourth president of the United States, James Madison. He also gave his blessing. In the letter delivering his approval, the secretary of war provided the twenty-nine-year-old reverend with precise instructions: "the agent will be directed to erect a comfortable school-house, and another for the teacher and such as may board with him, in such part of the nation as shall be selected for that purpose."[12] Crawford also shared thoughts about the ideological orientation of the curriculum: The indigenous students should be taught agricultural and domestic skills that would encourage life as farmers and homesteaders as opposed to more itinerant ways of living. Kingsbury must "furnish two ploughs, six hoes, and as many axes, for the purpose of introducing the art of cultivation among the pupils. Whenever he is informed that female children are received and taught in the school, and that a female teacher has been engaged, capable of teaching them to spin, weave, and sew, a loom and half a dozen spinning-wheels, and as many pair of cards, will be furnished."[13]

Enthusiasm for Kingsbury's proposal was evident by the fact that the war secretary set his sights on more than just a single institution. Even before the school was built, Crawford began envisioning an expanding US-sponsored native education program. He insisted that Kingsbury's proposed school could serve as a building block for more educational institutions down the line and he outlined a vision for an expansive, federally supported education program for dealing with the "Indian problem." Building on the missionary's proposal, Crawford suggested that Kingsbury would "be directed, from time to time, to cause other school-houses to be erected, as they shall become necessary."[14] Readers may recall the story of Goodland Academy, named in the introduction: a mission established by Kingsbury among the Choctaw nation in 1935. Goodland was the same school that eventually became an enrollment site of the Dawes Commission in the late nineteenth century, where Susan McCoy was written out of her rights as an Afro-native woman by white government actors.

The role of the federal government in Brainerd's story, particularly its ownership of the physical building, pushes against dominant historical interpretations. Such historical analyses tend to place greater portions of the responsibility of early native schooling on private actors in religious organizations, while understating the central role played by the state. Secretary Crawford's careful distillation of who was ultimately in charge is clarifying in this regard. He explained, "The houses thus erected, and the implements of husbandry and the mechanical arts which shall be furnished, will remain public property, *to be occupied and employed for the benefit of the nation*."[15] He continued, "If the persons who are about to engage in this enterprise should abandon it, the buildings and utensils which shall have been furnished may be occupied by any other teachers of good moral character."[16]

The secretary of war's words, that the proposed mission to be established with federal support were "to be occupied and employed for the benefit of the nation," makes clear the early investment of the state in the political project of settler schooling for native people.[17] This demands a revision to historical narratives that have suggested federal involvement in native schooling was primarily a post-1870s development, when the nation witnessed the rapid expansion of native schools and increased spending, as well as the move to replace missionary schools with government-led schools. While it is true that native schooling became more directly coordinated, expansive, and centralized by government officials after shifts in US Indian policy following the Civil War, federal funding and involvement had always been key to its development throughout the nineteenth century. Accounting for Brainerd as a government-constructed mission school underscores the state's broader role in expanding missionary schooling among native people prior to the nation's transition to government-run native education during the late nineteenth century—a period when the political goal shifted to dismantling tribal governments and making native people citizens of the United States.[18] Thus missionary education among native students, while privately operated, was quite often implemented with funding and coordination from federal actors.

A relational comparison helps illuminate the historical significance of using federal support to establish Brainerd. Secretary Crawford approved Kingsbury's proposal for funding during the same era when Thomas Jefferson's 1817 proposal for tax-supported universal education would be rejected in Virginia, and when education of whites was still highly decentralized and sparse around the country. The racial project proposed by Kingsbury, however, served more direct military aims, whereby the federal government justified supporting his experiment with native education as a matter of national security and expansion.[19] There were distinct political and economic motivations for native schooling as expressed by Kingsbury and the US secretary of war, and the actions of these two men were shaped by evolving racial ideology about "the Indian"—a racial category forged over and against a diverse set of indigenous nations who presented an inconvenient, and at times bloody, roadblock to the United States' nation-building project.

The secretary ended his letter to Kingsbury with a promissory note. Pending successful execution of the mission, explained Crawford, "it is probable that the attention of Congress will be attracted to the subject, and that the means of forwarding your beneficent views will be more directly and liberally bestowed by that enlightened body."[20] In other words, if Kingsbury's experiment with educating native students proved successful at alienating them from traditional indigenous ways of life and made them less resistant to settler expansion, Congress would likely formalize federal support for such endeavors on a larger scale in the future.

The US war secretary saw in Kingsbury's proposal a potentially scalable solution to a perennial problem. This was the settler-educational fantasy being dreamed up in the United States Department of War, a set of deliberations that involved a missionary, the highest-ranking military official, as well as a past, current, and future US president.

LOCATING THE LAND AND BUILDING THE SCHOOL

Having received his marching orders from the secretary of war, Kingsbury set out to find a location suitable for such an endeavor. To accomplish this first step, he traveled to Turkeytown—a settlement of the Cherokee nation, now part of present-day Alabama—in October 1816. Government officials in Washington likely informed Kingsbury about ongoing land negotiations in Turkeytown between leaders of the Cherokee and Chickasaw tribes and US state officials. They would have encouraged Kingsbury to use this occasion to secure land for the school he had been approved to build. In traveling to Turkeytown, Kingsbury's purpose was to obtain an audience with Cherokee leaders, in which he might request permission to build Brainerd and purchase the land for this specified aim.[21]

During this visit, the soon-to-be schoolmaster witnessed Cherokee and Chickasaw leaders, led by Cherokee Chief Pathkiller, sign the Treaty of Turkeytown—a historic event where these leaders ceded 3,500 square miles to the United States in what is now the northwest region of Alabama.[22] It was at this same meeting that Rev. Kingsbury secured the grounds to build a school on behalf of the United States and the American Board of Commissioners for Foreign Missions. The land purchased from the Cherokee nation to build Brainerd was a defunct farm on Chickamauga Creek, which fed into the Tennessee River. Kingsbury likely hoped this proximity to the water would make trading efficient—as there was always a desire for the school to be self-sufficient. It was also a practical location as it pertained to future school operations, as later records for Brainerd would detail goods received by the school through this pathway. More importantly, the location was near native people, particularly the Cherokee nation. While such proximity to native tribes would eventually be seen as an impediment to effective settler schooling by the late nineteenth century—for fear of students running away and being too close to the influence of their families—such concerns had yet to take root in the early years of Brainerd.

That the acquisition of land used to build Brainerd occurred at the same meeting where a massive ceding of native lands took place serves as a poignant reminder that US-sponsored native education was always part and parcel of indigenous land dispossession. Furthermore, the use of black enslaved labor to build the school reflects the reality that chattel slavery and settler-colonialism were mutually constituted procedures of racial domination shaping the yet developing schooling apparatus of the United States. Brainerd Mission, the first federally funded native school, was a settler-colonial project cloaked in missionary zeal, but it was also fundamentally a racial project. Its aim of civilizing native people was in fact about alienating native students from their heritage and land; a process of education where native students were racialized in close proximity with the two other racial groups in North America. As I will continue to show over the course of *American Grammar*, such racialization of native people was always being developed in direct relation to ideas of whiteness and blackness. Indeed, white missionaries like Kingsbury, and government actors like Crawford, carried very distinct racial ideas that linked blackness with slavery, as both relied on enslaved black labor in their personal and professional lives. In fact, Kingsbury defended the use of enslaved black labor for the building and operations of native schooling well beyond his time at Brainerd.

Kingsbury secured the land and quickly began building Brainerd within the Cherokee nation, and its development deeply reflected the political-economic linkages between the social realities between white Americans, indigenous populations, and enslaved black people.

BRAINERD MISSION LAYS THE GROUNDWORK FOR THE CIVILIZATION FUND ACT OF 1819

Kingsbury was not alone in appealing to the secretary of war for federal funds to civilize native peoples. American citizens who were familiar with the organization of the US government would know that the War Department had been responsible for "Indian affairs" since the decades immediately following American independence. As Secretary Crawford mobilized funds to help build a school for the

American Board of Commissioners to Foreign Missions, Quakers in Baltimore who were affiliated with the Committee of Friends on Indian Concerns—a Quaker organization concerned with humanitarian and "civilizationist" efforts among indigenous peoples—also wrote to Crawford for support. They sought financial assistance to continue educating a young Choctaw boy working in their dry-goods store.[23] The boy was fifteen years old at the time, and his name was James McDonald. Campaigns to support McDonald's education between 1816 and 1818 fed into a broader, concerted effort to persuade Congress to provide financial support for mission schools, culminating in the Civilization Fund Act of 1819. The story of Brainerd's founding and the rise of McDonald as a poster child for native schooling were both part of the cultural and political zeitgeist of the federal government's role of dealing with "the Indian problem."

Until this point, McDonald had been privately educated by Quaker missionaries in Baltimore. Yet they hoped McDonald might further his education and work toward a law degree. They encouraged him toward this dream, though McDonald reportedly wanted to be a farmer. Perhaps his attainment of this goal might provide necessary evidence that native people's intellectual abilities were not as frail as some believed them to be, thus helping justify further support for the civilizing project.[24] Either way, the possibilities for McDonald's future were being shaped by racial politics about who this native child could or should be, based on the gaze of white settlers.

Receiving no reply from the secretary of war, McDonald, originally from the Mississippi Territory and a slaveholding family in the Choctaw nation (because the Choctaw, like the Cherokee nation, also practiced racial slavery), continued working in Baltimore while taking classes in mathematics and philosophy.[25] Financial federal support for McDonald's education would not come until John C. Calhoun succeeded Crawford as secretary of war in December 1817, a year after the founding of Brainerd. It would be Thomas L. McKenney, head of the Indian Trade Office, and a fierce advocate for missionary education among indigenous peoples, who convinced Secretary Calhoun to authorize payment for the Choctaw boy's education.[26]

McKenney made it his personal mission to prove that "civilizing" native peoples was an achievable goal. Quaker missionary Philip Thomas introduced McDonald to his friend McKenney in 1818, and McKenney agreed to "adopt the youth" and support his continued education.[27] As I will later discuss, such "adoptions" were captive in nature, and driven by clear militaristic motivations, even when enacted by individual citizens, but especially when done by such political elites like McKenney and others in his network.

McKenney would later use McDonald as his walking billboard for the settler-schooling project he helped develop to serve the nation's agenda on US Indian policy and relations. McDonald was to serve as embodied proof that settler schooling could be an effective remedy to "the Indian problem." In a letter describing McDonald, McKenney proclaimed, "The acquirements of this young Indian afford *a gratifying evidence of Indian capacity*, and aptness for the attainment of the principles of Civilization, and of science. . . . To such as question the capacity of Indians for Civilization and improvement in science, no better argument need be offered. . . ."[28] McKenney would support McDonald in attending a law academy in Georgetown, though McDonald would finish his degree in Ohio in 1823.[29]

The boarding school at Brainerd Mission and the education of James McDonald bolstered Thomas McKenney's lobbying campaign for the Civilization Fund Act of 1819. Brainerd was the flagship institution based on the principles of manual labor, the Lancaster teaching model, which relied on proficient students to teach their peers, and Christianization, all toward the assimilation of native students into white Western ideals of civilization. McDonald, when placed before political elites, became a living text read as evidence that settler schooling might save future generations of native youth from their natal communities—settler schools, as conceived of by the likes of McKenney and Kingsbury, might alienate the native youth like McDonald from native adults, indigenous customs, and their tribal ties to land. Brainerd Mission and McKenney's promotion of McDonald would be used as evidence for claims about settler schooling's efficacy.

Missionaries' work to educate native students for civilization was not merely religious work taken up by private citizens of their own volition, and beyond the bounds of government. They were not merely religious fanatics working on their own accord. Such work involved the approval and authorized financial support of political figures working in the highest levels of the United States government. Missionary activity among native Americans, to be clear, traced back to the Colonial Era.[30] However, the Second Great Awakening of the late eighteenth and early nineteenth centuries, when the nation witnessed a Protestant revival that inspired many social reform movements, shaped the efforts of men like Kingsbury and McKenney. However, their work as missionaries, in the context of a newly united states, was not only about spreading the gospel; it was also about statecraft—building up and sustaining the nation, as it worked to ensure its longevity, global influence, and identity as more than merely a nation of former British colonies.

As one historian explained, both churchmen and rationalists (in the tradition of Thomas Jefferson) maintained nearly identical "views about the nature of the Indians and the possibility of their transformation. . . . One built on the philosophy of the Enlightenment . . . the other was a product of a surge of evangelical religion that came with the Second Great Awakening at the turn of the century, a new missionary spirit, a revivalism."[31] What's more, government officials and church leaders were of one mind on the matter: "the American civilization offered to the Indian was *Christian* civilization, that Christianity was a component of civilization and could not and should not be separated from it."[32]

Such missionary zeal among religious leaders and US politicians can be traced back to the era of George Washington, and it also expanded under the period of Thomas Jefferson's factory system, which sought to foster native people's dependence on manufactured goods, looking to commerce as a means of "civilizing" and thereby pacifying native nations.[33] Such paternalistic efforts among native people were in part motivated by national leaders recognizing the eminent conflict resulting from a rapidly growing United States population and what they perceived to be an inevitable infringement on the territory of indigenous peoples. Based on national census data, the US population rose from 3,929,214 in 1790 to 5,308,483 in 1800, and it would steadily increase by nearly 33 percent over the subsequent decades. In assessing such trends, Jefferson rationalized America's civilizationist work among native people, otherwise stated as a racial project premised on native dispossession, as follows: "to provide an extension of territory which the rapid increase of our numbers will call for . . . [the US must] encourage them [natives] to abandon hunting, to apply to the raising stock, to agriculture, and domestic manufacture, and thereby prove to themselves that *less land* and labor will maintain them in this better than in their former mode of living."[34]

Central to Jefferson's mission was the disruption of indigenous ways of being in relationship with land. He declared, "The extensive forests necessary in the hunting life will then become useless, and they will see advantage in exchanging them for the means of improving their farms and of increasing their domestic comforts."[35] Until 1819, Jefferson's factory system, which included trading goods with native peoples to facilitate profit from commerce and socialization into Western norms, along with the efforts of individual Indian agents, was the main vehicle by which the US sought to disrupt native lifeways and introduce them to "civilization." Jefferson's factory system, many hoped, would help root out traditional indigenous ways of doing and being. And though this factory system was constantly under threat of repeal, during the early nineteenth century there was relative political consensus around the civilizing mission of the United States.[36]

American leaders framed the period following the War of 1812 as a return to peace, as they looked westward, toward the frontier. However, from the perspectives of native peoples, who saw oncoming encroachment as they faced eastward at the US frontier, the period of Brainerd's establishment, McKenney's adoption of native students like McDonald—and others to follow—and his lobbying efforts on the part of missionaries was in many ways a continuation of war. We need only look to the words of the US president to understand it as such.

In 1816, President James Madison expressed his pleasure "that the tranquility which has been restored among the tribes themselves, as well as between them and our own population, will favor the resumption of the work of civilization which had made an encouraging progress among some tribes, and that the facility is increasing for extending that divided and individual ownership, which exists now in movable property only, to the soil itself, and of thus establishing in the culture and improvement of it the true foundation for a transit from the habits of the savage to the arts and comforts of social life."[37]

Madison declared that now that physical warfare had ended, the project of civilization could continue. Most notably, he emphasized that a major aim of settler schooling was to teach native peoples to understand "the soil itself" as property. This required that native students adopt a new, externally imposed worldview. The president declared native students must abandon indigenous beliefs about the proper ways of being in relationship with land—it was not to be seen as part and parcel of one's kinship systems but instead as property to be owned, traded, and subjected to mechanisms of human possession and extraction. Madison's declaration also required, ultimately, that native peoples abandon core aspects of their tribal identities, since the very idea of individual property was at odds with indigenous peoples' heritage and communal claims to land as sovereign nations.

Such aggressive civilizationist discourse was widespread among US political leaders, as we've seen in quotes from Thomas Jefferson and other government officials. What's more, this work of alienating native people from their natal communities and ties to land was usually framed in benevolent terms: as the preservation of physical life for native populations, just not the continuation of indigenous ways of life. Government officials often named what they understood to be an inevitable ultimatum: Indigenous peoples must either assimilate or be physically eliminated.

For native people "to remain Indian" on their own terms was, for the US government, no viable option at all. Hence the pedagogical aims of schools like Brainerd and those to be funded by the Civilization Fund Act of 1819. In schools like Brainerd, native students were taught to live domesticated lives, in homes, on patches of land that they cultivated as farmers, where they took on traditional Western gender roles, where they were Christian, where they were taught to conserve their individual earnings and resources to amass wealth, where they shed tribal identities and asserted themselves only as individual subjects, without collective ties to tribal customs and homelands.

In 1818, the House Committee on Indian Affairs explained, "In the present of our country one of two things seem necessary: either the sons of the forest should be moralized or exterminated. Humanity would rejoice at the former, but shrink with horror from the latter."[38] Such fatalistic rhetoric implied that the disappearance of native people was inevitable if the US did not take proper precautions to protect them from themselves. Education would arm the indigenous populations against "savagery" that threatened their futurity. The committee explained that if the nation "[p]ut into the hands of their children the primer and the hoe," then "they will naturally, in time, take hold of the plough; and, as their minds become enlightened and expand, the Bible will be their book, and they will grow up in the habits of morality and industry, leave the chase to those whose minds are less cultivated, and become useful members of society."[39]

As outlined by the 1818 House Committee on Indian Affairs, US leaders must target native youth, since they would become the future generations. Perhaps the young could be saved, as it was implied that those with "less cultivated" minds—those of the old Indian ways—would gradually die out. What the House committee effectively articulated was a formalizing strategy to remove native children from native parents and elders as a means of alienating them from their natal communities and kinship ties—which, it is important to stress, always included their relations to land.

Such civilizationist discourse reflected the leading ideology shaping US Indian policy, and it undergirded Thomas McKenney's idea for the Civilization Fund Act, which passed the following year, largely due to McKenney's successful lobbying. With Brainerd and McDonald as proof of concept, as well as memorials from several missionary societies pressuring Congress, the CFA, first proposed in 1818, would pass in 1819, setting a very important historical precedent.[40]

The act was intentionally crafted as education policy. The federal government was to allocate $10,000 annually to support civilization efforts among the native tribes, and it encouraged the proliferation of schools like Brainerd—institutions that encouraged conversion through religious education, taught the three R's (reading, writing, and arithmetic) using the Lancasterian educational model, and trained students in agricultural and domestic labor based on normative gender roles in Western society. Most importantly, this educational model also engendered distinct ideas about "land as property," challenging fundamental ways of knowing and being among indigenous peoples.

Pedagogical concerns about land in the project of settler schooling for native people is important to hold sight of, because it gets at the core of the political-economic motivations driving the actions of government leaders and many private citizens interested in the expansion of the United States. On the matter of the privatization of land, McKenney made his educational views explicit: "To make the plan effective, therefore, and to follow out its humane designs, it is respectfully recommended that, as these youths are qualified to enter upon a course of civilized life, sections of land be given to them, and a suitable present to commence with, of agricultural or other implements . . . to engage. They will then have become an 'intermediate link between our own citizens and our wandering neighbors, softening the shades of each, and enjoying the confidence of both.'"[41] The students educated in CFA-supported schools, according to McKenney, would learn to put down roots in private property and serve as a buffer between white settler society and its "wandering neighbors": native people who had yet to achieve civilization, who continued to relate to the land as a living thing as opposed to property, and who continued to engage in "the chase" for sustenance, as opposed to homesteading and more sedentary lifestyles. All the while, the question of land and its status as property was a central concern in white visions of settler schooling for native youth.

In 1820, Secretary of War John C. Calhoun produced a circular outlining criteria for parties interested in CFA funding. The national effort to build schools among native tribes was historic in that there was no comparable centralized effort for white or black education in the United States prior to its establishment. Indeed, this was nearly two decades before Horace Mann's appointment as the first secretary of the Massachusetts State Board of Education in 1837, and nearly five decades before the United States formed a national Department of Education in 1867. While white education was left to local efforts, native schooling formed as a national priority—with federal funding—and a centralized process for expansion with Congress's establishment of the CFA in 1819.

The Civilization Fund was widely advertised, especially among missionary societies. The circular explained, "[I]t will be indispensable, in order to apply any portion of the sum appropriated in the manner proposed, that the plan of education, in addition to reading, writing and arithmetic, should, in the instruction of the boys, extend to the practical knowledge of the mode of agriculture, and of such of the mechanic arts as are suited to the condition of the Indians; and in that of the girls, to spinning, weaving, and sewing. It is also indispensable that the establishment should be fixed within the limits of those Indian nations who border on our settlements."[42] National leaders prioritized settler schooling for natives bordering the American frontier, as they imagined such educational activities to serve an offensive strategy: helping to break ground and soften the walls of resistance among native people most immediately in the path of US expansion.

In 1820, the War Department under John Calhoun disbursed the first round of CFA funds to mission schools already in operation—Brainerd Mission was among the recipients. Schools in the Cherokee nation received the most funds, but the funds also supported missions among the Seneca and Tuscarora tribes in New York, as well as the education of four children's education at the Foreign Mission School in Cornwall, Connecticut.[43] While biased toward established schools, the CFA from the beginning supported new institutions as well: In this first year, CFA funds supported construction of schools in Valleytown of the Cherokee nation and in the Osage nation along the Arkansas River.[44] By 1822, Calhoun reported the US was sponsoring "[e]leven principal schools, with three subordinate ones, in actual operation;

and that three are in the state of preparation; and that the number of scholars at the last return . . . amounted to five hundred and eight."[45]

By 1824, the CFA supported over twenty schools in twelve nations, mostly in the American South and near the Great Lakes.[46] That year, the Bureau of Indian Affairs was created through the Department of War, largely to oversee the CFA and other "civilizing" work. Calhoun had long sought to consolidate the work of "Indian Affairs" under one superintendent, writing to Congress repeatedly in hopes of creating such a position either inside the War Department or a new "Home" Department.[47] Overseeing the CFA, factories, agencies, and treaties—along with the US military—was too monumental a task for one secretary of war.[48] Yet such tasks were all deeply intertwined, as the previous narratives reveal.

Acting on his desires Calhoun seized the opportunity to refine his department's internal organization when a clerk in the War Department died in 1824. He did not wait for congressional approval. He immediately hired Thomas McKenney to fill the vacancy, paying a clerk's salary to the nation's first Superintendent of Indian Affairs.[49] The move formalized a long-term alliance between the two men, bringing McKenney directly under Calhoun's supervision in the War Department and responding to increased demands associated with native schooling during this new phase of the Indian Wars. As such, the Civilization Fund Act led to the creation of a new organized unit in the federal government. This is no small detail. It underscores the federal government's role and investment in the project of settler schooling for native people as a political project of national importance.

McKenney, as leader of the Bureau of Indian Affairs, reported directly to the War Department—a practice he was quite familiar with through his previous endeavors. Indeed, the chain of command in the work of settler schooling reflected its political aims: It was a distinct model of education formed as a racial project for dealing with the problem of indigenous nations, a matter most immediately in the purview of the military, the repressive arm of the United States government.

For any given school, CFA funds made up a small portion of the operating budget relative to the private donations from pious Northerners and missionary groups. Nevertheless, the proliferation of federally funded schools during the 1820s situates this work as integral to the nation-building project. The sanction and support of the US government was a "gratifying and very encouraging assurance" that the work was in line with the vision of the state, as some missionaries reported from the field.[50] Just as private donors influenced the schools' operations—at Brainerd, for instance, pupils were sometimes renamed after their Northern patrons, with one child even bearing the name of the Northern newspaper, *Boston Recorder*—so too did federal support shape the pedagogy of mission schools.[51] In keeping with this example of naming practices, for instance, one finds in such records that many native students were also renamed after white government officials in CFA-funded missionary schools through the nineteenth century.

In 1822, Calhoun issued a circular to missionary organizations reminding them of the expectations accompanying receipt of CFA funds. He instructed missionaries "to impress on the minds of the Indians the friendly and benevolent views of the Government towards them, and the advantage to them in yielding to the policy of the Government, and co-operating with it in such measures as it may deem necessary for their civilization and happiness. A contrary course of conduct cannot fail to incur the displeasure of Government, as it is impossible that the object which it has in view can be effected, and peace be habitually preserved, if the distrust of the Indians as to its benevolent views should be excited."[52] With the promise of education came the forceful threat of US terror if native people did not comply. The secretary of war instructed missionaries to make this message clear in their teachings to native students in their schools built and sustained with federal dollars.

Secretary Calhoun declared that such schools must encourage among native students a friendly disposition toward the US government so that "peace [may] be habitually preserved." In the same breath, he reminded them of the forceful posture of the federal government; ultimately presenting a threat as to the nonpeace that would follow if native students (and the communities they represented) resisted settler schooling. The former presumably was the lesser of two evils.

Calhoun insisted that the mission and aims of the US government should inform the ideological orientation of native schools receiving federal funding. Yet, no such concerns or considerations were made for how these schools might account for the perspective or customs of indigenous nations. The priorities and views of the United States were to be taken on by the native students themselves. They were to internalize such standpoints as their own, as their framework for seeing and knowing. Schools contracted through the CFA were to cultivate in native students a settler gaze for viewing the world—its past, present, and future.

The CFA marked a formalized alliance between the federal government and missionary societies, and it advanced a very particular model of schooling for native Americans, making it an integral part of a growing schooling apparatus of the United States. Irrespective of what portion of missionary schools' budgets were made up of federal funds, the CFA signaled something greater than the distribution of material resources. It articulated a firm nod of approval from political leaders in the United States, who insisted that educational work among native tribes to the end of disrupting their traditional claims to land and quelled resistance to US expansion served the public good.

The CFA as educational policy nudged and encouraged the expansion of educational work taken up in what was technically foreign territory. For indeed, indigenous tribes were sovereign nations with whom the United States negotiated and formed agreements through treaty. Yet such educational activity was consistent with past federal policies, indicating that US state actors never fully recognized indigenous sovereignty. As evident by the political discourse above, US presidents, government officials, and missionary leaders deputized by the state, all engaged native peoples in an aggressively paternalistic fashion. This was characteristic of US policies toward native nations prior to and throughout the nineteenth century. For these reasons, scholars have long argued that white American paternalism has been the defining feature of US policy toward native peoples.[53]

The words and deeds of government officials reflected a shared understanding among settlers: The education of native people would help clear a path—literally and figuratively—for westward expansion. It would serve as a more effective solution to preventing more Indian wars, and it was of benefit to both the nation and the native peoples themselves. The lives of native people, settlers proclaimed, would be improved by shedding their tribal identities and enlisting themselves into the broader national project of the United States, as a newly essentialized racial group of Indians who deferred to the authority and supremacy of white settler society at the expense of their own indigenous identities and heritage claims to land. This logic is expressed with striking clarity in reports by government officials, as well as by missionaries moving in lockstep with the nation.

In 1823, the American Board of Commissioners for Foreign Missions reported the following to Congress: "When the southwestern parts of the United States are settled, it will be found, as we may rationally hope and expect, that the missions among the Cherokee and Choctaws had an important influence in promoting social order, and introducing the ordinance of the Gospel."[54] This missionary group understood their work to be about much more than saving souls. It was also about securing the future of the nation as it expanded into new territory—a destiny they understood to be ordained by God, but which would only manifest through the hard work of committed citizens.

Continuous expansion was imminent—in the minds of settlers. Schooling native peoples was just as essential as felling the forests. From the perspective of the US government—which at times deviated from that of missionaries, whose intimate relationships with native communities often led to varying degrees of internal moral conflict—the expansion of education among tribes bordering the frontier settlements was fundamentally about native land dispossession as motivated by the settler-colonial project. The CFA reflected a long-term strategy to avoid more Indian wars while facilitating dispossession, nonetheless.

Native education policy and the Indian Wars were deeply intertwined. This is perhaps most evident in the fact that the CFA and other educational activities among indigenous peoples were facilitated by, and directly accountable to, the US secretary of war. Such proximity between education and war in the context of US Indian policy is revealed in sobering fashion in a statement by Senator John Elliott, who professed, "It was then to be regarded as a struggle for *supremacy*, between savages and civilized men, between infidels and christians. But now, sir, when, by successive wars, and the more fatal operation of other causes, hereafter to be noticed, their power has departed from them, and they are reduced to comparative insignificance, it well becomes the magnanimity of a humane and generous Government, to seek out the causes of their continued deterioration, and, as far as practicable, to arrest its progress, by the application of the most appropriate remedies."[55]

According to Elliott, schools could be a tool for killing the Indians *and* a remedy for saving them. A means of war and, simultaneously, a medium for reconciliation. A method for arresting the progress of social factors that were "the causes of their continued deterioration." Seeing ongoing white efforts to displace and kill native peoples as having nothing to do with the matter, settlers identified native people's ways of life to be the primary cause of their misery. After such "settler moves to innocence," government leaders turned to settler schooling as being among "the most appropriate remedies" to save native people from themselves; to teach them to be otherwise.

•••

The story of Brainerd Mission as the first federally funded school as well as the Civilization Fund Act of 1819 are integral to the history of native land dispossession and settler colonialism, and they are integral to the story of US education policy. This is especially the case given that such educational projects were fiscally supported at a national level at a time when no similar model of national education existed for white or black Americans. The CFA is a key part of early education policy in the nation and a monumental development in the emergence of the schooling apparatus of the state. This more comprehensive view of the early landscape of education policy outlines a fact that is too often obscured: that schooling was a racial project in the United States from its inception, and that the origins of education as a foundational institution in American society can never be understood only through the frames of early white common schooling, but also require an accounting of the native and black presence in the story.

As previously mentioned, the story of the CFA is important to more than just the schooling experiences of indigenous people. This is immediately evident by the exploitation of black enslaved labor in the building of Brainerd—as well as many other missionary schools that followed. Beyond their use of enslaved labor in developing settler schooling for native students—and the practice of racial slavery among some native tribes—the government actors appearing in this chapter as architects of racialized education policy were also vocal defenders of slavery and advocates for the development of education for white citizens. For instance, when seeking support for Brainerd in 1816, Rev. Kingsbury consulted Jefferson on his plans, and we know that the latter held strong views about black intellectual inferiority while holding an equally strong, radical vision for universal education for white Americans. John Calhoun and Thomas McKenney both owned slaves, and the "civilization" that they hoped to promote in native nations was rooted in antiblackness. Indeed, part of the reason the Choctaw and Cherokee were considered closer to civilization than other native tribes—having been recognized among "the Five Civilized Tribes"—was precisely the fact that they owned enslaved black people, in addition to adopting other key features of white settler society, such as Western education.

Education policies like the CFA were being constructed in the minds—and offices—of influential men who were also invested in the domination of black people. The structural context of education policy in the United States derived from the minds of men who held complex views about distinct racial groups, as defined in relationship to one another in the broader social environment. The Civilization Fund Act's emergence correlated to racial projects enacted through white common schooling, and especially the criminalization of education for African Americans as motivated by the demands of the plantation economy.

The development of Brainerd and the CFA represent one piece of a three-pronged system of racialized educational policy in the earliest decades of the young republic. They contributed to a national landscape of schooling in service of a growing nation built on the domination of some to the benefit of and consolidation of power among others.

3

ANTI-LITERACY LAWS AND THE ROOTS OF ANTIBLACK EDUCATION POLICY

> A law of this tenor is absolutely necessary, and will continue to be necessary, until man can eat of the tree of knowledge and not know evil, or, in plainer parlance, until those of our negroes, who are taught to read the bible, shall be unable to read [David] Walker's pamphlet and other incendiary publications.[1]
>
> —Edward R. Laurens, South Carolina (1832)

Richard Parker learned to read and write through fugitive means, having been born enslaved on a Virginia plantation in 1806. Parker routinely kept a spelling book tucked away under his hat to avoid detection from prying white eyes, and he often received lessons from the daughter of his enslaver. Parker "was a favorite of hers," as he put it, so the young mistress tutored him regularly around three o'clock when she arrived home from school.[2] Parker's concealed curriculum and his playing school with the master's daughter—who would potentially inherit him as her property—were both forbidden actions according to his master and the state of Virginia.

On at least one occasion, Parker was discovered secretly playing school. For this, his enslaver ordered that he receive fifteen blows. Parker's flogging complied with the act signed into law by Virginia Governor Thomas Mann Randolph in 1819, which "reduc[ed] into one, the several acts concerning Slaves, Free Negroes and Mulattoes." This act included an anti-literacy statute, officially criminalizing reading and writing among enslaved people in the state, and it authorized whippings "at the discretion of any justice of the peace, not exceeding twenty lashes."[3] In 1831, shortly after a literate slave named Nat Turner led a revolt in Southampton, Virginia, the law became stricter, criminalizing all black education, including the education of free African Americans.[4]

Parker's memory of white suppression of black education is consistent with accounts from across the country, where African Americans were subjected to the decentralized enforcement of antiblack educational protocols in the United States. According to the testimony of formerly enslaved people, physical punishment and dismemberment were characteristic of white people's enforcement of anti-literacy laws and social customs—and I say "social customs" because even in the absence of anti-literacy laws, anti-literacy sentiments often prevailed anyhow. Some enslaved people recalled the cutting off of a forefinger.[5] Others told of children being whipped nearly to death, then being warned to forget what they had learned.[6] One overseer went as far as rubbing acid in the eyes of an enslaved boy caught reading under a tree.[7]

Ben Brown, a formerly enslaved man from Virginia, recalled how mere proximity to a book or loose sheets of paper led to punishment. "De slaves wuz not allowed any learning an' if any books, paper or pictures wuz foun' among us we wuz whipped if we couldn't explain where dey cum from," he recalled.[8] Minnie Davis, who was enslaved in Green County, Georgia, and who later became a teacher, recalled the town marshal attempting to whip her mother after learning she had been writing letters. Davis explained, "The Crawford children [children of her enslaver] were caught teaching my mother to read and write, but they were made to stop. Mother was quick to learn, and she never gave up. She would steal the newspapers and read up about the war, and she kept the other slaves posted as to how the war was progressing. She knew when the war was over almost as soon as Marse John did."[9]

Douglas Dorsey was born enslaved in Suwannee County, Florida, in 1851 to parents who were illegally captured in Maryland and sold into slavery. Dorsey had long been tasked with carrying the books of the Matair children on their way to school. While black education was criminalized, this did not stop masters from exploiting black enslaved labor in service of white education, which often created opportunities for subversion. One of the Matair children taught Dorsey to read and figure. After detecting Dorsey's literacy, the mistress in the Matair home decided to set a trap. She began writing on paper using a quill pen, then casually asked him to make out the words and the numbers. Dorsey "proudly answered in the affirmative, not suspecting anything." She asked Dorsey to name the letters and numbers, then to write them. What started as a simple demonstration of his recently acquired skills ended with Dorsey being struck in the face and Mrs. Matair threatening, "If I ever catch you making another figure anywhere, I'll cut off your right arm." To drive home the lesson, she took Dorsey and her own son, Willis, on the porch, beating them both to make the lesson stick.[10]

Dorsey was a slave. Willis, his future master. The literacy of the enslaved boy tugged at the instability of this relation. Dorsey's story points to the ubiquity of anti-literacy ideology as an expression of antiblackness during the antebellum period. Unlike other slave states during the antebellum period, Florida never established an anti-literacy law. Yet Douglas Dorsey's testimony joins several others, where formerly enslaved people from states that never formally criminalized black education—such as Kentucky—reported that anti-literacy laws were de facto across the South, even if such proscriptions were not written into state legislation.[11]

Anti-literacy laws reinforced black people's status as noncitizens. It fortified a prosthetic color line between those who were people and those who were, or could be, property. The intimacy between the enslaved and those deemed enslaveable manifested with great clarity in the national culture, especially when it came to literacy, schools, and the system of knowledge.[12] While such antiblack sentiments were endemic to the national educational landscape, it was most widespread in the Southern states prior to the Civil War, in part because it was in the South that the critical mass of black people—as men and women in bondage—resided.

Some scholars point out that anti-literacy laws were loosely enforced.[13] This point is well taken. In fact, I am unaware of any cases where violations of anti-literacy laws by black people appeared before a judge and jury. However, by overemphasizing this point, we run the risk of implying that these laws had minimal implications in the lives of black people, suggesting that a lack of formal enforcement meant anti-literacy laws were, as nineteenth-century slaveholder Richard Fuller called them "dead letters"—essentially laws on the books that were never enforced.[14] I treat such assessments with caution, because anti-literacy laws were widely meted out at the local level, by slave masters and overseers themselves—as was the case with Richard Parker, Minnie Davis's mother, Douglas Dorsey, and in iconic cases like that of Frederick Douglass, who was enslaved in Maryland prior to the state's adoption of an anti-literacy law.

Black people were vulnerable to surveillance and punishment by any person who chose to enforce widely accepted racial norms. White Americans were licensed to police the bodies and actions of black people, and account after account from the antebellum era emphasizes this point. While court records and the archive reflect little enforcement of anti-literacy laws, the proliferation of black testimony about the ubiquity of anti-literacy ideology, and the violence used to reinforce it, requires that we reconsider the implications of such laws and the work they did as part and parcel of an ever-expanding schooling apparatus of the United States. Anti-literacy laws have generally been treated as a feature of the peculiar institution of slavery, and as context for understanding black people's fervor for education after emancipation; however, I assert that anti-literacy laws are foundational to the national landscape of education policy in the newly united states. It is an integral part of the story of schooling and the building of the nation, where educational opportunities were intentionally imposed on some racial groups and withheld from others for distinct political and economic purposes, all of which were structurally entangled.

Anti-literacy laws are one of the oldest forms of education policy in the United States, with slaveholders coordinating across state lines to advance anti-literacy policies. For instance, Georgia's 1770 anti-literacy law was a near-exact copy of South Carolina's 1740 statute. Mississippi's 1823 law borrowed language from Virginia's, passed in 1819.[15] As historians have underscored, slaveholders used the Southern agricultural press, whereby publications circulated for those in the agricultural industry, to share advice on "slave management," including how to Christianize enslaved people without teaching them to read. To accomplish the latter, some stressed oral lessons to avoid arming black people with the unpredictable tool of literacy.[16]

In his 1849 slave narrative, Henry Bibb described the decentralized yet ambient nature of anti-literacy laws and the constraining impact they had on black educational life. While enslaved in Kentucky, Bibb references the Georgia's colonial law as precedent. "Similar laws [to Georgia's] exist in most of the slave States," Bibb observed, "and patrols are sent out after night and on the Sabbath day to enforce them." Bibb described how white mobs, or patrols, "go through their respective towns to prevent slaves from meeting for religious worship or mental instruction." Recognizing such antiblack educational policies to be about more than just the state of Georgia, Bibb declared, "This is the regulation and law of American Slavery, as sanctioned by the Government of the United States, without which it could not exist."[17] Bibb argues that anti-literacy laws were part of a formalizing national legislative context. It was not just a story about the South, not just a story about slavery. It was a story about how education developed as a key stratifying agent in the American social order, a process of stratification enacted by state actors and driven by racial ideologies undergirding slavery and, as the previous chapter has shown, settler colonialism as well.

On at least one occasion in Virginia, someone who violated the state's anti-literacy policy was found guilty and punished through the courts: Margaret Douglass, a white woman. A judge and jury found her guilty of teaching black children to read and write, between 1852 and 1853, at a school operating out of her home in Norfolk, Virginia. She would be fined one dollar and forced to serve a month in jail. It was extremely rare for a white woman to serve jail time during the antebellum era, especially in the South. As one scholar explained, "Seldom could more than one or two women be found in a Southern penitentiary" prior to the Civil War.[18] When they were imprisoned, it was because their actions were deemed so heinous, legal authorities felt the need to make an example of them—typically actions that transgressed the strict gendered moral code of the day or extremely violent crimes. Margaret's punishment was extraordinary for the 1850s, and it signals the severity of her crime in the eyes of the white male judge and jury who felt compelled to punish her even as they recognized Margaret to be "a female, apparently of fair and respectable standing in community."[19]

Unlike Richard Parker, Minnie Davis's mother, and Douglas Dorsey, Margaret Douglass was recognized as a citizen: a political subject entitled to the rights of habeas corpus. Despite her inferior status to white men in Virginia, Douglass was not (legally) vulnerable to the kind of unrestrained violence inflicted on the bodies of black people during this time. Such acts would have been deemed not only a violation of her individual rights, but also the entire project of the nation, as "the nation" itself was most intimately expressed—symbolically speaking—through the domestic sphere. The nuclear white American family, and the home, were understood as the most basic unit of the country, with the domestic sphere falling under the immediate purview of white women—those responsible for mothering the nation, and its future citizens.

Margaret Douglass was a single mother, a former slave owner, and a new resident in Norfolk, having been born in DC before marrying and raising her children in Charleston, South Carolina. Recognizing an opportunity to do some good, and likely in need of making a living for herself, now that she was a widow, Douglass started a school for free black children. However, Douglass was no abolitionist. She took no firm stance against the institution of slavery in her autobiographical writing nor her testimony in court. By her estimation, one could educate black people, especially free black children, and still maintain the institution of slavery. She later wrote of Virginia's anti-literacy statute, "This law, although connected with slavery as a Southern institution, has not necessarily anything to do with the abstract question of slavery itself."[20] In many respects, Douglass's story reveals broader limitations black (and native) people came to recognize about white paternalism and allyship throughout history. They recognized this in white abolitionists who disagreed with slavery in principle, yet still believed black people to be racially inferior. This is also evident among white missionaries like Brainerd's Cyrus Kingsbury, who questioned the ethics of slavery, but chose to be silent on the issue for the purposes of advancing his cause of native education while relying on enslaved labor to build and run his mission school. Douglass embodied contradictions that anticipate similar shortcomings of white advocates in the antislavery movement as well as those among "the friends of the Indians," both political spaces where white women gained organizing experience that would be appropriated toward the movement for women's rights during the late nineteenth and early twentieth centuries, leading to the Nineteenth Amendment; a long story exposing how white women, not just white men, benefited from the subjugation of black and native people.[21]

...

In the spring of 1853, students attending Margaret Douglass's school experienced the death of a classmate. The young black girl had been sick for some time, and her death seemed to be imminent, as she participated in the planning of her final rites. She selected six classmates who would dress in white and serve as pallbearers for her funeral. Margaret and her daughter, Rosa, developed an attachment to the young girl, having taught her in their school for several months. They even stayed up "night after night, with the suffering child"—for whom we have no name—during her final days. Given such affections, the mother and daughter decided to participate in the funeral procession for their student. This public ceremony of free black people in Virginia would have been viewed with suspicion and unease by white onlookers. That the crowd was racially mixed certainly heightened the discomfort of white townsfolk. Margaret and Rosa would likely have been aware that their public display of affection for a black person could be interpreted as incendiary, perhaps even an unintended expression of antislavery sentiments.

Margaret knew that Virginia and many other Southern states made it illegal to teach enslaved black people to read and write. However, she later expressed being "totally ignorant of any existing law prohibiting the instruction of free colored children." Margaret pointed out that prior to opening the school at her residence, she observed many of the churches in Norfolk "were actually instructing from books both slave and free colored children, and had done so for years without molestation." While aware of laws prohibiting instruction of enslaved blacks, Margaret believed them to have been leniently enforced. As a single mother, and a capable teacher, she saw an opportunity to make a living and, perhaps, do some good. She too would teach black children, but only those who came from free black families.[22] This was her story, as she later told it.

"I was careful to have no slaves among our scholars," explained Margaret. Despite this precaution, the reality is that since 1831, in the wake of Nat Turner's slave revolt in Southampton, it was illegal to teach both enslaved and free black people to read and write. Irrespective of when and how frequently the law was enforced, the mechanism was in place to suppress the education of all black people in Virginia, as lawmakers and their white constituents hoped to control and suppress the political aspirations of black people, minimize their exposure to abolitionist literature, and disrupt their ability to use the written word for coordinated action. As demonstrated by the case of Margaret and Rosa Douglass, such laws could also be used to target white people who appeared to be sympathizers of the antislavery movement.

Some days after the funeral, on May 9, 1853, Margaret answered a thundering knock at her door. Nearly all twenty-five students were assembled inside her home, her daughter, Rosa, sat at the pinewood desk ready to begin instruction.[23] When Margaret answered the door, she was greeted by the face of an officer who immediately inquired about who lived in the house. Margaret informed him that she and her daughter lived at the house alone. He then asked more direct questions, queries that got to the heart of the matter, exposing the true purpose for his visit.

"You keep a school?" he asked.

"Yes, sir," Margaret replied.

"A school for colored children?"

"Yes."

"I must see those children," the officer demanded.[24]

Confused, and surely a little frightened, Margaret wondered what business the officer could possibly have with the children in her school, or anything at her home, for that matter. The officer informed Margaret that he had been sent on direct orders by the mayor. Accompanied by a second officer, the constable asked no further questions, instead forcing his way into Margaret's home.[25]

The two large white men went into the classroom, demanding the names of each student and their parents. The black students were terrified. They knew all too well—likely more than their white teachers—the kind of violence and harm that could come from interactions with constables. After recording the names, the officers marched the group down to the mayor's office. Margaret tried to comfort them, though she herself had no idea what would happen. She arranged them into pairs and instructed them to march two by two, then turned them over to the officers and followed their instructions. The entire group made their procession to an unknown fate, the officers following them, clubs in hand.

This scene of twenty-five black children walking two by two under close police watch with their white teachers behind them stood in stark contrast to the image of these same students gathering in a public procession just weeks before to bury their classmate. Perhaps this public ritual of shaming the students and their teachers was a corrective to the disruption they previously caused to the social environment—a public display of police force to emphasize that (racial) order continued to be secure.

As they reached the mayor's office, the question of "What will happen to the students?" continued circling in Margaret's mind. She posed this question to the mayor, who assured her nothing would happen to the children or their parents. Margaret explained to the mayor that she was aware of laws prohibiting the teaching of enslaved people but had no knowledge that teaching free blacks was also illegal. Margaret wept and pled ignorance to the mayor. Perhaps her tears carried some power because the mayor decided on leniency. The pupils were immediately dismissed, and they "fled like so many little birds let loose from a cage," Margaret recalled. In the end, the goal on the part of Norfolk authorities seemed to have been the shutting down of her school. This goal was accomplished that day. Douglass's school, which operated for just under a year, closed for good.[26]

The mayor was forgiving. However, a grand jury learned of Douglass's offense and chose to indict her, and while Richard Parker was subjected to fifteen lashes at the hands of his enslaver for disobeying Virginia's anti-literacy law, Margaret Douglass, a single white woman, would meet her fate in the courtroom. Margaret's trial began on November 2, 1853, before Judge Richard Baker and a jury of a dozen white men. Margaret refused a lawyer and decided to represent herself in the courtroom. She stood by her decision to educate the free colored children of Norfolk, stating matter-of-factly, "I am a strong advocate for the religious and moral instruction of the whole human family!" Such broad statements by Margaret appeared not only unapologetic but were also interpreted as implying a commitment to social equality among the races. Her words not only irritated the judge and jury; they outright infuriated the men. Judge Baker condemned "the indiscreet freedom with which [Margaret Douglass] spoke of [her] regard for the colored race in general." He regarded such opinions "in the present state of our society . . . as manifestly mischievous." His ruling would express such stern discontent.[27]

The judge found Douglass's offense to be among the most heinous. Teaching black children was an egregious violation of the law that threatened the safety of all white people. According to the judge's assessment, Douglass's offense threatened the preservation of the very state itself. Honorable Richard H. Baker ruled in *Commonwealth of Virginia v. Margaret Douglass* (1854) that the accused was "guilty of one of the vilest crimes that ever disgraced society."[28]

...

While Judge Baker cited an 1835 precedent from the state of Virginia in his ruling, anti-literacy laws date back to nearly a century earlier. To appreciate the conflict at the heart of Margaret Douglass's case requires some context about the political-economic motivations behind anti-literacy laws, where antiblackness and emerging conceptions of education interacted and formed a distinct racial project during the slavery era in the United States.

Anti-literacy laws preceded American independence. In 1740, colonial South Carolina passed its historic anti-literacy law in response to the Stono Slave Rebellion of 1739.[29] White South Carolinians believed enslaved people used the written word to organize their revolt and plans of escape to Spanish Florida. Indeed, South Carolina's colonial legislature's belief that literate slaves led to "great inconveniences" anticipated Judge Baker's argument that restricting black people's access to intellectual development, particularly literacy, could help safeguard white supremacy and its key ancillary institution of chattel slavery.[30]

The criminalization of literacy and mental development was one of many reasons slavery in the modern world was distinguishable from its progenitors—for instance, in ancient Greece and Rome—in addition, of course, to increased value associated with racial difference. As nineteenth-century political theorist Alexis de Tocqueville writes of this distinction, "The immediate ills resulting from slavery were almost the same among the Ancients as among the Moderns, but the consequences were different. Among the Ancients, the slave belonged to the same race as his master and was often superior to him in education and enlightenment. Only freedom separated one from the other; freedom granted, they easily combined."[31]

This would not be the case with racial chattel slavery. In addition to the refinement of the slave category as indiscriminately associated with African-descendant people or those racialized "black"—whereby "the memory of slavery dishonors the race, and race perpetuates the memory of slavery"—the matter of education and intelligence also became an instrument drawing the line between free and unfree, black and nonblack.[32] It was a new structure, distinctly American, forged through the unprecedented journeys of the Middle Passage and the antiblack racial regime they ushered in. Education, schooling, and the system of knowledge—what I've referred to elsewhere as the schooling apparatus of the United States—emerged as vital instruments used to justify and reproduce this new world and the social relations that gave meaning to its form.

Criminalizing black education was critical to the institution of chattel slavery for conceptual and practical reasons. The policing of African languages and African-derived spiritual practices were closely aligned methods used to disrupt black independent thought and knowledge production. As historian Heather Williams explained, "Masters made every attempt to control their captives' thoughts and imaginations, indeed their hearts and minds. Maintaining a system of bondage in the Age of Enlightenment depended upon the masters being able to speak for the slave, to deny his or her humanity, and to draw a line between slave consciousness and human will."[33] Therefore, when it came to the matter of reading and writing in particular, the most widely recognizable forms of reason and intellectual development during the Enlightenment era, "The presence of literate slaves threatened to give lie to the entire system. Reading indicated to the world that this so-called property had a mind, and writing foretold the ability to construct an alternative narrative about bondage itself. Literacy among slaves would expose [unseen truths about] slavery, and masters knew it."[34]

White developers and enforcers of anti-literacy laws understood such legal mechanisms to be about the maintenance of chattel slavery. By constraining knowledge and policing educational opportunity, they believed, black resistance might be minimized and contained; black people's position as both slave labor and slave capital, and thus the source of large sums of white American wealth, would be secured. Denying black literacy was about the protection of white possessions—land, people, and other things they claimed as their property.

Laws criminalizing black education contradicted but also simultaneously reinforced racist ideas about black intellectual inferiority. Justifications for slavery hinged on false notions that black people were less intellectually capable than other racial groups; that they were more prone to criminality and more inclined toward sexually deviant behavior, among other racial myths that positioned black people as the antithesis of the reasoning human subject. However, if African-descended people were mentally inferior, there would be no need for such extreme measures to suppress educational opportunities among them. Nevertheless, by keeping black people uneducated and illiterate in a world that increasingly associated literacy with citizenship and civilization, such laws helped reinforce ideas that black people were mentally inferior. The logic was circular in this way.

At the heart of anti-literacy ideology was a peculiar conundrum. Evidence of literacy and the capacity to engage in high-order thinking among the enslaved troubled the very notion that black people were destined to be slaves. William Whewell, the white British polymath and master at Cambridge College, offers a succinct confession of this contradiction. In his antebellum writings, Whewell asserted, "Such laws suppose the capacity of negroes for intellectual culture, and are an implicit confession that it is necessary to degrade their minds in order to keep their bodies in slavery."[35] Francis Wayland, the white American president of Brown University, built on Whewell's assertion to point out how anti-literacy laws were self-justifying: "What must be [the slaves'] condition, when, having been by . . . prohibition rendered ignorant, stupid, and sensual, [and yet] this very ignorance, stupidity, and sensuality is pleaded as a reason why they should be held down to this degradation forever?"[36]

Thus far, I have elaborated on some of the conceptual reasons that white Americans implemented anti-literacy laws. But there were also practical reasons. Criminalizing black education was about mitigating the threat of black rebellion: to prevent enslaved and free African Americans from reading antislavery literature that might stimulate their dreams of freedom; to foreclose the possibility of them writing passes to escape; to prevent them from using the written word to coordinate rebellions across plantations, or indeed, from furthering the common wind of black revolt already sailing across the Atlantic world.[37]

Anti-literacy laws, as a form of early educational policy, and the contradictory racial logics used to legitimize them, were the product of white anxieties. For instance, Edward R. Laurens, a South Carolina slaveholder, politician, and self-styled public intellectual when it came to matters of managing enslaved people, articulated a widely shared perspective about reducing threats of black retribution. In an address to the Agricultural Society of South-Carolina on September 18, 1832, that was later published in the Southern press, Laurens explained, "[A] law of this tenor is absolutely necessary, and will continue to be necessary, until man can eat of the tree of knowledge and not know evil, or, in plainer parlance, until those of our negroes, who are taught to read the bible, shall be unable to read [David] Walker's pamphlet and other incendiary publications."[38] Laurens was a leading proponent of state intervention to regulate the relationship between slaveholders and enslaved people.[39] He believed, as did many others, that the manner in which white enslavers managed their property had implications for their entire class (and race) in a slave society.

Lauren's efforts, along with other lawmakers, resulted in the 1834 omnibus "law in relation to slaves and free persons of colour." This law included a revised anti-literacy law for enslaved black people, stating: "By the Act of 1834, slaves are prohibited to be taught to read or write, under a penalty (if a white person may offend) not exceeding $100 fine and six months imprisonment. if [*sic*] a *free person of color*, not exceeding 50 lashes and a fine of $50."[40] Laurens believed ardently in banning free black education as well. Traditional slaveholding legislators, who believed in spiritual instruction of black people, forced Laurens to concede this point and abandon the stipulation that would universally criminalize black education in the state.[41]

Laurens was not alone in his concern about the circulation of antislavery literature like David Walker's writings. Judge Baker raised similar concerns when ruling on the case of Margaret Douglass, spelling out the threat of abolitionist pamphlets circulating in antebellum Virginia. He addressed the court as follows:

> *Many now living well remember how, and when, and why, the anti-slavery fury commenced, and by what means its manifestations were*

made public. Our mails were clogged with abolition pamphlets and inflammatory documents, to be distributed among our Southern negroes to induce them to cut our throats. These, however, were not the only means resorted to by Northern fanatics to stir up insubordination among our slaves. They scattered, far and near, pocket-handkerchiefs, and other similar articles, with frightful engravings, and printed over with anti-slavery nonsense, with the view to work upon the feelings and ignorance of our negroes, who otherwise would have remained comfortable and happy. Under such circumstances there was but one measure of protection for the South, and that was adopted.[42]

Judge Baker's claim was only partly true: Radical abolitionist literature increased in circulation during the decades leading up to the Civil War. This caused great anxiety among white planters, motivating stricter anti-literacy measures. However, it was a complete fabrication to suggest that black people were comfortable and happy prior to the circulation of such literature. Antislavery writings were not poisoning the minds of black people but instead came to reflect in literary form a steady stream of radical critique long flowing in black culture and black consciousness.[43]

David Walker's 1829 *Appeal to the Coloured Citizens of the World* reflected this critique. In this text, he encouraged members of his race to take up arms and rebel against slavery. In addition to advocating for armed rebellion, Walker also articulated a radical vision of black education. He declared, "For colored people to acquire learning in this country, makes tyrants quake and tremble on their sandy foundation . . . [because] [t]hey know that their infernal deeds of cruelty will be made known to the world."[44] Walker lived in Boston and worked as a tailor, but his pamphlet was smuggled down the eastern seaboard, making its ways deep into the territory of slavery. Walker's *Appeal* was banned in many Southern states. Despite efforts to suppress its circulation, the text found its audience.

One might imagine "pamphlets ripped out" and "read aloud" (to borrow from poet Rita Dove), where some person decoded the audacious words of Walker in the presence of other black people on arrival in the

Carolinas, in Georgia, in New Orleans.[45] A similar scene of communal literacy appeared amid the historic plan for insurrection in Charleston, organized by Denmark Vesey in 1822. The revolt was squashed before it could be executed, but as Vesey's coconspirator explained, the leader "had the habit of reading to me all the passages in the newspaper that related to Santo Domingo [present-day Haiti, which led its own successful slave revolt in 1791]." Vesey also relayed stories about communicating with black cooks who worked on ships traveling between Charleston and Haiti, explaining that the Haitians would join in black Charlestonians' fight for freedom if they would just strike the first blow.[46]

Such histories linking black education and rebellion stoked anxieties among white Americans and informed their responses to events like the circulation of Walker's *Appeal*. Police officers confiscated Walker's pamphlet in several Southern states. The first documented account was in Savannah, Georgia, before Christmas of 1829, and similar reports followed. The hysteria surrounding Walker's pamphlet is well documented. After Savannah, one historian writes, "20 more copies appeared in Georgia's capital, then another 30 in Virginia. More materialized in New Orleans and Charleston two months later." By the end of 1830, "more than 200 had breached the Carolinas. Police scrambled but failed to confiscate most copies, despite in some instances sending undercover agents into Black communities."[47] It became evident that Walker's *Appeal* was spreading through networks of runaway slaves, providing ample evidence that, contrary to Judge Baker's assessment, the enslaved population was never happy and content. Indeed, their physical acts of running away were deeply connected to their mental acts of escape in the form of fugitive literacy and clandestine education. White people had always been aware of this, and therefore, were always in a state of panic. Yet the banning of Walker's book did not end the consistent flow of black radical thought and educational efforts.

This reality was not confined to the South, as cases also appear in Northern states and predate Walker's text. A New York City school founded through the Society for the Propagation of the Gospel was shut down in 1712 after a group of enslaved people led an insurrection in which nine white people were killed and several others wounded. Many believed the plot to have been orchestrated by enslaved people who received religious and literacy instruction at this school. This theory was quickly disproven, but the school was shut down anyhow.[48]

Two years after the publication of Walker's *Appeal*, in September 1831, the townspeople of New Haven, Connecticut, blocked a black-led effort to establish an "African College" by a vote of 700–4. White townspeople expressed their resistance to the idea by vandalizing a black-owned hotel, a black-owned home, and the home of a known abolitionist. Quite revealing was a local newspaper's coverage, which connected the town's refusal to welcome what could have been the nation's first black college to the recent Nat Turner–led slave insurrection in Southampton, Virginia, the month before. In the writings, Turner was depicted as "a shrewd fellow" who "reads and writes, [and] preaches." The story of this slave revolt was followed by another column, titled "Gabriel's Defeat." Gabriel Prosser was a literate blacksmith who organized an insurrection in Richmond, Virgina, in 1800, though it was unsuccessful, and his ability to read and write was also emphasized in the newspaper's accounting of the threat he represented.[49]

Black education continued to be linked with black rebellion in the white imagination. In 1833, the Connecticut legislature established its "Black Law," a piece of education policy that prohibited black students from traveling into the state to attend school.[50] While this was not an outright ban on black literacy, as was the case in most Southern states, such unrestrained hostility to black education in antebellum New England was part of a broader educational landscape where mechanisms of law and policy were used to criminalize and underdevelop educational opportunities for black people.

A throughline can be drawn connecting the dots of these prior events to the controversy surrounding Margaret Douglass's conviction for educating free black students in antebellum Virginia. Across all these stories, one gleans how white leaders employed policies to suppress and criminalize black education while at the same time expanding policies for native schooling through the US War Department as a settler-colonial project, and likewise, fiercely advocating for common schooling to expand white education as a public good. The subtractive schooling policies targeting black people are informed by their primary position in the United States' mode of production, as an exploitable group of enslaved laborers. Such investments were at the heart of the conflict in the state of Virginia, and the judge and jury in Margaret Douglass's case would make this explicit.

•••

Long-standing anxieties among white people linking black education and black rebellion shaped the Virginia law Margaret Douglass violated as well as the punishment she received: The Norfolk jury rendered a verdict of *guilty*, demanding a fine of one dollar. Judge Baker, however, insisted that Douglass would also serve one month in jail.

Baker's ruling was historic. He lamented, "I exceedingly regret, that in being called on, *for the first time*, to act under the law in question, it becomes my duty to impose the required punishment upon a female, apparently of fair and respectable standing in community."[51] Nevertheless, some meaningful punishment was necessary given the lack of remorse in Douglass's testimony, where she showed little appreciation for the necessity of anti-literacy laws or the legitimacy of the established racial hierarchies that conditioned the social world where such racialized educational policy were expressed and upheld. Baker declared that Margaret's "bold and open opposition to it [Virginia's anti-literacy law] is a matter not to be slightly regarded." Upholding and enforcing anti-literacy laws, which limited the intellectual instruction of black people, was "a measure of self-preservation and protection," he lectured. Douglass, like any other responsible citizen of Virginia, must have some understanding and appreciation for this position.[52]

Judge Baker, in his verdict, lectured Douglass and the court about why "every Southern slave State in our country . . . has deemed it wise and just to adopt [anti-literacy] laws with similar provisions." While acknowledging the importance of black people receiving religious instructions to make them moral and content, Baker carefully insisted that such education could take place without intellectual instruction, without black people learning the fundamentals of literacy. Religious lessons rendered orally were effective means for achieving such ends. Black education had to be criminalized, Baker insisted, because of the "abolition pamphlets and inflammatory documents" that circulated and clogged the mail.[53] He insisted such policy was the only pragmatic solution.

Having listened to Judge Baker's verdict, reflected on her actions, and served her month in prison, Margaret Douglass continued to find her predicament both laughable and terrifying. The idea that such a "dignified and aristocratic State" like Virginia would be placed in a perilous circumstance because "a few little negro boys and girls had learned" to read and write, or, furthermore, that its entire existence "was jeopardized in the year 1853" because of her running a school for free black children, was to Douglass not only hyperbolic, but most of all ungodly.[54] Shortly after her release, Margaret Douglass and her daughter, Rosa, moved to Philadelphia.[55] After all, she was a free white woman, able to move about the country as she pleased. The impact of anti-literacy laws in the lives of black students, enslaved and free, had a more lasting impact. The stories of Richard Parker and Douglas Dorsey told earlier this chapter are a reminder of such diverging fates when it came to the application and consequences of this law.

...

Like Parker and Dorsey, Mary Jane Wilson was also enslaved. She was born in Portsmouth, Virginia, around 1850 to a mother and father in an "abroad marriage," meaning they were owned by different masters and lived on different plantations. Though she had been a girl when the Civil War broke out, Mary Jane had clear memories of her distinct vulnerability as an enslaved child. She recalled how the man who enslaved her father took him to Norfolk to place him in jail so that he could be auctioned and sold. The woman who owned Mary Jane and her mother bought her father "so he could be with us," she recalled.[56]

While this incident resulted in her father being closer, it could just have easily ended with him being sold down the river, as was the case for many enslaved people whose families were constantly disrupted by the domestic slave trade. Mary Jane learned that though her parents were married, enslaved people had no autonomy over their lives—their marriage was never just the joining of two people, where two flesh became one. For marriages among the enslaved, there was always "the third flesh," as historian Tera Hunter explains, where the master's will and desires violently intruded upon the sanctity of the union.[57]

The Norfolk jail where Mary Jane's father was held would likely have been the same one where Margaret Douglass was imprisoned for teaching black children to read and write. Portsmouth was three miles south of Norfolk and just over the Elizabeth River. So, the site of Mary Jane's enslavement was not far at all from the school, where Margaret Douglass was "careful to have no slaves among [her] scholars." Mary Jane recalled how her status as an enslaved girl was particularly expressed through the denial of literacy and educational opportunity, explaining, "I didn't get any teachings when I was a slave."[58] The policing of literacy and educational opportunity along racial lines helped draw and reinforce the boundary between enslaved and free, black and nonblack. Such was the case in Virginia, as it was, to varying degrees, in the United States overall.

Like many enslaved people who arrived at a conception of literacy as a key instrument and expression of freedom, Mary Jane immediately sought out an education following the Civil War. "When I was free, I went to school," she proudly explained. "The first school I went to was held in a church. Soon they builded a school building that was called, 'Chestnut Street Academy,' and I went there. After finishing Chestnut Street Academy, I went to Hampton Institute. In 1874, six years after Hampton Institute was started, I graduated."[59]

Mary Jane came back to Portsmouth and started a school of her own. Her desire was to teach, having deeply understood what the denial of education meant for black people—it was not just about the denial of educational opportunity, it was also about the misrecognition of their humanity; the denial of an interior life. She detailed the story as follows: "I opened a school in my home, and I had lots of students. After two years my class grew so fast and large that my father built a school for me in our back yard. I had as many as seventy-five pupils at one time."[60] Mary Jane, having once been enslaved and forbidden from learning, now committed herself to cultivating the minds and souls of her people, as a means of refusing the violent history of slavery and its persistent encroachment on black life after the Civil War.

Many of Mary Jane's students continued in the same tradition as her and became teachers as well.[61] She taught them in the schoolhouse established in her home, then, as a final rite, the students graduated at the historic Emanuel African Methodist Episcopal Church in Portsmouth.[62] The church was a poignant place to send off her scholars; like other sites of black life and education in the American South, the original church—erected before the American Revolution—was burned down in 1856 "by wicked hands," only to be rebuilt the following year.[63]

Mary Jane's school operated in a black educational tradition that emerged in the shadows of anti-literacy laws and amid blazing white resistance. It was a beautiful tradition, but it was one shaped by an ugly and violent history—one where nefarious education policies criminalizing black education became integral to the schooling apparatus of the United States, as it expanded during the antebellum era. Mary Jane's story is one that has come to instill pride among many today, but it is important not to look past the way hegemony functions in the story itself.

The intertwined stories of Richard Parker, the enslaved boy who received fifteen blows for reading and writing, Margaret Douglass, a white woman imprisoned for teaching black students and violating Virginia's anti-literacy law, and Mary Jane Wilson, a formerly enslaved woman who would start her own school after the Civil War, present an important opportunity to reflect on the crucial role the political economy of slavery played in shaping the national educational landscape. The mechanisms of law and policy used to restrict black education were an integral part of the infrastructure of the schooling apparatus of the United States as it was yet forming, and such mechanisms were motivated by the political-economic interests of the white planter elite.

Like the Civilization Fund Act of 1819, which expanded the role of native education as a key US strategy for dealing with the "Indian problem," anti-literacy laws were also a form of education policy used to facilitate a racial project in service of the nation. What's more, such education policies informed by the political-economic demands of settler colonialism and chattel slavery were also hugely important for the development of citizenship education for white students. It is to this story, the development of white American education, that we will now turn in the following chapter, where the relational formation of race was central to the grammar of American schooling, and where education, as a racial project, functions as an integral part of the nation-building project.

4

NATIVE LAND, BLACK LABOR, AND THE DEVELOPMENT OF SCHOOLING AS A WHITE GOOD

While previous chapters traced developments in antiblack and anti-indigenous educational policy prior to the Civil War, what follows is an analysis of how mainstream white common schooling developed as a racial project through laws and policies that constructed public education as a system primarily meant to benefit white Americans. In this context, "schooling as a white good" functioned as an organizing principle for the schooling apparatus of the United States, though white schooling was not the only racial project constituting the national educational landscape, as evidenced by long-standing federal support for native schooling as well as the long history of anti-literacy laws that criminalized black education.[1] The political-economic motivations for the latter two phenomena, as this chapter will reveal, were in fact deeply intertwined with the story of white educational expansion—a story of expansion that was integral to the building of the nation. I argue that this relational history of race is part of the physical, fiscal, and epistemological development of white schooling.

The "founding fathers" shared a commitment to education as a national priority, though this commitment is not explicitly spelled out in the Articles of Confederation nor in the US Constitution.[2] Historians of education have long observed that the architects of the new republic desired to educate citizens of their individual rights, while also cultivating a deep investment in, and loyalty to, the nation.[3] They "regard[ed] the common school as the *sine qua non* [something that is absolutely necessary] of republicanism." So central to early US visions of republicanism was the common school that scholars insisted education was "in effect a fourth branch of government."[4] Education, according to early US political thinkers, was essential for internal development, coherence, and the long-term preservation of the fledgling new republic.

Constructing a unified nation out of a collection of rebellious colonies that had just risked everything to break away from the Crown, as well as the territories they continued to amass, was no small feat. They looked to schools as essential building blocks to be used in the process of constructing the nation—a strategy for holding together a geographically expansive public with an increasingly diverse set of priorities.

Early visionaries of US common schooling had a very particular group of citizens in mind. The architects of the American republic conceived of schooling as a public good, where white citizens were the ideal political subjects. Schooling, as a nation-building project, was conceived of as a white good, to borrow from education historian Benjamin Justice.[5] It was crafted with white students (especially white male students) as its primary beneficiaries. White students were to inherit the nation. They were the ideal citizen and, thus, the ideal student.

Political articulations of education as a key component of nation-building are found in the earliest years of American independence. Scholars agree on this point. For instance, David Tyack, Thomas James, and Aaron Benavot point to "the educational provision of the Ordinance of 1787," documenting: "As successive generations of Americans undertook their *errands into the wilderness*, they were *determined to carry with them the civilizing institutions* they had known in more *settled communities*."[6] While origin stories of American schooling do well to account for the political nature of education as a part of statecraft, the social reality of racial formation at the heart of this nation-building project generally goes unnamed. Whiteness is invisible as a racial category, and black and native people are only marginally related to the story—that is, when or if they are mentioned at all. Yet, upon closer scrutiny, such absences call attention to themselves.

The wilderness. Civilizing institutions. Settled communities. Such language used by scholars to narrate the historic development of common schools as a key building block in US expansion merits unpacking, because the renderings betray much about what is seen and unseen, said and unsaid, in the origin stories passed on about the roots of American schooling.

The wilderness paints a broad stroke of forests and trees—lands uninhabited and unconquered by human civilization—regions of the earth that have yet to be "known." The wilderness is also a biblical place: Christ was tested in the wilderness; God's chosen people were lost in the wilderness, wandering, until they found the Promised Land. White missionaries, for instance, often drew from biblical notions of the "wilderness" and "the chase" when describing their work with native people, seeking to justify and frame the urgency of their educational activities. Cyrus Kingsbury, founder of Brainerd Mission, the first government-owned mission school for native people, conceived of his mission as "civilizing & converting the savages of our wilderness." He marveled at his ability to disrupt "the chase" and assemble a classroom at Brainerd full of "these tawny sons and daughters of the forest."[7]

For missionaries, the "wilderness" was not simply a zone of waste devoted to "the hunt," but also a biblical wilderness where God was absent, and where temptation abounded. Despite differences in connotative depth, however, both the federal government and missionaries agreed that "the hunt" and the "wilderness" it necessitated were the marks of an uncivilized nation. It was a place waiting to be conquered by the hands and workings of human civilization, as they conceived of it. Meanwhile, the "civilizing institutions" and "settled communities" referred to by Tyack, James, and Benavot implied benevolent institutions meant to protect human life and construct stable, coherent communities to expand the nation. Settlers hoped to use these social institutions as they expanded into new "wild" geographies through harmless "errands." Yet the logic of the wilderness as both biblical and pastoral is key to understanding how native Americans and enslaved (native) Africans were understood as belonging to the wilderness and needing to be civilized, tamed, and made available for the expansion of white civilization and its capitalist order. Beneath such seemingly neutral language is a much more violent story of racial domination and educational development.

Such defanged characterizations of US imperialist expansion are consistent with dominant origin narratives of American schooling. They present a sanitized narrative that elides native land dispossession mobilized through military force and perpetual theft. Benjamin Justice's characterization of US settlers as holding "twin commitments to common schools and white supremacy," to the notion of education as a white good, however, offers an alternative framing for interpreting such early development of white American education.[8]

I find the silence on the political economy of race and its relationship to the development of white American schooling to be peculiar. Historians of early public education, for instance, passively note how school funds established before and after American independence were generally established through land grants or revenue generated from selling "public lands." Yet the notion of public lands (or "federal lands") appears in such narratives as a stable and natural event, as a neutral categorization. As detail unworthy of further explanation or inquiry.

Finding such details to be ripe for further unraveling, I ask the following questions: What happens to this history when we refuse to take for granted the idea of "public lands," having recognized how deeply entrenched racial domination was to early conceptions of the American public sphere? What happens when we trouble such terms in the historiography by taking seriously the role of aggressive US land grabs, and indigenous land dispossession more broadly, as the precondition for the creation and classification of such territories as "public lands"? What happens when we approach the history of white common schooling in a way that is more accountable to the history of indigenous peoples and lands, noting the centrality of their exploitation to the story? For indeed, this violent history of settler-colonial procedure is key to the building of white public education, having been a primary source for generating raw capital in service of a developing schooling apparatus of the United States.[9]

Relatedly, what happens when we ask questions about the role of property taxes in the early funding of American education, while attending to the realities of slave capital and *people who were property*? What happens when we inquire about school funds created to support white education that relied on investment bonds from banks that trafficked in the commercial enterprise of the trans-Atlantic slave trade? What happens when we acknowledge that US schooling is one of the most representative sites where the grammar of the American social order, and all of its attendant racial ideologies, was expressed, refined, and reproduced?

Certain language and prior understandings cease to hold meaning when we name the presence of settler colonialism and chattel slavery in our narrations of American educational development. Prior narrations fall flat when we take for granted that black and native people are always central to the story, rather than auxiliary to it.

When employing such questions to probe the historical record, one finds, with no level of uncertainty, that the early development of white common schooling, and the origins of American public education, cannot be understood as separate and apart from the two structural systems at the heart of the American social order. Slavery and settler colonialism were integral to the policies, funding, and construction of the national educational landscape.

Building on the insights from the previous chapters, this section provides a response to the previously outlined questions. It also demonstrates how white education formed through distinct relationships to the racially distinct educational projects imposed on black and native people. More specifically, I will expose the violence undergirding the formation of public education as a white good through its financial and physical development. Some examples are quite large and easy to trace, like the federal land grants that support public schooling to this day; or the reality that all states were deeply enmeshed in an economy reliant on the labor of enslaved black people. However, many examples are small and often local, requiring close assessments of school funds for individual counties or the land deals of a particular state. Yet, taken as a whole, these historical narratives paint a comprehensive picture of the many ways in which white schooling materially relied upon settler colonialism and chattel slavery, demonstrating how policies like the Civilization Fund Act and anti-literacy laws served as companions to laws and policies orchestrating the expansion of white education.

FISCAL AND PHYSICAL ROOTS OF SCHOOLING AS A WHITE GOOD

"Errands into the wilderness" may be a historical distortion, but it accurately describes the narrative tropes animating education policy in the early years of the United States. Such myths were crafted to animate political actions and achieve specific material gains. The nation's leaders envisioned more "settled communities" being established from sea to shining sea, and the "civilizing institutions" of America—schools in particular—would be instruments used to fell the forests of the "wilderness" as settlers pursued such ends. This destiny, they insisted, was inevitable, ordered by God. The educational mission embedded in the Land Ordinances of 1785 and 1787 reflected such settler worldviews, and these visions of national expansion were to be achieved by employing very particular instruments of racial domination.

Through the first ordinance, the federal government made public schools a consistent unit—or instrument, even—of US expansion as new townships, and ultimately states, were added to the union. The law made a commitment to public education in two clear ways. First, it granted "public lands" to be used for helping finance "common schools." Second, the federal government established a process for enlisting new territories to be states, requiring that public education be included in its internal formation.[10]

While some are familiar with the legacy of land-grant colleges as institutional manifestations of settler-colonial protocols, where the federal government apportioned seized native lands to fund higher education, the reality is that "the commodification of Native homelands to support common schooling overshadowed the higher-ed land grants by an order of magnitude." More specifically, "Between 1795 and

1912, state and federal governments granted 129 million acres of land for common schools—an area nearly the size of France."[11] The Land Ordinance of 1785 laid the groundwork for this historic development, where the expansion of public schooling as a white good grew through the extractive practices of settler colonialism and racial chattel slavery, which helped drive economic and geographic expansion.

The ordinance also outlined a system of surveying and selling native lands west of the Appalachian Mountains. It created the surveying unit of a township: a six-by-six-mile grid divided into 36 one-square-mile sections. Effectively, land was overlaid with the grid (Figure 4.1), and sections were designated for specific purposes. As it pertained to common schooling, the ordinance stipulated, "There shall be reserved the lot No. 16 of every township, for the maintenance of public schools within the said township."[12]

Congress almost invariably granted the sixteenth section of land to states for use in public schools—from Ohio statehood in 1802 to Alaska statehood in 1958—usually as part of the process for admitting new states. Initially, states were only allowed to lease the lands in support of schools. However, in 1827, Ohio petitioned the federal government to allow for the sale of sixteenth sections in support of schools, and subsequent enabling acts allowed for sale as well as lease.[14] Most states sold these lands and contributed them to a permanent fund in support of education, following a model established by Michigan.[15] The only states that did not receive land grants for schooling were the thirteen original colonies, as well as Vermont, Kentucky, Tennessee, Maine, Texas, West Virginia, and Hawai'i.[16] Important to note, many

36	30	24	18	12	6
35	29	23	17	11	5
34	28	22	16	10	4
33	27	21	15	9	3
32	26	20	14	8	2
31	25	19	13	7	1

4.1: Graph showing the numbering system for a six-by-six-mile township, a surveying unit used by the US for lands conquered after 1785.[13]

of the sixteenth sections were the least valuable plots of land in a given township, causing inequities to abound. This has less to do with education being undervalued and more to do with the imperfection of the section 16 strategy—for instance, there was no way to carefully predict which areas in future townships would be swamplands or contain other physical characteristics that made them unsuitable for schools or less valuable if sold. However, irrespective of the value this land had for the white communities who settled there, a mechanism was set in place whereby native land loss was to directly contribute to the financial development of schooling as a white good.

As the US empire expanded westward, forcing more native people onto discrete reservations, sixteenth section grants became less uniform. States often received other sections. Some simply received large sums of money, in lieu of the sixteenth sections occupied by Indian reservations or other claims.[17] Even with such variation of policy implementation, the fact remained: The sixteenth plot enabled the systematic creation of common schools, either by building a school on that parcel of land or by selling the plot of land and using proceeds as seed funding for a state school fund. Some states invested these monies, along with funds raised through taxes, into bonds to support the growth of resources for public education; thus expanding access to schooling for white Americans as the nation developed.

School funds that arose from sixteenth-section lands had varied success. Indeed, many states squandered federal land grants, failing to establish successful systems of white education from the initial capital. But in other cases, particularly in the American West, the proceeds from selling or leasing these lands continue to fund US public schools today. In 2020, states earned over $3.7 billion in revenue for their K–12 schools from federal land grants.[18]

Interestingly, this origin narrative of white common schooling and its development through native land dispossession complicates historical narratives that suggest early Americans were universally resistant to government regulation and redistribution. While the newly formed United States was "reluctant to adopt policies of *regulation* and *redistri-*

bution," given their history with the heavy-handed British Crown during the Colonial Era, "both federal and state governments were busy, however, *distributing* benefits," particularly when it came to education. This distribution of benefits was violently white supremacist in nature—a public resource generated by seizing native land and converting it into capital to benefit white education. To clarify this process, we might look closely at Connecticut's use of native lands to fund its common schools.

THE "WESTERN RESERVE" AND CONNECTICUT'S COMMON SCHOOL FUND

Colonial Connecticut mandated education for white citizens by 1650, but funding for such education was left up to towns and the people themselves.[19] Following American independence, however, the new state constructed plans for a permanent school fund. Like most early states, Connecticut claimed land west of the Appalachians prior to the American Revolution. Its charter, established by the British Crown during the Colonial Era, granted the colony land spanning from the Atlantic to the Pacific Ocean—indeed stretching all the way through present-day California. Given the preindustrial nature of the colonies, white settlers relied on agriculture as their primary basis for economic expansion and growth. Therefore, the need for more land was baked into colonists' frame for worldmaking.

Many settlers in the English-speaking colonies, anticipating access to new Western land claimed by France, took up arms for the British in the Seven Years' War (1756–63; also known as the French and Indian War), some going into debt to defeat the French and their indigenous allies. However, in 1763 the Crown sought to protect its indigenous allies by forbidding white settlement west of the Proclamation Line of 1763—a boundary drawn across the Appalachian Mountains. Thus, while many recall the conflict over taxation without representation to be a key motivating factor for rebellion against the Crown, Britain's decision to limit western expansion also played a role in stoking America's demand for independence. This conflict over native land, between the colonies and the Crown, rarely receives the attention it deserves, yet the story of Connecticut's school fund helps to expose its significance to social formations in early America.

Concerns for colonial Connecticut stemmed from the fact that its land claims were effectively sealed off by the British Proclamation Line. Surely this frustrated Connecticut's leaders, who saw in their western lands valuable territory to be commodified. Connecticut believed it had a very old claim to its "Western Reserve" lands, a claim going back to its 1662 charter under British royal authority. This charter was, of course, conditioned by the British Crown's refusal to recognize native nations as having any legal right to their homelands. Nevertheless, Connecticut's leaders insisted on the state's right to the Western Reserve through the eighteenth century, even though the land was the home of indigenous nations and generally untouched by white settlers.

The land was valuable. Connecticut's leaders were very aware of this. Therefore, after the American Revolution, they insisted that the newly formed federal government use its treaty-making capacity and military power to help the state lay claim to the West. After the American Revolution as well as rounds of dealmaking amid states with competing claims, Connecticut emerged with a claim to 3,366,921 acres of land along the south bank of Lake Erie.[20]

In the 1790s, selling this Western Reserve became a major consideration for the state's leaders. In May 1795, the future of the Western Reserve started to become clear: Connecticut's legislature voted to sell it and dedicate the proceeds to "be made into *a perpetual fund*, from which shall be, and hereby is, appropriated *to the support of schools* in the several societies constituted by law, according to the list of polls and ratable estates."[21] Under the twenty-four-year management of Seth P. Beers (1825–49), the fund rose to over $2 million (or the equivalent of more than $82 million today). By the 1850s the fund disbursed annually about $1.50 per pupil.[22]

A key detail in this story, however, is that the land was still home to several indigenous nations. Connecticut's Western Reserve lands, which the state slated for sale, was comprised of unceded native territory. This is not small fact to be glossed over. Yet and still, the state passed the legislation in May 1795, in expectation that the land would be sold to the United States shortly. In the minds of Connecticut's leaders, the question of native dispossession was not a matter of *if*, but *when*—indigenous removal was perpetually articulated as both natural and inevitable by white settlers. In August 1795, the United States finalized the Treaty of Greenville with the Wyandot, Delaware, Shawanee, Ottawa, Chippewa, Potawatomi, Miami, Eel River, Wea, Kickapoo, Piankeshaw, and Kaskaskia nations, which included a cession of about a third of the Western Reserve.[23] In October 1795, Connecticut finalized its sale of the Western Reserve to the Connecticut Land Company for $1.2 million.[24] In 1805, another treaty with the Wyandot, Ottawa, Chippewa, Munsee and Delaware, Shawnee, and Potawatomi nations provided for the cession of the remainder of the Western Reserve.[25] The Connecticut Land Company agreed to pay $175 annually to these nations as part of the treaty.[26]

Connecticut's sale of the Western Reserve reveals a web of relationships between private, state, and federal actors all built upon a shared goal of native land loss and the expansion of a settler state, and it was a process that coalesced around schooling as a key building block in the newly formed nation. However, what is revelatory about Connecticut's case is that all actors involved understood the goals of the settler state, and that they were comfortable making million-dollar transactions on the expectation that land would soon be ceded. What's more, history makes clear that such treaties were signed under coercion, when we account for the role of military force used to achieve such political goals. I've presented the story of Connecticut here, but as I will show in future pages, such stories can also be traced to places like New York, Mississippi, and North Carolina.

Connecticut's long-standing land claims were based on a refusal to recognize any legitimate claims on its "Western Reserve" by native nations who had long known it to be their homeland. As philosopher Bryan

Nichols explains, "in this (colonial) context, theft is the mechanism and means by which property is created." Through such negotiations and treaties, native people, as the dispossessed in this settler-colonial procedure only receive a status as prior owners as they are forced into sham negotiations, what Nichols calls a recursive dispossession, a "form of property-generating theft." Native people "are figured as "original owners," but only retroactively—that is, "refracted backward through the process itself."[27]

The state government's sale of its claim to the land also depended on an understanding that the federal government would soon negotiate a land cession from the native nations living there. This action by the federal government was crucial, as treaty-making in the colonial context conferred legitimacy upon settler land claims—the performance of a just and "civil" process of orderly and politically responsible negotiation—even as treaty negotiations were conditioned by the implicit threat of colonial violence by the growing military power of the United States. Nevertheless, these coercive land deals ensured white people could settle native homelands with the blessing and backing of the federal government. Under the federal government's authority, native land became white possessions—and sizable amounts of that property went directly to the development of white schools in the interest of developing a national polity committed to the perseverance of the new country and its settler future.

The Connecticut Land Company's purchase of the Western Reserve from the state of Connecticut was similarly conditioned on the federal government's theft of native land. In exchange, the federal government expected the company to help fund the annuities outlined by the 1805 treaty. The Land Company was then free to lease or sell the Western Reserve to eager white settlers. The capital from the initial payment was converted into Connecticut's school fund, and the profits from selling the reserve to settlers further enlarged the wealth of the state. This became a patterned practice—a scalable model for expanding the schooling apparatus of the United States that political leaders across regions agreed was a necessity for the good of the republic.

LAND TO PROPERTY, PROPERTY TO CAPITAL, CAPITAL TO SCHOOLS

The pattern revealed in Connecticut's case—where native homelands became white property, white property became white capital, and white capital funded schooling as a white good—was systemically enacted through the township structure of expansion. In many states settled before the Land Ordinance, however, similar processes appeared.

In 1795 the New York State Assembly passed an act to devote £100,000 over five years to support education. In this same year, when the state proclaimed its historic commitment to public education for white citizens, its legislature sent commissioners to sign several treaties with the Oneida nation requiring it to cede major portions of its land base.[28] The federal government warned the state's leadership that such treaties were in violation of the new US Constitution. Despite such injunctions, New York proceeded anyway. Governor George Clinton likely knew that the young federal government would do little to intervene. After all, as the concurrent Connecticut case made clear, the federal government shared the ultimate goal of native land dispossession, as it was deemed essential to the project of national development.

New York's bullish land grabs were integral to the state's plans for future spending—including its expansion of education.[29] It is estimated that profits from reselling native land made up between 48.3 and 60.7 percent of New York's annual revenue between 1791 and 1795.[30] The state allowed buyers to take out mortgages on these lands and proceeds from mortgages on the land of the "late Oneida" reservation contributed to the school fund into the nineteenth century—where state funds were disbursed to local towns and cities to assist with education-related activities and expenses.[31]

In the American South, early attempts to promote white education also relied on the process of seizing native land. North Carolina's 1826 Literary Fund, which helped support multiple common schools in the state from its inception until the Civil War, drew significant capital from the state's sale of Cherokee lands. An 1819 report by a committee created to study education recommended that the "lately acquired" Cherokee lands be leveraged to fund common schools, and the 1826 bill included the proceeds of Cherokee land sales among its funding sources.[32] In addition to the 1826 provision, the Literary Fund received regular influxes of cash from the interest on "Cherokee bonds" issued by the state to induce settlement of Cherokee land.[33] Most of these bonds were issued in two rounds, in 1836 and 1838.[34] By 1841, interest on these bonds made up a substantial portion of annual revenue for the Literary Fund.

Georgia began offering provisions for white education in 1817, allocating $250,000 to the support of schools for poor whites. The fund was created out of the state's general treasury, which had recently been greatly enlarged by the sale of Cherokee land claimed by the state.[35] The windfall of $756,000 in 1817 was undoubtedly behind Governor William Rabun's message to the state legislature that year, reminding them they would be hard-pressed to find "a more favorable opportunity to commence internal improvement on an extensive scale."[36] The state's school fund was one such "internal improvement" made possible by the seizure of Cherokee lands—a process that would ultimately result in the infamous genocide known as the Trail of Tears.

SLAVERY'S CAPITALISM AND WHITE SCHOOLS

The development of white common schools in both the North and South is inseparable from the history of chattel slavery in the United States, as taxes on enslaved people also generated revenue used to expand white schooling. In Alabama, for instance, the state helped fund poor white students' tuition at private schools in Mobile using the funds from a 2 percent tax "on all sales at auction of real estate, slaves, horses, mules or other objects."[37] In 1821, the "police juries" that governed Louisiana's parishes (the equivalent of counties or townships) were authorized to "lay a tax on lands and slaves within their respective parishes for the purpose of promoting education."[38] Louisiana did not have a central common school fund and it is difficult to ascertain whether parishes imposed taxes for enslaved people counted among property. However, given that the state generated 30–40 percent of its revenue from direct slave taxes, it seems quite likely that parishes followed suit with taxes of their own.[39]

As noted earlier, Georgia's 1817 school fund was drawn from the general treasury, which derived heavily from the direct taxation of slaves as property. For instance, by 1849 almost half (49 percent) of Georgia's revenue came from slave taxes.[40] What's more, in 1819 the state further enlarged its school fund by buying stock in the Bank of Darien, a financial institution chaired by slaveholder Thomas Spalding and deeply involved in the export of cotton produced on slave plantations.[41]

This relationship between the exploitation of enslaved labor and the growth of white public schooling was not contained to the American South. New York's common school fund, established in 1795, named the proceeds of "stocks" in various banks as a primary source of revenue, which were deeply entrenched in the trans-Atlantic slave trade. To identify this history requires that we follow the money and investment practices employed to manage and grow the state's school fund; when we do this, the connections are immediately apparent.

Multiple acts of the New York legislature in the first decades of the school fund's existence show a desire to enlarge the fund by tying its success intimately to stocks the state owned in various New York banks. An 1807 law, for instance, enabled the comptroller to invest in Merchants' Banks of New York, the dividends "arising therefrom" being "appropriated for the use and encouragement of common schools."[42] By 1813, the Common School Fund held stock in Merchants' Bank, along with the Bank of Hudson, the Bank of Columbia, and the Mohawk Bank.[43] By 1819 the legislature reported the school fund was invested in seven banks within the state. Returns from bank stock comprised roughly one-third of the school fund's revenue by 1813, and a similar figure in 1816.[44]

The fact that New York's common school fund benefited from numerous banks suggests it was not immune to the capital flow of slavery. The Merchants' Bank of New York, for example, partnered with Louisiana banks that in turn supported slave traders like Isaac Franklin, owner of several plantations and cofounder of Franklin & Armfield, the nation's largest slave-trading firm.[45] As old and recent scholarship on slavery and capitalism has shown, the business of slavery was not merely a Southern phenomenon; rather it flowed across regional boundaries and industries. Given such clearly traceable ties, whether white schooling was developed using dirty money is a closed question. The only questions worth asking is the matter of degree—a question of just how dirty the money used to fund early white schooling was.

When looking closer at lesser-known laws as well as local, on-the-ground narratives, we find instances of even more direct and intimate connections between chattel slavery and the development of white schooling.

Some wealthy slave owners carved out portions of their estate to be donated to educational efforts, at times allotting specific slaves to be sold for this very purpose. This practice can be traced to the oldest free school for white students in the United States, Hampton Academy, dating back to 1624—where wealthy planters in colonial Virginia bequeathed portions of their estate—including land, enslaved people, and other property—to establish a school for children of local colonists, and where poor white students could attend at free or reduced cost. Hampton Academy—not to be confused with the historically black college, Hampton Agricultural and Normal Institute, founded in 1868—was privately funded but operated for what was perceived to be the public good.[46]

This practice persisted through the antebellum era. Alexander Dickson of Duplin County, North Carolina, was one such enslaver. In 1814, Dickson died without any immediate family. He had outlined in his will that the enslaved people he owned be sold and that the "monies arising therefrom [should be used] to create a fund for establishing a Charity School for the Education of poor Children in the county of Duplin."[47] Dickson carefully explained that certain slaves, perhaps those for whom he had some greater affection, should be sold in family units: A woman named "Old Lucy" was to be sold alongside her children, Lucy and Frank, and a pregnant woman named Kitt was to be sold with her children. He left two enslaved women—Nancy and Amy—to his nephews and dictated that an enslaved man named Old Tarisman be "well treated by my executors and not let want for anything."[48] He then clarified, "The Negroes not herein named are to be sold separate to the highest bidder."[49] It is unclear how many enslaved people were sold, but by 1817 the Dickson Charity Fund reported a sum of $12,621.49 as generated from the sale of Alexander Dickson's land, slaves, and possessions. It is worth noting that through 1962, Duplin County schools continued to financially benefit from proceeds derived from the selling of Dickson's slaves during the prior century.[50] Relatedly, Hampton Academy, established in colonial Virginia, would become absorbed into Elizabeth City Schools after the Civil War, operating as the oldest public high school in Hampton, Virginia, today.

In 1855, the Union Baptist Association helped fund the construction of Warsaw High School in Duplin County.[51] The school was likely built on land donated by General William L. Hill, who made a name for himself by putting down a minor slave insurrection in 1821, in neighboring Onslow County.[52] In 1850, the general owned upwards of one hundred slaves, and his status as a slave owner and generous benefactor of Warsaw High School reveals a direct line between slavery's capitalism and the construction of this local high school.[53] The school was also constructed on land carved off from his plantation. What's more, given the number of enslaved people Hill owned, it is likely that enslaved labor was exploited for the construction of the physical school building. While this point about school construction is speculative—mostly because the sources are silent on the question—what we know for certain is that irrespective of the labor Hill's slaves were forced to contribute to the building of the school, the wealth generated by their labor allowed Hill to donate the 14.5 acres for the construction of Warsaw High School.

Thinking relationally about race in this early history of education in North Carolina (and Virginia) is important. It pushes us to trace the relationship between antiblack domination and the development of schooling for white students. The enslaved black people sold from the Dickson's estate to benefit North Carolina schooling, as well as the bondsmen and women whose labor helped make Warsaw High School possible, were systematically excluded from educational opportunity. Black education was criminalized by anti-literacy practices and legislation that made knowledge-sharing and congregating difficult. North Carolina adopted explicit anti-literacy legislation in 1832, finally joining its neighboring states in explicitly outlawing the teaching of slaves to read.[54] According to the legislature, "the teaching of slaves to read and write has a tendency to excite dissatisfaction in their minds and to produce insurrection and rebellion."[55] North Carolina legislators created a fine for white teachers and outlined corporal punishment for free black teachers. Though it codified the criminalization of education among enslaved black people with the 1832 bill, such legislation likely did not dramatically alter conditions for enslaved people, because even in the absence of explicit anti-literacy statutes, knowledge-sharing and assembly for instruction among enslaved people was often brutally repressed.[56] Such anti-literacy proscriptions as they pertained to black people were intimately bound up with the broader emerging landscape of educational policy in the state of North Carolina, and indeed the nation.

Duplin County provides two striking examples of the direct relationship between enslaved black people and white common schooling. In this one county, the sale of enslaved people and the labor of enslaved people directly contributed to the expansion of white education. Duplin County does not stand alone in this regard. Such stories abound in the history of early US education, though little space has been given in the scholarship to attend to whence the capital for white schooling derived. Instead, the historiography has generally been marked by silence and erasure. Yet the archive reveals how white citizens developed intricate laws and policies to suppress black education, while also expanding white schooling through extractive and exploitative measures imposed on black bodies.

Florida developed a process whereby improperly manumitted slaves could be seized and sold to support white schooling. In 1829, Florida's legislature authorized the state to seize black people who had been freed without their masters having paid a specified fine—a practice meant to discourage owners from manumitting enslaved people—and in 1851, lawmakers designated black people seized for this reason "as belonging to the Common School Fund."[57] This meant the proceeds from selling improperly manumitted slaves were to be used for the support of white common schools in Florida. The law was short-lived. Nevertheless, it provides a striking example of how the state may have used the direct sale of black people into slavery as a means of generating capital for the development of white schools. Furthermore, it should come as no surprise that the original revenue sources for Florida's school fund were intimately bound up with aggressive seizures of Seminole lands, reflecting broader patterns of native land dispossession serving as the foundational means for developing white schooling in the United States. The state of Virginia had a similar law to Florida's, where funds from the sale of unclaimed runaway slaves were to be claimed by the state's Literary Fund, established in 1811.[58]

White schools in the South were often built on or near plantations, which suggests that enslaved labor was likely used to build and maintain many of these institutions. This is another clear tie between slave capital and the development of white schooling. For indeed, private "neighborhood" schools, funded by neighboring plantation owners, were common prior to (and alongside) the propagation of more public schooling in the nineteenth century.[59] We know enslaved labor is inextricably linked to the built environment of the United States, especially when we consider the geography of the antebellum South. Therefore, despite poor documentation concerning the use of enslaved labor for building school infrastructure, an extensive accounting of this relationship in other aspects of American society helps fill in the gaps.

Recent public history work has uncovered the role of enslaved labor in constructing much of the built environment of the United States. Historians have chronicled the role of enslaved people in building the White House and other infrastructure in the US capital.[60] Multiple universities across the United States have documented how enslaved labor was used to construct buildings on their campuses. Brown University, for instance, has acknowledged enslaved people worked on its

University Hall, and the University of North Carolina at Chapel Hill has begun identifying the role of slave labor in constructing multiple buildings on campus.[61] Other educational institutions have noted deep economic connections to slavery, even when they have not uncovered evidence of slave labor in constructing physical spaces. Harvard University's 2022 report, *Harvard & the Legacy of Slavery*, found that enslaved people worked at the school between 1636 and 1783, and that the university benefited and continues to benefit materially from relationships with slaveholders.[62]

These findings are a reminder that capital generated through slavery was ubiquitous.[63] Renee K. Harrison has put the matter more pointedly, declaring that "enslaved and free Black people under the threat of harm and death helped build this nation, fiscally and physically."[64] Public education, or common schooling, as a vital institution and instrument in the building of the nation is no exception to this rule.

Furthermore, there are documented cases of white Americans using enslaved labor to build schools. While the relationship between enslaved labor and the fiscal and physical development of white schooling is strongly implied in the case of Warsaw High School, such connections were explicitly documented in the case of Bell County, Texas, where the Rock Church School was built by enslaved people in 1859.[65]A local history, compiled by retired teachers in Bell County, contains details about this construction, though they provide little information about the enslaved people exploited for this purpose in their account.

Readers might also recall previous accounts of white missionaries using enslaved labor to build mission schools for the purpose of "civilizing" native Americans. This was the case at the Brainerd Mission, a school financed by the US Department of War, and at Choctaw Academy in Kentucky, established in 1825 by Richard Mentor Johnson, a decorated general celebrated for his role in the Indian Wars.[66] In such cases, the domination of one particular racial group—enslaved black people—was mobilized by white leaders in service of the "civilization" and ongoing practices of land dispossession and elimination of another–indigenous peoples. What's more, the labor of enslaved people was used to build such schools, even as black education was explicitly criminalized through anti-literacy customs meant to surveil and control black people. The strategies of racial domination implemented through educational policies and practices were specific to the distinct racial groups, based on their political status with the social order, and especially their relationship to the mode of production from which capital was derived in the United States. Particular forms of racial domination, while relational, called for particular protocols of schooling. While native and black people both experienced racial domination in the realm of education in service of the expansion of white schooling, and the building of the nation, such experiences of domination were not analogous. They were distinct in kind. The political-economic motivations for one were settler fantasies for continued accumulation of indigenous lands, and for the other the continued extraction of value from enslaved black labor and slave capital.

•••

A comprehensive accounting of the extent to which America's schools arise from the exploitation of native land and black enslaved labor requires looking closer: considering individual treaties, individual schools, local histories, and now-defunct school funds. It also requires looking critically: looking beyond the bureaucratic language of bonds, general treasuries, and sixteenth-section lands to the antiblack and settler-colonial violence driving such procedures executed by local, state, and federal actors helping to expand the schooling apparatus of the United States. This violence generated the capital, and often directly the land and labor used to develop schooling as a white good in its earliest forms.

Yet as we saw in Part I, US legislators and policymakers also leveraged educational laws and policy in service of chattel slavery and settler colonialism to enforce the racially specific structural positions of native and black people within the United States as it was yet forming. The enslaved black people sold to support the schools in Duplin County were barred by law from receiving education. Viney Baker, a black woman born to enslaved people, personally recalled how this particular history in Duplin County shaped her family's history.

Baker's parents, Teeny and William McIntire, were enslaved in Duplin County. She once recalled the stories her parents told her of their enslavement, because she was too young to remember the experience herself, being only a young child when the Civil War ended: "Pap and mammy tole me marster and missus did not 'low any of de slaves to have a book in deir house. Dat if dey caught a slave wid a book in deir house dey whupped 'em. Dey were keerful not to let 'em learn readin' and writin'."[67] According to the stories passed on by her parents, anti-literacy and anti-assembly sentiments were enforced outside of plantations, as well: "Dey said de patrollers come to whare dey wus havin' prayer meetin' and beat 'em."[68]

Teeny was not owned by Alexander Dickson, and it is unclear who owned William. However, we can imagine the violent anti-literacy regime in Duplin County shaped the lives—and curtailed the freedom—of those whose sale helped fund the county's white schools. The suppression of black education was a mechanism of enforcing and maintaining chattel slavery. White schooling directly benefited from such distinct forms of racial domination. It was predicated on black and native dispossession.

The Cherokee land that North Carolina sold to support its Literary Fund in 1826 was also the site of the Valley Town Mission School, an institution run by the American Baptist Board that received funds from the US government through the Civilization Fund Act established in 1819.[69] I emphasize this point here because, again, the relational formation of race in American schooling is omnipresent when we look just beneath the surface. At Valley Town, white teachers promoted Christianity, Western gender roles, Western agriculture and labor practices, and private property. The educators at Valley Town acted as agents of the US government's "civilization policy," attempting to shrink Cherokee land bases by alienating native students from ways of doing and being that were consistent with tribal customs. Valley Town reflected a distinct history of educational policy predicated on the mandate of settler colonialism and it had implications for both indigenous peoples and the white students whose education received funding from the selling of Cherokee land. In this way, mission schools were a mechanism that helped drive ongoing native displacement, and white schools materially benefited, in a direct way, from such displacement.

Part I has revealed how early educational policy and funding practices were directly tied to the violent processes of chattel slavery and settler colonialism. The previous chapters provide the foundation for a new origin story of American schooling, and particularly how the grammars of race conditioned the policies constructed by state and federal actors as the schooling apparatus of the United States continued to expand its reach. They also spell out, in explicit terms, how native land loss and the exploitation of enslaved black labor economically contributed to the development of this national educational landscape.

This new origin story offers a long-overdue corrective to those that continue to frame historical scholarship and public memory. Those seeking to use education in the United States toward more just and equitable ends will benefit from cultivating a deeper understanding of the grammars of race and violence that gave rise to the schooling apparatus inherited by current generations. Reckoning with such history is critical, because our contemporary pursuits of educational justice first requires that we achieve an honest accounting of the injustice we hope to unseat.

PART II

EDUCATION AND THE AMERICAN INDIAN WARS

5

THE AIMS OF NATIVE SCHOOLING FOR AN EXPANDING SETTLER NATION

They must become as orphans . . . they must forget their parents as far as possible in order to abandon the habits of the Indians.

—Eugene C. Chirouse, Mission School Founder (1861)

Native American boarding schools have haunted my scholarly imagination since the age of seventeen. I wrote my first college essay at the University of California, Berkeley, on the subject—"Boarding Schools: Weapons of Cultural Genocide"—submitted for my Native American Studies class during the first semester of my freshman year. Prior to this course in 2006, I had no prior knowledge of this history. In fact, I only enrolled in the class because I needed to fulfill my freshman writing requirement. Having waited to the last minute to enroll in an R1A course, Native American Studies was one of the few options available. In hindsight, it seems I ended up exactly where I was supposed to be.

For this particular assignment, the professor tasked students with writing an analytical essay on a text assigned in the course. I chose to write about *Last Standing Woman*, by Ojibwe novelist Winona LaDuke.[1]

I can recall our class discussion about a scene in LaDuke's novel that inspired my conviction to write this paper. It involved one of the characters not being able to communicate with their grandparents on the White Earth Reservation. The Ojibwe student was forced to learn English from a young age in a native boarding school, as the institution forbade students from speaking their native tongue. This form of linguistic incarceration—to borrow from Malawian linguist Sam Mchombo—not only violated internal processes of cultural transmission among native communities, but also had the distinct effect of driving a wedge between familial and tribal relations, kinship systems bound through blood ties and other established forms of social connection. This rupture observed by LaDuke's fictional character was a literary rendering of the many voices of native students who named and experienced this violation in the historical record. That semester I also learned of General Richard Henry Pratt, a leading white reformer of native education in the late nineteenth century, and the founder of the infamous Carlisle Indian Industrial School in Pennsylvania, established in 1879. This boarding school was based on Pratt's educational philosophy of "Kill the Indian. Save the Man"—a slogan supposedly meant as a peaceful alternative to the ongoing Indian Wars, where native people's physical lives could be spared if only settlers could force them to shed their native ways of life, thus killing the Indian inside them.

I later learned that Pratt's philosophy for native schooling was not novel. He was, in fact, operating in a much longer tradition of white reformers empowered by the federal government to expand educational programs for native students as an extension of broader military aims to dispossess native people of their land and quell indigenous resistance. The ideological goals of native schooling coalesced with the repressive aims of US military aggression in the Indian Wars, and this was all part and parcel of the ever-expanding schooling apparatus of the United States. Behind Pratt's motto was a long-standing praxis among white settlers whereby the symbolic killing of indigeneity in the classroom was a companion to killing Indians on the battlefield. Settler schooling for native students has always been an act of war in this way.

Professor Kim Richards, an Apache woman and doctoral candidate whose research is dedicated to the survival of indigenous languages, was the lead instructor for my Native American Studies course. Professor Leece Lee, a Blackfeet/Choctaw doctoral student studying resistance strategies employed by indigenous communities against US settler policies, especially within a native American feminist tradition, served as the teaching assistant. Their expertise offered critical insights for appreciating native American literature in the broader context of anti-indigeneity, power, and education. They helped me and my classmates—likely all new to this subject—unpack the cultural critiques present in the historical literature we read.

Learning about the depth of violation and harm caused by native boarding schools for the first time was astonishing. We came to understand the boarding school as a site not only of physical violence, but also as one where kinship ties between students and their families were directly violated—a historical reality that has become particularly clarifying for me over the years. That federally backed schools intentionally alienated native students from their families seemed intimately violent in a way that was distinct from anything I had ever learned about education, pushing me to consider schooling as a site of suffering in ways I had never imagined. Education was not just about, or even primarily defined, through the lens of liberation and a matter of collective intellectual struggle, as I had come to understand it through a very particular African American tradition. Education could also be used toward nefarious ends, especially in the context of formal schooling. In fact, there was no way to understand state-sponsored education without thinking deeply about the powerful social forces shaping institutions and protocols of learning. The stories about native boarding schools forced me to see the political nature of education in more depth than ever before.

I was marked by this experience in my first Native American Studies course, both ashamed of my ignorance yet inspired by the new territory opening in my mind. I have found myself returning to this history at various points in my intellectual trajectory since that fall semester of freshman year. While learning of Pratt's violent philosophy was revelatory, as was LaDuke's writing about the intergenerational impact of settler schooling imposed on indigenous families, it was only recently that I began to appreciate this history as a fundamental expression of American schooling, which is to say, as more than just something that happened to native communities on reservations and outside the mainstream American political sphere.

The native boarding school story, as a distinct subject in educational history, is not entirely separate from the story of black segregated education or white common schools. Yet the historiography on American education, and studies of native schooling have generally framed it as such. This siloed thinking masks the intimate connection between native peoples' experiences with settler schooling as a distinct, politically and economically driven racial project promulgated by government officials who cut their teeth building the United States through the nineteenth century. It masks how native schooling, as a distinct racial project, formed relationally to other educational efforts driven by racial ideology, which collectively formed the national educational landscape.

Recall that native schooling contributed to the schooling apparatus of the United States in at least two distinct ways: It was a companion to US wars with native nations, primarily driven by settler desires for more accumulation of indigenous land, and such educational projects seeking to dispossess native communities of land were directly related to the development of a national public education system in the United States meant to benefit white citizens, in that the latter was significantly funded through the selling of seized native land. The native American boarding school and its various precursors—such as missionary schools and government contract schools—was one of three foundational racial projects that grew steadily and relationally through the early decades of the nineteenth century. It was structurally linked to the white common school, which was partially maintained by public school funds established with proceeds from sales of stolen native land, as well as the slow development of the racially stigmatized and materially inferior segregated black schools that developed over the nineteenth century.

Building from this line of historical argumentation, Part II reinterprets native experiences with settler-sponsored schooling as a central part of the national story of educational development, and as a racial project integral to the building of the nation. What's more, it looks to earlier periods than the post-1870s era of reformers like General Pratt, thus contextualizing this story within the origins of the national education system.

Nation-building, within the newly united states, was predicated on native land dispossession. This required undermining indigenous peoples' claims to land and neutralizing their resistance to violent settler encroachment. Federal leaders, missionaries, and various civilian groups partnered to develop settler schooling for native people that supported the nation's explicitly stated aims of physical expansion and dealing with "the Indian problem." Together they developed a federally backed native education system, largely administered by the US Department of War. Crucial to their strategy was their understanding that the education of native youth was a cheaper alternative to costly wars. Through schooling, settlers could eliminate indigenous ways of life by alienating students from their families, tribal communities, and heritage claims to land.

Settler schooling for native youth ran parallel to the development of American common schools, yet the extractive aims of the former helped to fund the latter. American common schools created a national white identity among diverse European immigrants, thus defining whiteness over and against ideas about indigeneity and blackness. Settler schooling for native people was an instrument to force native people into a new relationship with land—insisting that land was property to be individually owned, not a living thing to be socially integrated in kinship networks or claimed communally.

Like the common schools' flattening of ethnic European identities to construct a singular white national identity, settler schooling for native students functioned similarly as a racial project. It was used to flatten the heterogeneous identities among indigenous people while enlisting them into the American social order as "Indians" or "the red race." This racial category was always defined in relation to white and black Americans. Indeed, this founding racial triad conditioned the grammar of American schooling from its inception. As school policies and protocols evolved, this grammar persisted.

As the subsequent pages will show, indigenous people responded to settler schooling as one of the most comprehensive forms of settler-colonial violence in a variety of ways. From aggressive refusal to strategic appropriations of Western education, native students and families were political actors in this story. They studied the grammar of American schooling for themselves, choosing to engage on their own terms as they insisted on indigenous survival. This counternarrative of native resistance is central to native people's experiences with the schooling apparatus of the United States. Part II also tells this story.

JAMES MCDONALD'S ASCENT AS THE POSTER CHILD OF FEDERALLY FUNDED NATIVE EDUCATION

To understand the development of federally backed native American education in the nineteenth century requires that we take seriously how native children became targets in US Indian Wars—how the hearts and minds of indigenous children became extensions of the battlefield. The story of James McDonald is particularly revelatory of this historical reality.

In 1813, the US Department of War, under the leadership of John Armstrong Jr., began funding the continuing education of James McDonald, a twelve-year-old Choctaw boy from Mississippi Territory. With this support, McDonald traveled to Baltimore, where he was educated by white teachers over the course of five years. After this time, McDonald was "adopted" by US Secretary of Indian Trade Thomas McKenney, a historical figure readers will recall from previous chapters as the architect of the Civilization Fund Act of 1819. McKenney came to view the young Choctaw boy as living, breathing proof that civilization was possible for native people. He brought McDonald into his home, and this, for McKenney, served as a daily reminder that his mission to civilize native people was not in vain. McKenney once proclaimed, speaking of McDonald, "The acquirements of this young Indian afford a gratifying evidence of Indian capacity, and aptness for the attainment of the principles of Civilization, and of science. . . . To such as question the capacity of Indians for Civilization and improvement in science, no better argument need be offered."[2]

James McDonald was born in 1801 to a Choctaw woman named

Molly McDonald and an unnamed white European father, and he was raised amid a cohort of mixed-blood, landowning, and slaveholding Choctaws. His mother owned enslaved black people, and though land in the Mississippi homeland of the Choctaw was communally owned, she staked out a de facto claim to a tract by farming. Prior to moving to Baltimore and being adopted by Secretary McKenney, James McDonald received some formal education in Mississippi Territory, either in a school with other Choctaw children or possibly through individual studies at the home of a missionary—a practice not uncommon among the Choctaw nation.[3] McDonald was a member of a tribe increasingly viewed among white settlers as one of the more "civilized" and redeemable nations among native people—the Choctaws having been historically known as part of the Five Civilized Tribes, along with the Cherokee, Creek, Chickasaw, and Seminole nations.

After being tutored by white educators for five years, McDonald lived in Washington, DC, as McKenney's adopted son while also working for him, performing secretarial duties in the Indian Trade Office. The boy's time living in the home of McKenney was likely viewed as a natural extension of his education. There had long been a belief among settlers that the best way to educate—or civilize—native children was to remove them from their natal communities—their family and tribes, specifically—in order to immerse them in white culture. For this purpose, the homes of white settlers were deemed the ideal classroom. This process would be formalized in the late nineteenth century through General Richard Henry Pratt's "outing programs" at the Carlisle School, and it would become a staple feature of native boarding schools, where native students were placed in white homes or businesses as cheap laborers.[4]

McKenney stressed the importance of immersing McDonald completely in settler culture as his "adopted" son, alongside his biological son, Ben. He reported having made "no distinction between him and my son, in dress or attentions. He . . . took a seat with my family in the coach, rode with us to church, and visited where we did."[5] Such day-to-day activities of the McKenney family amounted to more than comfortable transportation and clothing. The trappings of elite white society, which included elaborate formal attire, carriage rides, and extravagant meals, were furnished in part through the forced labor of three black people McKenney enslaved.[6] Their presence too was a lesson in McDonald's education, in civilization. In fact, it was a lesson that was gradually being absorbed in the institutional life of the Choctaw nation to which McDonald belonged. The relationality between McKenney, the young native boy, and the black enslaved people forced to serve them provided important scripts about the racial grammar of American society, as well as its institutions of schooling. In his memoir, McKenney hints at interaction between these enslaved people and McDonald, recounting that the young Choctaw boy "was the idol of my servants."[7] In the nineteenth century, the black presence was part and parcel of settler schooling for native youth, just as the native presence was an integral part of the political economy of schooling for white and black Americans. Despite the siloed organization of historical narratives, the physical proximity between the three races was often more intimate than the scholarly literature implies.

Though he expressed a sincere desire to be a farmer, McDonald left to study law in Ohio after working in DC and living with McKenney for two years. This career choice was supposedly motivated by a desire to distinguish himself as a role model for other native children, a lesson certainly drilled into him by his "adopted" father. In a letter to McKenney, McDonald expressed that despite his plans to farm, "I must confess, I have some ambition to distinguish myself, some disposition to be useful, and a desire to free the character of educated Indian Youth (with some degree of Justice cast upon it) of a proneness to relapse into Savagism."[8] Such visions for McDonald's life were likely rehearsed over the course of his educational training and time living with the McKenney family. Indeed, the expressed fear of native students relapsing into savagism was a common expression among white missionaries and education reformers working with indigenous youth.

One can only imagine what it must have been like for McDonald, when people visited McKenney's home or when attending social events with his family. Thomas McKenney did not mask his desire to use his "adopted" son as a political prop when advocating for the civilization of native people. He took every opportunity to brag about the young Indian boy in his care, often noting McDonald's competency at his secretarial duties in the Indian Trade Office and emphasizing the young man's involvement in writing correspondences. One letter from McKenney, for example, bore the notation, "This letter is copied in haste by our little Indian."[9] Not only could "our little Indian" do the tasks put before him, but he could do them quickly and efficiently. McDonald was paraded around as evidence that native people could be reformed, and they could even become trusted and reliable workers. Proving this idea toward the mission of expanding settler schooling for native youth was McKenney's key objective.

McDonald returned to Washington only once after leaving the McKenney residence for his legal training. He traveled there in 1825 as a representative of the Choctaw nation to renegotiate a land deal, having become part of an elite group of Choctaws serving as intermediaries between the masses of Choctaw people and the US government. During this trip, McDonald used appeals to congressional authority to drive a hard bargain in renegotiating a treaty, and he submitted a piece of writing on behalf of the delegation, arguing against Indian Removal on the grounds that "for some great end, only known to himself, he [God] has permitted us to melt before you; but that the time must come when his interposing hand will be outstretched in our behalf, and we be made to become like white men."[10]

McDonald also confronted his adopted father on this trip. According to McKenney, the young Choctaw leader bemoaned his status as a "degraded outcast" lying somewhere between the "red and white races."[11] With his identity in crisis, McDonald began to name and express feelings of being torn between the world of settlers and the interests of the Choctaw nation. It appears he began to reach some level of consciousness as the differences between McDonald and his "adopted" father became more and more evident, a process that likely began long before this moment in DC, perhaps while they lived under the same roof.

Amid so much attention—with all the pointing and prodding—there must have been moments when McDonald was forced to encounter himself through the settler gaze, through the eyes of the white people around him, as they feasted upon him as their muse of Indian civilization. As the object of their pity and contempt for native people, as well as their hope for a future beyond costly wars, McDonald surely prompted small talk at social gatherings regarding pressing political issues of the day when it came to the Indian problem. Such topics were likely a recurrent theme, as it was the focus of McKenney's job. How would McDonald have responded to such encounters? Perhaps they became a source of pride for the young man, given his age and the need to feel valued and important during such a critical stage of adolescent development. Perhaps all the attention surrounding him could have been internalized as care, where affirmations that he was "our little Indian"—a good and desirable little Indian—could have been perceived as sincere parental doting. While deeply paternalistic and motivated by settler fantasies, it is possible that such affections shown McDonald may have initially landed in a positive and affirming way, despite nefarious intentions on the part of McKenney and white settlers.

One might also consider the kind of conflicts McDonald could have arrived at later in life as he negotiated treaties and advocated for native rights, and as he spoke out against efforts to remove native people from their homelands. Maybe such moments of conflict confirmed suspicions seeded years earlier, when McDonald caught glimpses of settler violence through the commentary of loose-lipped visitors in McKenney's network—as some would have certainly voiced skepticism about native people's intellectual capacity, or questioned whether any level of civilizing education could transform what some believed to be the innate inferiority of the Indian. Perhaps these too were moments when the Choctaw boy felt like a "degraded outcast" lying somewhere between the "red and white races," even if he did not have the language, at the time, to name it as such.[12]

Glimpses of McDonald's internal struggles appear through secondhand accounts. McKenney recalled a letter received from McDonald's brother in the Choctaw nation, Thomas Jefferson, where Jefferson informed McDonald that he cannot straddle both white and native identities. McDonald's brother declared to him, "The white man hates the Indian, and will never permit him to come into close fellowship with him. . . ."[13] According to McKenney, McDonald sobbed after reading the letter. He insisted that although McDonald agreed to study law, he continued to succumb to his own fatalism. The young McDonald reportedly lamented that "the seal is upon my destiny."[14] Such events suggest McDonald was deeply cognizant during his teenage years, if not resentful, of the racial status imposed upon him. He was personally aware of the ways his status as an Indian, no matter how much education he received, limited his opportunities in white society.

While he initially opposed removal, McDonald would sign the Treaty of Dancing Rabbit Creek in 1830, which required Choctaw people to leave their homelands in the southern region and resettle in Indian Territory out west. In the process, McDonald negotiated a deal for himself that allowed him to remain in Mississippi. While the rest of the Choctaw nation removed west to Indian Territory, McDonald stayed behind to oversee his family's farm and their slaves. He eventually lobbied to become a citizen of the state of Mississippi, while continuing to advocate for the civil rights of native people within the state.[15] In 1831, McDonald died after falling from a cliff. The circumstances surrounding his death are contested, and they raise many questions pertaining to the potential status of his mental health. Was it an accidental fall or was the cause of McDonald's passing death by suicide? Was the violence of his people's removal and the role he played in the process too much to bear? While such questions can never be fully answered, there is much to be learned from the life of this young man subjected to such a distinct kind of violence visited upon native students, over centuries, within the schooling apparatus of the United States.

James McDonald's life is a window that exposes the genocidal nature of US educational policies and protocols imposed on native students—educational programs motivated by the political-economic interests of the nation. And McDonald was not the first. Long before American independence, white settlers absorbed native children into the chaos of their fantasies of American expansion that were always predicated on disappearing indigenous ways of life. Since virtually the beginning of white settlement on the American continent, mission groups and local governments engaged in projects of cultural genocide, from sixteenth-century Catholic missions in Spanish-occupied South America to seventeenth-century praying towns in New England. Indeed, this is a history that preceded and extends far beyond the life of McDonald.

McDonald's experience provides a prism for studying native students' experiences across the nineteenth century, illustrating how they became conscripted into an educational system fundamentally based on *natal alienation*: a form of schooling meant to disrupt kinship ties between native students and their families, land, and nations.[16] Settler schooling, including its pedagogical strategy based on natal alienation, was a systematic process of turning native children into orphans, children in need of guardianship by white settler families and schools. These social institutions were deputized by the settler state to serve as adoptive parents and parental institutions, replacements for native parents deemed irredeemable by white school reformers, as native people who were too far gone—ruined and already beholden to old ways of the Indian. What's more, such systematic forms of natal alienation enacted through kidnapping, or what I will later refer to as *captive adoptions*, were inextricably linked to native land dispossession—as revealed through McDonald's signature on the Treaty of Dancing Rabbit Creek. Clearing a path for continued native land dispossession was always at the heart of settler schooling for native youth.

BEYOND THE RUSE OF ASSIMILATION

Like historian K. Tsianina Lomawaima, a leading scholar on native education and a descendant of boarding school survivors, I have arrived at a conceptual impasse with the language of "assimilation." During a roundtable on "Crosscurrents in Native and Black Educational Histories" at the 2023 conference for the Native American and Indigenous Studies Association (NAISA), Lomawaima voiced her skepticism, which

I invited as instruction. Wondering aloud during the question-and-answer portion of our session in which I was a presenter, she asked us to consider "if *assimilation* is even the right term for what we have been writing about." Her question resonated with me, having long found *assimilation*—the term widely used in historical scholarship and public discourse to characterize native boarding schools—to be a term in crisis. It is a conceptual framing of native education desperately in need of reconsideration because it conceals more than it reveals about settler-colonial procedures within the schooling apparatus of the United States. While assimilation names the process of native students being forced to incorporate aspects of Western Anglo-American culture into their ways of life, the language conceals the militaristic and political-economic aims driving the demands for students to shed indigenous ways of life as well as the motivation for creating distance between native students and the kinship networks of their natal communities, which, again, always included heritage claims to land.

While settlers publicly expressed their objectives to assimilate and civilize native students, having repeated such claims in tens of thousands of pages of documents, such claims should not be taken at face value. As Lomawaima has stated elsewhere, such claims were "rhetorical illusions fabricated to mask reality." She declares, "We must question the rhetoric of assimilation, because abundant practices worked to domesticate and thus preserve selected Indianness."[17]

Lomawaima names a contradiction in historical memory pertaining to native education. How is it possible that settler schooling aimed to assimilate native students into whiteness, while at the same time emphasizing their racial distinctiveness? Indeed, settler schooling for native youth was constructed for the special needs of these students as "Indians," a racial category used to flatten and essentialize indigenous peoples, who were extraordinarily heterogeneous in language and customs, among other notable distinctions. Settler schooling for native students was less about assimilating native students into whiteness and more about alienating students from their tribal communities, and ultimately their claims to indigenous lands, hoping to make them into a new kind of Indian—useful to the colonial project (perhaps as an intermediary) but nevertheless part of a racially subordinated group within the broader American social order.

Native American boarding schools, for instance, in their curricula and racially specific enrollment practices, emphasized that indigenous students were a distinct racialized group. This ran parallel to educational strategies imposed on ethnic European students, which sought to minimize ethnic distinctions among them and incorporate them into a national white American identity. In considering these nuances of settler schooling for native students, I insist that the language of assimilation, which is relevant to social processes of immigrant incorporation—particularly as it pertains to ethnic Europeans—is insufficient for understanding the distinct ways native people were enlisted in the American social order through the schooling apparatus of the state. Given the critical importance of native schooling as a key site for understanding the development of the nation—and for appreciating education as the underside of US empire—more revelatory language is essential.

Furthermore, while the language of assimilation suggests the incorporation of native people into whiteness, and white settler society, there is much evidence that suggests white settlers were deeply invested in preserving or "domesticating" certain aspects of Indianness. White settlers have always been invested in symbols and representations of Indianness—whether it be on US currency, through mascots, or as early colonists dressing up as native people to protest British rule. Such representations helped to dialectically define white identity in the United States, but the symbols and myths associated with "Indians" helped define the US as distinct from the English—its former colonizer. The white American national identity required preservation of "the native" as a prop, given its aboriginal closeness to the North American landscape and settlers' desires to be authentically American. By going through native people—through symbolic forms of consumption—white settlers intended to become the natural stewards of the land. Indeed, "playing Indian" and "going native" have been key phenomena in white settler fantasies over the centuries of US history—from the Boston Tea Party's

Mohawk disguises in 1773, as they rebelled against the British Crown, to the depictions of "noble savages" and "bad Indians" in foundational American literature, like characters Tashtego in *Moby-Dick* (1851) and "Injun Joe" in *The Adventures of Huckleberry Finn* (1884), as well as the very long list of present-day mascots.[18]

The language of "natal alienation" offers a corrective to the ruse of assimilation often used to characterize the aims of settler schooling imposed on native people. Natal alienation was a process through which indigenous children, as the future generations of native peoples, were intentionally targeted to disrupt genealogical and tribal ties between children and elders, as a means of disrupting the transmission of native heritage, which included indigenous peoples' relations to land and other natural resources. The actions of settlers (beyond what they said) suggest a general desire to "domesticate" native peoples into a more controllable group of racialized indigenous subjects.[19]

Boarding schools wanted native youth to remain Indian; however, they were to be carefully constructed versions of indigenous peoples that were more palatable to white settlers. Yet "the safety zone" of agreeable Indianness was a classification constantly in flux. For instance, at times native languages were used as a medium for transferring settler ideas. Other times native languages were banned. Sometimes native art and forms of creative expression were permitted. Other times they were frowned upon as savage. There are cases where "traditional" indigenous dress and ways of being were fetishized and incorporated into school performances and pageantry in stereotypical fashion. In other instances, they were vehemently forbidden through school policy. Indigenous Studies scholars K. Tsianina Lomawaima and Teresa McCarty offer "the safety zone" theory to describe such "swings of Indian policy." Indeed, when we look closely at the historical record, you can't help but notice such back-and-forth in native education policy, "an ongoing struggle over cultural difference and its perceived threat, or benefit, to a sense of shared American identity." Moving beyond assimilation and toward a more refined characterization of settler schooling requires that we account for the nuance in the story, how "the federal government has not simply vacillated between encouraging or suppressing

Native languages and cultures but has in a coherent way . . . attempted to distinguish safe from dangerous Indigenous beliefs and practices."[20]

I argue that settler schooling was a site for making indigenous youth into "noble" native students—a kind of offshoot of "the noble savage" archetype deeply entrenched in settler fantasies. It was a version of being Indian deemed safe and unobstructive to US national expansion. One of the primary methods of doing this was through the disruption of familial and tribal ties. Severing relations between native students and their families, as well as broader kinship ties within nations, was a first step, perpetually executed through repetition, in remaking native students in the likeness of such images constructed in the minds of settler-school reformers.

This objective of settler schooling is immediately apparent in the valorization of orphaned native children as the ideal native student in the discourse of white reformers. Colonel Thomas McKenney's adoption of James McDonald is a prelude to such logic, and it was also widely enunciated by government officials through the nineteenth century. As one Indian agent explained in 1848, "when separated from their people young," native children "are as susceptive of improvement as any other children." Writing from Minnesota Territory, the agent described his arrival at this conclusion after "adopting" several native children and while overseeing a school run by his sister among the Dakota.[21] In 1861, Eugene C. Chirouse stated the position in simpler terms. Having founded a school on the Tulalip Reservation in what is now Washington State, Chirouse declared, "Those who are orphans are the more tractable and better disposed." This observation led him to conclude, "The best way to civilize the children of the Indians is to keep them entirely removed from their parents and adult relatives . . . *they must forget their parents as far as possible* in order to abandon the habits of the Indians with less difficulty."[22]

While some native students were indeed orphans, by definition, others were subjected to a settler-schooling process intended to symbolically kill native parents and tribal relations in order to remake indigenous youth in an image that conformed to settler fantasies. For these reasons, I turn to "natal alienation," as opposed to assimilation, to characterize the primary strategy for schooling native students as a mandate of war. Natal alienation as an instrument of domination was a long-term strategy of neutralizing native resistance to settler expansion and helping to facilitate white Americans' predatory accumulation of indigenous resources.

NATAL ALIENATION AS AN INSTRUMENT OF RACIAL DOMINATION

Natal alienation is most notably associated with the history of trans-Atlantic slavery, where European traffickers intentionally disrupted kinship ties among African natives as a key method for turning people into property, as a means of killing the social life of black captives and asserting total control over their social worlds. When applied to the context of native schooling as an extension of settler-colonial procedure, however, the language provides significant clarity for analyzing this social phenomenon and its aims of disrupting native American relations and heritage claims to land. In his groundbreaking book, *Slavery and Social Death*, published in 1982, historical sociologist Orlando Patterson theorized natal alienation as a process of domination enacted through various physical and symbolic acts employed to facilitate and maintain a distinct form of social death universally experienced by enslaved populations. Enslaved people experienced "a secular excommunication," notes Patterson. Having been "alienated from all 'rights' or claims of birth, he [the enslaved] ceased to belong in his own right to any legitimate social order."[23] Such excommunication meant a rupture of genealogical ties and heritage that naturally accompanied blood relations and adjoining kinship networks.

Understanding race and racial ideologies as relationally formed—where racial ideas and experiences of one group are often intimately connected to those of others (for example, black, white, and native)—invites us to also consider how certain instruments of racial domination may be employed across racial groups, even when the application and aims are context specific.[24] Across black and native experiences, natal alienation was weaponized toward distinct political and economic ends, and it was animated by distinct forms of racial animus. While careful not to make false equivalencies between the two distinct forms of racial domination, I insist that this particular instrument of domination was applied to both black and native people as distinct racialized communities.

Patterson's sociological description of natal alienation is helpful for grounding this relational interpretation of antiblackness and anti-indigeneity. He professed:

> *Not only was the slave denied all claims on, and obligation to, his parents and living blood relations but, by extension, all such claims and obligations on his more remote ancestors and on his descendants. He was truly a genealogical isolate. Formally isolated in his social relations with those who lived, he also was culturally isolated from the social heritage of his ancestors. He had a past, to be sure. But a past is not a heritage. Everything has a history, including sticks and stones. Slaves differed from other human beings in that they were not allowed freely to integrate the experience of their ancestors into their lives, to inform their understanding of social reality with the inherited meanings of their natural forbearers, or to anchor the living present in any conscious community of memory.*[25]

Such genealogical isolation outlined by Patterson, as manifesting through the denial of natural blood ties, was facilitated through a process of reducing African people to chattel and employing methods of domination intentionally crafted to obstruct enslaved people's efforts to maintain relations with their established heritage and kinship networks. These violations aimed to reduce the enslaved to fungible objects, a "hybrid of property and person" to be bought and sold; a persecuted people, identifiable by their physical markers of African ancestry, who were forced to labor within the plantation economies of the Americas.[26] Such violation was experienced universally by enslaved Africans who suffered the trans-Atlantic slave trade and it applied to their descendants in the Americas, who endured ongoing violations of black family and kinship ties via, for instance, the domestic slave trade as well as exploitative labor and carceral practices in slavery's afterlives. That the condition of the slave followed that of the mother, whereby part of black women's labor was to continue to produce children who were to be property, children who could be taken at auction, further enunciated this social reality outlined by Patterson.

I understand natal alienation to be a strategy of domination applied to both African natives and American natives—because to be clear, the prior status of enslaved black people in the Americas was that of the African native stolen from their homeland and forced to make the journey of the middle passage. The African natives were extracted as a source of exploitable laborers, and because they were deemed useful for specific knowledge they brought from their native lands as it pertained to the cultivation of particular crops, as well as other cultural and industrial knowledge. For the African native-turned-black slave, on the one hand, the process of natal alienation was an experience of dispossession specific to oceanic movement, while on the other hand, this process of domination in the realm of native American experience was one of intracontinental movement. Though some tend to forget, there were two diverse groups of "natives" enlisted in the American project through the interactive processes of racial chattel slavery and settler colonialism. Natal alienation would serve particular ends for each group—one having to do with the exploitation of native American land as capital and the other having to do with the exploitation of enslaved African labor as well as enslaved Africans *as* capital.

NATAL ALIENATION AS A PEDAGOGICAL AIM OF SETTLER SCHOOLING

White architects of native schooling sought to obliterate native youth's ties to their parents and elders, effectively forcing them "to become as orphans" as a precondition for developing them into "noble" native students, students who would grow up to be amenable to ongoing projects of settler expansion and the shattering of native sovereignty. Settler school officials denied native youth the ability to freely integrate the knowledge and wisdom of their ancestors into their lives. By cutting off native tongues through restrictive language policies, officials hoped to ensure indigenous youth could not use the knowledge resources of their elders and ancestors to inform their understandings and interpretations of their social reality. And to be clear, such practices were about disrupting long-standing practices of indigenous education that preceded contact with European settlers. While it is a subject beyond the scope of *American Grammar*, readers should keep in mind that settler schooling is not the first form of education introduced to native people. Indeed, settler schooling was subtractive—just as much about taking away and undermining indigenous forms of education as it was about imposing the worldview and knowledge systems of settlers. Through such pedagogical procedures, practitioners of settler schooling sought to limit native students' ability to understand themselves as youth situated in historical context. They sought to deny native students any heritage that could be traced back. These strategies enacted by settlers upon native students were carefully constructed, intended to disarm the threat of indigenous people's tribal identities, particularly their collective claims and relations to land, as well as the ongoing threat of native resistance to white settler aggression.

Without conflating the distinct experiences of racial domination imposed upon indigenous people through settler colonialism with that of enslaved African people in the Americas, it is important to note that natal alienation was a method of domination weaponized against both groups, even if deployed toward ends specific to each one. The strategy of domination is similar, though the ends are not analogous because the native and black conflicts in relation to white racial supremacy are radically distinct. Native American people were conscripted into the development of the modern world on settler-colonial terms, principally through genocidal actions, where military aggression as well as mechanisms of law and policy were used to dispossess indigenous people of their land. This land then being turned into public and private property—as white possessions—all in support of a larger nation-building project. Alongside this development of native dispossession, African captives were enlisted in the American project through their commodification as human chattel to be bought and sold as the property of others, and used as fungible laborers in the plantation economy propping up the settler state and its slave society. Yet these lines of distinction having been drawn, the fact remains that instruments of domination used on one group are often taken up and used in the persecution of others, even if the application of such instruments, and the ends they aim to achieve, may vary. The playbook of power is actually quite small in this way.

LOCATING NATAL ALIENATION IN ACCOUNTS OF GOVERNMENT OFFICIALS, SETTLER TEACHERS, AND NATIVE STUDENTS

While the rhetoric of assimilation is indeed present in the archival transcript, there is also a clear record documenting how settler school reformers employed strategies to disappear indigenous ways of life by targeting kinship ties and traditional relations. Across the historical record we find evidence of state actors trafficking in the language of natal alienation. Descriptions of natal alienation are also found in recollections of teachers and students documented in a range of historical sources.

In his 1822 report, the United States secretary of war, John C. Calhoun, insisted that a line be drawn between younger generations of native students and their predecessors. Schooling efforts would likely be ineffective when it came to older generations; therefore, he insisted the work of civilizing native people required a paternalistic cultivation of indigenous youth. He asserted, "The present generation, which cannot be greatly affected by it, must pass away, and those who have been reared under the present system of education must succeed them, before its effects can be fully tested."[27] Civilizing the native—which also amounted to killing the old Indian ways—would be a gradual, slow death. It required putting distance between native children and "the present generation" of native elders. Indeed, schooling was a key weapon in the US arsenal when it came to the Indian Wars. The secretary of war's advocacy of natal alienation as a strategy for dealing with the Indian problem was shared by settler school reformers across the nineteenth century.

In October 1818, General Calvin Jones gave a heartbreaking account of a Cherokee grandmother turning her grandson over to the white educators at Brainerd Mission. Both the young boy and his grandmother sobbed as the school officials tried to console them while communicating through a translator. Jones recorded the following details: "An old Indian woman, who seems to have a vestige of civilization, brought a little savage, her grandson, to place at the school. When the former was about to depart she wept so much over her child, who cried to accompany her, that Mr. Hoyt apprehended she would not leave him, and through an interpreter, assured her he would in a few days be reconciled to his situation. She said that she had no intention but to leave him, that the parting was very painful to her, but she too well knew what was for the child's good."[28] In these instances, missionaries asserted themselves as new parents of native children, and the school communities, composed of other native students separated from their natal communities, were to form new family. This familial rhetoric was often implied, but it was just as often explicitly stated in the language employed by settler teachers.

This language of natal alienation appears not only in the words of federal officials but also in the words of teachers and students as they described experiences on the ground. An account published two months earlier portrays the same Mr. Hoyt using familial rhetoric when taking in a young Osage girl. According to missionaries who recorded the incident, on the afternoon of September 28, 1818, "word was sent that the little Osage captive was at a neighbors 4 miles distant" and the girl "would be sent to us the first opportunity." Instead of waiting, Hoyt "immediately went after her" after learning the girl's location, and "*on seeing the dear orphan who appears to be about 4 or 5 years old*, he directed her to be told in Cherokee (for she does not understand English) that *he would be her father*."[29]

Cherokee warriors kidnapped the young girl during a skirmish caused by the US government, which pushed Cherokee people to move west and encroach on Osage lands. The Cherokee "owner," a man named Aaron Price, sold the young girl to a white plantation owner from Mississippi, Lydia Carter, for $150.[30] This white woman also paid money to send the Osage girl to Brainerd Mission to be educated with the expectation that she would also be named for her. It appears that neither Lydia Carter, nor any of the other missionaries involved, made any attempt to reconnect the young Osage girl turned Cherokee captive turned adoptee of a white female slave owner with her family. We also have no record of the name given to the young Osage girl by her family and tribe, only that she was saved by a white benefactor who sent her to be civilized. She was to be turned over to a new family at Brainerd, and Mr. Hoyt was eager to assume the role as parent.

Hoyt's captive adoption of the young Osage girl recorded in *The Brainerd Journal* continues as follows: The young girl "fixed her eyes with great earnestness upon him for about half a minute." She then smiled and "reached him her bonnet as a token that she accepted the offer & would go with him. As he took her on the horse before him, she gave him some nuts she had in her hand, & leaned her head on his bosom as if she had really found a father. . . ." Mr. Hoyt soon introduced the young girl to her new family. When "first introduced to the family she seemed a little surprised on seeing so many gathered around her, but the children beginning to talk to her in a language she understood, her cheerfulness immediately returned, & she appeared to be quite at home." The missionaries understood this young Osage girl, like the other native youth at Brainerd, to be their adopted child. They insisted, "We feel ourselves bound, not only in duty, but by the feelings of our heart, to train her as our own child."[31]

White settler teachers often used familial rhetoric to characterize their relationship with native students, and such rhetoric was not unique to Brainerd. These characterizations should be interpreted as more than sincere or well-intentioned care for native children, but instead a paternalistic sensibility shared among missionary teachers and US representatives whose motivation for adopting native children emerged from fanatical ideas that white Protestant settler adults were superior to the parents and elders in the natal communities of indigenous students. This was not benign care and compassion. It was a desire to make native students as orphans—young people alienated from their tribal identities and elders, only to be immersed in a social context structured and totally constrained by white settler fantasies of who native people should be and become.

Mary Reed and Isabella Porter, enrolled at the Mayhew Girls School in the Choctaw nation (present-day Mississippi), were devastated when separated from their families in 1824. Missionaries described the scene of Mary becoming "adopted" by her female teacher. When Mary's parents "came again, and were about to go away, Mary shook hands with them, and then went and leaned her head on her teacher very affectionately, which her parents saw, and smiling said, 'She is your daughter now.'" According to the missionaries, Mary's family "all parted very cheerfully." Isabella Porter, however, continued to be heartbroken after being separated from her family. The girl sank into such a deep state of depression that the missionaries asked her mother not visit her again. The teachers insisted this would help Isabella get used to being without her mother and minimize distress. Recounting Isabella's mother's response, the missionary teachers explained, "She took her things as agreed, and went out. As she passed the window, the tear of affection stole down her cheek." Despite the troubles and resentment Isabella may have had from being separated from her family and her mother being warned against visiting, the missionaries felt their actions to be justified and in the best interest of the young girl. For "Isabella is a good scholar, possesses much of the native cunning, and appears to have a pleasant disposition."[32] These missionaries saw themselves as white mothers to a darker race of children, and they modeled a particular brand of white paternalism whereby white womanhood was mobilized in service of the patriarchal and settler aims of the growing nation. In this way, white women, though not the architects of native school policies, nevertheless played key roles in the removal and alienation of native youth from their natal communities.[33]

Such experiences of natal alienation also appear in the documented accounts by native students themselves. In June 1828, Cherokee student Elizabeth Taylor wrote a letter to Miss Abigail Parker at the behest of her missionary teacher exposing assimilationist rhetoric students were taught to internalize at Brainerd Mission as they were forced to distance themselves from their families and communities. Brainerd, readers may recall, was the first government-sponsored native school, and a model that Thomas McKenney used to help justify the Civilization Fund Act of 1819. It is from this school that Elizabeth writes to Miss Parker, emphasizing that "when Christians know how much we need the means of knowledge, they will feel the importance of sending missionaries." Native people needed these missionaries, Elizabeth explains, because some Cherokee people are "unenlightened" and they "dress in the Indian manner."[34]

As a Cherokee student, Elizabeth is required to frame her education as an effort to move beyond the unenlightened and retrograde status of her own family and community. The settler school teaches Elizabeth that her mission as a student is to strive for enlightenment, as defined by white educators, and to no longer dress in the Indian manner, as many of her people do. Her education seeks to alienate her from her natal community, to be a pioneer in laying the foundation for a new way of being Indian, one that is commensurate with a settler future. Though Elizabeth is Indian, she might take comfort in the fact that she too can improve and become civilized. Elizabeth writes, "But I have learned that the white people were once as degraded as this people [the Indian people]; and that encourages me to think that this nation will soon become enlightened." In the settler school, educators taught Elizabeth that white people already progressed along the stages of civilization, and that she and other Cherokee youth could follow their example. Through education, they could quickly progress in the stages of human civilization by looking toward a more enlightened race of people and away from their tribal elders and customs. Settler schooling could help accelerate the civilization process for native people. To do so, however, requires that Elizabeth condemn and abandon the unenlightened ways of the Cherokee.

Handwriting samples (Figure 5.1) of nine-year-old Cherokee girls Delilah Fields and Susannah Hanley reveal how deeply engrained the idea of changing native students was to the school's mission, and how transparent educators were in communicating this to native students. Both students wrote the following standard in neat and careful cursive penmanship: "Brainerd Mission. Youth is the time for improvement. I love them that love me and they that seek me surely shall find me. Bible."[35] Revealed through the script of these two students is a clear reference to the religious teachings at the school, as evidenced by the reference to Proverbs 8:17, but also an insistence that native students were studying not just to learn, but *to improve*. In a sinister fashion, the wisdom books of the Bible were employed to teach lessons of natal alienation, for the meaning of "improvement" in this context was layered. Such improvement was in reference not simply to general stages of child and youth development—a progress from early to middle stages of adolescence—but it was a specific vision of improvement constructed over and against flattened representations of the "unenlightened" and "savage" adult members of the students' communities; adults who, by Brainerd's standards, were the antithesis of improvement.

The realities of natal alienation appeared in student letters and written assignments, where native students were required to ritualistically condemn the culture and heritage of their tribal communities. They also appeared in documented accounts where settler school officials, missionary teachers in particular, aggressively assumed roles as parents of native students as a means of facilitating a process of disinheritance. Settler school officials and reformers sought to usurp the authority of indigenous elders who represented traditional native ways of life that settlers worked to disappear. Mission teachers, as parents, and mission schools, as new families, were to block the flow of indigenous heritage. For native students to follow in the traditions of their parents and tribal members would be the opposite of improvement, by settler standards. To become as their elders or follow in the teachings of their own nations would be a declension trajectory at odds with the civilizationist goals of US policies for native schooling.

Settler schooling for native students was an extension of the Indian Wars. As the following pages will show, this reality of racial domination manifested in the institutional structure of particular schools, and in intimate exchanges between individual teachers, students, and white reformers. However, the story evolves in varying directions, responding to the sea changes in US national politics across the nineteenth century; likewise, native people's strategies of resistance and modes of engagement also varied across time and space.

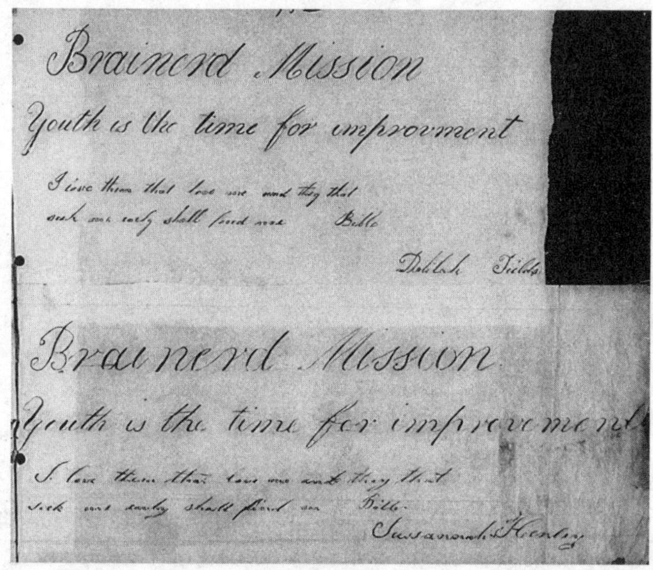

5.1: Handwriting samples from Delilah Fields and Susannah Hanley, nine-year-old Cherokee girls who arrived at Brainerd Mission in 1817. Transcription: "Brainerd Mission. Youth is the time for improvement. I love them that love me and they that seek me surely shall find me. Bible." The quote is from Proverbs 8:17.

6

SETTLER SCHOOLING AS AN ACT OF WAR

We are going to conquer the Indians by a standing army of school-teachers. . . .

—Merrill Gates, President of Amherst College and Lake Mohonk Conference (1891)

The claim that federally imposed native education during the nineteenth century was an act of war is not hyperbole. Native education, purportedly about "civilizing" the Indian, was always about American expansion and nation-building. To this end, federally sanctioned native education was fundamentally about the seizure of indigenous land. In this instance—in the realm of settler-sponsored native education, which I have referred to in shorthand as *settler schooling*—we see the mutually constituted ideological and repressive arms of the United States extending through its rapidly developing schooling apparatus into the lives of indigenous people, and in particular native children. The War Department's role in funding James McDonald's education in 1813 as a twelve-year-old Choctaw boy underscores native schooling's proximity to warfare during this period. It highlights a relationship that persisted throughout the nineteenth century.

The position that native schooling emerged as an expression of the US Indian Wars is substantiated in at least four ways. The secretary of war oversaw these efforts. White education reformers made explicit connections between native education and the aims of conquest in their discourse, often insisting that settler schooling was a cheaper alternative to costly wars. Settler schooling for native students often took place on or near US military posts. Lastly, high-ranking military officials played an active role in the direct oversight and enforcement of native schooling.

The War Department was at the center of a small cohort of actors which formed the official authority of US Indian policy during the first half of the nineteenth century. Native education policy was enacted through loose cooperation between private mission societies, state actions—many of which were illegal—and the federal government. This is to say, it was the result of collusion between government and private citizens, while also being motivated by public and private interests among white American society. This reframing is important, because for so long it has been easy to blame missionary groups as religious zealots and the primary perpetuators of harm inflicted on native children through protocols of settler schooling, as opposed to interpreting such actions as explicit expressions of state-sanctioned violence. And yet, while the enactment of policy was diffused across many actors, the creation of policy was concentrated in the hands of a small number of individuals in Washington, DC. For instance, during the era of the Civilization Fund Act of 1819, this included Secretary of War John J. Calhoun, his colleague and Superintendent of Indian Trade Thomas McKenney, as well as a handful of committed allies in Congress. Superintendent McKenney, the self-proclaimed "adoptive" father of James McDonald, positioned himself as the nation's authority on Indian issues. He used his position in the Indian Trade Office as well as the relationships he cultivated with multiple mission societies to establish his credibility.[1] In fact, Secretary Calhoun often sought McKenney's advice on native political issues, even as Calhoun seemed to be more inclined toward direct, aggressive military approaches when it came to dominating native people than his colleague was. Irrespective of their differences, the men regularly communicated on all things related to indigenous peoples.

•••

SETTLER SCHOOLING ADMINISTERED BY THE US WAR DEPARTMENT

When tracing correspondences between these various historical actors, analyzing official government documents, as well as following the chain of command and flow of federal funding to native education, one achieves an image of how business was handled. The general pipeline of operations took the following form: Missionary groups, Indian agents, and native leaders contact Thomas McKenney; McKenney lobbies Secretary of War John C. Calhoun on their behalf; Secretary of War Calhoun determines if a request merits support before allocating US War Department funds, at times lobbying Congress to establish some related policy.[2] Some gray areas and deviations exist, but one thing is certain from this flow of activity: The two essential tasks of warring with native nations as well as educating them were vested in the same person. After the president of the United States, the secretary of war was the final authority.

Leading government officials engaging in the so-called work of civilizing native people, through education, trade, and industry, had long reported to the War Department. This was the case before Secretary Calhoun established the Bureau of Indian Affairs in March 1824 and appointed McKenney, his friend and collaborator, as the first Commissioner of Indian Affairs. In the late eighteenth and early nineteenth centuries, the secretary of war oversaw the superintendents and agents working with indigenous nations. The secretary had the power to hire and fire those in such positions and he had the authority to assign them specific tasks. As historian Francis Prucha explains, "in the first decades of the new nation there was no formally established office charged specifically with Indian affairs. Dealings with Indians were considered a special category of the War Department's activities." In 1806, the Office of Superintendent of Indian Trade was established, quickly becoming the unofficial government office for dealing with Indian affairs, though still reporting directly to the secretary of war, "supplying information and advice to the secretary of war and corresponding with citizens who were interested in the Indians." With the newly created Commissioner of Indian Affairs in 1824, and specifically its role in administering funding from the Civilization Fund Act of 1819, the War Department formally became the official administrative hub for native schooling. Until the Indian Office was moved to the newly established US Department of the Interior in 1849, the structure established by Secretary of War Calhoun, in partnership with Thomas McKenney, persisted.[3]

Many members of Congress continued to advocate for the Indian Office to be placed back in control of the War Department after 1849. What's more, even after the Commissioner of Indian Affairs no longer reported to the War Department, War Department officials continued to have an outsized influence in the development and implementation of native educational policies, just as military leadership continued to be built into the infrastructure of native schooling operations. For instance, many native schools were built near or at military posts, and "the War Department continued to provide support and personnel to further the objectives" of settler schooling "even after Congress transferred responsibility for Indian Affairs to the Department [of the Interior]." This enduring relationship is reflected in various statutes passed in the second half of the nineteenth century. For instance, an act passed in June 1879 declared, "The Secretary of War shall be authorized to detail an officer of the Army, not above the rank of captain, for special duty with reference to Indian education." An act in July 1883 declared, "The Secretary of War is authorized to set aside, for use in the establishment of normal and industrial training schools for Indian youth from the nomadic tribes having educational treaty claims upon the United States, any vacant posts of barracks, so long as they may not be required for military occupation, and to detail one or more officers of the Army for duty in connection with Indian education, at each such school so established: *Provided*, That moneys appropriated or to be appropriated for general purposes of education among the Indians may be expended, under the direction of the Secretary of the Interior, for the education of Indian youth at such posts, institutions, and schools as he may consider advantageous. . . ."[4]

The task of warring with Indian nations while also deputizing government actors and private citizens to expand civilization among them through education seemed to cause no conflict in the mind of Secretary Calhoun. He moved between the two tasks with a noticeable level of fluidity. In the same letter, Calhoun could discuss tactical advantages for physically dividing the borders of the Creek, Choctaw, and Cherokee nations, to prevent an allied military response on the part of these nations—warning "they could raise at least fifteen thousand warriors"—while also lauding progress made in the area of settler schooling among these same tribes. The two, in Calhoun's mind, posed no contradiction at all. For, indeed, the Indian Wars and Indian education were different means toward the same end.[5]

President James Monroe's strong reference to native education—particularly Brainerd and the Civilization Fund Act—in his 1824 appeal to Congress regarding the federal government's commitment to dissolve Cherokee land titles in Georgia is also quite revelatory. Of critical importance here is the Compact of 1802, where the US ensured the state of Georgia it would clear Cherokee titles within the state's proposed borders. This effort to remove the Cherokee (and several other nations) gained momentum over the first decades of the nineteenth century. By the early 1820s, President James Monroe would include letters from Cyrus Kingsbury regarding Brainerd, among other documents pertaining to civilization efforts among native peoples to make the case that civilization policies could provide a path to peaceably extinguish the Cherokee titles.[6] President Monroe opposed forcible removal, calling it "unjust"—though he definitely wanted native nations to move west. In this instance, he made an explicit connection between Brainerd and ongoing attempts to "peaceably" extinguish the Cherokee title in Georgia. Settler schooling, he believed, was helping to break the ground or soften the force of native resistance. Documentation regarding the CFA and Brainerd was used to back up his urging Congress to be patient and allow the executive branch to keep negotiating land cessions and pursuing civilization policies. The US committed itself to removal of the Southeastern tribes in 1802—something tribal leaders were well aware of. Native leaders and US policymakers were constantly operating under the knowledge that removal seemed to be on the horizon. This is to say, such impending action loomed over any educational project among the Cherokee people in the early nineteenth century. The War Department funded Brainerd as a school within the Cherokee nation in 1816, and it began administering the CFA in the 1820s, but such action was motivated by this protracted vision of disappearing native people in the Southeast—both literally and figuratively. The US government formally adopted this plan of action—which included deciding the fate of native tribes in the Southeast—into its nation-building project decades before Monroe's management of this conflict in the 1820s.

By funding initiatives such as the continuing education of James McDonald and the establishment of Brainerd Mission School in 1816, the War Department actively lobbied for the Civilization Fund Act. It would then serve as the administrative entity for disbursing funds once the legislation was passed. These events on the timeline of native education must also be contextualized by the hovering threat of US force to remove native peoples in the Southeast. This dynamic is quite evident in political discussions around native education in Washington, within the War Department and beyond.

Top of mind for Secretary Calhoun were concerns about native nations living on the American frontier as well as the strategic uses of education as an instrument of US dominance. In a report to Congress in January 1820, Calhoun declared, "It is impossible with their customs, that they should exist as independent communities in the midst of civilized society. They are not, in fact, an independent people, (I speak of those surrounded by our population,) nor ought they to be so considered. They should be taken under our guardianship; and our opinion, and not theirs, ought to prevail, in measures intended for their civilization and happiness. A system less vigorous may protract, but cannot arrest their fate."[7] With this report, Calhoun included a circular that was to be distributed among mission schools and societies, exposing the ulterior motives of the Civilization Fund Act as an educational program targeting native people. In referring to the schools supported with such funds, he explained that "the establishment should be fixed within the limits of those Indian nations who border on our settlements." Calhoun spoke of this circular and the funding it advertised as a mechanism to "concentrate and unite the efforts of individuals and societies." This circular demonstrates how government officials hoped to enact a unified policy by wrangling many different groups involved in "civilizing" native people together. Calhoun administered this new policy as an effort to make settler schooling a systematic process for neutralizing native resistance and a strategy for penetrating the perimeter of the American frontier, helping to clear a path for further expansion.[8]

One can find records of CFA disbursements included alongside annual reports from Secretary Calhoun, where his assessments were surely heavily shaped by McKenney's thinking. Calhoun often framed schooling as an integral part of a more general strategy of extending US authority over native people in these reports. In 1822 he referred to schooling as "the foundation of all other improvements." Calhoun outlined how after settler schooling "a plain and simple system of laws and government" would gradually follow among the frontier tribes, "such as has been adopted by the Cherokees." This would also include "a proper compression of their settlements, and a division of landed property." This was all toward a larger goal of completely absorbing native peoples in the United States and trampling on indigenous sovereignty. Explicating this intention, Calhoun wrote, "By introducing gradually and judiciously these improvements, they will ultimately attain such a state of intelligence, industry, and civilization as to prepare the way for a complete extension of our laws and authority over them."[9]

The War Department's administering of the Civilization Fund Act set a historic precedent, not only because it formalized the national strategy of using education as a military tactic, but because it also established an educational program administered by the federal government. The US government devoted $10,000 annually (just shy of $250,000 today) and significant government oversight to developing a system of native schooling stretching across tribal boundaries—this was, of course, in addition to educational funding administered through annuities to tribes as outlined in treaties between individual nations and the US government. The CFA is an extraordinary development in that Congress passed this legislation amid postwar economic depression and long before the activist federal government of the Progressive Era, when we see concerted efforts to centralize American education in the mainstream US political sphere. I share these details to emphasize the political urgency surrounding native education in the minds of federal actors. In short, Congress established the CFA at a time when white education was haltingly being developed on a state-by-state or town-by-town basis. Such coordinated effort at a national level, and the commitment to federal oversight over settler schooling for native students, reveal its importance in the minds of the nation's leaders as a matter of political-economic expediency. Federal leaders conceptualized settler schooling for native students as a nation-building project, one with critical implications for national security, given the long-standing violent wars surrounding native removal and land dispossession. As such, settler schooling developed through the repressive arm of the state as an ideological project serving clear political and economic ends. The secretary of war's central role in the schooling of native youth betrays this political reality.

NATIVE LAND DISPOSSESSION AS A MATERIAL GOAL OF SETTLER SCHOOLING

The intimacy between the Indian Wars and settler schooling is further revealed in accounts by native students. These young people experienced schooling as inextricably bound up with warfare, even as many came to understand education as a mechanism of resistance and a strategy for indigenous survival. Both realities, while seemingly contradictory, could be true. This is strikingly evident in an 1828 Christmas letter from Nancy Reece, a Cherokee student, to Rev. Fayeter Shepherd. The letter suggests that some native students appropriated schooling as a claims-making tool, hoping to use their educational achievement to safeguard against further US expansion rather than encourage it. It's important to note that Reece's letter was written a month after Andrew

Jackson won the US presidential election, a political leader well-known for his miliary success over native people and strong advocacy for their removal from the Southeast.

Reece begins with contextual details about her time as a student, explaining, "I will tell you something of our happy school, so you may know how we shall feel if we should be separated from each other, and from our teachers and other missionaries." She paints a happy picture of schooling in her Cherokee homeland, constructing a portrait of "civilized" Cherokee life that would be destroyed if the looming threat of removal were to come to fruition. Reece also draws sharp conclusions about the evil visions of some settlers and the threats they pose to the future of the "happy school" and life she has come to know. She concludes, "I do not think that all the people are friends to the Cherokees. Miss Ames has been reading a part of the Presid. Message. . . . Miss Ames has been talking to the scholars and she felt bad and told them that they must get a good education soon as they can, so they can teach if they should be removed. . . . It seems that it will be a trying season to us and the missionaries if we should be separated from them. . . . I have been talking to the children about it and one says 'if the white people want more land let them go back to the country they came from. . . .'"[10]

Interestingly, while Reece advocates against removal on the grounds that she and her peers have demonstrated their capacity for civilization in "happy schools," she also reveals her awareness that such strategies had limitations. She points to the refusal of some settlers to appreciate the "happy schools" of Cherokee students as evidence of their worthiness to remain in their homelands. In naming this limitation of settler schooling, Reece effectively arrives at the conclusion that schooling for native students was not *actually* about civilization for civilization's sake, but it was always about separation; always about severing kinship ties and claims to land; fundamentally a process of dispossession.

Reece articulates an important line of indigenous criticism, not just of the hypocrisy of civilizationist rhetoric, but also in documenting the position expressed by some native students, that if settlers want more land, they should go back to Europe. While the repressive arm of the state employed settler schooling toward the ends of domination, native students appropriated skills acquired in these schools to speak back, using the written word and distinct rhetorical strategies to communicate their distinct position.

Contract schools, which were privately run mission schools that received CFA funding and reported directly to the US War Department, continued to expand through the Civil War era. By 1842 there were more than fifty schools operating for the sole purpose of educating native students, and according to reports by forty-two of these schools, there were at least 2,132 native youth enrolled. In 1877, there were approximately 3,598 native students in settler schooling in 1877; however, by 1900 the enrollment of native students reached 21,568.[11] Over the course of this time, the system of CFA-funded contract schools operated by missionary societies would slowly be replaced by a system of federally administered boarding schools in the late nineteenth century, though day schools and mission schools on or near reservations still operated, often as feeder schools. This boarding school system of Indian education, which formalized after the 1870s, was also a direct outgrowth of the Indian Wars. Indeed, there is much continuity between the strategies employed from the time of the CFA and Brainerd Mission in the first decades of the nineteenth century and late-nineteenth-century boarding schools like the infamous Carlisle Indian Industrial School, founded in 1879 by military leader General Richard Henry Pratt.

The intimacy between Indian education and Indian Wars in the United States persisted through the first full century of the nation. Such educational activity was an integral part of the United States' arsenal as it pressed forward in expanding from coast to coast. Settler schooling grew more and more formalized as the project of native land dispossession and US expansion intensified in strategy and scope. In this process, a rapidly growing number of native students became subjected to settler schooling as part of the first line of defense in American conquest. As a great Kenyan writer once explained of racial domination and colonialism, "The night of the sword and the bullet was followed by the morning of the chalk and the blackboard. The physical violence of the battlefield was followed by the psychological violence of the classroom."[12] What was true of the colonial context of Kenya, was also true of the settler-colonial realities of native American students during the nineteenth century.

Government officials beyond the era of McKenney, Calhoun, and Presidents Monroe and Jackson continued to frame native education as an integral part of ongoing native dispossession. We can look to any of the Commissioners of Indian Affairs after McKenney to illustrate this point. Thomas Hartley Crawford, commissioner from 1838 to 1845, is a prime example. During his tenure, Crawford oversaw the removal of Cherokee people and negotiated thirteen treaties to dispossess various nations. While engaging in this work, Crawford also drafted proposals for federally sponsored native education, including his advocacy for manual labor schools among tribes that would stress the importance of making native women "good and industrious housewives" to hasten the civilization process.[13] This focus on manual labor schools was a continuation of the CFA era, demonstrating how continuous the legacy of the Civilization Fund Act was even as financial contributions from the CFA to contract schools became less significant as a portion of the funding for settler schooling activities among native nations. Yet it is important to emphasize that federal funding provided more currency than the dollar amounts allocated. It signified federal endorsement of these schooling activities. The CFA created a policy nudge—an incentive structure, even—for private citizens interested in helping the United States deal with "the Indian problem."

Historian David Wallace Adams and others have demonstrated how the settler school reformers billed federal native education policy as a replacement for the bloody and costly Indian Wars of the mid-nineteenth century. In his iconic book, *Education for Extinction*, Adams declared, "The war against Indians had now entered a new phase. . . . The next Indian war would be ideological and psychological, and it would be waged against children."[14] However, the reality is that the particular tactics deployed in the battles waged against indigenous children through schooling from one period to the next were all part of a much larger, protracted war—and it always had physical implications in the material world. The use of schooling as a strategy of conquest was cyclical. The war waged in the classroom was neither episodic nor exceptional at any point during the nineteenth century. Settler schooling was a strategy of conquest with deep roots in nation-building projects across the Americas, even as it was refined and employed with increased precision; as it became centralized and implemented at scale by the federal government.

The US Indian Wars were ongoing up and through the era of President Grant's "Peace Policies" of the postbellum era, and certainly through the Wounded Knee Massacre of 1890, when hundreds of members of the Sioux nation were slaughtered by the US military. All the while, the classroom and the battlefield continued to be companion sites of conquest. The emergence of the United States as a leading capitalist power in an increasingly globalized market was contingent on consistent expansion. The nation's vision of growth was inextricably linked to a vision of displacement and disappearance of indigenous people. Such visions of settler futurity were intimately bound up with the shrinkage of native populations, and particularly their heritage claims to land. Their alienation—from the land and from indigenous ways of life—was a national priority.

THE MILITARY RHETORIC OF WHITE REFORMERS IN SETTLER SCHOOLING

Settler school reformer made clear discursive connections between fighting indigenous people and educating them. This was the case in the early nineteenth century with people like Cyrus Kingsbury and Secretary of War Calhoun, and the intimacy between schooling and warfare continued to be expressed in white political discourse by the end of the century. Merrill Gates, president of the Lake Mohonk Conference in 1891 (and the former president of Rutgers University and sitting president of Amherst College), offered one of the most iconic statements illustrating this throughline in settler rhetoric surrounding native schooling. At the event, white leaders and organizations gathered around their shared concerns about dealing with "the Indian problem." At such gatherings, the fate of native peoples was discussed by white elites who had the power to influence the direction of national policy because of their wealth and lobbying power in Washington.

Addressing members of the conference, Gates offered the following:

> *First, the time for fighting the Indian tribes is passed. There may be Indian riots to be quelled: let us have no more Indian "wars." We do not believe in a standing army, but it should be an army of Christian school-teachers. That is the army that is going to win the victory. We are going to conquer barbarism, but we are going to do it by getting at the barbarians one by one. We are going to do it by that conquest of the individual man, woman, and child which leads to the truest civilization. We are going to conquer the Indians by a standing army of school-teachers, armed with ideas, winning victories by industrial training and by the gospel of love and the gospel of work.*[15]

These words reflect the political ideology shaping the late-nineteenth-century era when native boarding schools proliferated as the pinnacle of the settler schooling project. It also resonates with words spoken by white architects of native education during the CFA era. Recall, for instance, the words of Rev. Cyrus Kingsbury, founder of Brainerd Mission School in the second decade of the century, during the aftermath of the War of 1812 and the Red Stick Wars with the Seminole nation. When appealing to Secretary of War William Crawford, Kingsbury explained that educating native people could be a more effective remedy for addressing the conflict between the United States and native nations. He insisted, "no other means could be so successfully employed to prevent the recurrence of expensive and bloody Indian wars" than education. Kingsbury believed native schooling would help ensure "permanent security to our frontier settlements."[16]

Education and war were two sides of the same coin when it came to matters of US Indian policy. This conclusion would be drawn by government actors and private citizens time and again as the United States expanded over the nineteenth century.

Settler school reformers were explicit in the connections they drew between native schooling and the Indian Wars. Secretary of the Interior Carl Schurz provides a particularly important example in 1881, making an economic argument identifying education as a cheaper alternative to war in a chillingly explicit fashion. Schurz concluded: "We are told that it costs little less than a million of dollars to kill an Indian in war. It costs about one hundred and fifty dollars a year to educate one at Hampton or Carlisle. If the education of Indian children saves the country only one small Indian war in the future, it will save money enough to sustain ten schools like Carlisle. . . ."[17] Schurz is a figure of crucial importance, though his time as secretary of the interior was brief. Schurz used his tenure at the Interior Department to fight against a concerted effort to move the Office of Indian Affairs back to the Department of War. Yet, while his successful organizing helped keep the Indian Affairs Office separate from the Department of War, Schurz was nevertheless actively involved in ongoing genocide. By his own admission, he did not view native education as far from the Indian Wars in its goals.[18]

In the passage above Schurz references two iconic institutions, both founded by US military leaders. Hampton Institute was founded by Samuel Armstrong, a white military general, to educate formerly enslaved people in 1868. Carlisle was founded in 1879 by Richard Henry Pratt, also a white military general, as a boarding school for native students. The latter grew out of the first "Indian Program" at Hampton, which originated from an educational program run by Pratt at a prison in Florida. The intersection of black and native education in this story reflects deep connections between the two racial projects, which will be explored in later chapters. However, for now it is important to note that the linking of these two institutions in the mind of Secretary Schurz reflects how race formed relationally through such projects of domination, since they were always structurally linked within the political economy of the nation while also being intimately connected in the minds of individual white educational leaders who wielded power through the schooling apparatus of the United States.

MILITARY OFFICIALS AS SCHOOL LEADERS AND MILITARY SITES AS SCHOOL GROUNDS

Not only did the white architects of native schooling position their program as a replacement for and at times an extension of the Indian Wars, but also the schools they created often emerged amid acts of military conquest and remained deeply connected to their military origins. If Rev. Kingsbury's Brainerd Mission was the model of contract schools during the CFA era, then General Richard Henry Pratt's Carlisle Indian Industrial School, built in former military barracks in Carlisle, Pennsylvania, served as the model for the Indian boarding school era of the late nineteenth century. As subsequent chapters will reveal, many native schools were built on or near US military posts. What's more, General Pratt's first cohort of "pupils" were prisoners of war, composed of a group of Cheyenne, Arapaho, Kiowa, Comanche, and Cadoo men captured during a series of skirmishes in 1874. He turned his prison at Fort Sill into a school for civilizing Indians with the assistance of two New England teachers, having been inspired by Progressive Era paternalism. Pratt's mission was to completely unmake the warriors held as his captives and then build them into a new kind of native people through formal education, especially through his "outings" program, which placed students in the surrounding white community in St. Augustine, Florida, as workers. Pratt would settle for nothing less than complete physical and cultural transformation, forcing the students to adopt white forms of dress and hairstyles, as well as the English language and an appreciation for individual property rights as opposed to tribal forms of communalism. All strategies, to be clear, were reminiscent of the contract school era initiated by the Civilization Fund Act of 1819.[19]

That most of the government officials working in the realm of Indian affairs were war veterans or actively working in the War Department further emphasizes the intimacy between settler schooling and warfare. This included influential Commissioner of Indian Affairs Thomas J. Morgan, also a Civil War veteran, whom scholars of native American history consistently rank as a person almost singularly responsible for creating a more centralized and expansive infrastructure for native education during the boarding school era of the late nineteenth century. Morgan helped establish a tiered native educational system, where students began at government-operated day schools and were promoted up and through off-reservation boarding schools. During the late nineteenth century, Morgan worked to get rid of the privately operated institutions from the contract school era and replace them with a highly centralized and efficient system of government-sponsored native education. Leaders like Morgan favored the residential boarding school, in particular, because it complemented the shift in late nineteenth century US Indian policy, wherein the political goal became explicitly about disrupting tribal identities and forcing native people to become US citizens or wards of the state. One of the main priorities of schools like the one developed by General Pratt was their emphasis on taking students away from their families and tribal nations for extended periods of time to strengthen the hold of the civilizing project. This was distinct from boarding schools on or near native reservations. The goal was to thoroughly alienate students from their natal communities, because indigenous genealogical and tribal ties fundamentally threatened the nation-building project of the United States, particularly given the kinship between indigenous lands and tribal heritage. Settler school leaders, who were often also military leaders, argued that proximity to native families and nations made it too easy for students to "relapse into savagery."

While there were some new aspects to the boarding school era of the late nineteenth century, the continuities from earlier Indian policy are quite striking. So much so, that long-standing arguments that a national US Indian education program was a late-nineteenth-century creation invites revision or, at minimum, a softening of such rigid temporal framings. Education was a persistent goal of policymakers in the nineteenth century because it was so intimately linked to native land dispossession throughout the 1800s. While it is true that the boarding school era witnessed more robust federal support for education, more standardized curricula, and a systematizing of tiered institutions—where day schools on reservations were at the bottom, then boarding schools on reservations stood above them, and finally off-reservation boarding schools ranked at the top—this "one best system" for Indian education was a model built on decades of settler schooling administered by federal actors concerned with military aims in partnership with their white civilian allies over the century.

The patchwork of educational sources fueling settler schooling among natives during the CFA era persisted into the boarding school era of the late nineteenth century. Private mission groups remained very active during these later years, and they worked in close coordination with government actors, particularly those with direct ties to the US military. The military aims of settler schooling were especially expressed through the disruption of native students' kinship networks, as natal alienation emerged as a particular strategy for severing native heritage claims to land. In some cases, mission schools were regarded as "in loco parentis" with regard to food rations and other resources distributed by the federal government. This is to say, rations and resources that would otherwise have been given to a family for a child were given to mission schools instead. This practice not only signaled a change in who the federal government recognized as guardians of native children, but this mechanism of resource distribution would also be exploited to compel native parents to keep their children in school once enrolled for fear that if their child returned home, they would be denied rations to feed them. The persistence of bureaucratic lag and the ineptitude of Indian agents is well documented, and many of them certainly chose to continue diverting rations to the school to induce attendance. Indeed, military officials at Indian agencies often encouraged such behavior, at times even proposing the strategy themselves. It also doesn't require much stretch of the imagination to consider how some missionaries and Indian agents might have used this structural dynamic to their benefit, to coerce native parents and communities into compliance.

Settler schooling for native students was education in occupied territory. It was conceived of and administered by the very governmental actors and war officials developing and executing military strategies to advance the nation-building project. Indeed, these were the same people aiming to expand the seizure and occupation of native land by white settlers and they hoped to do so while meeting the least amount of native resistance.

7

"BOARDING SCHOOL IS NOW THE ANCESTOR"

THE CAPTIVE ADOPTIONS OF NATIVE STUDENTS

White architects of native education subjected indigenous students to captive adoptions. They removed students from their natal communities for the distinct purpose of proving that indigenous ways of life could be rooted out, and disinheritance ensured. Captive adoptions were often the first step in a series of violating rituals meant to alienate native students from their families and tribal heritage, including renaming practices, haircutting ceremonies, and the removal of traditional tribal clothing. Captive adoptions were enacted on an individual level, where individual settlers "adopted" native students with the clear intention of erasing the heritage of these youth, and it was also systematically enacted through the schooling apparatus of the United States via educational institutions and policies. Such methods of natal alienation can be traced from the early nineteenth century, as embodied in the actions of education reformers and individual schools, through the late nineteenth century, as settler schooling for native students dramatically expanded, particularly with the growth of off-reservation boarding schools by the late 1870s. The story of a familiar figure provides a useful starting point to trace this throughline.

Readers will recall Colonel Thomas McKenney's adoption of Choctaw James McDonald in 1816, as discussed in previous chapters. McDonald's story provides an iconic example of this phenomenon, as his captive adoption fed McKenney's lobbying efforts to establish the Civilization Fund Act of 1819. However, James McDonald was not the only native student "adopted" by Colonel McKenney. In 1827, McKenney adopted two additional native children: one Euchee and one Creek. Similar to McDonald, he took these young boys into his home and appointed himself as their father. Their adoption reflects the interpersonal arm of McKenney's work extending from the 1819 Civilization Fund Act. And while I will emphasize such captive adoptions in the life of Colonel McKenney, it is important to note that there are many documented cases of white government officials "adopting" native children.[1] Evidence suggests captive adoptions may have been more widespread, and that they were often done informally. Despite the absence of precise numerical figures, we know that the violence of native schooling was intimately expressed through such adoptions, and that they modeled, in the private life of white education reformers, the logics of natal alienation that eventually became expressed through a federally run school system for native children.

Arbor was ten years old when Colonel Thomas McKenney adopted him in 1827. Arbor was the boy's "Indian name," according to McKenney; a name given by his family, who were members of the Euchee tribe, a people closely allied with the Creek. At the instruction of white missionaries, however, Arbor should only respond to "Lee Compere." They insisted Arbor was an Indian name, and therefore should be replaced.

White teachers renamed the boy Lee Compere after the Baptist missionary who founded Withington Station, a mission near Montgomery, Alabama, and likely the school previously attended by Arbor. Withington Station was one of two mission schools in the Creek nation, the other being Asbury Mission School.[2] White teachers often renamed indigenous students after white political figures, especially missionaries who committed their lives to "civilizing" Indians. These educators believed that Arbor, the young Uchee boy, should aspire to the likes of Lee Compere. So they changed his name. Arbor, the name given by his family, as far as they were concerned, carried no meaning, or at least none worthy of respect.[3]

On Friday morning, October 26, 1827, Arbor stood in a state of confusion after arriving at the Creek Agency at Fort Mitchell, just along the Chattahoochee River. Like many Indian agencies and government trading houses, the Creek Agency—and likely the school where Arbor received his new name—stood in "the shadow of a military post."[4] This was no coincidence, as the education of native children fell under the jurisdiction of the War Department. It was on these grounds, a direct extension of the repressive apparatus of the United States, that Arbor was handed off to Colonel McKenney.

Yet the lives of the colonel and the young boy were intertwined well before this fall morning. As we know, McKenney was the man responsible for establishing the Civilization Fund Act in 1819—the very legislation establishing federal funding to support contract schools like the one where Arbor was renamed Lee Compere by white missionaries. Reports by the Commissioner of Indian Affairs for 1827 list the two missions in the Creek nation among forty "Indian Schools" supported by the Department of War, and therefore funded by the CFA.[5] As such, McKenney had a direct impact on Arbor's life well before their first encounter at the Creek Agency. The same could be said for the other indigenous youth McKenney adopted on this day: a thirteen-year-old Creek boy referred to as William Barnard in McKenney's diary.

According to McKenney, he adopted Arbor and William "at the request of their parents and friends." Like James McDonald, these two native boys enter the historical record through their relation to McKenney. It is primarily his accounts that frame their lives in the settler-colonial archive—an obvious limitation for historical recovery. While limited in its perspective, however, we still find glimpses of Arbor's and William's perspectives through documented accounts of their behaviors and embodied responses to this captive adoption, as described by McKenney. Even as Arbor's and William's words are absent, their actions left impressions in the record. The marks left by these two native boys reveal details about the agency of native students who strained against the grips of the settler state and its schooling apparatus.

We know that William tried to comfort Arbor as they prepared to enter the stagecoach with the three passengers accompanying them on the first leg of their journey from the Creek Agency in Alabama to Georgia in October 1827. Thomas McKenney was accompanied by his son Ben and Alabama Senator William R. King. We also know that after traveling nearly thirty miles, McKenney became distracted from his conversation with King because "the little fellow [Arbor] gave signs of great restlessness." Arbor "kept muttering something in Uchee." William, having sufficient command of English and Uchee, translated Arbor's message for the group: "He wanted to go home," the boy said.[6]

Finding this amusing, McKenney decided to himself, "I would test the self-relying feeling which I had often heard attributed to Indians, even of his tender age. . . . I knew he could have no knowledge of the way he had come, for he, and William, and Ben, had occupied the front seats of the stage, and have travelled backwards." McKenney asked the driver to stop, then instructed William to "tell Lee he can go home, if he wishes to go." Before William translated a word, Arbor was headed for the door, having made out what McKenney said with the limited English picked up during his time at the mission school. Arbor "seized his bundle, and was, in a twinkling, out at the side of the stage, and going down over one of the fore-wheels." Irrespective of which direction they were traveling, it seems Arbor knew that the desired direction was away from the coach taking him from his family and tribe. Before he could get too far, McKenney commanded his son to fetch Arbor. Ben followed his father's orders, pulling Arbor back into the coach. Their journey continued. According to McKenney, Arbor "was inconsolable, and remained so" until the group reached their destination in Augusta, Georgia.[7]

Like Arbor, many indigenous youth attempted to run away.[8] They refused captive adoptions facilitated by the schooling apparatus of the United States. While the historical record is replete with stories documenting settler school officials working to alienate native students from their natal communities, there is always, in the shadows, a continuum of resistance among native students haunting the state's paternalistic narratives and political posturing. Running away was a common expression of native students' resistance to captive adoptions meant to destroy their kinship ties and deny their heritage as indigenous people. However, the paternalistic hand of the settler state was persistent.

William and Arbor immediately received haircuts and new clothes in Augusta, Georgia, where they stopped before eventually traveling to McKenney's home in Washington, DC. McKenney gave Ben "directions to clothe them in the best manner, and to buy for each a plaid cloak, and a handsome cap." Ben then took William and Arbor "into a chamber of the hotel, and gave them a thorough cleansing." When Ben finally presented the two boys to his father, they were "dressed, not in a very handsome suit of clothes, only, but in smiles." According to McKenney, "A couple of prettier boys could be found nowhere."[9]

There is no indication in McKenney's record that his grooming of William and Arbor or his description of them as "pretty" had anything to do with sexual intent. However, it would be irresponsible not to name the possibility of sexual violation in the context of captive adoptions and settler schooling. There is a known history of sexual vulnerability and violation suffered by native students in such contexts. While the historical record may be silent on the questions of sexual violence in nineteenth-century settler schools and adoptions, we know from later oral histories that such violations were indeed part of the reality of indigenous youth in the homes of white families and in boarding schools.[10]

The rituals of haircutting and cleansing and dressing native students described by McKenney were deeply symbolic, even as they transformed the physical appearance of indigenous youth. The actions aimed to shed external markers of native identity. McKenney's description of William's and Arbor's transformations proves instructive when thinking about procedures of natal alienation. They were forced to travel far away from their homeland in a disorienting manner to decrease the chances of a solo return. The haircuts often violated internally held cultural meaning associated with hair and dignity. The clothing they were forced to wear engaged in a sartorial politics meant to assert gender norms aligned with Western ideology, while also erasing tribal identities expressed through dress. So, beyond physical separation from their natal communities, native students went through various processes of physical and symbolic transformation to alienate them from the social worlds they were to leave behind. While such rituals took place in the familial context of settler families who "adopted" native youth, as I will show later in this chapter, such practices were eventually incorporated as rituals for initiating native students into settler schooling. As institutional features of settler schooling, such rituals expanded most dramatically in the boarding schools of the late nineteenth century. Readers should also keep in mind that these latter institutions were indeed meant to be replacements for native families and tribes. They were often described as a scaled-up version of white settler families—where white teachers served as new parents while employing the same methods of natal alienation as those employed by the McKenney family.

From Georgia, McKenney traveled with Ben and his new "adopted" sons to their family home in DC. According to McKenney, "these little boys were made part of my family; and were adopted by the government."[11] As with James McDonald, the first student adopted by McKenney in 1816, the colonel's guardianship of Arbor and William in the late 1820s primarily centered on their education. McKenney explains, "Their education, and the supervision of their entire circumstance, devolved on me. I sent them to school, at that time kept in Georgetown, and upon the principle of the West Point Academy."[12]

CAPTIVE ADOPTIONS AS A KEY FEATURE OF SETTLER SCHOOLING

If federally sponsored native schooling was an expression of the Indian Wars, as the previous chapter indicates, then the hearts and minds of indigenous children were a key battleground for such warfare. Indeed, captive adoptions were a primary method of conquest. Time and again, the logic behind such methods were spelled out by Indian agents. For instance, in 1848 Indian Agent Thomas S. Williamson declared that when indigenous children are "separated from their people young, they are as docile and as susceptible of improvement as any other children."

Therefore, he recommended taking children as a first step in civilization—an old practice, repurposed in the context of his time. Such disruption of kinship ties was not merely a means of degrading native people and demonizing their ways of life, but also was motivated by distinct political-economic motivations. It was a means of dissolving links to tribal identity and thus disappearing indigenous ways of life, particularly their relations to land.

In a letter to the Commissioner of Indian Affairs, Williamson argued for the application of the logic undergirding captive adoptions to a boarding school for native students. He insisted that schooling would only be effective for students of the Dakota nation if more permanent distance could be created between students and their tribal communities. Williamson especially complained about the disruption caused by the tribe's "autumn hunt." To help resolve such issues, Williamson insisted that part of the treaty annuities paid to the tribe by the US government "cannot be better expended than in erecting and supporting a manual labor boarding school." Williamson stressed that he was not the first Indian agent at Kapiosa to make such a recommendation. He cited reports by his predecessor, Major L. Taliaferro, back to the 1830s, where Taliaferro made similar requests for a boarding school. To Williamson's knowledge, "The authorities in Washington have often expressed themselves in favor of such schools. I know of no reason why one has not long since been established for these Indians, except the opinion of your predecessor that it would be difficult to get the children from their relatives and retain them in the school."[13]

Williamson argued that when students regularly left school to freely engage in the cultural life of their tribal communities, the work of settler schooling was undermined, and even undone.[14] Therefore he advocated for removing Dakota students from their families and placing them in homes of white families, or in institutions where white settlers functioned as parental figures. According to Williamson, this would not only help them learn the English language, but it also offered the necessary context for important ideological lessons. Only in such controlled environments might native students "learn something of the economy, of civilized life." From 1848 to 1851, across several letters, Williamson argued that only through removing native children for extended periods of time could the pedagogy of settler schooling have the totalizing effect desired by white school reformers and the federal government.

Such logics undergirding captive adoptions of native students during the first half of the nineteenth century laid the ideological groundwork for the formalized structures of native boarding schools typically associated with the late nineteenth century in historical scholarship. By the late nineteenth century, the practices and ideas expressed by men like Thomas McKenney and Thomas S. Williamson would be scaled up and form key features of the more expansive schooling system imposed on native communities. Thus, despite historical scholarship's focus on the post-1870s context, when the number of boarding schools rapidly expanded, the story is indeed continuous—a history of protracted war waged on the hearts and minds of native youth, where indigenous kinship ties were directly targeted.

Writing forty years after Indian Agent Thomas Williamson, Indian Agent Fletcher Cowart repeated a similar rationale for boarding schools in 1885: "The hope for effective work lies with the children. The Government should turn its chief attention to them. School facilities should be enlarged, the children divorced effectually from camp life, and with a plain English education instructed well in farm and mechanical labor. In this way the next generation will see them fairly civilized and ready for citizenship." Cowart echoes Williamson's sentiments, but he also has an additional goal for native students: citizenship within the United States as opposed to native nations. This goal became much more pointed during the late-nineteenth-century boarding school era, though the boarding school as an instrument of domination employed within the schooling apparatus of the United States had long been debated and implemented.[15] Readers will recall that Brainerd Mission School, established in 1817, was the first federal boarding school for native students, and it was developed with funding from the US Department of War.

• • •

THE BOARDING SCHOOL'S PRESENCE IN NATIVE LIFE

While the roots of the Indian boarding school can be found in earlier iterations of settler schooling—in missions and day schools, in government contract schools, on and off reservations—the institution grew most expansively in the late nineteenth century, becoming an integral part of native students' coming-of-age experiences. A key historic event marking this shift in native education policy is General Richard Henry Pratt's founding of the Carlisle Indian Industrial School, which grew out of Pratt's educational experiment with native prisoners in Florida beginning in 1875. The latter experiment evolved into his partnership with General Samuel Armstrong to establish the Indian Program at Hampton Institute in 1878 before Pratt left Hampton to establish Carlisle in 1879. Across the trajectory of native education within the schooling apparatus of the United States, from its most nascent stages to its rapid development in the last decades of the nineteenth century, settler schooling was a disruption to the natal communities of indigenous students. It was a school system based on the methods of captive adoptions modeled by early white school reformers like Thomas McKenney. As historian David Wallace Adams lucidly explains, "[A]fter the first generation of students returned home, the boarding school became a less mysterious institution; veterans of the system could now prepare the next generation for the ordeals that lay ahead." He adds, "[P]aradoxically, by the turn of the century, boarding schools had become part of the Indian experience. To be an Indian in white America meant being carried off to a faraway place where the white man cut off your hair, put you in uniform, and told you that your ancestors were savages."[16]

Settler schooling became so widespread by the late-nineteenth-century boarding school era, such a dominant feature of native life, that we might read the institution as a forcefully imposed replacement for the ancestor. Indeed, boarding schools became a scaled-up version of the captive adoptions of years prior—a protracted war waged not only in the physical world, but also in the symbolic and spiritual realms. The aftermath of such warfare waged through settler schooling continued to abound among survivors and their progeny, leaving marks on individual students as well as the communities surrounding them. My point here extends from Ojibwe scholar Brenda Child, who writes, "Boarding school is now *the ancestor* in a direct *genealogical line* of terrible *offspring*—alcohol abuse, family and sexual violence, and other social dysfunction." Such schools were institutions crafted to facilitate a process of native disinheritance. For indeed, disinheritance was the primary objective, even more so than their intention to assimilate native youth into settler society. Settler schooling was built on a sociological model of reconfiguring, and at times unmaking, native kinship ties.

As a descendant of boarding school survivors herself, Child continued, these institutions "did, after all, align federal authority with the zealotry of religious missions, and suppress Indian cultures in an English-only way while *opening the door of alienation from land* and the extension of everyday Anglo-American culture into the lives and souls of Indian people."[17] Alienating native students from land, as Child emphasizes, was a key aim of settler schooling. Settler schooling set out to teach indigenous students to be in new relationship with land—to recognize land as property. Prior attachments to land among indigenous peoples were rooted in communal stewardship and not individual ownership; and kinship networks among native people also extended from the land. It was a living thing, and one that factored prominently in indigenous creation stories. To reduce such a force in the social life of native people to merely an inanimate object, as property to be owned, was a fundamental violation of indigenous ways of life. It alienated individual native students from their natal community and its ways of doing and being.

Contextualizing the conflict pertaining to native relations to land, another historian explains, "The land issue was linked to what reformers regarded as the biggest obstacle to Indian assimilation, the reservation system." White reformers came to deplore the reservation—which was a settler creation—because "it perpetuated Indians' attachment to the tribal outlook and tribal institutions. Most notable in this regard was the high value placed on community property holding and gift giving, traditions that reformers viewed as anathemas to the emergence of self-reliant individualism."[18] Thus settler schooling set out to inculcate native students in Western notions of the liberal individual subject and individual property ownership, which were fundamental to settler society. Importantly, forcing native people to break up communal lands into individual property also allowed for more opportunities for the buying and selling of land, therefore helping to break up tribal claims on land as a roadblock to settler expansion.

Child's invocation of ancestor, genealogy, and offspring to discuss the boarding school as a broader metaphor of settler colonialism in the Americas aligns with key features of natal alienation as a weapon of racial domination. This language points to key features of the captive adoptions experienced by native students in the homes of white settlers and the schools they built. Such alignment also emphasizes the utility of natal alienation (as opposed to assimilation) as a more generative term for characterizing settler schooling as a historical atrocity with expansive implications for native life.

INTENSIFICATION OF NATAL ALIENATION DURING THE BOARDING SCHOOL ERA

The white architects of native schooling continued to discuss ways of limiting parental involvement and alienating students from their natal communities through the nineteenth century. Such practices became far-reaching and more systematic as settler schooling grew more bureaucratically sophisticated and larger in scope in the last decades of the 1800s. The federal government increased spending on native education as more rigid reforms developed after the 1870s; all the while, native student enrollment in settler schools increased dramatically. These numbers tell an important story of how natal alienation through white-led settler schooling became more and more intrusive in the collective experiences of indigenous people in North America. While there were fifty-two Indian schools listed in federal reports in 1842, forty-five of which claimed an enrollment of 2,132 students, this number continued to increase over the years, especially after the 1870s. Between 1877 and 1900, annual federal funding for native education increased from $20,000 to $2,936,000, and student enrollment increased nearly 600-fold from 3,598 to 21,568.[19]

In the last three decades of the nineteenth century, federally backed native schooling became more targeted and refined in the context of a new era of US Indian policy. The goal of late-nineteenth-century policies toward native peoples increasingly turned to weakening the organization of tribal governments as sovereign entities and absorbing native peoples more fully into the American body politic as individual citizens, thus attempting to do away with tribal identities altogether. During this period, strategies of natal alienation, which had been used and refined in the earliest years, when the US system of native schooling was fledgling in form, became weaponized in more dramatic fashion.

It should come as no surprise that the Indian boarding school—and particularly the off-reservation school—emerged as the apex of US native education policy. This institution embodied what white reformers deemed the most totalizing strategy for alienating students from indigenous heritage—an institution based on the model of captive adoptions. Settlers identified the boarding school as the best method for killing old Indian ways that stood in the way of the nation-building project and, ultimately, white fantasies of a settler future. For these reasons the off-reservation boarding school became a defining feature of the period widely known as the Allotment and Assimilation Era, when Congress passed the 1887 Dawes Act, which provided allotments of land to individual native families. The Dawes Act was a direct assault on collective tribal identity, and a seemingly inconspicuous effort to further dispossess native people of their land.

Natal alienation defined the very institutional ethos of the Indian boarding school, as it was conceived of in its earliest iterations. White reformers refined the institution over the nineteenth century as they worked to create a more efficient and centralized program of native education as a necessary alternative to the costly American Indian Wars. And again, white school leaders and government actors often commented on the boarding school's promise as the ideal institution for usurping the influence of native parents and tribal communities. They insisted that early and sustained separation would allow for a more thorough alienation of students from traditional native ways of life, clearing a path for white teachers to mold native children in a manner commensurate with a settler future.[20]

BOARDING SCHOOL RITUALS OF NATAL ALIENATION

The disruption of native students' social ties to their heritage and natal communities manifested through settler schooling's infringements on parental rights of native people, and the physical distance white education reformers intentionally created between native youth and elders. However, natal alienation was also weaponized against native students in more symbolic ways. This was done through ritualized haircutting. The shedding of tribal wear and adornments. The formal religious instruction and verbal condemnation of indigenous ways of life. The renaming practices. All of these symbolic acts of violence became characteristic of native boarding schools of the late nineteenth century, and all can be traced back to earlier methods of settler schooling.

Readers may recall how missionaries changed Arbor's name to Lee Compere in memorial of a celebrated white missionary. Native students before and after Arbor would be subjected to this same ritual of natal alienation. Sometimes renaming practices were used to cultivate financial support from white benefactors. At Brainerd, for instance, native students were named after individuals and organizations that helped sponsor their education, to memorialize the care of white benefactors. One Osage girl was "adopted" by Father Hoyt at Brainerd Mission School in 1819. The nine-year-old child was renamed after the Mississippi plantation owner who purchased her from the Cherokee man holding her captive. The young girl's name was decided before she arrived at Brainerd. According to missionary reports, "It was understood . . . that, if obtained, she should be called

Lydia Carter, the name of the benefactor lady of Natchez who contributed so liberally for her redemption."[21]

Brainerd's missionaries formalized this renaming process as a way of linking individual students with individual sponsors. Renaming rituals also served as a fundraising strategy, since it allowed settlers to feel more intimately connected to native children whom their money helped civilize. Donors gave money and expected native students to be named after them, just as contemporary donors give money to educational institutions in expectation that buildings or scholarships be named in their memory. Brainerd's leaders made it a point to swiftly assign names to students shortly after they arrived, because they did not want "to keep . . . benefactors in suspense any longer." The school's leaders "learn[ed] that money has been sometime since contributed for the support of children to bear these names." In September 1823, the missionaries listed dozens of white benefactors' names given to native students. They ranged from John Emmerson and Thomas Witherspoon to Elizabeth Kean and Louisa Battelle. One of the most extreme cases of this paternalistic ritual, however, was the case of one student named "Boston Recorder," a name given in recognition of a Northern newspaper that made a financial contribution to Brainerd. The missionaries proudly announced this student's story, explaining, "Boston Recorder is now able to read the paper, if his benefactor please to send it to him."[22] Such renaming rituals alienated indigenous children from their natal communities, and the names chosen often memorialized white settlers whose legacies centered on dispossessing indigenous peoples. In this way, native children were transformed into walking billboards.

Renaming was one of many rituals used to initiate native students into settler schooling. White school reformers also celebrated stories that highlighted the outward transformation of students, insisting that alterations to these youth's physical appearance symbolized an inward transformation achieved or in process. Such examples were continuous throughout the nineteenth century.

These narratives often focused on the sartorial, describing how settler educators covered native students in new clothing as one of the rituals performed to shed their Indianness, as a means of putting distance between these students and their natal communities. As is always the case, such clothes were "scriptive things."[23] In the context of settler schooling for native students, clothing carried very specific ideas about race, about whiteness and Indianness, about civilization and savagery, about Western notions of gender. They also came with a script about how native students were expected to behave, as well as who they were striving to become once they wore such clothing, once they had been thoroughly converted, or alienated from whence they came.

An illustrative example of this appears in an 1818 account by General Calvin Jones, who documents the educational activities among native students at Brainerd Mission School. Jones provides a detailed account of one student whose inner and outer changes demonstrated her successful alienation from her traditional Cherokee roots. According to Jones, this success was most immediately represented by her sartorial (and linguistic) transformation. He was "no longer skeptical" of the settler school's effectiveness, having "witnessed the success of the attempts which [were being made] to instruct and humanize" the Cherokee nation. Jones declared, "I renounce my Darwinian error. I firmly believe, if the efforts now making are duly seconded, the little that remains of a brave and unfortunate nation will be rescued from barbarism, suffering, and utter annihilation." There were forty-nine students at the school, he reported. Of this number, the majority were between the ages of eight and twelve. However, Jones was most inspired by the oldest student of the group, a Cherokee girl named Catherine Brown. Catherine represented, in his mind, the kind of native person younger students might aspire to become. Writing of the girl he believed to be a model student, General Jones explained, "This last was a young woman of such merit, she read well, conversed sensibly, was grave, dignified and graceful in her matters, handsome in person, and would be an ornament to almost any society. I was told at their female society meetings when asked to pray, she always unhesitantly did so, and in a manner peculiarly fervid and eloquent. Her name is Katherine Brown. *Not four years ago she wore the dress, spoke the language and had the manners of her nation.*"[24]

General Jones's before-and-after sketch of Catherine Brown was echoed by Jeremiah Evarts, treasurer of the American Board of Commissioners for Foreign Missions. "Her parents are half-breeds, who have never learned to speak English," Evarts explained of the girl's background. Of her manners upon arrival at the school, he offers, "She was vain, and excessively fond of dress, wearing a profusion of ornaments in her ears." However, after a thorough immersion in the school, Catherine would overcome her faults and the limitations of her genealogy, he emphasized, for "[s]he can now read well in the Bible, is fond of reading other books, and has been particularly pleased with the Memoirs of Mrs. Newell. . . . Since she became religious, *her trinkets have gradually disappeared*, till only a single drop remains in each ear. On hearing that pious females have, in many instances, devoted their ornaments to the missionary cause, she had determined to devote hers also. In coming to this determination, she acted without the influence from the advice of others."[25]

In four years, Catherine successfully shed her Indianness—or she had at least dialed it back from "a profusion of ornaments in her ears" to "a single drop remain[ing] in each ear." This reduction in traditional Cherokee adornments in the narrative are meant to capture a change in physical appearance that also reflected an inner transformation. The heritage of Catherine's natal community was replaced by the customs of civilization defined by Brainerd's teachers, from whom students received "literary, religious and moral instruction" as well as lessons in "practical farming and . . . habits of industry, and art and virtue unknown among savages." The removal of Catherine's traditional clothes and ornaments, for General Jones and those concerned with settler schooling before and after his time, represented a transformation whereby the Indian was killed, but the life of the young woman spared. Through a thorough process of natal alienation facilitated by settler schooling, white government officials believed indigenous youth might be made into noble native students.

In another example from June 1826, mission school leader Abel Bingham celebrated his students' new affinity for settler clothing as evidence of their progress in civilization. When describing his work with thirty native students at the "Indian School at Tonawanda," Bingham proudly boasted that "Considerable improvement has been made in their mode of dress. I judge that twenty or more of them wear pantaloons and vests, and some of them are now able to cut out clothes." Yet despite his success, Bingham decried being run off his mission post by none other than the famous Seneca chief and celebrated orator Segoyewatha. Ironically, Segoyewatha was most popularly known as "Red Jacket," because of the distinguishable coat he wore, having received it as a gift from the British Crown for valiantly fighting against the United States during the American Revolution. According to Bingham, the Seneca leader was unrelenting in his demands that all missionary work cease among his tribe. Red Jacket is reported to have gone to great lengths to throw obstacles in the way "to prevent the instruction of the people." Bingham reports being personally threatened by the chief "that the young warriors shall be let loose upon [him]" and "that our buildings shall be burned."[26] As evident in Red Coat's resistance to the mission school, the wearing of settler clothes—whether they be given by the British or American settlers—was no proof of the inner transformations many white school reformers hoped for.

Early-nineteenth-century accounts of sartorial transformations anticipated strategies employed in the late-nineteenth-century boarding schools. Speaking to the power and effectiveness of boarding schools, in 1885, John Oberly, the US superintendent of Indian schools, turned to sartorial language to metaphorically describe native students' transformation as they prepared for a settler future through settler schooling. His sartorial metaphors were meant to emphasize the effectiveness of the boarding schools model. Oberly declared,

> *These schools strip from the unwashed person of the Indian boy the unwashed blanket, and, after instructing him in what to him are the mysteries of personal cleanliness, clothe him with the clean garments of civilized men and teach him how to wear them. They give him information concerning a bed and teach him how to use it; teach him how to sit on a chair, how to use a knife and fork. . . . While he is learning these things he is also learning to read and*

> *write, and, at the same time, is being taught how to work, how to "earn a living."*[27]

Government officials continuously looked to settler schooling as the most effective means of dealing with the Indian problem over the nineteenth century, and the architects of such schools continued to identify success by pointing to markers that suggested natal alienation was taking place—that the sociocultural, epistemological, and physical distance they imposed between native students and those to whom they were connected by birth resulted in a more totalizing and lasting assimilation. Clothing continued to be seen as an outward manifestation of such inward transformations desired by white school reformers. In Oberly's report, the contrast between "the blanket" and "the clean garments of civilized men" was to make this distinction between native savagery and settler civilization, between filth and cleanliness. The rigid contrast drawn by Oberly is deeply ironic given the troubled history of the intentional spreading of deadly smallpox among native people through the distribution of infected blankets by European colonists.

The story of Emory, a young Hopi boy, helps complicate Oberly's framing of native forms of adornment—the blanket, in particular. Emory was stripped of a colorful blanket made by his grandfather, after being kidnapped in the middle of the night without the consent of his parents in the late 1880s. Emory's story reflects how such captive adoptions became systematic by the late nineteenth century, while also underscoring how the removal of indigenous forms of adornment carried physical and symbolic implications. Emory was forced to wear military-style uniforms once he arrived at boarding school. This story of Emory's disrobing was recorded in his wife's memoir. She recalled, "When Emory was five years old he was sleeping with his little brothers on the second floor terrace of his home in Old Oraibi. One September morning, early, without his mother's knowledge, the school police took little Emory, still asleep, wrapped in a brand new blanket that his grandfather had made for him." She declared, "This was Emory's initiation into the white man's way of education."[28]

Emory never recovered the blanket made by his grandfather, yet he later lamented, "My beautiful new blanket with colored stripes was gone . . . [but] I saw it later, in the possession of the wife of the superintendent."[29] This latter detail is important, because surely the blankets of native youth were not as filthy as white school administrators described, if these same garments could be turned into suitable clothing accessories for white women of status. Emory's emphasis of this detail is a reminder that theft had always been an integral part of natal alienation. Theft of children. Theft of their cultural inheritance. Theft of their heritage claims and relations to land. Theft of intimate objects that carried symbolic value about who they were in the world and in relation to others, whether it be Emory's blanket from his grandfather or Catherine's traditional adornments used to decorate herself as an expression of her Cherokee identity.

White school officials often justified cutting the hair of native students as a matter of hygiene; however, their commentary often exposed deeper nefarious intentions as well. In the words of one superintendent, "the long hair was a symbol of savagery."[30] Such rituals were a site of contestation between settler views of native students as people with no culture and ways of knowing and indigenous people's deep-held beliefs associated with hair as well as their tribe's beliefs and value systems.

Yankton Sioux writer, educator, and political activist Zitkala-Ša (originally named Gertrude Simmons) explicitly detailed her experiences of natal alienation in settler schooling, and particularly the violent haircutting ritual she experienced. The cutting of her hair was the first major violation she experienced after arriving at White's Manual Labor Institute, a Quaker boarding school in Wabash, Indiana, in 1884, at the age of eight years old.[31] Shortly after arriving at White's, Zitkala-Ša's friend who only "knew a few words of English" gave her "a terrible warning." Her friend "overheard the paleface women talk about cutting our long, heavy hair." Zitkala-Ša was immediately disturbed at the thought of her hair being sheared off. It went against Sioux customs, according to her mother's teachings. Zitkala-Ša explained, "Our mothers, had taught us that only unskilled warriors who were captured had their hair shingled by the enemy." Thinking from the Sioux standpoint, Zitkala-Ša grew perplexed as to why teachers would debase students in such a way. Further explaining the symbolic meaning of cutting hair among the Sioux, Zitkala-Ša declared, "Among our people, short hair was worn by mourners, and shingled hair by cowards!" She insisted that neither category applied to her. For these reasons, Zitkala-Ša told her friend, "No, I will not submit! I will struggle first!" As the time for her haircut approached, Zitkala-Ša hid in a dark room, hoping the threat would pass. The teachers eventually found her and immediately subjected her to the demoralizing haircutting ritual—a violating ritual of settler schooling undergone by thousands of native students before and after her. Zitkala-Ša explained, "I remember being dragged out, though I resisted by kicking and scratching wildly." Despite her best attempt, she "was carried downstairs and tied fast to a chair." Zitkala-Ša was forever scarred by this moment. She recalled: "I cried aloud, shaking my head all the while until I felt the cold blades of the scissors against my neck, and heard them gnaw off one of my thick braids."[32]

Just as shedding indigenous attire was part of a politically motivated process of alienating native students from their tribal identities, so too was the process of cutting their hair, which carried distinct meanings among various indigenous nations. When writing to Sukulai homar (meaning "Young Plant"), a former Mojave student at the Fort Mojave Boarding School, Superintendent S. M. McCowan described the dramatic scene of the student receiving a haircut for the first time.

Referring to Sukulai homar as Pete Lambert in the letter, the name given to him during his boarding school days, McCowan offered the following account:

> *I can remember when I first took you into the Ft. Mohave school and what a time I had in cutting your hair for the first time. I can see now all the old Mohave women standing around crying, while you covered your long hair with your arms and told me that I wouldn't dare to cut that hair off, but the hair was cut in spite of all your efforts and the direful predictions of the Mohave women. I compelled you to have your hair cut off, not because of any objections to the long hair in itself, but merely because the long hair was a symbol of savagery.*[33]

Cutting hair was about killing a symbol. Through the settler gaze, this symbol represented indigenous ways of life and, indeed, the indigenous ancestor. Cutting native students' hair was a settler ritual of eliminating the native. It was a refusal to recognize "the direful predictions" of the elder Mojave women about what would happen to the young man in the line of succession to be their future leader, and their clan, if he was debased in such a way. However, for Superintendent McCowan such loss of connection to ancestors, wisdom, and other internal characteristics of bravery valued by the Mojave were the very things from which he hoped to distance Sukulai homar.

Cutting hair from the head of an individual child is one thing. The work of cutting off a symbol is another matter entirely. The latter invites a level of violence far beyond what meets the eye, far beyond the literal hair on the head of any student, whether it be Sukulai homar or Zitkala-Ša. Indeed, the cutting of Sukulai homar's hair was not only a violation against him as an individual. As someone who would one day officially be the hereditary and elected great chieftain of the Mojave people, "the Aha macave pipatahon," this ritual was a broader assault on Mojave heritage. In fact, such rituals of natal alienation, which were so foundational to settler schooling, expressed a deep commitment to the idea that native students descended from a people absent heritage. Students like Sukulai homar and the elders attempting to prevent the superintendent from cutting his hair, were understood to be immersed in a social world defined by savagery, a social life deemed unworthy of recognition by settler school leaders.

Through such processes of natal alienation in settler schooling, we witness an attempt by white school officials to make native students a kind of "genealogical isolate," to borrow from historical sociologist Orlando Patterson. "Formally isolated in his social relations with those who lived," Sukulai homar was also "culturally isolated from the social heritage of his ancestors."[34] Such violations were about erasing and flattening that which came before in order to open a path for constructing some new desired version of the (now) disinherited.

The occasion for McCowan's letter was to congratulate "Pete" on his "elevation to the honorable position of chief of the Mohave tribe of

Indians." He explained to Sukulai homar, "I am glad because of your promotion and hope that you will be the means of leading the younger Mohaves out right into the bright light of our best civilization." He hoped the former student would do his part and "always stand for the schools and education and enlightenment." McCowan urged the newly elevated chief to "see that your people send their children to the Mojave school first, and then after five or six years insist upon these children going to some larger and more advanced school." He urged Sukulai homar to be unapologetic in making decisions that violated the old Mojave ways, even if met by resistance among his people. McCowan declared, "I hope you will be just as firm and emphatic in your commands, when you know you are in the right, as I was in insisting upon the cutting of your hair." The chief must insist that as many Mojave children as possible be subjected to the same rituals he experienced in settler schooling. McCowan urged Sukulai homar to be a fierce champion of the Mojave Boarding School. He instructed, "When Supt. McKoin asks you to bring him 150 children or any number of children, don't rest either night or day until the Superintendent's request is obeyed."[35]

Such rituals or natal alienation required repetition, because the work of building the nation's settler future was ongoing. Native identities and tribal claims to land continued to pose threats to such fantasies.

PHOTOGRAPHIC NARRATIVES OF NATAL ALIENATION IN INDIAN BOARDING SCHOOLS

The boarding school grew to have an ancestral presence in native life because the institution became so intertwined with the stories told and retold about native peoples' survival of settler-colonial violence, but also because of the visual narratives constructed around these institutions and the impact such visual narratives have had in shaping public memory. The visual archive of boarding schools was intentionally constructed by settler school officials. White reformers used images to tell photographic narratives of natal alienation. Such visual narratives of progress were integral to their campaign for more boarding schools.

McKenney's tale of Arbor's and Williams's transformations in the 1820s, and his previous advertisements of James McDonald's educational achievements, anticipated white school reformers of the late nineteenth century who intentionally used before-and-after photos of indigenous students to promote the success of native boarding schools. This late-nineteenth-century strategy of circulating narratives of native student transformation was a carryover from earlier strategies employed by white settlers. To emphasize this throughline, one historian refers to such narratives of transformation as an "essential ingredient" for civilization campaigns during the colonial era. "The planning stage [for schooling efforts] demanded the involvement of at least one Indian. When this individual displayed some degree of competence in the basic tenets of Christianization and civilization, the success of the project was almost assured. The Indian's skills provided the exemplary model, which was then advertised by the missionary/schoolmaster for the express purpose of attaining financial support."[36]

While Colonial Era and early-nineteenth-century narratives of native transformation appeared primarily in written form, or by the physical presence of indigenous students at settler gatherings—as walking billboards, like James McDonald—photography eventually became the most effective medium for such campaigns in the late nineteenth century. These photos indexed a much longer history of killing native people and disappearing indigenous ways of life, and this long memory among settlers shaped how they interacted with and read such images of native students. This is to say, white settlers brought long-established racial story lines and cultural myths with them—distinct points of reference—which shaped their interpretation of the photographs.

Such photos were also a ritual, along with the haircutting, the shedding of traditional clothing, and the changing of names. Native students were forced to sit as props in settler-colonial fantasies as white school officials rehearsed those fantasies on the native student body. The performance of such images—in their circulation—helped build momentum for the boarding school movement. The use of such photographs at the Carlisle Indian Industrial School, the most notorious boarding school from the nineteenth century, founded by General Richard Henry Pratt, helps to illustrate this point.

General Pratt began his education program with native students at Fort Marion in Florida with native men from several tribes held as prisoners by the United States. Pratt transferred his work to Hampton Normal and Industrial Institute in May 1878, a school originally founded in 1868 to educate African Americans after the Civil War, where he collaborated with Hampton's founder, General Samuel Armstrong, to establish an "Indian Program." Within the first few months of this effort, Pratt and Armstrong developed "an ingenious public relations scheme" to secure funding for their educational efforts with native students. They used "photographs to illustrate the conditions of the Indians both 'before' and 'after' their institutionalization." Writing to Pratt, as he traveled to recruit more native students to bring back to Hampton, Armstrong encouraged him to "be sure and have them bring their wild barbarous things." The goal was to include these artifacts in the before photographs. Armstrong explained, "[t]his will show whence we started."[37]

Behind the camera's aperture was the gaze of white settlers. The settler gaze was anthropological in the most imperial way, as a cultural politics of race played out through these photographs, reflecting evolving ideas about race and culture in the emerging fields of American social sciences. Native people featured in "before" photos were believed to represent "a stage of culture on the road to civilization," but not yet there. Such embedded claims about native people's cultural inferiority—which gradually replaced older claims of native people's biological inferiority—were used to justify interventions enacted upon native people by a more civilized race. Such racialized logic informing these educational reform strategies came from leading white social scientists of the period, whose academic scholarship formed a "scholarly" basis for such settler-colonial procedures, including native boarding schools, along with other racial projects in American education.[38]

The "before" photo portrayed a native student in traditional indigenous attire, with "their wild barbarous things" and with long hair. These photos are noticeably darker than their companion photographs. Sometimes photos depicted a group of native students, staged in a manner that reflected their presumed natural state, though many bore traces of impoverished conditions brought about by various wartime hardships, accumulated experiences of removal, as well as the starvation resulting from forced dependency on the US government after accumulated dispossession, materially and culturally. Such critical context, to be clear, was studiously absent in the captions and narratives accompanying photos of native students. An honest analysis of the material realities of settler-colonial violence stood at odds with stories white Americans clung to as interpretive frames for such images. Instead, white reformers relied on the settler imagination to inform reception of such photographs. The settler imagination had long been formed and molded through stereotypical narratives circulated by white schoolbooks, newspapers, folk songs, and political discourse.

The "after" photo portrayed the image of a native youth, or a group of students, on the other side of their great transformation. These photos are noticeably lighter. They project the illusion that students' skin complexions grow rapidly closer to whiteness, as though students had been cleansed of the darkening filth of savagery. New haircuts and formal Western dress, often military-like uniforms, symbolized the newly constructed native students, or at least the aspiration of what settler schooling aimed to accomplish. These photos served to visually represent native youth's alienation from their natal communities—images denoting how remnants of the Indian past could be washed—or violently scrubbed—away. Sometimes the before-and-after photos may have even displayed the new names given to the children. These photos visually represented natal alienation, helping to expand the campaign for boarding schools, and the broader racial project of native education within the schooling apparatus of the United States. In the minds of settler school officials, these photos documented and reminded them of their mission to make "noble" native students of "savage" Indians.

The eyes of the students imply a different story, however. When

Tom Torlino—Navajo, "As he entered the school in 1882" and "As he appeared three years later." Courtesy of the Carlisle Indian School Digital Resource Center.

Rose White Thunder, Sioux student, before and after at Carlisle (1885). Courtesy of the Carlisle Indian School Digital Resource Center.

Wounded Yellow Robe, Henry Standing Bear, and Chauncy Yellow Robe in 1880s, Sioux students, before and after. Courtesy of the Carlisle Indian School Digital Resource Center.

looking—and listening—to such images, carefully, one might also see—and hear—a perspective from the standpoint opposite the camera lens, where native students actively confront the settler-colonial gaze. While the boarding schools formed an ancestral presence in native life, as it became employed by the United States to disrupt kinship systems among indigenous nations, there was also a persistent tradition of native student resistance to boarding schools that also formed as part and parcel of this heritage. This too sits just beneath the surface of such staged photographs of natal alienation.

This perspective is audible through the words and actions of native students in the historical record. Arbor's attempt to run away in 1827 while insisting—in Uchee—that he wanted to go home is but one example. Arbor's refusal anticipates that of Zitkala-Ša nearly sixty years later, when she "resisted by kicking and scratching wildly" as settler teachers pinned her down to perform the haircutting ritual repeatedly employed in the process of unmaking indigenous relations, as a means of severing ties to native communities—as a means of killing what settlers deemed to be a symbol of the Indian.

Such cracks in the settler-colonial narrative, where the agency of students like Arbor and Zitkala-Ša come through, provide an alternative historical standpoint for interpreting captive adoptions of native students and broader efforts by settlers to alienate students from their natal communities.[39] The accumulation of such stories provides new resources for interpreting the Civilization Fund Act of 1819, which McKenney successfully lobbied for, and they provide powerful counter-narratives that juxtapose the before-and-after photographs of native students during the boarding school era, as well as the anti-indigenous narratives attached to them. Such perspectives we might access, even in the colonial archive, even in photos produced through the frame of white settler fantasies.

It is difficult to look at these photographs and not see longing and confusion and, often, heartbreak. Hard to listen to these images and not hear witness of the violence, suffering, and ongoing resistance of indigenous youth, as documented by their testimonies and their practices of refusal recorded in settler reports over the centuries.[40]

While the boarding school carries a haunting ancestral presence in native education, there is also an opposing force that must also be accounted for. Native student resistance constitutes a steady stream in this story. Stories of the rebel native student emerged as a kind of folk hero in native education, when read from the perspective of native communities. Zitkala-Ša's writing of her own resistance in her autobiographical essays published in 1900 is but one example of this. With the publication of "The Impressions of an Indian Childhood," "The School Days of an Indian Girl," and "An Indian Teacher among Indians" in *Atlantic Quarterly* in February and March 1900, Zitkala-Ša distinguished herself as the first indigenous writer to educate the American public about the violent realities of settler schooling imposed on native youth. Zitkala-Ša not only offered a critique of settler schooling, but she also asserted a countervailing narrative of native resistance, one where native peoples' political and intellectual agency are always present. Her story is one of many, helping to construct an archetype of a heroic historical figure, one narratively constructed across a multitude of stories about native student resistance.

In contradistinction to the boarding school, I argue that the heroic figure of the rebel native student is also an ancestor in native educational life. This presence in native education is a key political force in the early history of race and power in the schooling apparatus of the United States. The next and final chapter of Part II explores this history of native student resistance. For indeed, it is a distinct and distinguishable heritage. Within this lineage, students such as Arbor and Zitkala-Ša represent a discernible tradition, where native learners developed strategies to resist settler schooling and its pedagogy of natal alienation.

8

NATIVE STUDENT RESISTANCE AND THE ROOTS OF NATIVE AMERICAN LITERATURE

> I had a secret interview with one of our best medicine men, and when I left his wigwam I carried securely in my sleeve a tiny bunch of magic roots. . . . So absolutely did I believe in its charms that I wore it through all the school routines for more than a year.
>
> —Zitkala-Ša, "The School Days of an Indian Girl" (1900)

From the very beginning, native students and families resisted the violence of settler schooling. As Zitkala-Ša explained in her autobiographical essay "The School Days of an Indian Girl," many "resisted by kicking and scratching wildly." Native students employed a range of strategies to resist. However, running away from settler schooling was the most widely cited of their most direct actions of refusal. Readers will recall how Arbor, the nine-year-old Uchee student, attempted to escape Colonel Thomas McKenney's captive adoption in 1827, after being taken from the Creek Agency in Alabama. Arbor was one of many. Indeed, accounts of native students running away are found throughout the nineteenth century. Even at Brainerd Mission, the first government funded boarding school, established in 1817, one finds early reports in the settler-colonial archive of native students running away and disrupting the protocols of settler schooling.

On July 5, 1822, teachers at Brainerd Mission complained that three boys had been absent from school that day. According to reports, the boys were seen playing a few miles away from the school, presumably with other youth not enrolled at the school. Brainerd's teachers wanted to limit interactions between Brainerd's students and other native youth and Brainerd's policy was very clear: Off-site activities with other native children were forbidden.[1]

Some native students knowingly disobeyed these rules and regulations, and such rebellious activities frustrated the school's teachers. In this instance, an older student at Brainerd named Tilman Rose snuck away to attend an off-site event with other classmates. The teachers denied Tilman's initial request but he went anyway. Brainerd's teachers deemed Tilman's offense more egregious than those of his peers who went with him, because he consciously broke the rules. For this blatant act of defiance, the missionaries expelled him. They reasoned that the risk of him continuing to influence other students to break rules was a bigger threat than giving up on the work they'd done to "civilize" him. This was particularly frustrating to Brainerd's teachers because Tilman was a veteran at the school. He had been enrolled there for multiple years and was well accustomed to the school's norms. The fact that he was the ringleader of the runaways reflected poorly on the school, potentially calling Brainerd's effectiveness into question. The teachers wanted to make an example out of Tilman, and they described explaining their actions to the entire student body, insisting, "We endeavored to make all the scholars understand the reason of our proceeding."[2] But the students learned lessons from Tilman's actions, just as much as they did from the words spoken by the missionaries.

Tilman's influence over his peers who were newcomers to Brainerd invites one to speculate about the kinds of lessons and information native students shared with one another beyond the surveillance of settler teachers. Just as older boarding school students mentored native youth coming behind them about what to expect at these institutions and how to navigate such hostile social environments, students also shared knowledge that reinforced pride in native identity. They exchanged information to help other native students develop their own analysis of settler schooling and the realities of colonial violence. At times students also encouraged direct forms of resistance.

Individual acts of native student resistance should be seen as part of a continuous and collective endeavor. It reflects a countervailing educational tradition developed in response to the schooling apparatus of the United States. This persistence can even be traced at Brainerd, because though missionaries expelled Tilman Rose, they failed to solve their problem of native students running away.

The following year, in April 1823, two small boys had run away and made it back to their homes. In this instance, Brainerd's teachers believed that both the students and their parents were at fault. Because of this, they deemed it necessary to compel parents to send students back to Brainerd, threatening them with a fine if they failed to do so. The teachers hoped to avoid setting a precedent that might undermine the school's authority. In this instance, the missionaries coerced parents to return students, or else they would be forced to pay whatever amount the school calculated as expenses related to their children's education. Knowing that such fines would be difficult for many parents to pay, Brainerd placed parents in a challenging situation; this strategy was similar to those applied by Indian agents years later who threatened to withhold treaty annuities or food rations as a means of forcing parents to enroll their children in school. I refer to such actions of school officials as coercive because they knowingly exploited the precarity of native families to achieve their aims of settler schooling. Four days after the students ran away, and after the teachers threatened to impose a fine, the father of the two students brought them back to the Brainerd Mission.[3]

Native resistance took many forms.[4] It ran the gamut, from outright refusal and running away to various ways of co-optation, where native students and communities appropriated elements of settler schooling to resist further settler encroachment or to mitigate the impact of accumulated devastation within native communities. Tracking resistance in native student histories requires careful reading. At times it appears in unexpected forms, such as native learners performing scripts of civilization prepared by white settlers as strategies for survival, at times doing so alongside assertions of native sovereignty and refusing ideas of white racial supremacy. When looking to native student voices in the historical record, particularly from the boarding school era of the late nineteenth century, we also find everyday forms of resistance. For even when students did not run away, native students recounted secret student meetings and organized plots to disrupt school operations to gain unplanned holidays and time off. Students also preserved and passed on traditional stories among their peers. They reveled in the triumphs of heroic native leaders, some of whom they bore relations to. Students held initiations for secret social groups they formed among themselves, engaged in forbidden romantic relationships, and took pleasure in speaking freely in their native tongues when they reached a safe distance from the surveilling ears of settlers. In short, native students not only taught one another how to survive settler schooling, but passed down strategies to resist settler schooling while insisting on meaningful relations to their tribe and, eventually, to their race constituted by a set of intensifying pan-Indian political commitments. For indeed, the roots of what would later be called "Red Power" can be found in such early forms of resistance.

APPROPRIATING SETTLER SCHOOLING TO RESIST SETTLER VIOLENCE

English language and literacy are the most immediate markers of settler schooling, as native students were generally forbidden to speak their native tongues. While English was weaponized as an instrument of racial domination, it was also appropriated by survivors of settler schooling as "a generative tool for expressing diverse ways of seeing, saying, and believing."[5] It is important that we acknowledge the violent racio-linguistic history indexed by the prevalence of English among native peoples while also seriously considering "what students did with the language after they learned it."[6]

Native students across generations used English language and literacy to represent themselves, but also to bear witness to the actions of white settlers from indigenous perspectives. Native students used English and literacy as a means of writing (and speaking) back to the white supremacist narratives shaping the modern world, especially as it pertained to characterizations of native people. Writing of the nineteenth century, one historian explains, "Among the first generation of native young people educated at boarding schools were hundreds of graduates who used their facility with English, their 'civilized' appearance, and their understanding of American institutions to enter political life." Many of these native students went on to use the knowledge acquired through settler schooling in service of their communities, often to advocate against the violence of settler colonialism as it manifested through ongoing native removal, land dispossession, and inhumane schooling practices. More specifically, they "participated in tribal and village councils, circulated petitions attacking the policies of the Office of Indian Affairs, and employed the American legal system to pursue community objectives."[7]

Choctaw James McDonald is a prime example of this legacy. Readers will recall that McDonald appeared as the poster child for the Civilization Fund Act of 1819 and as the adopted son of Colonel Thomas McKenney. McDonald, who became an attorney, represents an important legacy of indigenous leaders who worked to resist continued dispossession of native people by making direct claims, in pragmatic fashion, on the settler state. This too must be understood as an important form of native resistance that ran parallel to other direct forms of resistance on the battlefield. As historian Frederick Hoxie sharply explains, "While not denigrating nineteenth-century warriors like Tecumseh or Chief Joseph," it is important to note that "since 1492 Native people spent far more time negotiating, lobbying, and debating than they spent tomahawking settlers or shooting soldiers." Indeed, we must also locate the important strategies of native resistance and survival found in "the stories of men and women who adapted ancient traditions to new circumstances or married new phenomena like Christianity and Western technology to the needs of their people."[8]

James McDonald was one of those native people who saw opportunities in Western education to advance the interests of the Choctaw nation, and native people more broadly. For instance, McDonald leveraged his personal connections and education to renegotiate the Treaty of Doak's Strand, in which the Choctaw nation ceded about half of its original homeland. During the process, McDonald and a delegation of Choctaw leaders went to Washington, DC, and renegotiated a payment of $216,00 in January 1825, which was a significant increase from the US government's original offer of $45,000.[9]

McDonald pioneered and experimented with new legal arguments building on insights gained through his engagement with the schooling apparatus of the United States. Thus, despite settler schooling working to strip him of his native identity, he acquired strategies for contesting the American government using its own tools along the way. As his biographer explains, McDonald was "the first Native activist to make the case for Indian 'rights' directly to American political leaders and to negotiate for a recognition of those rights in a formal agreement." He also made several important contributions to American political thought. McDonald "pointed out the contradiction between the Americans' public allegiance to the ideals of democracy and constitutionalism and their participation in extralegal assaults on the dignity and humanity of the continent's first people." He also developed a distinct approach to advocating for native rights through the law: "rather than defend the Choctaws as diplomatic actors on the international stage," McDonald "made the case for a tribal presence, and tribal rights, within the boundaries and institutions of the United States."[10] This emerging political strategy is most immediately apparent in an open letter to US Congress from the Choctaw treaty delegation that was ghostwritten by McDonald in February 1825.[11] This political document represents an early text in the native American literary tradition, and the legacy of settler schooling is apparent in both the form and content of the letter itself.

Schooling was warfare, and schooling was natal alienation. Schooling was also, at times, understood as strategically necessary for native people's survival. The open letter from the Choctaw delegation to the

US Congress reflects this legacy of resistance in native American literary history and nineteenth-century political protest. For this reason, I have included an abbreviated version of the letter below:

APPLICATION OF THE CHOCTAW TRIBE FOR AID FROM THE UNITED STATES IN IMPROVING THEIR CONDITION.

To the Congress of the United States:
WASHINGTON, February 18, 1825.

As the representatives of the Choctaw nation and (in part) of the aborigines of this country, we feel ourselves impelled alike by duty to address you at this present crisis. . . . You are an assembly which we have been taught to consider the most august in the world, and into whose hands are committed the destinies of our people. To whom, then, could we more properly address ourselves on the great point connected with our happiness and prosperity?

We have long been sensible of our weakness, and we know that, should Government of the United States rise in hostility against us, we must inevitably be exterminated or driven to the west. . . . We have been tempted to ask, Why should this be so? Has the Great Spirit frowned upon his red children, that they should thus have withered in your presence? Yet we have been told from the good book that he loves all his children alike, and that his greatest attribute is that of infinite mercy. This we are most willing to believe . . . that the time must come when his interposing hand will be outstretched in our behalf, and we be made to become like white men.

. . . .

We have but small tracts of territory remaining, and our numbers are comparatively few. The majority of those east of the Mississippi are turning their attention to agriculture, are settling themselves, and would in time become useful citizens. We admit, at the same time, that a large number still continue

> a wandering life, are wretched and degraded. These it would give us pleasure to see settled west of the Mississippi. It would be better for them, and better for those who remained. But you cannot persuade all to remove. . . . The important question then presents itself, What will you do with those that remain? . . . It is this great point to which our address is intended principally to direct your attention.
>
> As connected with the subject and with the question just proposed, we are constrained to say that in several of the southern States we are denied privileges to which, as members of the human family, we are of right entitled. However qualified by education we may be, we are neither permitted to hold offices, nor to give our testimony in courts of justice, although our dearest rights may be at stake. Can this be a correct policy? Is it just? Is it humane? When schools are multiplying among us; when we have made liberal appropriations of money for education of our children; when we are forsaking the chase, and turning our attention to agriculture, and are becoming an orderly and social people; does it comport with an enlightened and liberal policy to continue the imposition of those degrading restrictions upon us? Should not inducements be held forth to our young men to qualify themselves to become useful citizens of your republic? Should not the portals of honorable distinction be thrown open to them as well as to their white brothers? . . .

The Choctaw delegation's letter written by McDonald is an important document in native American literary and political history and underscores a fundamental relationship between this literary tradition and the history of settler schooling. The letter also reflects how some indigenous nations worked to model and perform civilization to resist ongoing aggression by the US settler state. Settler schooling is directly referenced and is also implied by its form. By form I am referring to McDonald's skilled use of the English language, particularly the rhetorical strategies common to political writing of the period, as well as his strategic use of settler narratives about native people. The relationship with settler schooling is also apparent through McDonald's direct references to the Choctaw nation's engagement with formal education—a point he references as a basis for critiquing settlers' unjust treatment of the Choctaw—and especially his assertion of the Choctaw nation's larger desire for more education. The position taken in the letter is one of endorsing settler schooling as a means of bolstering the delegation's requests for protection against threats of being removed from their homeland.

The strategies of literary and political resistance employed by McDonald often trafficked in the civilizationist rhetoric of white settlers. As the letter demonstrates, McDonald's appeals were often couched in anti-indigenous tropes, where he characterized some natives as willing to change and become "civilized" over and against those who continued to model "uncivilized" lifestyles. How much of this was an expression of McDonald's sincere belief and how much was McDonald strategically appealing to a white audience whom he hoped to persuade is impossible to determine. Yet, given the duress under which the letter is written—particularly the impending threat of forceful removal—its contents, which include statements such as "time must come when . . . we be made to become like white men" should be read with caution—without immediately assuming the Choctaw delegation's willing acceptance of white superiority. Indeed, the delegation's critiques of settler hypocrisy evident in the letter provide sufficient basis to cast doubt on such a conclusion.

Despite the strategies employed by activists like McDonald to appeal to the democratic ideals of equal protection and rights among all, the US government continued to trample on the rights of native people—whether it be their rights as sovereign nations independent of the United States or as native people who made claims for tribal rights within the boundaries of the United States. McDonald expressed his frustrations as this reality became more and more apparent to him. A year after the open letter to Congress, McDonald sent a letter to Colonel McKenney—the man who "adopted" him—explaining his fear and anger as demands for Indian Removal continued to grow in number and force. McDonald wrote, "The clouds appear to be gathering from every quarter and ready to burst over every fragment of the Indian race. . . . I see applications to congress from half the states in the union for the extinguishment of Indian titles to land—and to my mind it looks like a bitter and endless persecution."[12]

Outright resistance was never futile, but it was costly. As an alternative, many native people saw in Western education opportunities to advance the interests of their nations, and at times their own survival. Settler schooling was about alienating native students from their heritage; however, some indigenous people also saw in settler schooling opportunities to learn about a social order crafted by white Americans who were intent on their dispossession. Settler schooling was violent and abductive, certainly, but it also exposed windows of opportunity, large and small, to resist the genocidal expansion of the United States—from native students secretly speaking in their tribal tongues and singing traditional songs, to McDonald's national leadership in experimenting with new legal strategies to mitigate the damage of settler violence. In the context of some nations, especially the Five "Civilized" Tribes—which included the Choctaw nation, as well as the Cherokee, Chickasaw, Creek, and Seminole nations—adoption of Western education was a means of performing civilization, and thus rebutting common justifications by settlers for their displacement. Such performances of civilization were one of many strategies of resistance. This politics of civilization—akin to the politics of respectability in the African American tradition—were deemed useful by native people striving to make use of the resources, political and cultural, at their disposal, as they experimented with new ways of organizing their lives within a rapidly changing world. While such strategies of resistance have been widely criticized today, in hindsight it is important to note such political tactics were understood to be useful by many communities striving to carve out dignified lives for themselves and their people while facing extremely violent and dehumanizing experiences.

NATIVE STUDENT RESISTANCE AND THE ROOTS OF NATIVE AMERICAN LITERATURE

Contrary to common arguments about the assimilationist aims of settler schooling, one of the key lessons forced upon native students is that "they learned to write 'Indian.'" This reference to "writing 'Indian'" is about the literal word used to racially categorize the heterogenous groups of indigenous nations, as well as writing from the political and cultural perspectives emerging from the social position of that distinct racialized identity. For instance, James McDonald and his peers wrote to Congress "[a]s the representatives of the Choctaw nation and (in part) of the aborigines of this country," thus expressing a pan-Indian identity. Native students came from many nations, with different languages, creation stories, and natal communities; however, settler schooling, as a colonial institution meant to alienate them from their tribal heritage, became a shared experience. Across tribes, native students resisted settler schooling in various ways, and in doing so forged a literary tradition in the process. As they were literally forced to write the word *Indian* in the English language, as a means of linguistically representing themselves—and thus forced to encounter all the racial storylines about "Indians" handed over to them by teachers and missionaries—native students also came to impose their own interpretations and ideas on what it meant to be Indian. As they learned to write "Indian," there also emerged a countervailing intellectual tradition that pushed back against anti-indigenous ideas perpetuated by white settlers.[13]

The Indian boarding school maintains a permanent presence in native American literature.[14] The first writers of native American literature in English were survivors of boarding schools, and many of their writings detail experiences with settler schooling. The trend is not only characteristic of the nineteenth century, but it persisted well after the boarding school era of the late nineteenth and early twentieth centuries. Native writers in the twentieth and twenty-first centuries continuously turned to the boarding school and native youth's experiences navigating them as major themes in the literature they produced. As one scholar explains, native scholars writing during the mid-twentieth century and after would "portray boarding-school students as being both resistant and in possession of a remarkable degree of power and agency. These representations are set in context by focusing on the explicit connection the texts make between writing and tribal survivance." Thus, in multiple ways, "[t]hese contemporary retellings elucidate the ongoing centrality of the boarding-school experience to the American Indian literary tradition."[15]

I argue that what emerges as a twentieth- and twenty-first century trope in native literature has much longer roots, to the nineteenth century and before. Indeed, the boarding school is present, even when it is not explicitly named in native American literature because all native literature in English is written in the shadow of settler schooling. As the Laguna Pueblo scholar Paula Gunn Allen explains, "Like the long, long war and the extended period of its aftermath, often called the Reservation era (together they spanned well over three hundred years), *the Indian boarding school and its effect form a major subtext in Native American narrative.*"[16] The boarding school is always implied in native American literature, as the texts are written in English, which carries, for indigenous people, the marks of settler schooling's past and present. Thus settler schooling is widely represented topically in the stories and scholarship by native writers, and it constitutes a permanent subtext in all native American literature because of the violent history of English-only language policies imposed on indigenous nations.

The first writers of native American literature were all subjected to settler schooling in some form. Likewise, they all used their writing to speak from their distinct social location as native people—documenting important aspects of their worlds, and offering clear critiques of settler-colonial violence. These first waves of native writers experienced informal adoptions by white families experimenting with "civilizing" native people or they were enrolled in institutions of settler schooling, either government-backed boarding schools or white schools that permitted native students to enroll. For instance, William Apess, a member of the Pequot tribe, and of mixed-race ancestry, became the first native

American to publish a self-authored autobiography in 1829. Apess was taken from his Pequot family early in life and indentured by a European American family who sent him to school during the winter months. His autobiography, *A Son of the Forest*, was written at a moment when American politicians were in deep deliberation about removal policies, where native people from the eastern part of the United States would be removed from their original homelands to territories farther west. Apess's writings about his conversion to Christianity and religious commitments became a basis for his critique of white America's ill treatment of native (and black) people. Four years later, in 1833, he published his seminal essay, "An Indian's Looking-Glass for the White Man." In this text, Apess "let readers know in no uncertain terms that their behavior did not measure up to biblical standards, especially their treatment of Native Americans and African Americans." Apess published five books before his death in 1841, and according to native American literature scholar Lawana Trout, he was "the most significant Indian author in the early nineteenth century," having also been "one of the most forceful protest writers of his day," in that he preached and wrote "against prejudice and injustice."[17] Just as McDonald referenced the educational achievements among the Choctaw tribe as evidence that they were civilized and therefore fit for citizenship within the boundaries of the United States, native writers like Apess used his conversion to Christianity to bolster his critiques of white America's unjust treatment of indigenous peoples.

In 1883, a little more than fifty years after Apess's *A Son of the Forest*, Sarah Winnemucca published *Life Among the Piutes: Their Wrongs and Claims*, becoming the first native American woman to publish an autobiography. Similar to Apess, Winnemucca's exposure to settler schooling took place within the domestic context of a white family. After several of her family members were killed by the US military, Winnemucca's grandfather arranged for her and her sister to live and work for a wealthy white family in Carson City, Nevada. In this context, Winnemucca refined her command of written and spoken English, while also gaining more familiarity with the ways of white settler society. She would use these skills for the remainder of her life.

As Trout explains, "She mastered English, acted as an interpreter, and became a political activist, lecturer, and educator." Winnemucca insisted on opening her own school, as opposed to simply working under the direction of white settlers, and for a short time she achieved this goal. What's more, Winnemucca's autobiography preserved what is now "a rare eyewitness account of four decades of encounters between Paiutes and Euro-Americans."[18]

Francis La Flesche's autobiographical account, *The Middle Five: Indian Boys at School*, published in 1900, and Zitkala-Ša's autobiographical essays published the same year are iconic examples of this legacy of native students learning to write "Indian." They also provide rich accounts of native student resistance in boarding schools during the late nineteenth century. While these texts document La Flesche's and Zitkala-Ša's initiation into the world of racist ideas about native peoples via boarding school curriculum, they also trace these students' participation in a subculture formed among native students as a distinct group of racialized learners within the schooling apparatus of the United States. Their accounts demonstrate how much of the resistance engaged in by students was also linked to social systems among native tribes, revealing how these youth resisted efforts of white school reformers to obliterate their identities as indigenous peoples. Such *boarding school narratives*, like much of the literature written by native thinkers beginning in the nineteenth century, reveal how native students appropriated skills they acquired in settler schooling, particularly English language and literacy, to critique the violence of such institutions.

Native American literature written in the English language develops, formally and most expansively, during the twentieth century.[19] Yet, while this literary tradition blooms after the foundational years of settler schooling in the nineteenth century, the writers publishing during the twentieth century were the products of these schools, or were the children and grandchildren of boarding school survivors.[20] Thus Brenda Child's contention that "the boarding school is now the ancestor" is quite revelatory, in that the institution carries an ancestral presence in native American literature. It is an ancestor that carries a haunting presence, to be clear, but a permanent presence nonetheless. And fortunately, it is not the only permanent force in the literary traditions indigenous peoples created using English language and literacy.

The story of native student resistance also carries an ancestral presence, and it is particularly evident in the native American literary tradition. Indeed, one of the key interventions of literature by native survivors of settler schooling—such as La Flesche and many others—was their preservation of indigenous stories, knowledge, and other cultural resources passed on by elders through oral tradition, now to be preserved in written form. In doing so, native survivors of settler schooling merged oral literature and storytelling traditions that carried much longer roots in indigenous cultures with new expressive forms acquired through their Western education.

Native students preserved old stories and ways of knowing passed on by ancestors in their tribal communities using new educational resources. This countervailing tradition in native education is also an essential part of native students' experience within and critique of the schooling apparatus of the United States.

THE BOARDING SCHOOL NARRATIVES OF FRANCIS LA FLESCHE AND ZITKALA-ŠA

Abraham Lincoln stood nervously before his audience. The young Omaha boy's name, in memorial of the recently assassinated United States president, was likely given to him by settler teachers at the Presbyterian Mission School in Thurston County, Nebraska. On this particular occasion, Abraham was being administered a pop quiz while standing before his schoolmates, the white teacher, and four unexpected white male visitors, sometime during the mid-1860s. The public examination was motivated by the teacher's desire to put on a show for "the white-chests" (a name the Omaha used to describe settlers, referring to the white shirts exposed beneath their suit jackets). The lead educator of the Presbyterian mission was a man whom students referred to as Gray-beard, because "his beard was iron-gray." Gray-beard wanted the students to make a good impression, to assure visitors that the Indian children left in his care were acquiring foundational knowledge and key lessons of settler schooling. He wanted to assure guests that, in addition to taking new names, students were shedding their Omaha identities. He hoped to display that his students were making good progress internalizing white ways of knowing and behaving.[21]

Demands for such public demonstrations at the command of white visitors were commonplace for native students in settler schooling. Such spectacles helped put white anxieties about native people at ease, providing momentary evidence that settler schooling was working. Writing of these frequent tours by white guests, one boarding school survivor described how white men and women of varying social status, from "city folks with canes and eyeglasses" to "the countrymen with sunburnt cheeks and clumsy feet," enjoyed "gazing upon the Indian girls and boys bending over their books," emphasizing how "[b]oth sorts of these Christian palefaces were alike astounded at seeing the children of savage warriors so docile and industrious." This former student recalled how "white visitors walked out of the schoolhouse well satisfied," so proud that "they were educating the children of the red man!"[22]

Gray-beard began the quiz with a simple query, asking Abraham a question he assumed all the students could confidently answer: "Who Discovered America? . . . Abraham, you may answer." Shifting his weight from one foot to the other, Abraham fidgeted with his hand tucked away in his pocket. A look of embarrassment on the boy's face suggested he lacked confidence in his answer. He eventually responded: "George Washington!" Disappointment painted Gray-beard's face red. This was not the start he had hoped for. Quickly pivoting to clean up the mess, Gray-beard tapped a more reliable student, an orphaned boy named Brush who attended the mission school as early as 1857 when he was four years old, indeed when his name was still Mat-zhe-zin-zah. Having been without family and relations since a young child, Brush's complete dependence on the "white-chests" at the mission made him particularly vulnerable, possibly leading him to trust the mission's leaders out of necessity, placing full confidence in their teachings. It was for these reasons that white school reformers often valorized native orphans as ideal students. Continuing the pop quiz, Gray-beard asked, "Brush, can you tell us who discovered America?" The boy promptly gave his answer: "Columbus."

The boarding school narrative recalled above is documented in the memoir of Brush's and Abraham's schoolmate Francis La Flesche, also a member of the Omaha tribe. La Flesche recalled various scenarios like the one above, where school curriculum and policies attempted to alienate native students from their tribal communities and customs. Through his writing, La Flesche reveals how teachers insisted that native students adopt a white curricular standpoint on history and abandon traditional ways of native people, including their languages. Boarding school narratives written from the perspective of indigenous people are an important form of resistance, as they have been vital resources in the development of counternarratives on native history, culture, and experiences. These stories, in their written and oral forms, preserved a body of knowledge that could be (and has been) mobilized against the genocidal logics of settler schooling imposed on native people. Furthermore, such narratives are foundational to the early development of native American literature and native studies, as they came to be expressed in written form.

But to be clear, native students' resistance was not only a belated endeavor manifesting through their contributions to American letters. It did not begin with their retrospective accounts as boarding school survivors in memoirs and autobiographies—though these texts are important and continue to gain more attention by scholars of native American and indigenous studies. The counternarratives and social thought in boarding school narratives—like those in their African American companion, of slave narratives—were extensions of a much longer continuum of resistance that precede such literary expressions. Indeed, like many other authors of boarding school narratives, La Flesche reveals various ways native people, and students in particular, resisted the violent pedagogies of settler schooling meant to alienate them from their Omaha heritage. The scenario that began with Abraham's failed public examination unfolds in a way that elucidates this point.

The same day Abraham Lincoln failed to recall that essential lesson of settler schooling—that Christopher Columbus "discovered" America, and its embedded claim that indigenous people possessed no independent capacity for knowing, and that they too had been *discovered*—the Omaha students displayed an impromptu act of reclamation. It was a display of embodied sovereignty revealing lessons learned outside of the two-story structure of the Presbyterian Mission School. Abraham, Brush, La Flesche, and their classmates engaged in a demonstration that further undermined claims of European discovery and the notion that knowledge and human culture were nonexistent on the North American continent prior to 1492.

Much to Gray-beard's delight, the students successfully spelled words and answered trivia questions about white American history, helping to redeem them after Abraham's forgetfulness. Thinking the public examination had come to an end, and that they would soon achieve some relief from the intruding gaze of the four white visitors, a final question was put before the students. One of the men asked if the students were taught music. The superintendent, who was among the four guests, explained that while the children "can sing nearly all of the Sunday-school hymns," music was not a subject taught in the school. The visitor then posed his follow-up question directly to the students: "Have your people music, and do they sing?" Bypassing Gray-beard's authority as the key mediator of this exchange, and choosing to speak for himself (and for his people), one of the older boys among the group boldly answered, "They do." The visitor continued, "I wish you would sing an Indian song for me. I never heard one."

Moments like these exposed the contradictory messages from white settlers, where their fetishization of native life at times clashed with the colonial aims of settler schooling. In this moment, the visitor requested that the students offer up a performance of Indianness for his momentary consumption—a desired display of "noble savagery" in service of the settler gaze. The visitor would quickly regret his request.

Students were surprised and a bit nervous. They were never asked to sing Omaha songs. They were also strictly forbidden to speak the Omaha language. Singing an Omaha song seemed to be a violation of this rule, which was often reinforced through physical punishment. Nevertheless, the students were moved, perhaps even excited, to oblige the invitation.

"Suddenly a loud clear voice close to me broke out in a Victory song," La Flesche recalled. Then, "before a bar was sung another voice took up the song from the beginning, as is the custom among the Indians, then the whole school fell in, and we made the room ring."

One small prompting by an unexpected visitor and the entire school of native children whom Gray-beard worked so hard to civilize seemingly relapsed into their old ways. Indeed, fears of such relapses were constantly discussed among missionaries and government officials, serving as one of the primary reasons they expressed preference for boarding schools. The constant surveillance in these institutions, they hoped, could ensure social control of native students. Yet, right before their eyes, the white spectators observed this seemingly converted group of native youth begin to sing in unison while embodying the pride of a sovereign people, thus challenging the very aims of settler schooling.

La Flesche never forgot the feeling of this moment. The feelings that gave the song life were more important than its literal meaning. La Flesche declared, "We felt, as we sang, the patriotic thrill of a victorious people who had vanquished their enemies." In this moment, the Omaha students displayed a kind of knowledge that was deeply engrained in them, a way of knowing that challenged lessons drilled into them through the rote learning methods employed by missionaries. In a split-second display of their prior knowledge—seemingly unrehearsed—the students channeled a repertoire of feelings, understanding, and ways of being that threatened the entire project of Gray-beard's lessons. The students demonstrated that they had not been completely undone by the rituals of settler schooling meant to strip them of their heritage. Collectively, they embodied an archive of song, but also knowledge that gave meaning to the song and the very act of singing it. The Omaha students' victory song formed a meaningful response not only when coming back from the battlefield, but also in the classroom.

The looks of disgust plastered across the visitors' faces were unforgettable. They shook their heads in disapproval, before one abruptly shouted, "That's savage, that's savage! They must be taught music."

What he just heard from the children, he insisted, was nothing of the sort. Soon after this incident, the mission school required students to spend an hour in singing lessons each day, and it eventually acquired instruments to establish a band. School officials hoped, it seems, that new instruments and instruction in music customs of the settlers might instill new sounds and new songs in the Omaha children. New sounds might drown out the old ones, they hoped. Settler teachers, at this Presbyterian mission and hundreds of others across the country, were willing to do whatever it took to suppress whatever it was that possessed the children the day they sang the "Indian song."[23]

The son of an Omaha chief, La Flesche arrived at the mission with a great sense of pride in his identity. His father hoped La Flesche would combine what he learned in the "House of Teaching" with the wisdom and traditions of the Omaha for pragmatic reasons. As the number of white settlers continued to grow, and as Omaha land continued to shrink, his family arrived at the conclusion that the Omaha would have to find ways of communicating and protecting themselves against "the white-chests." La Flesche described his sense of duty when heading to school by recalling the elaborate clothes he put on to prepare for the new phase of boyhood. Like many other Omaha students, La Flesche arrived in "[h]is buckskin suit, prettily fringed and embroidered with porcupine quills of the brightest colors, indicat[ing] the care bestowed upon him by fond parents."[24]

As a matter of political necessity, some native parents encouraged their children to develop a command of the English language and the customs of white society; not to become white, but to acquire skills that might help mitigate the devastation caused by ongoing dispossession, the economic and health challenges brought about by European contact, and, overall, to advocate for the interest of their communities as the written culture of US laws, policies, and contracts continued to be used as instruments to economically exploit native people and their resources.[25] The goals Omaha families had for sending children to white-run schools would be trampled on, however, by the larger agenda of the United States and settlers acting in the interest of the broader nation-building project. The aims of the latter were the alienation of native students from the very communities who sent them to school for the collective benefit of indigenous nations. As one scholar aptly explains, "against the wishes of Native parents," native students were subjected to an education that was "subtractive rather than additive. . . . Students were expected to learn English not as an additional language but rather as the only language worthy of acquisition. They were not to become bicultural but rather to substitute the Christian majority culture for their own."[26] This conflict gradually revealed itself to students and families. While La Flesche did not fully grasp the violence of Gray-beard's lessons about who founded America or the renaming of students in real time, he certainly arrived at such conclusions by the time he recorded these stories in his memoir.

In addition to the story of native students singing a traditional Omaha song, La Flesche describes multiple accounts of students running away from the mission school. According to La Flesche, some Omaha youth and families resented the fact that school leaders forbid students from attending traditional ceremonies and events. As a result, La Flesche and a group of classmates chose to run away to attend "the annual summer buffalo hunt" during the 1860s, and by the 1890s, Indian agents continued to complain about Omaha students running away for this same event.[27] La Flesche's accounts of Omaha students running away to be part of the social life of their tribal communities reflect a broader pattern. As one historian notes, "Students learned the time and whereabouts of these events in various ways: surreptitious message from a relative; the glow of firelight in the distant sky; the sound of drums reverberating against the mountains." When the will of students grew strong enough, and when the alienation experienced in settler schooling became most intolerable, "even walls, gates, barred windows, and padlocked doors could not hold the determined runaway. The promise of freedom and the pull of family were simply too strong."[28]

Students also found ways to escape within boarding school walls. La Flesche recalled how his group of friends, who went by "the middle five," and a group of older students, "the big seven," held after-hour gatherings in a deserted room, to talk about life in camp or listen to peers tell stories of the Omaha tribe passed on through oral tradition.

They also snuck out to the village to gather food, community information, and other things that helped maintain their relations. La Flesche explained, "From time to time through the winter we had these nocturnal banquets, taking turns in going to the village for our supplies." The meetings were quite lively. The boys took an oath of secrecy to one another. They spoke in the Omaha language—openly defying this cardinal rule of the boarding school. They told stories of Omaha victories and folktales. La Flesche recalled, "We laughed heartily at the mishaps of Ish-té-ne-ke, a comical character that figures in the folktales of the Omaha, as they were vividly portrayed in language and gesture."[29]

Students could be harshly punished for violating school rules. However, even moments of punishment, on occasions, evolved into further displays of resistance on the part of students. While being caught and reprimanded could be demoralizing, they could also become moments where students displayed great bravery, inspiring resistance in other students. La Flesche recalled one such event, after Gray-beard caught a student climbing out of the window in the middle of the night. Knowing this young student had not acted alone, Gray-beard attempted to identify his coconspirators. An older boy named Aleck, the leader of the Big Seven, confessed to making the younger student climb out of the window. Another student from the Middle Five followed his lead. These two boys insisted they acted alone, though their schoolmates knew several students were involved. Gray-beard decided to physically punish them with a hickory rod in front of the entire class. This was a traumatic experience for the students being punished as well as those forced to witness. Settler school leaders encouraged such harsh disciplinary practices for rebellious native students in hopes that such extreme enforcement of rules might serve as a form of collective punishment to quell future acts of resistance.[30]

Despite the intentions of white school leaders, La Flesche recalled being inspired by the bravery of his two schoolmates, especially Aleck, who took the blame for the collective group, many of whom were younger than him. Aleck stood out in manner and stature. According to La Flesche, "He was tall and muscular, with prominent nose and cheek-bones." In addition to his commanding presence, he rarely showed emotion. His schoolmates "never knew him to change the expression on his face, either in pain, anger, or mirth." Aleck took on a kind of mysterious quality among the students, and it was rumored, according to La Flesche, that "the boy had ceased laughing since the killing of his father by the Sioux, and that he was reserving his laugh for the time when he should take revenge." So, while Gray-beard chose to physically punish the most revered student, Aleck refused to give him the satisfaction of being broken in front of his peers. According to La Flesche, Gray-beard "dealt blow after blow on the broad shoulders of Alexander," and the young leader "gave no sign of pain." La Flesche recalled, "The boy stood unmoved, every muscle relaxed, even his hands were open, showing no emotion whatever. The stick was worn out, and Gray-beard threw the stump on the floor." While many of the students feared Aleck before, because they did not understand him, they all came to respect him for standing up in such an honorable way for his younger comrades. After the whipping, Aleck went back to his desk and continued to work silently.[31]

•••

Zitkala-Ša's three autobiographical essays appeared in the *Atlantic Monthly* in January, February, and March of 1900, just months before the publication of *The Middle Five*. They spanned her early experiences among the Yankton Sioux tribe of the Lakota people, being raised by her mother, then her experiences across four different schools, including two native boarding schools, a predominantly white Quaker college, and finally, her time working as a teacher at the Carlisle Indian Industrial School. This educational trajectory is reflected in the titles of Zitkala-Ša's essays: "The Impressions of an Indian Childhood," "The School Days of an Indian Girl," and "An Indian Teacher among Indians." With these essays, Zitkala-Ša distinguished herself as the first indigenous writer to educate the American public about the violent realities of native boarding schools and settler schooling more broadly.[32] Using skills acquired in settler schooling, as well as intellectual resources gained from native people, especially her mother, Zitkala-Ša "[r]eject[ed] any notion that full assimilation into American civilization was desirable" and "sought independence from the ideological confines of her white education."[33]

Zitkala-Ša was born Gertrude Simmons in February 1876. She was the last child of her Yankton Sioux mother, Ellen Simmons, and a product of Simmons's third marriage to a Frenchman from whom she separated quite early in Zitkala-Ša's life, possibly before she was born. While of mixed-race heritage, Zitkala-Ša was raised by her indigenous mother and deeply immersed in Sioux customs.[34] Choosing to emphasize her Sioux heritage, around 1898, in an act of reclamation she changed her name to "Zitkala-Ša," which translates to "Red Bird" in Lakota. The name change was a forceful and unapologetic assertion of her cultural identity, as well as a direct response to her violent initiation into settler society. While her Lakota name was intercepted before birth, she witnessed other students stripped of their Lakota names at boarding schools, and after critically reflecting on her experiences in settler schooling, Zitkala-Ša decided to reverse the course when it came to the spelling of her proper name. She explained that Simmons was not even the name of her biological father; what's more, it reflected a history of European colonization of native peoples. For these reasons, Zitkala-Ša explained, "I choose *to make* a name for myself."[35] Zitkala-Ša's rejection of her English name was intimately connected to her rejection of the boarding school's aim of alienating native youth from their natal communities. In fact, she changed her name just as she began publicly writing about the violence of settler schooling.

At the age of six, Zitkala-Ša was enrolled in the Presbyterian bilingual school at the Yankton Agency, near her home, only two years before traveling east at the age of eight to a Quaker boarding school hundreds of miles from her family and tribe. While Zitkala-Ša documents the many indignities experienced in settler schooling, she also provides many examples of native resistance. For instance, while she described being subjected to a demoralizing haircutting ritual at White's Manual Labor Institute, she also describes her resistance to this violation. Zitkala-Ša recalled "being dragged out" of her hiding place, where she had hoped to evade the violating ritual, as she "resisted by kicking and scratching wildly."[36]

It is worth noting that native parents also resisted settler schooling when they learned about the harsh treatment of students. Parents from Zitkala-Ša's community engaged in an act of protest after the death of Zitkala-Ša's schoolmate, which raised concerns about the conditions at White's boarding school. According to the Indian agent, news of the young girl's death caused a great uproar among tribal leaders and family members. Yankton Sioux parents refused to send any children to the local agency school in protest, declaring that until the remaining students, including Zitkala-Ša, were brought back home, they would not comply with orders to send their children to the day school run out of the Yankton Agency.[37] J. K. Kinney, an Indian agent, ultimately threatened to take extreme actions if parents continued to violate the terms of their tribe's treaty with the US government, which required enrollment at the agency school for nine months out of the year. His threats likely included withholding annuities and other resources. Given that Zitkala-Ša completed the full three years at White's before seeing her family again, it appears the Indian agent refused to honor the demands of Yankton Sioux leaders that the children be returned.

Like many students, Zitkala-Ša refused to completely turn away from Sioux traditions and spiritual practices, even as boarding schools forbade students from engaging in what white school leaders deemed "heathen" activities. Around the age of fifteen, Zitkala-Ša prepared for her journey back to boarding school, and to do so, she also sought protection from a Sioux medicine man. Though she attended Christian-based settler schools for several years, Zitkala-Ša returned to Sioux customs as a source of identity, security, and as a means of grounding herself for the hostile experience she was sure to encounter when returning east. Zitkala-Ša writes, "I had a secret interview with one of our best medicine men, and when I left his wigwam I carried securely in my sleeve a tiny bunch of magic roots. . . . So absolutely did I believe in its charms that I wore it through all the school routines for more than a year."[38] Zitkala-Ša kept the roots tucked away and out of sight from the missionary teachers at White's because she knew they would certainly disapprove of her having them. Like Tilman Rose at Brainerd Mission in the 1820s, as well as Francis La Flesche and his classmates at the Omaha boarding school during the late 1860s, Zitkala-Ša knowingly went against well-established rules of settler schooling that violated her heritage as a young indigenous woman.

Zitkala-Ša also subverted settler ideology in her essay (and through her actions in real time) by including details of her decision to accept roots from a medicine man while a student. The inclusion of such narratives destabilize the settler gaze as a controlling mechanism in her writing. For indeed, the settler gaze was openly hostile to indigenous spiritual and healing practices. In boarding schools, students were required to ritualistically condemn such practices as part of their conversion to Christianity and "civilization." Zitkala-Ša refused this demand for self-censorship, choosing to think otherwise, and to represent her engagement with traditional Sioux customs as a means of protection against the hostilities of settler schooling and white teachers.

One of the unique things about Zitkala-Ša's autobiographical essays is that she not only reveals her experiences as a native student in settler schooling, but also discussed her early experiences as a native teacher at the Carlisle Indian Industrial School. Thus her criticisms of boarding schools spoke to the particulars of her experience at White's, but also experiences at the institution most celebrated among white school reformers. Zitkala-Ša's resistance as a student translated to her perspective on native education as a teacher.

In the summer of 1897, at the age of twenty-two, Zitkala-Ša decided to, as she put it, "spend [her] energies in a work for the Indian race . . . to teach in an Eastern Indian school." This journey would put her face-to-face with the most iconic leader among the white architects of settler schooling for native people. About a month after Zitkala-Ša's arrival, General Pratt explained his plan for how he might use her charisma and skills as a gifted communicator. It appears he wanted "the little Indian girl" (as he referred to her) to help increase student enrollment at the school. Zitkala-Ša never forgot one particular statement Pratt shared when issuing this assignment. Speaking to Zitkala-Ša as a new native teacher, Pratt declared, "I am going to turn you loose to pasture." He was sending her west "to gather Indian pupils for the school." And, as Zitkala-Ša emphasized for her readers, "this was his way of expressing it."[39] His language likened Zitkala-Ša and native communities to animals, revealing deep-seated racist beliefs informing his leadership of Carlisle.

Despite Pratt's intentions, this recruitment trip would be a turning point in Zitkala-Ša's internal development, leading to a political awakening that shaped her future writing and political organizing. When Zitkala-Ša arrived to Yankton in August 1897, it was her first time home in several years. What she witnessed on the trip was startling. With her own eyes, she witnessed the ramifications of rapid settler encroachment. This along with story after story shared by her mother left Zitkala-Ša mortified. Not only had white settlers continued to rush in and illegally occupy Sioux lands, but her brother Dawée, who worked as a government clerk for the reservation, had been fired and replaced by a white man. Zitkala-Ša offers her mother's assessment of her brother's misfortune, writing, "[T]he Great Father at Washington sent a white son to take your brother's pen from him. . . . Since then Dawée has not been able to make use of the education the Eastern school has given him."[40]

Ellen Simmons's stories about the rapid dispossession of indigenous lands, alongside the challenges of Zitkala-Ša's brother in the Indian Service and in dealing with the federal government, were deeply concerning. They sharpened her gaze as she returned to continue her work as "An Indian Teacher among Indians" at a boarding school led by a white man who deemed it appropriate to liken her and all native people to animals roaming the grasslands.

The dispossession Zitkala-Ša witnessed at home and the dispossession she witnessed at Carlisle were inextricably linked. With her mother's lessons, Zitkala-Ša began to "look back upon the recent past" and "see it from a distance, as a whole," as she put it.[41] The ongoing theft of native land back on the reservation and the theft of native students' identities and spirit in boarding schools, all done with the aiding and abetment of the US government, were mutually constitutive.

Zitkala-Ša's outlook became more critical as she returned to Carlisle. While Zitkala-Ša did enjoy some aspects of her work—especially interacting with young native students—and while some of the relationships she developed felt sincere, the larger aims of General Pratt's school tugged at internal conflicts she'd long possessed, from the time her hair was cut as a little girl.[42] One documented classroom encounter reveals how Zitkala-Ša's private battles made their way into her lessons for native students. In January 1898, Zitkala-Ša "held a subversive debate on 'whether or not the treatment of the Indians by the early settlers caused King Phillip to make war'" in a class with the sixth-year students.[43] As evidenced by an earlier speech she gave while a student at Earlham College, this class activity was not the first time she questioned settler interpretations of history. In her speech, given just months before arriving at Carlisle, Zitkala-Ša drew attention to the specificity of ongoing native dispossession across the centuries, while insisting on the legitimacy of native people's commitments to sovereignty and social equality between the races. Speaking to a roomful of white college students and adult judges, including alumni from Harvard and Yale, Zitkala-Ša proclaimed:

> *The white man's bullets decimated his tribes and drives him from his home. What if he fought? His forests were felled; his game frightened away; his streams of finny shoals usurped. He loved his family and would defend them. He loved the fair land of which he was rightful owner. He loved the inheritance of his fathers, their traditions, their graves; he held them a priceless legacy to be sacredly kept. He loved his native land. Do you wonder still that in his breast he should brook revenge, when ruthlessly driven from the temples where he worshipped? Do you wonder still that he skulked in forest gloom to avenge the desolation of his home? Is patriotism only a virtue in Saxon hearts?*[44]

In addition to noting anti-indigenous violence inherent in settler society, in this same speech, Zitkala-Ša also pointed to the violence met by other marginalized groups, particularly referencing the violent history of enslavement. "Let it be remembered," she said to the audience at this oratorical competition, "before condemnation is passed upon the Red Man, that, while he burned and tortured frontiersmen, Puritan Boston burned witches and hanged Quakers, and the Southern aristocrat beat his slaves and set blood hounds on the track of him who dared to aspire to freedom."[45] Zitkala-Ša spoke these words even as white college students from rival schools shouted racial slurs at her and held up a banner bearing the word "Squaw"—a racial epithet hurled at native women—to remind her of the place she occupied in their minds and in settler society.[46]

Zitkala-Ša found herself growing more sensitive to the actions of the white educators when she returned to Carlisle from her visit home. She began to study them more closely, concluding that their individual actions expressed a larger phenomenon of settler expansion at the expense of indigenous people. Zitkala-Ša explains how in the months after her visit with her mother, she "slowly comprehended that the large army of white teachers in Indian schools had a larger missionary creed than [she] had suspected." White teachers' efforts among native people were, more than anything, self-serving. Their faith "was one which included self-preservation quite as much as Indian education." Noting observations that justified her claim, she writes, "When I saw an opium-eater holding a position as teacher of Indians, I did not understand what good was expected, until a Christian in power replied that this pumpkin-colored creature had a feeble mother to support." Zitkala-Ša also described white teachers engaging in abusive behavior toward native students. In taking stock of the macro and micro dynamics conditioning settler schooling, Zitkala-Ša's patience began to shrink at a rapid pace. While there may have been some good among white teachers, it became more and more difficult to locate. Her exhaustion, and anger, left little room for grace or sympathy for settlers working in Indian schools. Zitkala-Ša decided her energy needed to be spent on something other than trying to rescue the work being done by white teachers in settler schooling. Expressing her limited patience for white people, Zitkala-Ša declared, "My illness, which prevented the conclusion of my college course, together with my mother's stories of the encroaching frontier settlers, left me in no mood to strain my eyes in searching for latent good in my white co-workers."[47]

The ultimate resolution to Zitkala-Ša's conflict with settler schooling appears in her third essay. In her resolve, Zitkala-Ša pointed to native refusal and self-determination. After achieving her new level of consciousness during her time working at Carlisle—the epicenter of settler schooling during the late nineteenth century—Zitkala-Ša decided that quitting her job as a teacher was the only option. From her position at Carlisle, she saw no opportunity to engage in meaningful work that was accountable to the needs of native students and their communities. Zitkala-Ša described finding "a new way of solving the problem of [her] inner self."[48] Having learned the English language and literacy in settler schooling and having developed a critical awareness of her position as a racialized native woman, Zitkala-Ša used what she acquired through her educational journey to condemn the form and function of settler schooling in her writing. Zitkala-Ša's essays, alongside a host of other boarding school narratives and other forms of writing by the survivors of settler schooling, formed the basis of native American literature.

Zitkala-Ša's life helps reveal the haunting presence the boarding school carries in native American experience. It also demonstrates how native students' resistance to this violent institution shaped a new course of study for native American education—a new course of study revealed, with astonishing clarity, in literature produced by boarding school survivors.

•••

Boarding school survivors who became native writers, like La Flesche and Zitkala-Ša, experienced a burden of representation as they entered the literary world. Anything they wrote would be seen as a representation of an entire race of people, despite the diversity among indigenous nations. Their works would be interpreted as either reinforcing certain stereotypical narratives about native people or disrupting them—each coming with their own set of ramifications. What's more, there were forceful external pressures working to influence what former boarding school students wrote based on narrow ideas about who native people were and how they should appear in literature.[49] This kind of pressure came not only from the publishing world, but especially from the white architects of settler schooling. While excited to see boarding school students engage in such "civilized" activity as publishing literature, white reformers grew anxious to control the topics former students wrote about and the positions they might take on said topics. White school reformers believed native students' representations of themselves would reflect positively or negatively on the settler schooling project.[50] While some white education reformers willfully misread La Flesche's book—focusing on moments in the text that could be interpreted as supporting assimilationist objectives, while ignoring his criticisms of how boarding schools denigrated native cultures and abused students—Zitkala-Ša's essays provided little opportunity for such misreading. Her discontent was unequivocal. For this reason, Zitkala-Ša's essays were attacked by white school reformers. They called her a hypocrite, suggesting she was ungrateful for the very people who sacrificed to give her access to a better life. Couched in a paternalistic rhetoric characteristic of white settler commentary, these school officials insisted they saved Zitkala-Ša from the depths of savagery and a life of squalor on the reservation.

Richard Henry Pratt was a vocal critic of Zitkala-Ša. He wrote scathing reviews of her essays and short stories, and he proclaimed that everything in the way of skills and ability the woman did have for the literary arts and culture "she owes to the good people, who, from time to time, have taken her into their homes and given her aid. Yet not a word of gratitude or allusion to such kindness on the part of her friends has ever escaped her in any line of anything she has written for the public." Pratt insisted that Zitkala-Ša's actions had the capacity to harm the important work being done in settler schooling: "By this course she injures herself and harms the educational work in progress for the race from which she sprang." Pratt's criticisms written privately to his colleagues in the Indian Service were even more harsh, displaying deeply held anti-indigenous views, particularly toward native women. He declared, there was "a great deal of feeling throughout the Indian service against" Zitkala-Ša for her public writing about boarding schools, because it undermined the "cause of right Indian education." Pratt insisted Zitkala-Ša would be nothing without the help of white educators like himself, declaring, "But for those she has maligned, *she would be a poor squaw in an Indian camp*, probably married to some no-count Indian."[51]

Despite such criticism and pressure from white education reformers, native students continued to bear witness to their experiences of settler schooling, and they did so from their perspectives as indigenous people. No longer physically confined by the boarding school, native students went out into the world and made independent decisions about how to represent themselves, indigenous cultures, their encounters with boarding schools, and other aspects of the settler-colonial conflict, as they saw it.

Here lies the risk always embedded in processes of education. For even when such educational projects are constructed with nefarious objectives, there is always some modicum of freedom when it comes to matters of the mind.

Portrait of Zitkala-Ša by Gertrude Kasebier c.1898. Courtesy of National Museum of American History, Smithsonian Institution.

NATIVE EDUCATION AND THE SCHOOLING APPARATUS OF THE UNITED STATES

The white architects of native schooling built institutions and established policies that extended from ongoing acts of war and conquest against indigenous peoples. Such protocols of settler schooling aimed to disappear native ways of life, particular native claims on land, and one of the primary methods for facilitating such dispossession was to alienate indigenous youth from their natal communities early in life, and in the most totalizing ways possible. Settler schooling as a method of natal alienation was supported by the federal government directly, though often executed and expanded by private entities, such as missionary organizations, who received financial and moral reinforcement from the federal government. Native education was a national priority because it served the political-economic interests of national expansion, in that schooling was a mechanism for alienating native youth from tribal identities and heritage claims to land, thus reducing native resistance to settler encroachment. And while all of this is true, regarding settlers' deployment of education as a tool of racial domination among native people, it is also true that native students and communities resisted such efforts to disappear indigenous people and indigenous ways of being.

Just as McKenney's captive adoption of native students and experimentations with native schooling reflects how settlers used education as a method of dispossessing native people, the details of Arbor's attempt to flee and refuse the hand of the settler state are also integral to this history. It marks a perspective of settler schooling from below, whereby native people, and native students in particular, articulated a politics of education within, and in relation to, the American school. From such perspectives emerged a countervailing tradition, a politics of indigenous survivance in education, through which native students appropriated resources they acquired through settler schooling to document and bear witness to the depth of violation employed through these institutions, just as they used skills acquired in settler schooling to make political claims on behalf of indigenous communities to resist the ongoing domination and intrusion of the settler state. What's more, native students like Zitkala-Ša also employed strategies of resistance that held roots in indigenous customs and traditions. They merged ways of knowing and being to respond to their distinct needs as native people.

The history of native education is not a story at the periphery of the schooling apparatus of the United States, but it is in fact a central part of its development. Integral to this story is the countervailing tradition of native studies emerging from the centuries of indigenous students' refusing to be alienated from their people and lands.

PART III

BLACK EDUCATION IN INDIAN TERRITORY

9

RACE, SLAVERY, AND EDUCATION AMONG THE FIVE "CIVILIZED" TRIBES

I was not looking for black people in the Commissioner of Indian Affairs reports. Yet, there they were. During the summer of 2020, in the midst of the COVID-19 pandemic, my student researchers and I met via Zoom as we mined digitized collections of government reports to analyze developments in settler schooling imposed on native students through the nineteenth century. These government documents were addressed to the US secretary of war and detailed, among other things, settler-led educational activities among indigenous tribes. Having noticed sporadic references to enslaved and free black people in these reports, particularly in narratives pertaining to "the Five Civilized Tribes"—which included the Cherokee, Choctaw, Chickasaw, Creek, and Seminole nations—we became interested in learning more. Furthermore, the black presence in the records of native schooling led to a series of unavoidable questions.

How did the grammars of race and schooling in the United States influence the relational dynamics of race and schooling within the internal context of native tribes that enslaved black people? What were the educational experiences of black people, before and after emancipation, among slaveholding tribes? How did the educational experience of black people living within native nations align with or depart from black experiences in the United States more broadly? And how does the history of black education in Indian Territory relate to the schooling apparatus of the United States, given its formation "outside" of the nation?

In pursuing such questions, I learned to appreciate the story of black education among the Five Tribes as both a part of and apart from the national story of US education. This is necessary given the simultaneity of indigenous sovereignty and the heavy-handed paternalism endemic to US policies toward these sovereign nations. While the grammars of American schooling, particularly its racial logics, certainly influenced black people's educational experiences among the tribes, there were distinctions to black-native relations that had to be treated on their own terms. This was necessary even when accounting for the invisible hand of whiteness structuring the tensions between the two racialized groups.

My students and I came across the blog of Angela Walton-Raji in 2021 as we sought out primary sources pertaining to black education in Indian Territory. At the time, Walton-Raji was a sixty-nine-year-old black woman of Choctaw heritage whose research focused on "African-Native American genealogy" and black experiences among the Five Tribes. She immediately responded to our request to meet.

We gathered on Zoom—one of the conveniences that became a new normal during the early phase of the pandemic. The conversation included Walton-Raji, Anna Kate Cannon (my undergraduate research assistant), and myself. During our introductions, Anna Kate shared that she was a member of the Choctaw nation, which prompted a conversation between her and Walton-Raji about this relation they shared. The two exchanged a few sentences in Choctaw. I proceeded to tell Walton-Raji that all three of us have ties to Oklahoma, explaining that my paternal grandfather, Jarvis Ray Givens, for whom my father and I were named, was born and raised in Chickasha, Oklahoma, and that my grandfather's mother, whom we called "Mama Jewel"—named Jewel (McCoy) Givens—was the granddaughter of a Choctaw man named Oliver "Boss" McCoy and a formerly enslaved black woman named Susan (Guess) McCoy. The genealogist in Walton-Raji immediately awakened, and she shared her familiarity with some of the family names. Susan McCoy (later Susan Brashears) appears in one of Walton-Raji's blogs and other writings about freedmen among the Five Tribes, because—as readers may recall from this book's introduction—Susan filed a petition in 1906 to have her children's names transferred from the Choctaw freedmen roll to the list for Choctaw citizens by blood, claiming that her former husband, and her children's father, Oliver McCoy, was a citizen by blood, therefore making them full citizens of the nation. Susan's case demonstrates how formerly enslaved people within the Five Tribes worked to advocate for themselves within their respective tribal nations, and also reveals the complicated politics of race and citizenship they were forced to navigate.

Following this original conversation with Walton-Raji, I learned that my family's connection to this history is even thicker than I initially understood. I have since learned that Mama Jewel's husband, James Reese Givens—my great-grandfather—was also the descendant of Choctaw freedmen. James's great-grandfather Solomon Givens was enslaved, along with thirty-two other black people according to the 1860 census, by a Choctaw man named Solomon W. Givens. Given the shared names, this man who owned my great-great-great-ancestor was likely his father.

After our brief genealogy conversation, Walton-Raji seamlessly transitioned to thoughts she wanted to share with Anna Kate and myself about how we might refine our approach to studying black education among the Five Tribes. She provided names of specific schools that might be of interest—like the Tullahassee Mission School in the Creek nation (present-day Oklahoma)—and noted trends that were representative of key parts of the story, like the comparative difference between the treatment of black people in one tribe versus another. Walton-Raji also expressed how these historical narratives were deeply bound up in her own family's history. She told us about her journey, over decades, conducting research to help make the story of Afro-native people more visible in public memory about the nation's past.

Walton-Raji declared her Choctaw heritage was "no stranger to me." She grew up in Fort Smith, Arkansas, during the 1950s and '60s, and she recalled that her great-grandmother was a fluent speaker of the Choctaw language. Walton-Raji's earliest childhood memories were of her great-grandmother sitting with her brothers, where "they would sit out in the backyard, dipping snuff and smoking corn-pipes, speaking Choctaw to each other." Walton-Raji regularly visited family in the Choctaw nation, just south of Fort Smith. She was black *and* she was Choctaw. This had always been her identity.[1]

As an adult, Walton-Raji began to take seriously the work of researching her family history and in doing so learned more about the complicated past of Afro-native identities. It was in the National Archives, for instance, that Walton-Raji first encountered the term "Choctaw freedman," used by the federal government to denote black people who historically lived in the Choctaw nation, mostly the formerly enslaved people of Choctaw elites. She encountered the term while trying to find her people in the Dawes Rolls—a list of tribal citizens created by the United States when it forcibly divided native nations into privately owned land allotments in the late nineteenth century.

Walton-Raji's quest to find her people indexes an archival and genealogical impulse shared by descendants of enslaved Africans in the Americas—a diasporic people forged, in part, through cyclical patterns of rupture in familial ties initiated by chattel slavery. However, as Walton-Raji's labor attests, the identities of African-descended people in the Americas have also been shaped by their resistance to such violation of kinship ties, through strategies of mending, recovery, and ingenuity. Black people's quest for self-knowledge—for family history and counternarratives about their race—became integral to the aims of their education in the context of American schooling. The pursuit of self-knowledge—like the work taken up by Walton-Raji—carries distinct meaning in the politics of education across the African diaspora, and it is intimately bound up with black identity formation. The case is not different when it comes to the educational lives of black people who are descendants of Choctaw (and Cherokee, Creek, Chickasaw, and Seminole) freedmen.[2]

"We never used the word *freedman*" growing up, Walton-Raji explained. She had always understood herself to be, simply, Choctaw. This was not necessarily something to be understood apart from her identity as a black woman. It was only after Walton-Raji failed to find her family in the Dawes Rolls for "Choctaws by Blood" that she turned to the "Choctaw Freedmen" rolls. In these documents she found her ancestors enmeshed in a complicated historical struggle for native sovereignty couched in antiblackness, both on the Choctaw and US side of the struggle. This label, "Choctaw freedman," points to the entanglement of African slavery among the Five Tribes—an intimate part of Walton-Raji's history, which she has written about extensively—and yet the history beneath such categorization also reveals important insights about the racial politics of education among the Five Tribes, as they worked to resist unyielding settler encroachment.[3]

When unpacking the complicated and long-standing nature of antiblackness among the Five Tribes, Walton-Raji shared the story of a young girl—who she believed to be Creek—that was denied entry to the Carlisle Indian Industrial School because she was "half Negro." The school's rejection of the Afro-native girl in the early 1900s reflected long-standing antiblack sentiments embedded in the racial politics of native schooling. Readers may recall that enslaved black people were used to build Brainerd Mission, but they were not allowed to attend the school. Walton-Raji counseled that this young girl was hardly the first denied entry, declaring: "You will not find other people who were freedmen at Carlisle, ever."[4]

Walton-Raji's suggestion that the experience of this young girl was likely shared by others was true. After doing a little digging, I learned that Carlisle administrators sent home a group of Afro-native students from the Shinnecock nation four days after they arrived on September 4, 1892, even as they were legally recognized as Indian. Their student cards preserved in the Carlisle archive listed the reason for the denied enrollment of these Afro-native youth. In plain language, the school administrators listed the "cause" for their denial: "Negro" or "too much negro" was the explanation provided.[5]

Apparently there were limits to Carlisle's civilizing power. While the school's founder insisted on "killing the Indian" in order to "save the man," there appeared to be no similar path to civilization for black students: One could not kill the Negro and save the man. This incompatibility was a feature of a settler-colonial project propped up by and developed in relation to African slavery, which carried over to its

Name Grace Bunn
File No. En.
" " G.-3071
" " D.
Indian name
Tribe Shinnecock Age 13 Blood 1/2
Agency
Father Warren Bunn
Arrived 9-4-'92 Departed 9-7-'92 Cause Negro
Class entered Class left
Trade Outing
Character
Married Deceased
Remarks over
YAWMAN & ERBE MFG. CO., ROCHESTER, N. Y.

Grace Bunn Student Information Card, Carlisle Indian Industrial School, a member of the Shinnecock nation, who entered the school on September 4, 1892, and departed on September 7, 1892, National Archives and Records Administration, RG 75, Series 1329, box 6.

Name Herbert H. Smith
File No. En.
" " G.-1722
" " D.
Indian name
Tribe Shinnecock Age 16 Blood 1/2
Agency
Father Henry C. Smith
Arrived 9-4-'92 Departed 9-8-'92 Cause Too much negro.
Class entered Class left
Trade Outing
Character
Married Deceased
Remarks over
YAWMAN & ERBE MFG. CO., ROCHESTER, N. Y.

Herbert H. Smith Student Information Card, a member of the Shinnecock nation, who entered the school on September 4, 1892, and departed on September 8, 1892, National Archives and Records Administration, RG 75, Series 1329, box 14.

afterlives in the United States and in Indian Territory. Indeed, these relational politics of race are at the heart of Carlisle's founding. It is important to note here that General Richard Henry Pratt abandoned the Indian Program at Hampton Institute in 1879 after one year because he strongly disagreed with black and native students being educated with one another. Such proximity to black students would lead to native students being stigmatized by association, therefore undermining his goal of absorbing native people into white society. The point here is not to express a desire that Afro-native students would have been accepted at Carlisle—for indeed, I experienced some relief when Walton-Raji shared the young girl's story of rejection—instead, the lesson is that native schools, like Carlisle, while constructed with the violent intentions of alienating native students from their natal communities, could also engage in the work of antiblack domination by virtue of exclusion. Native students' proximity to whiteness and distance from blackness served the interest of a white supremacist civilizing project for indigenous peoples in the settler society conditioned by racial slavery. Multiple racial projects were at play in the context of a single institution.

This complicated story from Carlisle harkens to a history of antiblackness and schooling among the Five Tribes. This was Walton-Raji's reason for sharing. She declared that the antiblack policies of the Five Tribes, as it pertained to slavery and later segregation, "would spill over into educational policy" among these nations throughout the nineteenth century, before and after black emancipation.

Walton-Raji stressed that antiblackness was a persistent force in the educational lives of African-descended people among native tribes; however, the stories she shared, along with scholarship by historians such as Tiya Miles and Alaina Roberts, also clarify how such antagonisms in black and native relations were structured by a larger force of white supremacy in the United States. Such realities of racial domination took on distinct form in the context of indigenous nations—where, similar to the United States as a whole, whiteness, indigeneity, and blackness were fundamentally relational, even when dealing with intimate histories of direct interaction between native and black people. For even at moments when "the conflict seemed bilateral, it was in fact triangular, holding in tension Indian experience, black experience, and an invisible, structuring white presence."[6] This is to say, the realities of antiblackness in nineteenth-century education among the Five Tribes was always intimately connected to the schooling apparatus of the United States. Just as the Afro-native girl was denied enrollment at a school for native students founded by a white American military general, the schooling systems developed among the Five Tribes were also directly influenced by white missionaries, education reformers, and US government officials.

Running against this current of antiblackness in education policy among native nations was a countervailing tradition—the story of black people's struggle for citizenship and freedom through education among the Five Tribes. Though this history of black educational resistance is similar to narratives in the broader United States, the distinct political context of native sovereignty in the nineteenth century requires nuance and specificity when telling the story. Like Walton-Raji, many of the freedmen among the tribes understood themselves to be members of the nations in which they were enslaved and freed—not the United States. Furthermore, black men and women among the Five Tribes were negotiating power not only with leaders in native nations, but also officials representing the US settler state. This is a lesson I learned from Walton-Raji, but also from a flowering of scholarship on this critically important subject.[7] Most importantly, it is a lesson I have learned from the voices and actions of Indian freedmen in the archival record.

AN AFRO-NATIVE SCHOOL STORY: TULLAHASSEE MISSION AND THE FAMILIES OF PHILIP AND ELZORA (FULSOM) LEWIS

"Education was a major concern" for the Indian freedmen and their ancestors, as Angela Walton-Raji explained, "and a few schools were established to provide basic education" following the Civil War.[8] Tullahassee Mission School, situated in the Creek nation, eventually became one of those "few schools." The story of this institution's founding, and the histories of the people connected to it, provide windows into the story of black education in Indian Territory.

Philip Lewis was an educator at the Tullahassee Mission School in the late 1880s when he met, and eventually married, Elzora Fulsom. He was an assistant teacher at the time and later served as the school's superintendent. However, at the time of Tullahassee's founding in 1847, black students like Philip and Elzora Lewis would have been excluded from enrolling. The Creek established Tullahassee as a national school at a time when this tribe—along with the other slaveholding tribes—discouraged, by law or custom, education for black people out of fear that it would stoke the flames of abolition. After Reconstruction, the Creek council repurposed the school to meet the demands of Creek freedmen who organized for more educational opportunities.

Tullahassee's evolution, as well as Philip's and Elzora's family histories, reveal the shifting terrain of black education in Indian Territory over the course of the nineteenth century. The intertwined fate of this family and of Tullahassee is one I will trace throughout Part III of *American Grammar*, because their particular story helps ground important lessons about the shifting racial politics within the Five Tribes as well as the role that education—institutions, policies, and ideology—played in the process. However, the following chapters are not just about the history of a single family or that of an individual school. The narrative will pan out from this story at key moments to analyze details about black and native relations, relations that were also structured by the intrusive presence of whiteness as a settler-colonial force. This context outlines the social forces that conditioned the experiences of Philip's and Elzora's families, and the institutional history of Tullahassee. For instance, these stories require context about the complex history of slavery and captivity among the Five Tribes. For slavery in Indian country was shaped by internal dynamics among the tribes, particularly indigenous conceptions of captivity, but it was also significantly shaped by the external forces of US civilization policies through the nineteenth century and the distinct iteration of racialized captivity modeled by European settlers. Together, this information helps clarify the role race and schooling played in the nation-building project of the Five Tribes, how they used education as a means of negotiating settler-colonial constraints, and likewise, how the people they enslaved also engaged in a power struggle through education, to challenge a social order within Indian Territory built on black subjection. This social order formed internally, within the Five Tribes, but it was also conditioned by the schooling apparatus of the United States. Yet, even as the story delves into the detail of the social context, I will always return to the intimacy of this family's history and to the particular narrative of Tullahassee, because they allow for a thicker description of the general story. Together they reveal a story of how education functioned as a tool of racial domination, but they also shed light on a persistent quest for self-determination, self-knowledge, and human flourishing through educational struggle.

Husband and wife Philip and Elzora Lewis were Afro-native. Both descended from families who were enslaved within the Creek nation, though Elzora's father was a Choctaw freedman. When sitting to be interviewed in 1937, as part of the United States' Works Progress Administration's Indian-Pioneers Program, the couple entered their family histories into the archival record, providing stories that stretched back to the pre-removal Creek nation. Philip and Elzora were born during the era of Reconstruction, 1869 and 1871, respectively. Yet as is true of everyone born at every time, they were made of histories and stories that preceded their birth—formed through narratives about, and passed on by, their predecessors.[9] All the family members recalled by Philip Lewis, who preceded him in birth, were enslaved by Creek masters. Elzora's family lineage was more diverse. She described free Afro-Creek women, like her mother Elizabeth Scott Fulsom and maternal grandmother, Susie Scott, as well as nonblack Creek men. Elzora's father, Louis Fulsom, had been enslaved in the Choctaw nation before the Civil War, demonstrating the intertribal experiences of some black people living among the Five Tribes. Taken together, Philip's and Elzora's lineages include native people and free and enslaved black people, as well as racial and tribal intermarriage.[10]

Before meeting one another, Philip and Elzora enrolled in freedman schools. Such institutions resulted from years of activism among the freedmen of the Five Tribes who demanded educational facilities that paralleled those offered members of the Creek nation—that is, members of the Creek nation who were not known to be or visibly appearing to be of African descent. In the Creek nation, elites pursued efforts "to consolidate wealth and power and impose a form of racial nationalism," explained historian David Chang. So, the aforementioned advocacy by the freedmen for education took place against efforts by elites within the Five Tribes to perpetuate antiblack domination following emancipation. Also writing about the Creek, Rowan Steineker emphasized that a primary mechanism for expressing and constructing this racial nationalism was through the unequal opportunity for freedmen's participation in the Creek school system. After the Civil War, leaders within the Creek nation "incorporated freedmen schools into its new, national public school system and provided funding for them out of the national fund, but did so gradually, reflecting the tenuous position of former slaves." The Creek operated twenty-four national schools in 1870, none of which admitted freedmen. Due to political organizing of the freedmen, the nation operated five segregated schools for black people by 1874. Yet these students were still denied enrollment at boarding schools like Tullahassee, which were understood as institutions offering advanced educational training.[11]

The aforementioned story of Afro-native students being sent home from Carlisle reflected this much longer history of antiblack exclusion within the racial project of native education as a direct extension of the schooling apparatus of the United States. Such dynamics were present even among the Creek nation, a tribe generally understood to be more lenient in its treatment of freedmen. Such claims of leniency, however, can be misleading. For instance, there were no Creek laws on the books establishing de jure segregation. This meant that the Creek national schools barred black students from enrolling based on social custom or unspoken laws. Yet other nations among the Five Tribes adopted more formal measures. For instance, "Immediately after emancipation, Choctaw and Chickasaw leadership enacted legal codes designed to replicate the dehumanization and coercion of slavery."[12] The legacy of slavery in Indian Territory continued to shape the experiences of freedmen and their descendants, both because of the laws enacted by the tribes as well as the antiblack sentiments that carried over from a period when blackness was deemed synonymous with slaveness, which was also an expression of kinlessness. People like Elzora and Philip, though born during Reconstruction, continued to be close to slavery—their proximity was constituted by stories they inherited from their families that taught them lessons about their heritage as Afro-native people. In addition, their precarious status as citizens within tribes pointed to this recent history.

Philip and Elzora met during a period of intense political advocacy among freedmen within Indian Territory, but their family histories reflect a decades-old tradition of black people negotiating racial hierarchies within the nations. Sitting for his interview in 1937, Philip recalled the story of King and Rachel Kernel, the parents of his paternal grandmother, Rachel Lewis. Philip's great-grandparents were born enslaved in the late eighteenth century and died in the last decades of the nineteenth century, with King passing in 1873 and Rachel in 1885. Stories shared by and about Philip's formerly enslaved elders made a lasting impression on the young man, who, notably, had only known the world after slavery was abolished. One of the most memorable narratives was of Rachel Kernel describing how she and her husband met. The story begins on the auction block.

Rachel was brought to a slave market with other enslaved people to be sold. As she stood on the platform, anxious about her unknown fate, Rachel noticed "a very large young fellow in the crowd who seemed to never be looking at anyone except [her]." The young man was King, who was enslaved by a Creek man named Sookey Kernel. King made his way closer to the platform, and when a moment presented itself, he asked Rachel, "If I persuade my master to buy you, will you marry me?" By Rachel's account, it was the attraction she felt for the young man that compelled her to say yes. This we might appreciate, even as the very notion of "choice" in this matter is fraught, as it was bound by the material (and psychic) realities of human captivity.[13]

Insisting on self-advocacy and trying to make a good life, despite his condition, King moved hurriedly through the crowd, looking for the Creek man who claimed ownership over his life. He hoped to convince him to purchase Rachel, the woman he hoped to marry. As it was in slavery across the United States, marriage between an enslaved man and woman was formed by more than the flesh of two people; for indeed, the third flesh of the white enslaver was always present—even if visible sometimes and invisible at other moments. In such an arrangement, people who were property never possessed true autonomy over their bodies. The threat of its disruptions—through the selling of husband or wife, as well as other intrusive violations—always loomed about, threatening the permanence of such unions.[14]

King returned with his enslaver, and Rachel recalled what happened next as follows: "They approached my master, and shortly I was the property of a new master, who was the owner of the man to whom I had given the answer 'yes,' King Kernel. Our Master took King and I to his place and we were married immediately thereafter. Though in slavery, we were happy." Like enslaved black people elsewhere in the Americas, those held captive within native nations attempted to advocate for themselves and build meaningful lives. They continued, as best they could, to pursue love and companionship. Philip learned this story from his great-grandmother, Rachel, in her final season of life. Both she and her husband relayed such stories to their great-grandson, Philip, as they lived out their final years on the other side of slavery in the Creek nation.[15]

SLAVERY AND RELATIONAL FORMATIONS OF RACE AMONG THE FIVE TRIBES

Rachel and King were enslaved in the Creek nation but their story is connected to a broader history of slavery among the Creek, Cherokee, Choctaw, Chickasaw, and Seminole tribes. While one cannot conflate experiences between the Five Tribes, and must use specificity between them when possible, social and political developments within the individual nations were deeply influenced by what happened among them collectively. Tribal leaders shared strategies across national boundaries. For instance, when the Creek Council faced increasing pressure to leave their homelands in the 1820s, they consulted with leaders in the Cherokee nation about strategies for resisting. The Creek leaders decided to "follow the pattern of the Cherokees," insisting that they refused to sell "one foot of our land." Their public statement spelled out a refusal to any further land cessions and simultaneously proclaimed an "increase in the arts of agriculture and civilization" among the tribe.[16] Embracing lifestyle shifts, including settler schooling, was an integral part of the Five "Civilized" Tribes' strategy for thwarting further encroachment by white settlers. Creek leaders, like their Cherokee peers, hoped that demonstrating their adoption of Western practices would rebut settler arguments for native removal. Settlers often used native people's supposed lack of "civilization" as a reason for their displacement, with arguments swinging between declarations that native people had no legitimate claim to their land and those insisting that native people needed to be protected from the vices of civilized society. To be clear, such arguments were never genuine motivations so much as they were justifications for the land grabs of settlers. However, native leaders understood that public opinion was important, and they hoped to forestall or defeat removal by dismantling benevolent-sounding rhetoric and asserting a posture of civilization legible to US settlers, which included expressions of antiblackness.

Slavery in Indian country deviated from slavery in the United States, in practice and in the ideology underpinning captivity among the tribes. To appreciate the distinctions requires reckoning with the context of human captivity among the Five Tribes that preceded contact between indigenous peoples and European colonizers. As historian Christina Snyder explains, "slavery was already present" in indigenous American societies "when the first Europeans and Africans arrived in the sixteenth century." However, she also explains that these earlier forms of native bondage and captive-taking were not racial or hereditary; the status of a captive was not passed down from one generation to the next. It was in the late eighteenth century that slavery and race became intertwined among the Southern native tribes, and while the face of slavery came to take on a distinct racial character, as introduced through white settlers, the very idea of captivity continued to carry

FAMILY TREE OF PHILIP AND ELZORA LEWIS

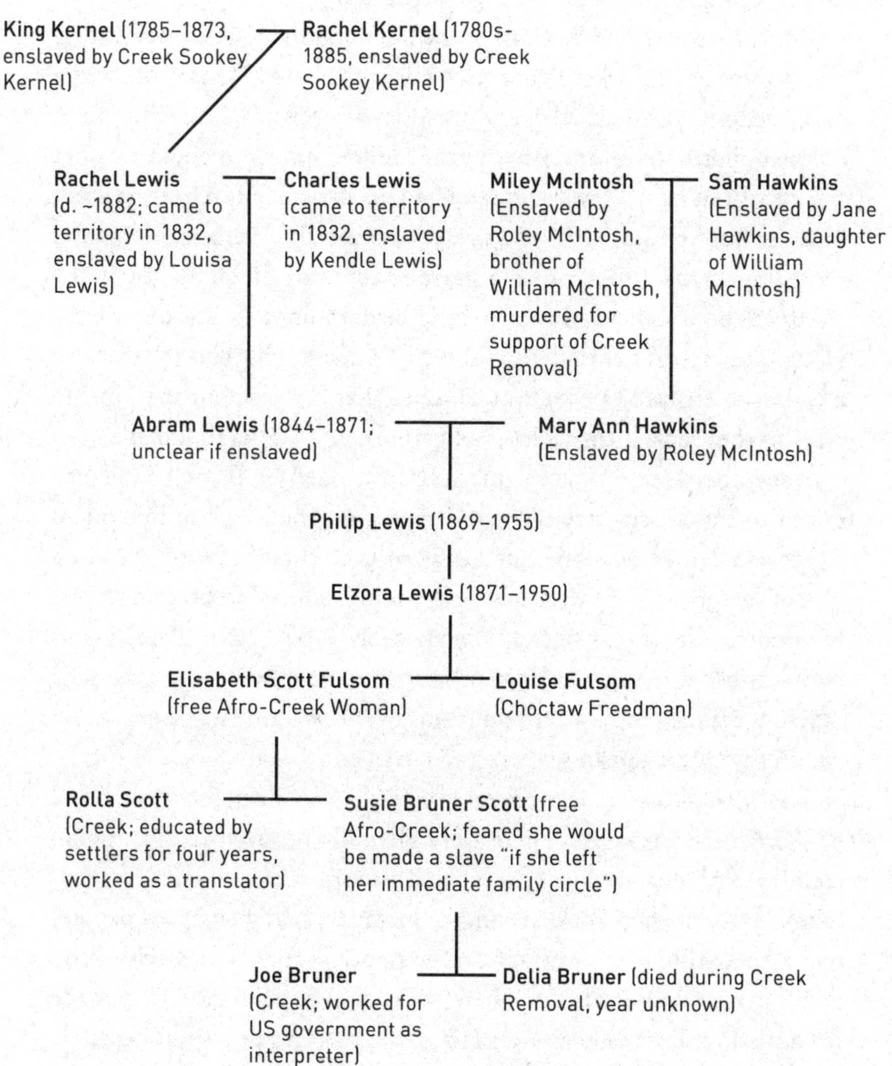

distinct meaning among native nations, pulling from its earlier meanings, prior to the late eighteenth century. Such meaning and values associated with captivity were more than a slight deviation from slavery among European settlers, ideologically speaking.[17]

Contrary to modern notions of the liberal individual subject, indigenous ways of being were not framed by the Western binary of slavery and freedom. While slavery and freedom are generally understood to be the opposite of one another in the United States, freedom was not the antithesis of slavery among indigenous people. For native nations, kinship was the opposite of slavery. Membership in a clan was the most important affiliation in a person's life, not individuality or the ability to be unbounded to anything beyond oneself and one's individual desires. In contradistinction to a person who had relations to a clan, the enslaved person, or captive, "had no place in the kinship system; they lacked the rights, obligations, and status that came with clan membership."[18] The stigmatization carried by black people enslaved in Indian country did not derive from their lack of individual rights and denied personhood; it derived from their being marked by a lack of relations. They were a kinless people reduced to objects owned by others. This status became inextricably linked with blackness as native tribes ceased to enslave other native people, having gradually developed a pan-Indian consciousness over the centuries of persistent conflict with European settlers and enslaved African people.[19]

The Five Tribes' enslavement practices also differed from those of the American South. There were virtually no overseers in Indian country, and enslaved people also had more opportunities for economic gain. In the Creek nation, for instance, many enslaved peoples operated without an overseer and supported themselves with food and clothing by tending to their own "squaw patches." This made for a distinct experience of enslavement, inviting one to understand that captivity existed on a "continuum" for much of native American history, to borrow from historian Kendra Field. What's more, prior to emancipation, African-descended Creeks—enslaved and free—also served as cultural brokers, ministers, warriors, interpreters, and negotiators as the Creek contended with tribal divisions, native removal, and the Civil War. Then, following emancipation and bolstered by the promise of citizenship and an equal share of tribal funds, black Creeks established themselves as subsistence farmers, as well as traders, merchants, and cattle ranchers, in Creek country.[20]

There was variation between slavery among the Five Tribes and the American South, and there was also variation across the tribes themselves. For instance, "while the Seminoles legally owned slaves, they treated them differently from the other Indian nations. . . . People of African descent owned by Seminoles lived apart from their owners and were able to cultivate their own agriculture and possess their own livestock." Therefore, while black codes restricting the movement of the enslaved may have been feasible among other native nations, and in the American South, this was not the case among the Seminoles.[21] While such distinctions existed, especially when thinking about black and native relations before the nineteenth century, the differences grew noticeably narrower. With the encroachments of white settlers, indigenous elites began to more closely mimic white logics for captivity, and the tribes worked to assert a posture of civilization defined over and against black people. Despite early deviations in slavery between the Five Tribes and white American settlers, nineteenth-century US civilization policies fundamentally reshaped notions of captivity among the Southern tribes.

With a consolidating pan-Indian identity in response to settler aggression, as well as increased civilization policies imposed on native nations—including a commitment to private property and an agriculturally based economy—antiblackness became grafted on to practices of enslavement. In this way, black chattel slavery became formalized among the Five Tribes. Writing carefully about such transformation, Snyder explains, "By the early nineteenth century, nearly all captives were black, and in many ways, bondage in Indian country mirrored the slavery practiced by their white Southern neighbors. But the transformation was not complete, nor did it happen overnight. If escalating racism encouraged Indians to distance themselves from those of African descent, kin ties pulled many back. Indian societies, and even individuals, maintained contradictory attitudes about race." While native nations "grafted ideas about race onto their captivity practices . . . the process was slow and uneven, leaving those of African descent in an ambiguous position."[22]

This ambiguity of kinship and tribal status reflects the lived experiences of Philip and Elzora Lewis, as well as their ancestors. Their families had both indigenous and enslaved lineage, as the two were not exclusive. As historians have observed, "Many Creek freedpeople had been both slaves and relatives of their Indian slaveowners."[23] Elzora's grandmother helps illustrate the ambiguous status of Afro-native people among the Five Tribes. Susie Bruner Scott was "a free Negro of mixed Indian blood," according to Elzora. As a young woman during the era of Creek removal, Susie resisted going west with her Creek husband Rolla Scott. According to the story passed on to Elzora, her grandmother Susie "feared being made a slave if she left her immediate family circle." Nevertheless, Susie eventually relocated with her Creek father, Joe Bruner, and mother, Delia Bruner. Susie's fear of leaving without close kin underscores the importance of kinship ties among the tribes, especially as a form of protection against captivity for Afro-native people prior to emancipation. Susie's freedom hinged not only on race, but also on her ties to others, particularly her Creek father.[24]

New grammars of race reconfigured old notions of captivity in Indian country by the nineteenth century. Such rules governing and stratifying the social world would also influence education policies and practices among the Five Tribes. In the early 1800s, native nations had yet to outline any formalized education system, whether it be for black or nonblack children within the nations. There were certainly some mission schools that received verbal and occasional financial support from native leadership, but education largely took place in the context of families, doubling down on the emphasis of kinship. During this era, black people living among the tribes pursued education as a means of liberation, and just as they faced violent repression when pursuing education among white Americans, black people would also experience violence and repression from native people. As the ideas about race and relationality continued to shift, black pursuits of education threatened their status as property, and it ran the risk of threatening the civilizationist posturing of the tribes. In other instances, native leaders resisted black education—and all settler schooling—because it threatened traditional native customs that some factions sought to preserve. Indeed, there were competing logics at the heart of this racial conflict, and they moved in many directions.

EARLY DEVELOPMENTS IN BLACK EDUCATION AMONG THE FIVE TRIBES

Black people, enslaved and free, living among the Five Tribes pursued education, and literacy in particular, as a matter of social and intellectual advancement and to affirm their humanity. In 1822, Jedidiah Morse, having been tasked by the US Department of War with observing and reporting on activities among native tribes living along the US border, gave the following account of black people he encountered within the Seminole nation: "The negroes, who dwell among these [Seminole] people, as their slaves, are intelligent, speak the English language . . . and are much pleased with the proposal of having their children taught to read; because, as they believe, it will increase their influence and their comforts."[25]

Religious instruction at mission schools became one source of educational opportunity for black people among native tribes. Some learned to read through Sunday school instruction and access to written texts in the form of Bibles and hymns. Representatives at Brainerd Mission School, for instance, reported the following of black students at their Sunday school in 1818: "A man of thirty years, who only knew the alphabet when the school commenced, can now read a chapter, or a psalm, very decently. A boy of fifteen, who did not know a single letter, can now read very well in the Testament. Several others have begun to read the Bible. The greater part come six miles, or more, to meeting; some fifteen or twenty on foot; and none less than two miles and a half." Even more extraordinary is the case of an unnamed black man who seems to have been employed as a Sunday school teacher at Brainerd in 1818; missionaries reported he "promises great usefulness to his coloured brethren. His heart is fixed & much engaged to instruct them all he can."[26]

It was reported that one Cherokee student who applied for admission to Brainerd was "found able to spell correctly words of 4 & 5 letters." The missionaries took care to note that the young boy had "been taught solely by black people who had received their instruction in our Sunday-school." Readers may recall Brainerd was established with funding from the War Department in 1817 to educate native students in hopes of minimizing the threat of more Indian Wars in the future, and it was built on recently seized Cherokee lands on the frontier. Given Brainerd's proximity to the United States, it is likely that enslaved people from both the Cherokee nation and the US came to the mission's Sunday school classes for educational instruction. Black people reportedly outnumbered native worshippers at some missions, such as Bethel Mission, situated in the Creek nation. And while it does not seem to have been common practice, some black people attempted to enroll at mission schools for education beyond Sunday school lessons. This is implied in the minutes from an 1820 meeting between Brainerd missionaries and representatives from the Moody Hall of Taloney Mission: "Resolved that it be left to the discretion of the teachers at the local schools whether they admit black children into their schools or not."[27]

While permitting black student enrollment at mission schools was still an open question by the 1820s, there seemed to be little reservation about using enslaved black labor at these institutions. Missionaries at Brainerd and other schools supported by the American Board of Commissioners for Foreign Missions (ABCFM) used enslaved people hired out by their native masters to help build the structures and carry out day-to-day operations. The ABCFM's Prudential Committee, for instance, considered the practice of hiring enslaved labor in 1825, responding to the inquiry of missionaries to the Choctaw nation. The committee concluded they "do not see cause to prohibit the practice; but, on the contrary, they are of the opinion that it may be expedient, in some circumstances, to employ [*sic*] persons who sustain this relation, by contract with their masters and with their own consent; it being understood, that all the members of the mission family at each station should feel the obligation of treating the persons thus hired with kindness, and laboring to promote their spiritual good."[28]

Such references to the use of enslaved black labor were not uncommon in the minutes of missionaries. As with the use of enslaved labor in the building of white American education, such practices were likely more common in the history of native schooling than detectable in the historical record. Black enslaved labor was an integral part of building the United States, fiscally and physically, and white missionaries working in Indian country brought many of the same taken-for-granted practices of nation-building with them as they engaged in the process of building settler schooling among native tribes. Nonetheless, passing references such as "we endeavor to hire a black girl," as found in the records of Brainerd in 1822, can also be found in the records of many missions. Later this same year, administrators at Brainerd sent a missionary to Washington, DC, to pick up an enslaved couple whose owner, a Mr. Rawlings, agreed to let them work at the mission in exchange for their eventual emancipation. The records of Brainerd are littered with references to "hired" labor, which were more often than not references to enslaved people.[29]

Rev. Cyrus Kingsbury, who founded Brainerd with funding from the federal government in 1817, defended the hiring of slaves at missions and boarding schools in 1848. He argued that the labor of enslaved people was crucial to the missionary project. Kingsbury declared:

> *In the year 1818, at the commencement of this mission, African slavery was in existence in this nation. The early missionaries were called to make it a subject of inquiry and prayer. There was no avoiding all contact with it. The large boarding school establishments, and other multiplied and constant labors, in a hot and sickly climate, then as well as now, made the employment of considerable slave labor indispensable. . . . We have made expensive efforts to hire free people, and again we have failed. In our situation we need help that can be relied on. And thus it will be while we remain here as missionaries. Good free help for us, in our situation, is very rare in this land.*[30]

Kingsbury's justification for relying on slave labor privileged the education of native students over the freedom of black people, and also implied that black people were better suited for "constant labors, in a hot and sickly climate." The development of white-led settler schooling among the Five Tribes was indispensable from slavery and the racial ideology that conditioned the peculiar institution.

As Western education became more engrained among the Five Tribes, the politics of race continued to evolve, and schooling was a key site of such racial formation. The complicated past of captivity and loosely defined boundaries of racial difference caused tension as the Five Tribes continued to undergo transformation in response to US civilization policies, where the tribes incorporated race as a central category of identity. This past was evident in the phenotypical diversity among the tribes by the early 1800s. A white woman named Jane Hill observed this while teaching at a mission school in the Creek nation. Speaking of a Creek student named Mary Ann Bettis, Jane recalled that the young girl's "mother is the daughter of a black woman her grandfather was half white & half indian. Mary Ann's father was white & she is the fairest female I have seen in this nation." Given this observation, Jane was shocked to meet Mary Ann's family because they were all noticeably of a darker hue. She explained, "nearly all of them [are] extremely dark people & her mother has some children who have black fathers."[31]

Jane made these observations in a letter to the secretary of war in May 1828, where she requested permission for Mary Ann Bettis to remain at the Asbury Mission rather than go west with her family. Historian Tiya Miles argues that this request, and Bettis's strong desire to stay at the mission, were likely a response to a recent attack on a mission at Withington Station, motivated by the presence of black people worshipping and studying there. Perhaps Bettis and Hill understood that an Afro-Creek Christian convert, especially a female one, might face violence in Creek country, given that a black girl was sexually violated during the attack at Withington Station. Therefore, the teacher advocated for the student to remain in present-day Alabama.[32]

Creek leaders had long been antagonistic toward the school at Withington Station run by Baptist settlers Lee and Susannah Compere. They expressed disapproval of what they perceived to be the racial agenda of the school curriculum, particularly the role of student labor in the educational program. In 1826, Lee Compere reported losing students to a neighboring Methodist mission school that did not include manual labor in their curriculum. Compere assessed, "The very idea of work always frightens the people, and whenever they think of it in connexion [*sic*] with our school system, they always associate with it the idea of slavery."[33] Compere's statement echoes similar accounts by white settlers regarding race, education, and labor among indigenous nations. In a 1823 book recounting travel among the Five Tribes, Adam Hodgson recounted, "One of the chiefs [whose son was admitted to Brainerd] offered to find a slave who should work all day, if the missionaries would excuse his son from agricultural labour between school-hours. . . ."[34] Similarly, Rev. William Capers, founder of Asbury Mission in old Creek country, insisted that Creeks were suspicious of manual labor schools because they believed such an educational program was "a suspicious contrivance to prepare [their children] for enslavement."[35] Importantly, some white school leaders used such views among native peoples to inform disciplinary tactics. For instance, Rev. Wheelock, founder of Dartmouth College, occasionally forced native students at his mission school in Hanover, New Hampshire, to work alongside the enslaved black people he owned as an effort to cure their "bad habits."[36]

While Creek leaders may have resisted attendance at Withington Station because of their growing discomfort with the role of manual labor in the curriculum, they also had concerns about the presence of black worshippers at the mission. As in the United States, black people living among the tribes embraced Christianity, yet "many Indians saw it as a form of imperialism or as a tool of insurrection for their slaves." Therefore Creek leaders attempted to bar black people from attending worship or receiving education at Withington Station at several points. The culmination of this backlash occurred in a violent conflict in 1828.

In May 1828, about two dozen Creek men burst into Withington Station as the Comperes worshipped with a group of Afro-Creeks. The men ransacked the building "under the pretense of searching for the black people." When they gathered the black worshippers, the Creek mob "tied them with cords and belts" and eventually "fastened them to a post in the yard, where they beat them unmercifully."[37] This act of antiblack educational and religious suppression was also gendered in very distinct ways. For one, the Creek mob was reportedly composed of all men. Furthermore, when the mob discovered a twelve-year-old girl among the worshippers, they forced her to witness the beatings of her fellow black converts before sexually assaulting the young girl at the same whipping post. The mob "led her like the rest to the fatal post, turned up her clothes and tied them fast around her neck." According to the account, the men assaulted her with "licentious examinations."[38]

The status of black people in Indian country was precarious, particularly as the aggression of US civilization policies intermingled with the internal social and cultural politics of the Five Tribes. Black people existed between nations, often in a form of statelessness. At Withington Station, violence was done against black people as representatives (objects even) of the settler state, though these black people were assumedly owned by Creek enslavers. Kinlessness meant powerlessness. As historian Rowan Steineker has argued, violent acts against black learning within the Creek nation, in this instance, functioned as an expression of Creek nationhood and kinship, as resistance against the settler state and the intrusion of civilizationist policies through education and religion more broadly, even as this act of retribution was enacted upon the bodies of Afro-native worshippers.[39] The conflict here was not bilateral. It was indeed triangular. This violent conflict at Withington Station, between black worshippers and Creek leaders, was facilitated by "an invisible, structuring white presence."[40]

Susannah Compere mourned the loss of religious education for the black converts after the 1828 attack. She said, "The case of our colored friends deserves compassion. Anxious to enjoy gospel privileges, their spirits are much depressed at the idea of our leaving them. They would rather submit to any thing than lose the word of God. Pray for these few Ethiopian brethren and sisters, that the Holy Spirit, the Comforter, may dwell with them to establish their minds and direct them in the midst of much darkness." Yet, while religious worship may have been important for the black converts, they were surely mourning the loss of educational opportunity presented at the mission as well.[41]

The attack at Withington Station was believed to be ordered by Opothleyahola, a traditionalist Creek leader, whose story helps one further appreciate the complexity of racial politics among the Five Tribes. As we will see in a later chapter, Opothleyahola would become a leader of an anti-Confederate band of Creek and Cherokee people who sought to escape behind Union lines during the Civil War. In this later instance, Opothleyahola and the "Loyal Indians" welcomed black people and freed any enslaved people who joined them. Opothleyahola's role in both events—the antiblack attack on Withington Mission in 1828 and the liberatory fight of the Loyal Indians in 1861—at first glance seems puzzling; however, it actually reflects Opothleyahola's shifting methods for conserving Creek culture. He was a leader making decisions based on what he believed would conserve the authentic character of the Creek nation. In 1828 he believed black education to be a threat to the Creek nation's way of life. In 1861 he was concerned about the Confederate-aligned Creek elite. Yet irrespective of his motivations from one period to another, the reality is that black people's precarity was based on their position in the political imagination of Opothleyahola, just as their vulnerability was also tied to their shifting position in the minds of other Creek leaders.[42]

Black people in Indian country were between a rock and a hard place. Opothleyahola's targeting of black students emphasizes this point. In the case of Withington Station, black education threatened the expansion of chattel slavery, which posed major concerns for Western-leaning Creek elites. At the same time, traditionalists saw black education as a threat to traditional Creek ways of life—because of the teachings and values embedded in such education. Therefore, on both sides of the continuum among Creek leaders, anxieties about tribal futurity manifested through violent repression of black people's learning as well as violent assaults on their bodies.

The ancestors of Philip and Elzora Lewis navigated this complicated racial landscape among the Five Tribes. Some were enslaved, others free; some were of mixed-race heritage, and others were the product of intertribal unions. Their family histories reflect the ever-evolving racial politics among the Five Tribes, and certainly some of the distinctions that existed across the tribes. For instance, many of Philip and Elzora's ancestors were likely considered *Estelvste*, "the Creek word invoked to refer to African-descended people of the Creek nation." Estelvste shared cultural practices—language, food, worldviews—and kinship ties with the Creeks. By the early nineteenth century, this category became increasingly associated with the shifting position of African-descended people among the nation, as a portion of the Southeastern tribes adopted agricultural practices of Southern plantations and increasingly associated Afro-Creek people nearly exclusively with slave labor and a people to be exploited for the wealth accumulation of elite Creek families.[43] These shifts in the political-economic arrangements of native societies as it pertained to race had direct implications for all institutions situated in this social context.

While it is unclear how the black ancestors of Philip and Elzora interacted with education, they were living during a time when Creek leaders—like others among the Five Tribes—explored the possibilities of building a national education system to fend off increasing encroachment of white settlers, as a tactic of resistance. These ancestors would have likely been privy to such conversations, as enslaved people were usually owned by the most elite among the tribes—indeed, the same people with the most at stake in determining the educational policies of their nations.

•••

The Five Tribes offer a very specific case of native-black relations, and it is an illuminating case for understanding the relational dynamics of race in education. However, it is important to emphasize that such histories cannot, and should not, be read onto all indigenous histories. Black people's level of freedom varied by nation, even among the Five

Tribes. Thus, accounting for tribal specificity and the liminal nature of the frontier is key. This is evident in the story of James Stewart, a black preacher who was adopted into the Wyandot tribe.

Born free in Virginia around the turn of the nineteenth century, Stewart eventually became a Methodist minister and set out to preach to native people. He arrived in Wyandot territory (present-day Ohio) in 1816. Unattached to any particular missionary group, Stewart was seemingly motivated by genuine religious commitments. The preacher would experience antiblack aggression by both white and native peoples in his journey as a minister. It was reported that Stewart had once been captured by slave-catchers in 1817 when traveling to visit his family; and an 1827 tract about the minister's work claimed Chief Two Logs of the Wyandot tribe "would sometimes tell the people, it was really derogatory to their character, to have it said, *that they had a Negro for their preacher*, as that race of people was always considered inferior to Indians." Nevertheless, it appears the Wyandot people adopted Stewart as a brother, even raising money to support him. In 1820, Stewart joined forces with a white minister of the Methodist Church and established a mission school among the Wyandot people with support from the Civilization Fund Act established by the US Congress just a year before.[44]

I share Stewart's experience because it provides a useful counterpoint—a narrative that is in many ways set apart from black educational narratives among the Five Tribes. Stewart's story calls attention to the diversity and shifting racial politics between black and native peoples in the early decades of the nineteenth century. The Wyandot people's varied treatment of Stewart illustrates that even as antiblack ideas reached most native peoples, adoption of settler-style racial hierarchies varied by tribes and were unsettled during the first decades of the nineteenth century. A remarkable part of this story—perhaps tragic, even—is the fact that Stewart, a black man, laid the groundwork for the first federally funded settler school in Wyandot territory. This layered reading of race, power, and education reveals the relations between the two subjugated groups within the founding racial triad to be in flux—constantly evolving, and perpetually unstable. In this instance, Stewart's role as a minister and school founder—irrespective of intentions—became part and parcel of a much larger colonial project whereby settler schooling was imposed on native people in service of the broader mission of the American Indian Wars. Indeed, the funding for Stewart's school came from the Civilization Fund Act, established by Congress in 1819, and administered by the Department of War. Stewart's story also reveals how native people could understand black people as both oppressed—by white settler hierarchies (enacted by white and nonwhite people)—and simultaneously a threat to native sovereignty—by aligning with key expressions of settler colonialism, such as the mission school.

Black education in Indian country was a shifting tale of schooling and power. It moved on a sliding scale conditioned by complex interactions between slavery and settler colonialism. When assessing such interactions between black and native people, one must always understand that even when such interactions seem to be bilateral, this is never the case. The founding racial triad at the heart of the American social order was always in play. The tensions between black and native experiences in education, in and across tribes, were always structured by a white presence. Even when invisible, whiteness was present in the material realities of native land dispossession and the violent realities of chattel slavery, overlapping systems of racial domination that conditioned black and native relations in these early decades of United States history. The narratives presented in this opening chapter provide a window into the shifting dynamics of race in Indian country during the first decades of the nineteenth century, as formal education systems began developing among the Five Tribes. As the next chapters will demonstrate, these dynamics continued to evolve as the period of Indian Removal took place, thus altering the world of these nations and the people they claimed as their property.

10

BLACK EDUCATION IN THE POST-REMOVAL CHAOS OF INDIAN TERRITORY

The period of Indian Removal was devastating for indigenous tribes. Several nations were forced to abandon their homelands in the southern region for newly allotted territory out west. Removal was also particularly harsh for black people enslaved by tribes being forced to relocate. According to historical estimates, more than three thousand black people, mostly enslaved, lived among the Five Tribes at the time of the Indian Removal Act of 1830, though their stories are often overlooked in recollections of the Trail of Tears.[1] Amid this chaos, the function of education as a racial project intensified. Pan-Indian identities solidified among the tribes, and these nations turned to education as an essential tool for rebuilding in the new territory. Schooling was both a means of asserting civilization among the tribes and a key social institution that stratified native societies along various axes within the matrix of domination: between tribal elites and non-elites, "civilized" and "uncivilized," black and nonblack, enslaved and free. A key development in this process would be the formalization of anti-literacy laws within tribal constitutions—similar to antiblack laws criminalizing black education in the US South—and in other instances, where such laws were not established, the suppression of black education intensified through social customs among the tribes. The grammars of race in Indian country were shifting, so too was the functionality of schooling within the nations, and the chaos of Indian Removal, against the backdrop of chattel slavery, made for very distinct experiences among black people as they sought out education and a life beyond bondage and condemnation.

The Indian Removal Act of 1830, largely constructed by the ruthless longtime removal advocate President Andrew Jackson, facilitated the process of conceptualizing and executing removal treaties with the Southern tribes, which could (and did) include the use of military force. Through this process, the American government forced the Five Tribes, and several others, to move into territories occupied by western indigenous nations, making for a chaotic experience on multiple levels. In the years preceding removal, most of the Five Tribes split into factions of traditionalists who believed in resisting forced removal to the bitter end and the often younger, US-educated faction who believed relocation was inevitable and favored a negotiated surrender. The latter groups in the Cherokee, Choctaw, and Creek nations became known as the "Treaty Party" because their leaders ultimately signed treaties agreeing to remove west—and such agreements took place, of course, under threat of US violence. These factions, intentionally aggravated by US agents, would continue to shape native politics long after forced migration. What's more, removal demanded that entire nations of people uproot themselves and trek across the country, leaving behind lands their people had always known to be home, while simultaneously placing these vulnerable populations in direct conflict with other indigenous tribes who were being displaced by this process of native resettlement.[2] Such removal policies had a kind of domino effect, essentially forcing indigenous nations struggling for their own survival to participate in the very process of native displacement and removal they sought to refuse. In such a context, native displacement begets more native displacement, compounding the violent impact of the settler-colonial procedure.

The ancestors of Philip and Elzora Lewis were among the enslaved black people forced to resettle with native Americans who claimed them as property. Philip's paternal grandparents, Rachel and Charles Lewis, traveled the Trail of Tears to the new Creek territory in present-day Oklahoma. Rachel was the daughter of the enslaved couple Rachel and King Kernel, who appeared in the previous chapter for their unconventional union, having met at the slave auction where King urged his Creek master to purchase Rachel, in hopes of marrying her.[3] As slaves of prominent Creek planter Kendle Lewis, Rachel and Charles were part of the first group of Creeks to settle the land promised them in exchange for leaving their original lands in the Southeast.

The Creek fought removal for decades. They tried to convince a land-hungry US empire to abandon their ambitions to seize the land of the Five Tribes, often using civilization politics to do so. The seizure of native land was central to the settler future of the United States, especially in the Southeast: The plantation economy of the era required wide swaths of soil, and US presidents throughout the entire nineteenth century faced considerable political pressure to steal indigenous land for US planters. For instance, with the Compact of 1802, the federal government guaranteed Georgia that it would "extinguish, for the use of Georgia, as early as it may be peaceably obtained on reasonable terms, the Indian title to all the lands within the State of Georgia."[4] While this compact mostly applied to Cherokee land claims, it was a clear signal to each of the Five Tribes, and others along the American border, that the US intended to seize their homelands. By the 1830s, President Jackson saw this aim through. It goes without saying, this goal was not achieved "peaceably" or "on reasonable terms" by any stretch of the imagination; especially when assessed from the perspective of the dispossessed.

It is likely that Rachel and Charles experienced similar hardships as other enslaved people forced to make the journey with their native American enslavers. Historian Tiya Miles recounts the following of bondsmen and women owned by the Cherokee: "In addition to bearing the hardships of the journey, slaves were enlisted to do the additional work of hunting for their masters, nursing the sick, preparing meals, guarding the camps at night, and hiking ahead of the group to ensure passable roads." When the Five Tribes arrived in what was to be their new homelands, the processes of rebuilding would also mean intense labor for their enslaved populations, as they were forced to build up new government buildings, homes, and schools. Enslaved black people made up significant percentages of the overall population among the

Five Tribes: By 1860 they ranged between 10 and 18 percent of the total population for each of the individual tribes. The largest number of enslaved people were among the Cherokee nation, where members owned 2,511 slaves, amounting to 15 percent of the tribe's population; in addition to 2,349 enslaved people among the Choctaw; 1,532 among the Creek; and 975 among the Chickasaw nation, which amounted to 18 percent of that tribe's population.[5]

Couched in the history of the Trail of Tears is the story of a doubly dispossessed people. Enslaved Africans were forced to make the journey from places they too had known as their homes, while also being used as instruments to help mitigate the calamity that this forced removal caused for their enslavers. Yet black people enslaved by the Five Tribes had been forced to make many journeys: marches from the interior of Africa to its coastal regions, the trans-Atlantic journeys of the Middle Passage, the coffles of the domestic slave trade within the United States, as well as being sold from the United States into Indian country, and now the Trail of Tears. This story of enslaved black people within the larger narrative of Indian Removal is a submerged history, and it is critical to the history of black education within the tribes, just as the history of slavery is critical to understanding the embattled experiences of black education in the United States more broadly.

Through the Indian Removal process, the Five Tribes increasingly began to present and understand themselves as racialized nations. In attempts to resist the settler state's "voracious demand for land," historian Christina Snyder explains, native leaders combined "Indigenous notions of nationhood" with "republican ideology, redefining their nations as territorially bounded polities populated by individual citizens."[6] A key component of this defense was antiblackness: Elite members of the Five Tribes banded together with other native nations to establish cross-tribal political groups, established miscegenation laws to criminalize sex between members of their nations and black people, and worked to suppress black education as a perceived incubator for abolitionist sentiments.[7]

Rachel and Charles traveled west with a changing Creek nation, during a period that scholar Theda Perdue has called "post-removal chaos," referring to the entire period from removal through the Civil War, but especially the 1840s. Yet periodization can be faulty, as some may question whether such an era of "post-removal chaos" ever ceased to exist.[8] As Lakota scholar Nick Estes writes, "Indigenous people are post-apocalyptic" because they "have undergone several apocalypses." For the Lakota people, he explains, "it was the destruction of the buffalo herds, the destruction of our animal relatives on the land, the destruction of our animal nations in the nineteenth century, of our river homelands in the twentieth century." Such apocalyptic stories vary across native nations, with their own specific historic references; yet and still, "if there is something you can learn from Indigenous people," Estes declares, "it's what it's like to live in a post-apocalyptic society."[9]

Every tribe was devastated by the chaotic and apocalyptic experiences of removal. However, in the Creek, Cherokee, Choctaw, and Chickasaw nations (as well as, to a lesser extent, the Seminole nation), tensions between treaty parties and anti-removal factions continued long after their arrival in the West. Skirmishes and assassinations were common, sometimes sanctioned by law. Yet, as we will see later, such political violence and factionalism amid native removal provided opportunities for enslaved black people to free themselves or assert their personhood. For citizens of the Five Tribes, however, it meant their nations were in desperate need of unifying institutions. Just as the United States turned to common schooling as a means of creating cohesion and strengthening internal development as it expanded through the seizure of more and more native land, native leaders also turned to education with even more vigor amid post-removal chaos.

ANTI-LITERACY LAWS AND ANTIBLACK EDUCATIONAL PROTOCOLS AMONG THE FIVE TRIBES

The Creek nation paralleled the other Five Tribes in their turn to education as a method of building a unified nation that could resist continued US aggression. Rachel and Charles, along with other members of Philip's and Elzora's ancestors, would experience life in an

Indian country where antiblackness was persistent and widespread, and expressed, increasingly, through educational policy. One of the most direct expressions of increased racial politics among the Five Tribes was the redefinition of their nations through the subjugation of black people, and anti-literacy laws and social custom became a key expression of such antiblack sentiments.

Reading and analyzing such laws and educational practices meant to suppress black freedom among the tribes is likely to shock and spark outrage in most readers. Such practices are easy to align with popular recollections of the American South during nineteenth-century slavery, but their existence among native nations will likely be disorienting for some (as this was certainly the case for the author). Then, after outrage, one is also likely to feel as though such laws and practices connecting the subjugation of black enslaved people among native tribes with developing education systems feels like more of the same—directly reminiscent of the kinds of anti-literacy laws that proliferated in the US South, as well as antiblack policies in the antebellum North, as recalled in Part I. Recognition of such patterns speaks to the growing influence of the schooling apparatus of the United States beyond its borders, and in the context of the Five Tribes. While these nations worked to rebuild themselves in new territory, they continued to appropriate institutions, strategies, and mechanisms of law and governance employed by the US with even more vigor, especially as they became more dependent on the United States to support them in working through new conflicts arising between their nations and the indigenous tribes they had come to displace in the West.

The first recorded anti-literacy law among the Five Tribes can be found in the Choctaw nation, as early as October 1836. According to the law, "teaching slaves how to read, to write or to sing in meeting-houses or schools or in any open place, without the consent of the owner, or allowing them to sit at a table with him shall be sufficient ground to convict persons of favoring the principles and notions of abolitionism." While this law effectively criminalized black education—as nearly all black people living among the tribe were enslaved—there were also laws where proceeds from the selling of enslaved people directly flowed into funding streams for public expenses, including expenses related to building the nation's education system. For instance, on October 8, 1840, the Choctaw nation passed "An Act providing for the apprehension and disposal of negroes suspected to be runaways." This law deputized any Choctaw "to take up a negro whom he may suspect as a runaway" and potentially collect a reward, either from the owner or from a district clerk representing the Choctaw nation. If a runaway were to go unclaimed, the law provided that the captive could be sold to the highest bidder to support public expenses within the said district. According to the law, "if no owner appears in six months after the apprehension of said runaway negro, it shall be the duty of the light-horse-men to expose such runaway or runaways to public sale. And it shall be the duty of the captain of the light-horsemen to execute a bill of sale for such negro to the purchaser. And the proceeds thereof shall be used to pay the expenses of apprehending, securing and advertising such runaway, and if there remain a balance of the proceeds it shall be put into the district funds for public purposes."[10] Readers may recall similar laws discussed in previous chapters from the US South, where the funds obtained from selling fugitive slaves or improperly manumitted slaves flowed directly to state literary and school funds. Such parallels in antiblack education policy between the US South and the Five Tribes reflects the many exchanges—of institutions, racial ideologies, and mechanisms of social control—between white settlers and native leaders working to craft a "civilized" nation amid the persistence of native dispossession.

In a similar vein, the Choctaw nation passed a law in 1846 indicating that free blacks, if found in the Choctaw nation, could be sold and used for national expenses, including schooling. Choctaw leaders created the law to discourage masters from emancipating their slaves. If Choctaw slave owners acquired approval by the General Council to free their slaves, the newly emancipated person would then be required to "leave this nation within thirty days after the passage of the act." Freed slaves were forbidden from returning to the Choctaw nation, despite having family members and other kin still living within the Choctaw nation. The consequences for returning would be reenslavement. According to the law, "in case said free negro or negroes should return into this Nation afterwards, he, she, or they shall be subject to be taken by the light-horse-men and exposed to public sale for the term of five years; and the funds arising from such sale shall be used as National funds." Such laws demonstrate how the Choctaw nation, like the other Five Tribes, came to increasingly understand itself as a racialized nation.[11] The laws express a clear articulation of blackness and slaveness as coterminous, and that social life within the nation was an entitlement only for non-black people—natives and whites deemed absent of negro blood—for indeed, there were no similar laws for white people among the Five Tribes. As written laws became formalized within the nations, as they worked to rebuild themselves, race became central to the nation building project, and antiblackness in particular. Education, as a key institution of social reproduction—within the United States and in Indian Territory—emerged as a critical site for the expression of such fortified racial grammar.

On October 22, 1841, the Cherokee government passed "An Act prohibiting the Teaching of Negroes to Read and Write." According to this law, it was illegal "for any person or persons whatever, to teach any free negro or negroes not of Cherokee blood, or any slave belonging to any citizen of the nation, to read or write." While the earlier Choctaw law criminalized education for enslaved black people, specifically, the Cherokee law applied to all black people—though, to be clear, the Choctaw law had implications for the suppression of education among free black people as well. The Cherokee law stipulated that offending parties would be required to pay a fine of five hundred dollars. An amended law passed in 1848 stipulating harsher punishments. Based on the amendment, "any white person, not a citizen of the Cherokee nation" would be forced to leave the Cherokee nation altogether. This law was primarily meant to target white missionaries whom the Cherokee nation deemed the main culprits for teaching black people to read and write, and it was part of a broader set of Black Codes meant to police and control the social activity of black people, free and enslaved. In fact, the Cherokee nation passed a law requiring that "all free Negroes who may be in this Nation" (except those legally freed by members of the Cherokee nation) to leave "the limits of this Nation" by January 1, 1843. The law was especially harsh for black people suspected of encouraging rebellion and escape among the enslaved. The Cherokee nation declared that "should any free negro or negroes be found guilty of aiding, abetting or decoying any slave or slaves, to leave his or their owner or employer, such free negro or negroes, shall receive for each and every such offence, one hundred lashes on the bare back, and be immediately removed from this Nation." Thus the criminalization of black education among the Five Tribes was part and parcel of a broader set of legal and social codes meant to maintain racial hierarchies integral to chattel slavery, as well as the civilizationist ideas that came to inform the political strategies of the Five Tribes as they worked to cope with the chaos and uncertainty of the post-removal context.[12]

While the Creek nation never formally established an anti-literacy law, Creek leaders did express anti-literacy sentiments. Suppression of black education among the Creek overlapped with general concerns among some leaders about the loss of traditional Creek values that might come with the intrusion of Western education, while others likely feared that intellectual and religious instruction might encourage abolitionist ideas. Recall here Opothleyahola's attack on black worshippers at Withington Station, where they received literacy and religious education from white missionaries. The attack was motivated in part by an effort to block the influx of Western ideas that threatened traditional Creek ways of life. However, there are other cases where Creek leaders explicitly suppressed black education, even going so far as to verbally express the idea that there may have been explicit laws or widespread lawlike social customs criminalizing literacy among the enslaved. The case of Rev. John Fleming demonstrates this point. Fleming taught black and native students at a mission school in 1833 before his instruction of black students was contested by a Creek chief. Of this incident, Fleming recalled the following: "The first chief assaulted me one day with a great fury for teaching their slaves and said it was contrary to their laws, but when he'd convinced himself that I knew the law as well as he did upon that point, he became apparently calm and rode off. But I deemed it prudent that I should cease to educate the slaves which I did." It is likely that this Creek chief's assumption about the illegality of black education may have been more widespread. From such an example, we can infer that even in the absence of explicit anti-literacy laws, anti-literacy ideology was present in the context of the Creek nation, where black education was targeted as a violation of Creek customs in a de facto manner.[13]

As in the United States, some masters in Indian Territory defied anti-literacy laws and taught their slaves to read and write. Their reasons for doing so varied. Some relied on enslaved people to help run their businesses, which required that they be literate and able to do math, thus serving the financial interests of those who claimed them as property.[14] Narratives from men and women enslaved among the Five Tribes also emphasize that some masters turned a blind eye when enslaved people pursued literacy. Phoebe Banks, born to enslaved parents in 1860 and owned by prominent Creek enslaver Mose Perryman, recalled, "Lots of the slave owners didn't want their slaves to learn reading and writing, but the Perrymans didn't care; they even helped the younger slaves with that stuff. Mother said her master didn't care much what the slaves do; he was so lazy he didn't care for nothing."[15]

In their reflections on slavery in Indian Territory, some black people also expressed a deep awareness that native people viewed black education with suspicion, and they explicitly referenced anti-literacy laws established among the Five Tribes. Betty Robertson, enslaved by Joseph Vann in the Cherokee nation, recalled the following: "Young Master Joe let us have singing and be baptized if we want to. . . . But we couldn't learn to read or have a book, and the Cherokee folks was afraid to tell us about the letters and figgers because they have a law you go to jail and a big fine if you show a slave about the letters. . . ." She went on to emphasize that one of the greatest things that came after the Civil War was the ability of her family to gain access to education, insisting, "I'm glad the War's over and I am free to meet God like anybody else, and my grandchildren can learn to read and write." Sarah Wilson, enslaved by a white man with a Cherokee wife, recalled that her ancestors were brought to Indian Territory from Tennessee. In addition to detailing the complexity of her family's history, she also refers to the criminalization of black religious worship and literacy in the Cherokee nation. Master Ben Johnson, whom Sarah described as "a devil on this earth," owned most of her relatives. It is possible that Ben Johnson was also her mother's father. In fact, as Sarah implies in her testimony, many of her relatives were likely the product of coerced sexual encounters by Master Ben and his family members. Sarah's father was Ned Johnson—potentially her mother's half brother, as Ned was the son of Master Ben Johnson and his Cherokee wife. While Sarah participated in a culture of dissemblance, similar to other black women before and after slavery, when it came to memories associated with the man that owned her family, declaring, "I don't want to talk about him [Ben Johnson] none," she did describe details about the suppression of black education and social life among the enslaved in the Cherokee nation.[16] Sarah recalled, "Before freedom we didn't have no church, but slipped around to the other cabins and had a little singing sometimes. Couldn't have anybody show us the letters either, and you better not let them catch you pick up a book to even look at the pictures, for it was against a Cherokee law to have a Negro read and write or to teach a Negro."[17]

That Sarah and the other enslaved people "slipped around to the other cabins" to engage in unsanctioned religious worship is revelatory of the subversive means black people engaged in to insist on their own dignity while striving to live on their own terms. Their actions reflect broader trends in slave religion across the United States. What's more, this "invisible institution" described by Sarah was essential to the educational imagination of black people during the era of slavery, not only among the Five Tribes but also across the United States. This too was part and parcel of the schooling apparatus of the state—the emergence of countervailing, and often heroic, traditions of teaching and learning, the likeness of which is rendered through the voices of those from below, but also inscribed as the subtext of anti-literacy laws. For indeed, such proscriptions were generated as a response to the spiritual strivings of the captives, a people seeking out education as a means to live free and meaningful lives. Reading such laws against the grain, especially by placing them alongside the voices of Sarah Wilson, Betty Robertson, and others, unveils a story of agency just as it reveals the realities of constraint.[18]

TULLAHASSEE MISSION: A "CIVILIZING" SCHOOL BUILT BY SLAVES IN THE POST-REMOVAL CREEK NATION

Antiblackness became institutionalized in the national education systems established among the Five Tribes during the post-removal era. This was done not only as it pertained to criminalizing black education through anti-literacy laws, but also when we consider the exploitation of black labor in the process of building new educational institutions for nonblack members of the Five Tribes. After arriving in Indian Territory, the enslaved were forced to build schools, homes for the wealthy, government buildings, and more. One account recalled the use of enslaved people to build government buildings for the Chickasaw nation in the 1850s, describing how "slaves of the Chickasaws toiled in the dense oak forests cutting down the finest trees and hewing them into shape."[19] Likewise, the tribes developed national education systems and they forced enslaved black people to build these structures while excluding them from educational opportunities and therefore asserting a posture of civilization propped up on black subjugation.

Tullahassee Mission School, where Philip Lewis eventually taught after the Civil War, began as one such institution in the Creek nation. Tullahassee emerged amid the "post-removal chaos" of the 1840s and '50s, a time when black people enslaved by the Five Tribes experienced increasing racial hostilities, and when factions among the tribes competed for power as the nations worked to reimagine themselves in relationship to their new western homelands. This was a tall task, one requiring the mitigation of both new and old challenges. The civilization politics of the pre-removal era persisted. Leaders of the Five Tribes increasingly emphasized the national character of their tribes and the extent to which they adopted settler ways of life. The tribes hoped that embodying settler notions of nationhood would finally persuade the US that they were sovereign and worthy of engaging with on equal terms. Doing so also meant codifying racial ideology in their construction of citizenship. As one historian writes, while "[i]nclusion was the genius that ensured the growth of the nations during the eighteenth century . . . that model no longer worked in the nineteenth century when Native people faced an increasingly powerful American state with a voracious demand for land." Native leaders built on indigenous notions of nationhood and "incorporated aspects of republican ideology, redefining their nations as territorially bounded polities populated by individual citizens." What's more, "as racial exclusion, in particular, became a component of national identity, people of African descent were no longer welcomed members."[20]

Such national politics became particularly pronounced in education. Antiblack exclusion in education, long used as a mechanism of domination in the slave society of the United States, became an instrument of nation-building and racially exclusive citizenship formation among the tribes. In this way, the schooling apparatus of the United States made an indelible imprint on the national education systems formed in Indian Territory.

As previously mentioned, Creeks were largely suspicious of education in the pre-removal era. By the 1840s, however, as other tribes like the Choctaw and the Cherokee began establishing national schools, Creek resistance to education gradually waned. Creek elites, likely influenced by elites in their neighboring nations, began to embrace educational institutions aligned with Western culture as a means of building and strengthening the nation. Observers like Creek agent J. L. Lawson took note of this shift in 1843:

> *For many years, there has been a decided opposition on the part of the chiefs to ministers of the gospel and missionaries, to public religious observances, and, I may add, to education. They [missionaries] were rigidly excluded from the nation—a necessary consequence of which was, an increased degree of idleness, licentious-ness, and immorality,*

> *measurably checked by the moral and religious tendencies of a very small portion of the nation, chiefly through the agency of negro preachers. A very decided change has taken place in the nation in the last twelve months, as respects the habits of the people generally, and the disposition of the chiefs. There is a growing desire for moral and religious instruction, and a stronger interest manifested for the education of children, which, if properly encouraged, must be productive of very decided benefit.*[21]

This "very decided change" continued. In 1848, Chief Chilly McIntosh, whose family enslaved Philip Lewis's maternal grandparents—Miley McIntosh and Sam Hawkins—joined with other prominent chiefs to end the Creek nation's official opposition to Christianity. This move was the culmination of decades of slow adoption of settler education on the part of Creek elites. Creek leaders widely acknowledged that those who were literate could better engage in diplomatic matters with the United States. Therefore, literate citizens began to garner social and political capital among some Creek communities. However, it is important to note here that English-speaking and writing Creeks constructed a political image of a nation that was "far more unified on paper than it was in reality." Most glaringly was the exclusion of enslaved and free black people from that nation.[22]

Philip Lewis's grandparents, Miley and Sam, must have understood that their master's endorsement of education was not for their benefit. As testimonies from other enslaved people have shown, they carried an awareness of how their enslavers' embrace of education was part of the same nation-building project that furnished anti-literacy practices they faced. As was the case in the United States, black people in Indian Territory recognized how the simultaneous expansion of education for citizens in the Creek nation and the systemic suppression of black education were two sides of the same coin. Within this racially stratified context of the Five Tribes, the educational opportunity created for some was inextricably linked to the substrative schooling policies used to suppress others. As formal education increasingly became an integral part of nation-building strategies employed by the tribal leaders, the denial of education for African-descendant people helped to reinforce their newly emerging racial politics of citizenship. The Tullahassee Mission School, which Miley and Sam's grandchild would eventually lead, was the flagship institution in this effort.[23]

The Creek nation began building the Tullahassee Mission School in 1848 near the plantations of several wealthy landowners. It was situated half a mile north of the Arkansas River and twelve miles from Fort Gibson. In 1847, a year prior to beginning the school's construction, the Creek council negotiated a contract with the Presbyterian Board of Foreign Missions to manage the school, stipulating that the costs of Tullahassee would be split between the Presbyterian Church and the Creek school fund, through which the US government gave $3,000 annually for the education of Creek children. A board of trustees was appointed, which became responsible for managing the school's faculty. One boy and one girl from each of the forty Creek towns were chosen to attend Tullahassee.[24]

When Tullahassee opened its doors for the first time on January 1, 1850, only English-speaking students were admitted. This practice was consistent with the rest of the Creek nation's manual labor schools, which meant the students who enrolled were overwhelmingly children of the Creek elite, particularly those in the Treaty Party, which more readily embraced settler schooling. Such division existed before the period of removal, and it was perpetuated after removal, as the power of the elite continued to expand due to inequitable access to education. Recall here that it was the elite members of the Creek Treaty Party who strongly favored civilization policies, and it was these same elites who had the material and political interest in defending slavery.[25]

Tullahassee deeply reflected such intratribal class politics. As one scholar noted, "The list of students reads like a roll call of future leaders of the tribe. In general . . . it was only the mixed bloods [of white and native ancestry] that attended the boarding schools, and their training therefore increased the cleavage that was already apparent within the nation." Yet, while Tullahassee mostly served the interests of the Creek elite, it was also integral to a broader effort to unify and build up the nation in Indian Territory. For instance, in 1856, after an influx of cash from selling land to the Seminoles, the Creek nation "immediately established seven day-schools under the administration of a native superintendent in each of the two settlements, and several graduates of Tullahassee received appointments as teachers." The Creek "now had a national system of education with a possibility of bridging the gap between the progressive and conservative members of the tribe." At the same time, it is important to note that the missionaries running Tullahassee were, like most missionaries, committed to a program of alienating native students from traditional customs. It is imperative that we not lose sight of this. Like other schools, Tullahassee was an institution created to strip children of their culture, even as this institution—as a tactical embrace of schooling—was integral to the dominant Creek strategy for survivance.[26] This conundrum abounds in the story of strategic uses of schooling by native tribes and conflicting aims of white settlers often serving as teachers and school administrators.

Unsurprisingly, Afro-Creek students were not permitted at Tullahassee when it was founded, even as the tribal leaders and missionaries relied on enslaved black labor to run the school. Some students took note of such racial politics of schooling in the Creek nation. Lilah Denton, a student of mixed Creek and white heritage, began attending Tullahassee just before her twelfth birthday. She recalled many details about her time at the school, including chores students were required to perform as well as servants who worked at the school. Denton recalled that female students were broken into two groups of twenty: the "up-stairs girls" were tasked with laundry and ironing, and the "kitchen girls" were responsible for washing dishes and "otherwise assisted" a black cook who goes unnamed in her account. Denton detailed various dishes made by Tullahassee's black cook with the help of "the kitchen girls": corn bread, quail, prairie chicken, and an "old Indian dish" made of corn called sofkey. Denton recalled how "the girls and teachers all thought a great deal of this Mulatto cook," who eventually left Tullahassee to get married. Before the black woman left, the teachers planned "a real show wedding" for her, which took place in the chapel.[27] Another black woman was responsible for laundering and ironing the teachers' clothes. She also laundered the boys' clothes, which the "up-stairs girls" then mended. The larger boys were responsible for felling trees and chopping them up for firewood under the supervision of a director of farming.[28] As was the case in settler schooling across all native tribes, rigid notions of gender were drilled into students not only through the ways in which they were required to dress, but especially through gendered division of labor at the schools; a gendered division of labor that was to teach native boys and girls what they were expected to do in the nuclear homes they were to lead as "civilized" men and women. In a world structured by settler colonialism and chattel slavery, such ideas of gender were always already raced as well. The presence of the black cook and launderer working for the school, though unable to attend, emphasized such intersectional lessons about race, gender, and citizenship within the tribes.

Records do not specify whether the black cook or black laundress were enslaved; however, it is likely that they were. Several slaves worked at Tullahassee prior to the Civil War, usually "hired" from Creek slave owners to provide labor for the school. Given the proximity of Tullahassee to the plantations of wealthy slave owners, it is also likely that slave labor was used to construct the physical structure of Tullahassee, which comprised of a three-story brick structure for the main school building, meant to accommodate forty male and forty female students, and which included stables, a workshop, a tool room, and an orchard.[29]

The use of enslaved labor is also likely given the proslavery stance taken by the Presbyterian Board of Foreign Missions, which helped build and maintain the school. In fact, missionary involvement in the development of Tullahassee reveals important dynamics surrounding black education and the question of slavery among the Five Tribes, and particularly in the Creek nation. Missionary groups took different stances on the slavery question. Their varied stances were based on their own ideological leanings, but also their perceptions of how native leaders viewed slavery's centrality to the success of their nations. Tullahassee was built around the time that the American Board of Commissioners for Foreign Missions, the largest and most powerful missionary group, became more vocal in their rebukes against slavery, and during this same time, the emergent Presbyterian Board of Foreign Missions maintained "neutrality" (if such a stance was possible). The debates among these groups reveal the complexity of the matter, and also provide necessary context for understanding Creek leaders' decision to partner with one mission group over another.

In the pre-removal context, black education among the Five Tribes can be characterized by limited opportunities, and limited government control over black learning. In such contexts, some black people enslaved in native nations became educated. They were "self-taught" or received educational instruction at missions. Some missionaries, like Cyrus Kingsbury, who founded Brainerd Mission School, were interested in the education of black people as well as indigenous peoples. In his autobiography, Kingsbury recalled being a young man finishing seminary, when his "thoughts had been directed to the condition of Indians in our country, & also to that of the Africans, particularly of the slaves." A classmate of Kingsbury's, Samuel J. Mills, shared this sentiment. Mills tried to educate and preach to enslaved people in the American South, but there were far more resources dedicated toward the education of native people—largely because it served the military and imperialist aims of the US nation. Lee and Susannah Compere, whose mission school at Withington Station was attacked in 1828 due to the presence of black learners, are another example of missionaries actively educating enslaved people.[30] However, the matter of slavery and the educational work of missionaries came into sharper focus after removal.

Missionary societies received increasing pressure to take a stance on slavery in the wake of Indian Removal. The Baptist and Methodist churches fractured over slavery. Presbyterians, of which the ABCFM was part, attempted to avoid the issue altogether. By the 1840s, however, the ABCFM was constantly debating its stance on slavery. Members, donors, and other groups, such as the American Anti-Slavery Society, urged the board to rebuke slavery. Some demanded the end to the use of slave labor at mission schools where native students were educated. Others argued that the board should preach against slavery and ban slaveholders from churches and schools. Missionaries like

Kingsbury urged a "neutral" stance, arguing that their work depended on avoiding the ire of native leaders, many of whom supported slavery. He also believed enslaved people were the only means of reliable labor to help with the grunt work on the day-to-day that came with running schools.[31]

I share this context to help situate the Creek nation's intentionality in choosing the missionary society they worked with in developing Tullahassee. The Presbyterian Board of Foreign Missions (PBFM), which contributed to the development of Tullahassee, was founded in 1837 amid such debates and deliberately positioned itself as a slavery-friendly alternative to the ABCFM and other groups. When the ABCFM eventually distanced itself from proslavery or so-called "neutral" missionaries in 1859, the PBFM absorbed these proslavery missionaries into their operations, taking over the patronage of several Choctaw missions, for instance. In short, the role of the PBFM in the founding of Tullahassee reveals a deep investment in slavery's persistence as a priority among leaders in the Creek nation.[32]

Missionaries had good reason to fear the consequences of preaching antislavery ideals at their missions. Backlash against missionaries for espousing abolitionist sentiments was not limited to the 1828 attack on Withington Station detailed in the previous chapter. The Old Fountain Church also became a target of suspicion among Creek leaders in the 1830s. Old Fountain was originally established as Muscogee Church and located at the Baptist Ebenezer Mission in the Creek nation. John Davis, a Creek Baptist and alumnus of Withington Station, led the mission and the church. Davis was very close to Lee Compere and frequently attended Withington Station, so it is possible Davis was present during the 1828 attack. At the very least, he had heard about it from his friend. For these reasons, Davis developed concerns about the growing number of black worshippers at his church, which at one point amounted to more than half the congregation.[33]

As Old Fountain became a house of worship and a site of education for its black congregants, some members of the Creek nation took offense. Writing to his friend and fellow preacher, Isaac McCoy, Davis reported in June 1833 that a "[g]reat many people disapprove of our teaching the black people to read." Two years later, in 1835, amid escalating anti-missionary sentiments, US Superintendent of Indian Affairs William T. Armstrong ordered all missionaries to vacate the Creek nation because he feared for their safety. Given his "pure" Creek blood, Davis remained in the nation, relying heavily on the support of black congregants for aid and protection. He would also, by virtue of his Creek heritage, escape the 1837 Creek Council Law, which stipulated that "any person of color who held a religious meeting or prayed in public would receive fifty lashes on the back"—a de facto ban on black preaching, since white preachers by that time had fled the country. To clarify, in the context of the Creek nation, Davis as a man of "pure" Creek blood would not have been considered a person of color as outlined in the law.[34]

The practice of teaching and preaching to black enslaved people continued to meet Creek resistance through the 1840s, as did the act of preaching more generally. Yet as Creek leaders expelled some missionaries, they also increasingly came to value education as essential to their national project. This, they hoped, could be done without firm ties to religious teachings. A Creek chief reportedly told a missionary: "We want a school, but we don't want any preaching; for we find that preaching breaks up all our old customs." Davis, despite his Creek blood, was forced out of missionary work by 1839 and took a post as a federally sponsored teacher near the Canadian River.[35]

In the years following the Civil War, Afro-Creek Baptists reestablished a church on the grounds of John Davis's long-closed Muscogee Church. What would become the Old Fountain Church claimed the heritage of Davis and his congregants, and the leaders of the church quickly organized a school for black children in the surrounding area. It was at this school that Philip Lewis would begin his education in the 1870s. The freedmen school at Old Fountain built on a long legacy of black resistance and educational striving in Indian country. Along this historical continuum, black education continued to be met by native resistance, since such educational projects were interpreted by leaders of the Five Tribes as undermining their recalibrated nation-building project in the new territory that was fundamentally a racial project formed through deep-seated antagonism between native, black, and white people. The racial grammar of the Five Tribes' new national education systems was formed through notions of civilization that were both imposed and imported from the schooling apparatus of the United States. Education was a racial project in Indian Territory, and it was fortified in the post-removal era by fierce antiblack sentiments expressed through schooling policies and practices.[36]

BLACK EDUCATION AND RESISTANCE ACROSS THE FIVE TRIBES

Black people in Indian Territory were not passive victims, even amid the chaos of the post-removal era. In these tumultuous years, native leaders looked to settler-style education—complete with its antiblack foundation—as part of their strategy to build up their nations out west. During this same period, when antiblackness became institutionalized through laws and policies within these nations, enslaved and free black people among the Five Tribes resisted, pursuing freedom through fugitive education, religious worship, and at times through outright rebellion.

Many black people developed a sophisticated understanding of the political terrain in Indian Territory, particularly those who were multilingual and served as translators between native leaders and US officials who only spoke English. Black people were aware that many native people frowned upon them being educated, and yet, as evidenced by previous accounts, they pursued what they believed to be a meaningful education anyhow. Similar to their educational pursuits, black people living among the tribes also used religion as a mechanism of resistance. They repurposed Christianity to affirm their humanity and sense of self-worth, just as they did in the United States. As in the classroom, black people could assert their dignity in religious meetings and envision a future in freedom.

So strongly did black people gravitate to religion in Indian Territory that when missionaries were expelled from the Creek nation, "blacks assumed the role of preachers, often holding clandestine religious meetings for black and Creek believers."[37] One white settler observing a worship service in North Folk town (present-day Oklahoma) in January 1842 described an Afro-Creek religious meeting as follows:

> *They commenced by singing a hymn in Creek to Creek music. It was rather more plaintive than solemn; after that several hymns in English were sung to Methodist or Baptist tunes; words were simple and apparently made by themselves: "Farewell Father," with a chorus and then "Farewell, Mother" and so on sister, brother, preacher, "I'm bound to go on," was about all I could hear of one hymn. I went into the room just a moment. A negro after I came out made a prayer with considerable energy.*[38]

The slave spiritual referenced in this account, titled "Bound to Go," implies deep connections between the black religious practices in the US South and those among the Five Tribes. Despite the development of laws meant to suppress black social life—in religious, education, and various other contexts—the enslaved and free black people living among the tribes continued to seek out means of escape, pursuing opportunities for human flourishing and sustenance.

Instruments of antiblack oppression flowed across national boundaries, and so too did strategies of resistance developed by black people to defend and assert their humanity. Many of those enslaved among the Five Tribes could have previously been enslaved in the United States. Recall, for example, Henry Bibb, whose comments on anti-literacy practices in the South were referenced in Part I. After several escape attempts in Kentucky, Bibb was sold to Cherokee owners, then ultimately freed himself following the death of his Cherokee enslaver. Furthermore, the physical proximity of the Five Tribes and US settlements prior to removal meant many slaves in Indian country likely shared lineages with those in the South.[39]

In the fall of 1842, two Quakers visiting Creek country recalled an incident similar to the previous account from North Folk Town, where a black preacher led a religious ceremony for a group of black and native worshippers. The two men recalled, "Many of the slaves and Indians appear sober and religious. Some of the slaves are approved preachers and hold meetings regular on first-days. We attended one of these meetings, which was conducted in a moderate and becoming manner. It was composed of Indians and slaves and their masters; their minister was an uneducated slave. All seemed interested in the meeting, and several much affected, even to tears."[40] Formerly enslaved people also recounted the role that religion played in enhancing black social life and mental stimulation even when more formal education seemed out of reach. Johnson Thompson, enslaved in the Cherokee nation, would recall, "I went to a subscription school for a little while, but didn't get much learning. Lots of the slave children didn't learn how to read or write. And we learned something about religion from an old colored preacher named Tom Vann. He would sing for us, and I'd like to hear them old songs again!"[41]

Education and religion were not the only features of black resistance. In 1842, the largest slave revolt ever recorded among the Five Tribes took place in Indian Territory. It began with twenty enslaved people from the Cherokee nation. By the end of the uprising, however, the group of rebel slaves included perhaps forty black people from the Cherokee, Creek, and Choctaw nations. The revolt can partially be attributed to the influence of a group of enslaved blacks who were "living like free people" near Webbers Falls, a town in present-day Oklahoma, situated in the southwest region of the Cherokee nation, placing it at the border of the Choctaw nation (directly south) and the Creek nation (directly west). And the revolt was likely triggered by the increasingly strict laws meant to further suppress black social life, which included the anti-literacy law passed by the Cherokee nation in October 1841.[42]

Whatever the cause, on November 15, 1842, a group of twenty Cherokee slaves raided a local store near Webbers Falls to gather supplies in preparation for their escape to Mexico. In moving southwest, the group of fugitive slaves crossed into Creek country, where they encountered resistance from a Creek slave-catching force, revealing the cross-national, class-based connections in Indian Territory across the tribes. In this instance, the Cherokee slaveholders were aided by Creek slaveholders, who helped chase down the runaways.

This intertribal collaboration, however, worked both ways. The Cherokee runaways sought common cause with Creek slaves, nearly a dozen of whom joined them. The Creek slaves shed blood to fend off a Creek slave-catching force. This journey for freedom continued. The group of fugitives, now more than thirty escaped slaves from the Cherokee and Creek nations, moved south, encountering more native masters and black enslaved people on the way. In yet another display of solidarity, the runaways killed two captors who were escorting a family of Choctaw slaves back to their masters. They freed the family, who joined the escape. Almost two weeks after the revolt began, a Cherokee militia caught the runaways seven miles north of the Texas border. Famished and outgunned, the rebels surrendered. Five were executed for their role in the revolt.[43]

This revolt was part of a longer history of resistance among black people enslaved within indigenous nations, despite historical claims that slavery was milder in such contexts. For indeed, prior to removal, "Cherokee-owned slaves had escaped as individuals and in pairs, refused to perform tasks, and manipulated their masters." One formerly enslaved woman echoes these sentiments, recalling various acts of resistance among fellow captives. According to Patsy Perryman, who was born enslaved in the Cherokee nation, she often heard tales of "other slaves getting beaten for trying to run away or too lazy to work." Indeed, such everyday forms of black resistance to enslavement also existed in an ordinary way. Patsy's recollection identifies resistance as a quotidian feature of black life in Indian country.[44]

The 1842 Slave Revolt would not be the last time enslaved people struck a blow at freedom. As one scholar has written, "For enslaved Blacks, the unrest of these early years [following removal] presented a long-awaited window of opportunity; in spite of serious risks, some chose to pursue freedom. . . ."[45] Slaves continued to run away, even as such attempts at freedom could easily end in them being killed. For indeed, tribal officials employed violent means to recapture black runaways and to preserve the institution of slavery.

I share this history of black resistance at length because it was partly the cause of the harsher laws and policies developed to constrain black social life among the Five Tribes. While perpetually deemed a slave race, and used in the propping up of white civilization in the United States, as well as native nations working to resist settler encroachment, black people engaged in sustained acts of resistance that made their pursuits of education a target. Indeed, it was in this context of continued resistance that black education was deemed a threat: an expression of black social life and assertion of self-determination linked with black rebellion and abolition.

In December 1846, *The Cherokee Advocate* included an article written by Cherokee Chief John Ross describing an incident where Cherokee slave-catchers pursued a group of black runaways. The slave-catchers quickly surrounded the location, then chased one man who tried to evade capture. The enslaved man's "pursuers however soon overhauled him, demanding a surrender." Refusing to surrender, the man presented "a large knife in one hand and a club in the other." He is reported to have used defensive language toward his opponents, perhaps hurling expletives of the day, assuring the Cherokee slave-catchers that he would fight to the death before accepting a continued life in bondage. The runaway dared the slave-catchers to approach him, insisting that he would not comply. Documenting the final seconds of this encounter, Ross explains that "with guns presented" the slave-catchers "insisted on his submitting. He then attempted to run. They fired—and he was killed."[46]

Runaway slaves were far from uncommon among the tribes, especially during the post-removal era. According to Cherokee Chief John Ross, the Cherokee nation in 1846 was "traversed by numbers, who have escaped from their rightful owners; either of the nation or the State, or the Creek country." Cherokee citizens were encouraged to do everything they could to help maintain order when it came to the enslaved population. Ross addressed this message to all, even those who did not own slaves. Speaking to nonslaveholders, he explained "it is but right that you use the utmost vigilance in ferreting out and arresting all who cannot give a good account of themselves." That is to say, all members of the Cherokee nation were deputized to police the actions of black people. Whether they be free or enslaved, black people were treated with suspicion, and could be stopped and forced to give an account of themselves to prove that they were not a runaway, that they were not in the wrong place at the wrong time, that they were not exceeding the bounds of what they could and should do as people who could be property. Chief Ross declared, "We would by no means advocate murder," but "We think nevertheless that it is time, high time that some thing be done toward regulating such property in the Cherokee country. It is not our place to discuss the right or wrong of Slavery. That it exists among us, is a matter of fact—and existing, they should know the relations they bear to free born citizens." He continued, "We would suggest to those who own negroes, that they be kind, yet strict in the enforcement of proper regulations . . . it is really essential to the maintenance of good order and quiet among some portions of the community."[47] Ross was a very powerful leader in the Cherokee nation; thus his editorial on dealing with the problem of fugitive slaves was the expression of an influential viewpoint.

Despite such oppressive conditions, black people continued to find ways of pursuing freedom. Irrespective of the supposedly milder treatment enslaved people endured among the Five Tribes in comparison to the South, they employed similar tactics to challenge their status as a people who were property. Such was the case for a group of Cherokee runaways who joined a band of fugitive slaves from the Seminole nation. It was reported that these Cherokee and Seminole runaways were "under the guardianship" of General Thomas Jessup, a military official who commanded American troops in the Seminole Wars. According to *The Cherokee Advocate*, "the mere face of being thus protected, has infused into them a spirit which leads them with the most bare faced impunity to trespass upon peaceable Cherokees."[48] General Jessup's motivation to protect these runaways likely stemmed from a desire to weaken the Seminole tribe, as opposed to any abolitionist vision or aim of social equality between the races. Irrespective of his motivations, however, these fugitive slaves accepted his protection. For indeed, it was to the idea of freedom that they were most loyal, not any particular nation, whether it be Seminole, Cherokee, or the United States.[49]

•••

Neither Philip nor Elzora referenced ancestors who participated in the 1842 revolt nor any who escaped at other times. Their ancestors were clustered by the Verdigris River, north of where the 1842 rebels passed through Creek country. However, resistance took many forms. Philip and Elzora's interviews suggest that their ancestors diligently passed down stories documenting their history of survival in the uncertainty of post-removal chaos. Such oral traditions were part and parcel of the countervailing tradition of black education developed in the shadows of slavery, offering a history from below that might shape the political formations of their progeny. As the Five Tribes increasingly defined themselves as nations on racially specific terms, and as they built schools like Tullahassee to unify and educate their populations, ancestors like Rachel and Charles Lewis, Miley McIntosh and Sam Hawkins, and Susie Bruner Scott, among so many others, looked to oral tradition to tell the story of their family. Violently denied education, these ancestors saw to it that their story was preserved. Because of their witness, when Philip Lewis took charge of Tullahassee as superintendent, he understood the complicated history of the place that he would lead.

11

A CREEK SCHOOL BECOMES BARRACKS FOR THE CONFEDERATE ARMY

White missionaries were ordered to leave Tullahassee and the Creek nation on July 20, 1861. Missionaries were met with growing hostility for decades, as many among the Five Tribes believed them to harbor abolitionist beliefs. They had experienced pressure to leave before; however, on this occasion the political climate intensified the threats, as the emergence of wartime violence in the United States made matters more urgent. On this day in July, white settlers in charge of Tullahassee chose to comply.[1]

The leaders of Tullahassee Mission School packed up and left. Rev. Loughridge, who served as the superintendent of Tullahassee since the time it opened, went to Texas. Under Loughridge was a married couple who taught at the school. Missionary societies preferred married couples to head their schools, when possible, or they "encouraged single missionaries to find a spouse upon their arrival."[2] These married couples could serve as examples of traditional gender roles, thus modeling an important lesson of settler schooling. Rev. William Schenck Robertson, the first principal teacher, and his wife, Anne Eliza (Worcester) Robertson, the child of missionaries among the Cherokee nation and born at Brainerd Mission, both went to Kansas. All students returned to their homes.[3]

The Robertsons relied on Simon Brown, an enslaved black man, to drive their wagon and facilitate their safe passage out of Indian Territory. Brown was owned by a nearby Creek woman and he was often hired out to work at Tullahassee. When escorting the Robertsons to the Verdigris River by wagon, he would have learned why they were being forced to leave, causing his mind to race over his own fate as he returned to Tullahassee on foot. Sensing that things were taking a turn, Simon likely studied the paths he traveled, believing that such knowledge might be useful in the future. Black enslaved people like Simon became accustomed to negotiating their position between white and native people, both of whom benefited from their status as property, using them to advance their distinct political and economic agendas—and in this instance, to secure their safety, despite Simon's distinct vulnerabilities as it related to the war unfolding around them.[4]

Two decades after the chaos caused by Indian Removal, a new period of tribal conflict and devastating violence emerged. Like the period of removal, this new political dynamic was directly linked to US social forces. Both native and black people in Indian Territory experienced such devastation, though the terms of such devastation were distinct. Native peoples would be pushed and prodded as ongoing victims of settler-colonial violence and US paternalism, and black people continued to be deemed a race of slaves, enlisted in national politics through various forms of coercion and objectified in processes of political negotiation between nations to which they held few meaningful claims other than kinship ties that bound them to one place or the other.

Dreams of black freedom, indigenous sovereignty, and white supremacy continued to interact in the geographic context of North America, and Tullahassee continued to be an institution right in the middle of the chaos. Yet the upheaval of the Civil War also provided black people with new opportunities to free themselves, organize, and emerge from the war with new visions for black life in Indian Territory. During the uncertain period of the Civil War, the freedmen experimented with building a new life as they crossed the threshold from slavery to emancipation—some by proclamation and many by their own doing. Education was an integral part of black people's experimentation with freedom amid wartime chaos. At the same time, the Tullahassee Mission School became repurposed as barracks for the Confederate army. Such conflicting developments amid the Civil War reflected the past of black education in Indian Territory just as much as it anticipated its future.

THE FIVE TRIBES JOIN FORCES WITH THE CONFEDERATE STATES OF AMERICA

The Creek council formally joined forces with the Confederate states on that solemn day in July. Yet signs of this alliance were abundant in the preceding months. On February 29, 1861, the council passed a new slave code, hoping to bring African Creeks under more complete control. The code declared that slaves were to be confined to their masters' land. It also required that any slave traveling outside those lands to carry a pass. If they failed to produce a pass, enslaved people could be detained by Lighthorse, a form of mounted police.

The code included proscriptions impacting free black people as well. In fact, the very notion of black freedom became a criminal offense. The law demanded that all free African Creeks must select a master by March 10, 1861. If they failed to self-enroll into slavery and use to their benefit the luxury of "choice" by identifying their own master, these black people in the Creek nation would be sold to the highest bidder. Officers were appointed to oversee these "returns" to slavery. No slave was allowed to own livestock or property or to hire themselves out as laborers. Every free black person returning to slavery—or being enslaved for the first time—was to dispose of their property prior to such return. While black religion had long been targeted and policed, it came under severe attack and increased scrutiny. Slaves were only allowed to attend church services on or near their master's land. African Creek preachers were forbidden to preach to mixed congregations.[5]

The Creek nation was not alone in strengthening its surveillance of free and enslaved black people. The remaining Five Tribes also sided with the Confederacy. The Chickasaw legislature in May 1861 declared its allegiance to the Confederacy, urging its neighboring "red brothers" to take up arms "in order to secure the independence of the Indian nations and the defense of the territory they inhabit from Northern invasion by the Lincoln hordes and Kansas robbers."[6] This expression of racial solidarity between the native tribes—denoted by "red brothers"—emphasized a sense of common cause among the nations, and it reflected the current formation of their newly fortified governments that were based on explicit racial logics, one intensely defined through the subjugation of black people and strategic collaborations with white settlers.

On June 1, 1861, leaders from the Creeks, Chickasaw, Choctaw, and Seminole nations who sympathized with the Confederate states joined as "red brothers" against the Union—and decidedly against the abolition of slavery. These tribal leaders met at North Fork Town to create a constitution for the "United Nations of the Indian Territory." Under this new political body, the principal chief of each nation attended meetings to recommend legislation and report on tribal matters to the United Nations. It was decided they would grant free passage to Confederate troops. Each nation also promised its own troops in order to repel "the *invading forces of Abolition hordes* under Abraham Lincoln."[7] It appears no Cherokee delegates attended the meeting where this agreement was created, but the nation was also undergoing a strong internal debate about where they stood in relationship to the Confederate States of America. Stand Watie, the Cherokee chief most in favor of the Confederacy, began organizing units as early as June 1861, however. Cherokee Chief John Ross did not sign a treaty with the Confederate states until October 1861.[8]

A few days after the constitutional meeting of the United Nations of Indian Territory, Albert Pike, the Confederate envoy to native nations, negotiated a treaty between the Confederate States of America and the Creek nation. This treaty promised to assume the annuities previously paid by the US government, legalized slavery, and more explicitly protected against territorial government and allotment, meaning the Confederacy would not attempt to govern the Creek nation and that the nation could hold its land in common as long as it pleased them to do so. Notably, the Confederacy promised to protect against the ongoing threats by the United States to extend control over Indian Territory. The rights of native nations to be self-governed would, purportedly, be akin to states' rights in this way. Upper Creeks refused to accept the new treaty. Even so, it was ratified on July 20, 1861, the same day the Creek Council forced the Presbyterian missionaries at Tullahassee and Coweta to leave the Creek nation.[9]

The same day Tullahassee was forced to close its doors, Creek leaders gathered fifty miles south in North Fork Village to ratify a treaty of alliance with the Confederate States of America. Creek leaders made this decision despite strong opposition from many within their nation. Despite internal debates among the tribe, this single action made one thing clear: The Civil War had come to Indian Territory. This war was not merely a conflict between the North and the South; it also involved indigenous nations, particularly those that trafficked in the business of owning and selling African-descendant people as property.[10] The tribes' decision to side with the Confederacy was two-pronged, about native sovereignty as well as a desire to continue as slaveholding nations.

THE EVOLUTION OF NATIVE SCHOOLS AS SITES OF WAR

Tullahassee Mission School became barracks for both Creek and settler Confederate forces during the Civil War. After the Creek nation split into pro- and antislavery factions, those who sided with the Confederacy took over Tullahassee and forced the white missionaries to leave due to accusations that they were abolitionists; then the chiefs repurposed the school building to support their fight to preserve slavery and fend off the heavy hand of the US government. They used Tullahassee as a barracks and a hospital, and part of the lower rooms were used as a stable. In many ways, the school metaphorically represents how enmeshed slavery was in the political economy of Indian Territory, given the Creek council's selection of a proslavery white missionary society to oversee the school in its origins, as well as the exploitation of enslaved black labor to run the school prior to the war. The Creek chief's repurposing of the school as barracks for the Confederacy is consistent with its history, and it aligns with the politics of the Creek leaders who helped found it.[11] This development had parallels across Indian Territory.

Many schools were transformed into tactical and political bases during the war. Armstrong Academy, situated in the Choctaw nation, for example, became the temporary capital in 1863. The school was farther west than the previous capital, in Doaksville, and was more centrally located with regards to the other Five Tribes, which made it a more pragmatic location. Indeed, Armstrong Academy is where the United Nations of the Indian Territory met in 1861, the site at which they made the historic decision to side with the Confederacy. Schools were symbolically important national sites within the Five Tribes, but they were also well built and more defensible structures. Readers may also recall the story of Goodland Academy in the Choctaw nation from Susan McCoy's narrative in the beginning of *American Grammar.* While Goodland became an enrollment site for the Dawes Commission in the 1890s, it was also a camp used by Confederate soldiers during the Civil War.

Educational institutions had always been literal and figurative sites of US warfare among native nations. During the Civil War, schools were explicitly appropriated as political sites for warring against the United States in partnership with states that seceded from the union and defended slavery. It would not be until 1865, as union victory loomed and black, native, and white members of the First Indian Regiment reclaimed much of Creek country and established a camp near Tullahassee, that the institution no longer served Confederate forces.[12]

The Five Tribes were internally divided, even as prominent factions of each nation pledged allegiance to the Confederacy early in the war. Many factors motivated their alliance with the slaveholding South. Some scholars point to defense of slavery, particularly among native elites, as a big motivation. Others suggest the influence of US Indian agents played a major role, as many of these government officials were from the South. On a broader level, some note the general antigovernment sentiments shared by native nations, who were tired of the US imposing its foreign agenda, trampling on indigenous sovereignty.[13] It is likely that the native leaders were motivated by a combination of such factors.

In most cases, the tribal factions on either side of the Civil War mapped on to divisions that emerged during the era of Indian Removal. The pro-removal "Treaty Parties" pushed for alliance with the Confederacy. Unsurprisingly, this faction tended to be composed of more slaveholders. Those who opposed removal, like the Ross Party in the Cherokee nation, were more favorable to the union as they often had fewer slaveholders. As previously mentioned, a Cherokee faction led by Stand Watie, longtime leader of the Treaty Party, pushed Chief John Ross to ally with the Confederacy. Ross, though a slave owner, initially urged neutrality on the matter of whether the Cherokee nation should take a stand. He gave in to pressure in 1861, however. Ross signed a treaty with the Confederacy, hoping this might maintain political stability among the tribe. Watie and John Drew, Ross's ally, both commanded armed Cherokee regiments. The two regiments rivaled one another, but they both fought for the Confederacy.[14]

Divisions were clear in the Cherokee nation. Many men from John Drew's unit deserted, and Chief Ross granted them amnesty. After union forces captured the Cherokee capital of Tahlequah in 1862, Ross quickly negotiated an alliance with the United States and stood down. The following year, the Cherokee council nullified its treaty with the Confederacy. In doing so, they freed their slaves and pledged allegiance to the Union. Stand Watie, however, continued to wield his political and military power, insisting the nation was still allied with the Confederacy. His regiment would not surrender until 1865. Before this time, Stand Watie and his warriors raided the nation and engaged in devastating guerrilla warfare.[15]

The Creek nation's alignment with the Confederacy was also a divided cause. Old lines drawn between the anti-removal Upper Creek and pro-removal Lower Creek once again flared up, the Lower Creeks urging loyalty to the slaveholding South and a group of Upper Creeks siding with the Union army. During this time of unrest, a familiar figure in the history of Afro-Creek education reappeared. Opothleyahola, the Creek leader and slave owner believed to have ordered the attack on black learners at Withington Station in 1828, was part of the Upper Creeks who opposed the alliance with the Confederacy. Opothleyahola and the Upper Creeks declared the treaty established between the Creek nation and the Confederacy to be void.[16]

Opothleyahola's involvement in both events—his attack on black education and religion as well as his opposition to an alliance with the Confederate states—reveals the complexity of racial politics in Indian Territory. In November 1861, four months after Tullahassee closed and the formal alliance with the South was established, Opothleyahola began recruiting Creeks and Seminoles to travel north to Union lines, assuming they would be safe there. Opothleyahola also invited black Creeks, free and enslaved, to join him and the group of "Loyal Indians" he led. It was declared that any slave who joined them would be free. Opothleyahola's decision to lead a free black exodus to the Union army—even though he himself was a slave owner and allegedly ordered the anti-literacy attack at Withington Station—reveals, more than anything, the strength of his traditionalist beliefs. Having fought in the Red Stick War—which involved opposing factions of Creek warriors, the United States, and European colonial powers in the early 1800s—and having fiercely opposed removal, Opothleyahola's support for the Loyal Indians was likely rooted in opposition to his political rivals more so than any commitment to the liberation of black people.[17]

SELF-EMANCIPATED AND SELF-TAUGHT: THE AGENCY OF AFRO-NATIVE PEOPLE DURING THE CIVIL WAR

African Creeks were aware of Opothleyahola's history. Nevertheless, they made similar tactical decisions, looking for opportunities that presented their best chance at freedom. Black people in Indian Territory freed themselves, refusing to wait for the war to be fought and their fates decided by others. Some Creek owners furnished slaves departing with supplies for their journey to Opothleyahola's camp, reflecting the varied ways in which Creek masters approached slavery. However, most black people making the journey took matters into their own hands.

This theme of self-emancipation is critical context for the educational work that black people took up during and after the war. This same spirit of self-determination can be traced to the self-initiated educational and religious activities in years past. Indeed, the pursuit of self-possession in the mind and spirit has always been tied to the freedom of body for the enslaved. This is a lesson that can be traced through the history of black life in American slavery, both in the United States and in Indian country.

Unaware of what awaited them, several hundred enslaved black people and pro-Union Creeks made their trek northward, beyond the Creek nation, in late November 1861. Confederate forces targeted the group. They engaged in three skirmishes as the group of Loyal Indians, primarily made up of families, slowly moved north. The Loyal Indians gained more supporters when they entered the Cherokee nation. These additions included enslaved and nonblack Cherokees who defected from Confederate battalions rather than fight against their families and kin. The Loyal Indians would effectively be defeated by Confederate attacks come early 1862; however, many smaller groups from this larger faction successfully reached Union lines.[18]

The efforts of African Creeks to join the Loyal Indians' exodus was a continuation of black resistance in Indian Territory. Black people freed themselves to join Opothleyahola, and the group's path northward was nothing short of an emancipatory event. Gilbert Lewis, who was enslaved alongside Philip Lewis's paternal grandparents on the plantation of Kendle Lewis, escaped in the fall of 1861 and crossed the Creek nation with his family to join the Loyal Indians. Simon Brown, the enslaved man who drove the white missionaries as they left Tullahassee by Creek decree, put his knowledge of the landscape—gleaned, in part, from his transport of white missionaries out of the nation—to good use. Brown planned his own escape path, and in November 1861, he did just that. He, along with his family, escaped to join the Loyal Indians.[19]

Brown was one of several enslaved black people working at Tullahassee, and he would not be the only member of this group to escape. Robert Johnson worked at Tullahassee under an agreement that would allow him to eventually buy his freedom. This deal disappeared when the white missionaries who had brokered it were exiled, as Johnson was reenslaved by his owner John Humper, a Confederate-allied Seminole chief. Despite this unfortunate phase of delayed freedom, Johnson eventually escaped in 1864. He fled to Union lines with the help of black and native allies, then joined the First Indian Union Battalion, serving as a highly valuable interpreter-soldier for the remainder of the Civil War.[20]

What is clear from the stories of Gilbert Lewis, Simon Brown, and Robert Johnson is that black people fled whenever they could during the years of the Civil War. They participated in the general strike waged by enslaved people across the American South, and in Indian Territory, where black people stopped work and fled plantations, as well as other sites where their labor was exploited by those who claimed them as property. Sometimes they absconded as individuals. At other times they fled as small groups, having planned escapes in secret, deploying the same methods of fugitive planning they used to educate themselves.[21]

Simon Brown and his family and many others were part of a broader exodus of black people in Indian Territory who became self-emancipated. The scene recalled by the white Union major Albert Ellithorpe emphasizes this point. He recalled the self-emancipation of almost four hundred black people after the battle of Prairie Grove in December 1862. "They make their escape in all conceivable ways," he recounted, "some on foot, carrying their children upon their backs and in their arms; in ox teams, mule teams, upon the backs of ponies, donkeys & etc." Major Ellithorpe explained that the runaways included "Old and young—the infirm and crippled, of all shades of color—Creek, Cherokee, Seminole, Chickasaw and Choctaw, male and female . . . they seem willing to endure any hardships . . . pressing forward towards a strange land—for what? Simply so that they may say *we are free.*"[22]

Though the Loyal Indians were defeated, many black and native people did successfully make the journey to Union lines during the war. The First Indian Home Guard was created in 1862, and it included units with black and nonblack soldiers. Black men, like Robert Johnson, played a crucial role as interpreter-soldiers in the First Indian, and black refugees of all genders were important intermediaries in refugee camps behind Union lines. Whether or not they were literate, Afro-native people were often bilingual and more comfortable navigating different cultural settings. They secured subsistence for themselves and native people, and they administered medical services because many native people did not trust whites to do so.[23]

Internal dynamics among the Loyal Indians during the war illustrates how black people were part of the national polities of the Five Tribes even before they were formally granted citizenship. Black and native people fought side by side in the group's rear guard to defend their black and native families. While not yet citizens of any of the Five Tribes, black people had varying degrees of kinship therein, and in the eyes of many native people, black people were more natural allies than the Confederates. Importantly, Afro-native people maintained their identities as members of indigenous nations. For instance, when the War Department ordered black soldiers in the First Indian Home Guard to be moved to the Colored Troop unit, many refused to do so. Most Afro-native soldiers, and their commanding officers, ignored this order. Until the end of the war, freedmen insisted on serving side by side with native people in the First Indian Home Guard.[24]

Black people from the Five Tribes were eager to continue their education during the war. For many, the war presented the first opportunity to openly pursue an education free of persecution. Simon Brown, who had worked at Tullahassee prior to the war, and who likely leveraged his connections to the white missionaries there, joined forces with a black Creek man named Monday Durant and the white missionary Hannah Worcester Hicks to advocate for black education in the refugee camp. They found a patron in the American Missionary Society's Freedmen Relief Association, which began funding Sunday schools for black children in early 1864 at Fort Gibson, in Indian Territory. During the summer of 1864, over 5,000 refugees from Kansas camps returned, where they camped with approximately 10,000 black and native refugees who were already at Fort Gibson amid poor living conditions. As with refugee camps across the American South, black people who fled to Union lines from the sites of their enslavement in Indian Territory also pursued education for their communities through self-advocacy and were self-taught. This trend persisted in the years to come.[25] Racial lines were still intact when it came to education, even if such boundaries were more flexible on the battlefield. Nonblacks from the Cherokee and Creek nations each had their own school sessions, but Afro-natives, presumably from across the tribes, learned together as black students. Such racial divisions existed even as the school, it appears, was created at the urging of Afro-native people.

RESISTANCE TO BLACK EMANCIPATION AMONG THE FIVE TRIBES

Black enslaved people in Indian Territory were not freed by the Emancipation Proclamation, nor by the Thirteenth Amendment. They were formally emancipated by treaty, which came much later. Even after the enslaved people in Galveston, Texas, learned of their freedom on Juneteenth, most black people enslaved by the Five Tribes had not gained their liberty. The Seminole and Creek nations settled treaties with the United States in 1866, freeing their slaves and granting freedmen "all the rights of native citizens," according to the Seminole nation, and "all the rights and privileges of native citizens, including an equal interest in the soil and national funds," as stated by the Creek. Many Seminole and Creek slaves were, of course, self-emancipated, having already effectively freed themselves by joining Opothleyahola or by taking advantage of wartime chaos.[26]

The Cherokee nation ended slavery first. As part of their attempt to switch allegiance to the federal government, the tribe abolished slavery in 1863 by an act of its national council. Then, in 1866, the nation signed a peace treaty outlining that black people residing in the nation, whether formerly enslaved or otherwise, "shall have all the rights of native Cherokees."[27]

The Choctaw and Chickasaw nations fiercely resisted efforts to free their slaves. They especially despised the idea of making them citizens. These two nations were long distinguished as the most severe in their treatment of black people, enslaved or otherwise, when compared to their peers among the Five Tribes. Nevertheless, both nations put forward plans for emancipation in October 1865, and in an 1866 joint treaty, both nations were induced to "adopt" freedmen and give them the rights and privileges of tribal citizens. However, both tribes refused to grant full citizenship to the freedmen.

Some black people noted the tribal nation's differential treatment of enslaved people and freedmen, which provides context for the Chickasaw and Choctaw resistance. Mary Grayson emphasized such distinction when recalling her family's time living in Chickasaw country after her father and uncles absconded and eventually joined other colored troops in the fight against slavery. She explains, "Pretty soon we were in Chickasaw country, and everybody was friendly to us, but the Chickasaw people didn't treat their slaves like the Creek did. They was more strict, like the people in Texas and other places."[28] Consistent with Grayson's account, the Chickasaw and Choctaw nations seemed to express greater resentment to the idea of accepting the freedmen into their tribes as citizens. The federal government attempted to induce adoption of freedmen as citizens, offering the nations $300,000 in exchange for doing so.[29]

The Choctaw government adopted freedmen in 1885—twenty years after the Civil War ended—making them the last of the Five Tribes to do so. The Chickasaw nation *never* adopted the freedmen as citizens. The US government unilaterally gave Chickasaw freedmen some privileges of Chickasaw citizens, like land allotments under the 1898 Curtis Act, but these black men and women remained on tenuous ground, effectively a stateless people.[30]

The federal government also turned to education as an effort to integrate the freedmen into the Choctaw and Chickasaw nations. The US attempted to induce adoption of the freedmen by providing $10,000 for freedmen schools in 1882. Yet, to be clear, as with the school organized by Simon Brown, Monday Durant, and their allies, this effort to start schools for the Choctaw and Chickasaw freedmen was also a response to popular organizing among the former slaves. In his 1883 annual report, Commissioner of Indian Affairs Hiram Price noted, "The freedmen themselves have held conventions and sent delegates to Washington, asking the protection and assistance of the Government in securing all the rights in the respective nations to which they are entitled by treaty." Knowing education to be one of the rights to which they were entitled, the freedmen did what they could to pressure the US government into holding the Five Tribes accountable to making opportunities available for their people.[31]

That the freedmen made claims upon the settler state surely presents a complicated political history, one where layered power dynamics become increasingly evident in relationships between black people, native nations, and the paternalistic white American settler state. The Afro-Chickasaw historian Alaina Roberts provides a useful assessment of this complicated moment in US and native American history. "When the United States forced them to free their slaves, the Five Tribes then found ways to keep people of African descent from fully accessing tribal membership," Roberts explains. "The emancipation and enfranchisement of Indian freedpeople that culminated in their receipt of land was the result not of Indian nations' decisions but of progressive Americans wrestling with the question of Black citizenship and fulfilling Black freedom and advancement within Indian nations in a way that they would not in their own country." This hypocrisy named by Roberts is strikingly apparent, especially when we read the federal government's forceful hand in requiring native nations to comply with demands to include freedmen as equal citizens alongside actions of the United States. For instance, just a few years earlier, in 1877, the US removed federal troops from the South, effectively ending its own enforcement of Reconstruction, and offering no protections to Southern black people exposed to threats by violent white mobs working to restore racial hierarchies reminiscent of the slavery era. According to Roberts, such demands by the US "both violated Native nations' sovereign right to define their own tribal membership" while also "provid[ing] Indian freedpeople with rights they would not have obtained otherwise." In this situation, black people again found themselves negotiating their position between white Americans and indigenous members of the Five Tribes, both of whom owned them as enslaved people, and both groups having used them to advance their distinct political and economic agendas. A tortured reality of black life in Indian country, indeed, and one deeply reflective of the general status of black personhood in the modern world more broadly.[32]

A NEW DAY BEGUN: EDUCATION AND NEGOTIATIONS OF FREEDMEN FUTURITY IN INDIAN TERRITORY

The Civil War was a tumultuous time in the United States, but also in Indian Territory. The war exposed old political rivalries within the Five Tribes, where removal-era factions among its leaders landed on opposite sides of the war. While the removal era primarily surfaced questions about territory, the Civil War added new questions about the future—political, economic, and racial—of Indian Territory. Afro-natives took up arms alongside the indigenous people who enslaved them when they joined the Union's fight. They did this because at the end of the day, they had one ultimate goal in mind—the freedmen fought for a vision of freedom they began pursuing long before the war broke out, and certainly before it ended. Their prior acts of fugitivity, insurrection, as well as their repeated acts of self-emancipation during the Civil War tell the story. Furthermore, their assertion of knowledge as translators, teamsters, soldiers, and advocates for themselves (and others) through the organization of schools behind Union lines reveal glimpses of the world they were hoping to make for themselves.

Afro-native people began building a reality of freedom in Indian Territory. As one historian writes, "Significantly, unlike during the previous years in the Creek Nation, [worship] services [at Union camps] were segregated into Indian and African congregations, a trend that accelerated after the war. Under the dire circumstances then, the African Creeks were beginning to put their community back together, and, in doing so, they created a different kind of community."[33] In this context, recently fortified racial boundaries between black and non-black, produced through racial policies in Indian Territory before the war, continued to hold, and the freedmen worked to organize in the most meaningful ways possible under such conditions.

After the war, the freedmen of the Five Tribes attempted to construct their lives as full members of their respective native nations—though they would meet degrees of resistance within each. In this process, Afro-native men and women looked to schools as a key site for imagining and enacting visions of freedmen futurity. Just as in past years, education continued to be a site for negotiating power within Indian Territory. Relationships between race and power were made and remade through education. This politics of education was about schools, but it was also about black people's negotiation of racialized geographies, education policy, as well as the inner workings of faith-based education and an emerging intellectual tradition organically developed and preserved among the descendants of enslaved people in Indian Territory, where counternarratives were passed down—a countervailing educational tradition that inspired and sustained a political tradition among Afro-native people in the years to come.

•••

Tullahassee Mission School was barely standing when the war concluded. When Williams Robertson returned to Tullahassee in 1866 with Reverend J. R. Ramsey on assignment from the Presbyterian Board of Foreign Missions, they found the school grounds to be "in a most deplorable condition" due to its use during the war.[34] Mr. and Mrs. Robertson reopened the schools in March 1868, and they would be joined by Miss Nancy Thompson, an educator previously connected with the school. This reunion occurred only after the new Creek constitution allocated $6,000 for the repairs of Tullahassee and the nearby

Asbury Mission early the same year. Thirty scholars attended during the first term, and enrollment increased once more missionaries arrived at the school during the summer. By October, the school could house eighty-one students. Nearly 160 Creek students had applied for admission, and according to a report by the Commissioner of Indian Affairs, "between seventy and eighty" had to be rejected by the board of trustees. It seems the chaos of the war in Indian Territory led to an increased demand among Creeks to attend Tullahassee. As some advocated in years past, learning the ways of the white man could be a strategy for refusing him.[35]

Tullahassee continued to be a site of antiblack exclusion, even after the Creek abolished slavery and adopted freedmen as citizens. Afro-Creek students were not allowed to enroll when the school reopened. It would also continue to employ settler-style education, whereby indigenous ways of life were disparaged, and where native students were forced to shed traditional native customs and become immersed in white Western culture. In his letter to the Creek agent reporting the great number of students, the new superintendent of Tullahassee, Leonard Worcester, emphasized renewed confidence in the power of the school's project of natal alienation, just as white leaders of settler schooling had always done. He insisted that the increased interest in education among the Creek was "encouraging" because in the past "it was almost impossible to keep up the desired number of scholars, on account of the indifference of both parents and children." He continued, "We have been much encouraged, also, by the interest manifested by the scholars themselves, and the progress made in their studies. We trust the day is not far distant when, in the providence of God, this people shall become truly a civilized and enlightened nation; when the 'busk,' the 'stamp dance,' and the ball play shall be among the things of the past."[36]

As it did before and during the war, Tullahassee continued to reflect sea changes in the political landscape of Indian Territory following the Civil War. In the last decades of the nineteenth century, the school became a key site in the freedmen's struggle for education and equal opportunity in the Creek nation. This struggle would be waged in tandem with black political struggles across the Five Tribes (and within the United States), as native nations continued to experience a shifting political landscape conditioned by settler-colonial policies supporting an ever-expanding US empire. The story of Tullahassee, as well as the family history of Philip and Elzora Lewis, will continue to reveal key shifts in the educational life of black people in Indian Territory.

12

EDUCATION AND FREEDMEN FUTURITY AMONG THE FIVE TRIBES

In 1868, missionaries reopened the doors of Tullahassee. This same year, Abram Lewis and Mary Anne Hawkins, the parents of Philip Lewis, were joined in marriage. The simultaneity of these events, both transpiring during a critical era of Afro-native political activity, widens our understanding of the relationships between the development of racialized education policies in Indian Territory and the intimate lives of black freedmen. Education was never just about learning in the classroom; what happened in schools was always inextricably linked to family, to home, and community. While historians concerned with black life in the post-emancipation era rightfully look to the US South, the story of the freedmen's struggle for equal citizenship, opportunity, and for Reconstruction was also waged among the Five Tribes.[1]

Mary Anne was enslaved by Roley McIntosh, a prominent Creek planter, and Abram was born to enslaved parents who were owned by the Lewis family in the Creek nation, so it is very likely that he too was enslaved. Abram and Mary Ann Lewis married just two years after the Creek nation abolished slavery through the 1866 treaty with the United States. This was a year after the Thirteenth Amendment abolished most forms of slavery in the United States. Philip Lewis's ancestors on both his mother's and father's sides lived in the Creek nation for generations, as both Abram's and Mary Ann's families traveled the Trail of Tears with Creek enslavers who owned them as property. As black people in Indian Territory, Abram and Mary Anne, like so many formerly enslaved people after the Civil War, struggled to craft a new life for themselves as newly freed people. This struggle for self-definition was waged in the public sphere, as newly recognized citizens of the Creek nation, but it also transpired in the private sphere, within the realm of family and kinship ties. For indeed, the institution of chattel slavery violated not only their rights as human subjects deserving of equal political recognition, but also intruded on the most intimate parts of the human experience. Building a future, as freedmen, meant insisting on new political opportunities in the public sphere; it also required cultivating space and belonging in more private ways. As it was elsewhere, the public and private lives of black people in Indian Territory were deeply bound up in this way.[2]

Tullahassee reopened its doors to the exclusion of black people. This was consistent with broader efforts among the Five Tribes to rebuild their nations on antiblack terms, where they excluded the thousands of newly freed black people like Abram and Mary Ann for opportunities afforded other citizens. As it was during the post-removal period, Creek leaders looked to education as a national project that might heal bloody divisions of the Civil War. They also anticipated new US efforts to undermine their sovereignty. In the decades following the Civil War, US policymakers resurrected their long-standing political commitment to privatizing native lands, which historically had been held in common among indigenous nations. This process of allotment would not be realized until the 1890s, when the federal government divided tribal land using a list of tribal citizens called the Dawes Rolls—which readers will recall from the story of Susan McCoy in the opening pages. As with removal, however, the writing was on the wall far earlier. As US leaders debated if and how to incorporate emancipated slaves into their citizenry, indigenous leaders sought to refuse inclusion in the US state altogether. All the while, antiblackness remained a primary vehicle by which native leaders looked to chart their nation's future. Leaders within the Five Tribes employed strategies to place themselves alongside whites on equal (or superior) footing, which also required placing themselves in opposition to those who had been marked as slaves.[3]

As Indigenous Studies scholar Brian Klopotek explains, "tribes hoped there would be economic and political value to distinguishing themselves from blacks in the U.S.," as well as within their own tribal nations.

He insists such efforts were also matters of political pragmatism, "Losing their status as Indians altogether would threaten their legal claim to sovereignty and political equality," so "tribes saw distancing themselves from blacks as a useful political strategy." As a result of this, "anti-black racism seeped deeper still into the construction of Indian identity," and it conditioned the political terrain in Indian Territory in the afterlife of slavery.[4] The sentiments informing such practices of nation-building in Indian Territory, where black bodies were deemed fungible to the political cause of native sovereignty, were structured by legal, political, and economic factors facilitated by settler-colonial procedure.

Tullahassee became an institutional embodiment of such antiblack ideology. The school no longer relied on the slave labor, yet the institution continued to function as an instrument that relegated Creek freedmen to the lower rung of the social ladder. At the same time, formerly enslaved people like Abram and Mary Anne worked to build up their families and their communities, as a people in pursuit of full human recognition—among themselves, but also the nations in which they were living and striving.

AFRO-NATIVE ORGANIZING AND EDUCATIONAL ADVOCACY DURING RECONSTRUCTION

In the wake of the Civil War, education became a key site for the freedmen's political struggle among the Five Tribes, a site for contesting their subjugation as black people. The battle would be uphill. The freedmen's agitation and self-advocacy was met with violent resistance, from both white and native people. The story of Richard Brashears, a Choctaw freedman, and James Ladd, another black man, believed to be a Cherokee freedman (though he does not appear in the Dawes Rolls), makes for a historic example of such resistance to black self-determination.

The two men were arrested in November 1869 by Deputy US Marshal A. H. Carson for organizing and promoting a convention of Chickasaw and Choctaw freedmen.[5] Like Abram and Mary Anne Lewis, Richard Brashears was born enslaved in Indian country, having been forced to travel west along with his Choctaw enslaver, Vaughn Brashears, in 1831.[6] James Ladd was likely owned by a member of the Cherokee Ladd family before emancipation. While they were no longer enslaved, their status as citizens within their tribes was precarious at best; for Richard Brashears, it was literally nonexistent, as the Choctaw nation refused to recognize freedmen as citizens until 1885.

The convention being planned by Brashears and Ladd was to take place on December 16, 1869, near Armstrong Academy in the Choctaw nation. For their organizing, Deputy Carson charged Brashears and Ladd with sending "messages, circulars and letters to individuals in the Indian country with intent to disturb the peace and tranquility of the United States." Carson based this assertion on a letter from the two men, where they called for "a convention to take measures to obtain [our] rights as men and citizens of the nations and lay [our] grievances before Congress." The freedmen proclaimed, "Now is the time for action. If we do not work for ourselves, who will?"[7]

The convention was not the first of its kind. Brashears and Ladd helped plan two similar conventions in the months prior, at Skullyville in the Choctaw nation. These conventions planned by black people in Indian Territory paralleled the growth of colored conventions in the postbellum American South, which have been well chronicled in the work of Black Studies scholars such as P. Gabrielle Foreman, who explains that "as the Civil War came to an end and 4 million once-enslaved people could move and mobilize in ways that previously had been impossible, conventions spread across the South in the wake of Rebel soldiers' retreat." Formerly enslaved people "claimed full citizenship as equal political partners not just through their demands but through the process they used to collectively articulate and circulate them."[8]

As the case of James Brashears and James Ladd reveals, such political action was not limited to formerly enslaved people on US soil. The convention movement among black people also extended to their organizing among the Five Tribes. Such political struggles were intimately connected with those waged within the United States, as the paternalistic relationship between the federal government and native tribes had long infringed upon indigenous sovereignty. As Barbara Krauthamer writes, free people were keenly aware of US ambitions to weaken native nations, which "opened an avenue for the Choctaw and Chickasaw freedpeople to pursue their interests as former slaves." The demands black people made at their conventions in Indian country reflected this complicated dynamic, where the assembled freedmen appealed to the United States to aid them in achieving full citizenship in their respective native nations. Freedmen like Brashears and Ladd claimed membership in native nations while asking the American settler state to undermine indigenous sovereignty in order to cement such claims.

Radical republican and Union Army general Oliver Otis Howard—the white man for whom Howard University is named—described the violent response to the political action taken by the freedmen: "[T]he Indians, having taken alarm at the claims set up by their former slaves, determined to prevent the assembling of the convention, and crush out by force, if necessary, any attempt of the colored people to even peacefully deliberate on their sad condition. For this purpose, they sent out parties to tear down posters stuck up to call the convention, and throughout the country told the negroes that it was against the laws of the United States and their own country for them to hold conventions, and that any one venturing upon it would be killed." Thus it was the action of both native peoples and a representative from the US settler state, via Marshal Carson, that blocked the convention being organized by Brashears and Ladd. Due to antiblack intimidation tactics, the freedmen postponed and relocated their convention, to January 1870 at Skullyville.[9]

The freedmen convention's organizers likely chose Armstrong Academy for its symbolic importance as a national site within the Choctaw nation. In this same vein, the backlash they experienced may have been motivated by similar reasons. Armstrong Academy was an important political symbol for its historic role as a seat of Choctaw political power and a cornerstone for the tribe's project of national schooling. As previously mentioned, such educational institutions were part of a broader concerted effort among the tribes to rebuild themselves as a civilized nation in the post-removal context. Such schools excluded black students, before and after the Civil War, though they relied on black labor for their construction and maintenance. Thus the political struggle being waged by the freedmen at this specific location carried layered meaning.

Choctaw leaders looked to Armstrong Academy to be a flagship institution of the national education system they founded in 1845, and this was an institution that built off a long legacy of national schools, stretching back to the pre-removal era. Recall the story of Choctaw James McDonald, poster child for the Civilization Fund Act. In 1825, McDonald and his allies among the Choctaw elite led the charge to establish Choctaw Academy at Great Crossings in Kentucky. The tribal leaders intended for the school to be an incubator for Choctaw leadership. Building off this legacy, Armstrong Academy was developed to educate the next generation of Choctaw students, providing Western-style education to nonblack Choctaws—much like Tullahassee in the neighboring Creek nation. Like Tullahassee, Armstrong Academy also relied on enslaved black people to work at the school. According to an account recorded in an 1860 Commissioner of Indian Affairs report, the Armstrong Academy employed "five negro women and one man; salary of man, $150—women, $100 each—*all belonging to citizens of the [Choctaw] nation*."[10] As with Tullahassee, Armstrong Academy was part of an effort to rebuild a nation—one with antiblack domination at its foundation.

Armstrong became repurposed during the Civil War, when in 1863 it was declared the capital of the Choctaw nation. Confederate soldiers were stationed in the school's buildings, and the Confederate-aligned leaders of the Five Tribes met at Armstrong on several occasions. After the war, Armstrong remained the Choctaw capital until 1883. Therefore, when Brashears and Ladd set their sights on Armstrong, these two men and their co-organizers were not only bringing their political struggle to the doorstep of the Choctaw council. They were contesting a space that had long served as a symbol of antiblack domination within the nation they claimed as their home. What better location to discuss their demands? This was the place they intentionally selected to "claim citizenship of their native country and equal political rights with the Indians, and an equal share in all the benefits of citizenship, including educational facilities," as observed by General Howard.[11]

Abram Lewis and Mary Anne Hawkins married the same year Tullahassee reopened its doors in the Creek nation in 1868, and their son, Philip Lewis, was born the following year, in 1869—the same year freedmen were violently targeted and arrested for planning a political convention. Black life persisted even as freedmen's pursuits of justice and civic recognition continued to be met by violent antiblack resistance on the part of natives and white people. This was the conundrum of black life in Indian Territory, which Philip Lewis was born into. The same can be said for his future wife, Elzora, who was born two years later, also in the Creek nation.[12] The political organizing reflected in the convention movement in Indian Territory had a direct impact on the lives of the couple, particularly when it came to the development of new educational opportunities.

Much of what can be known about the life of Philip and Elzora Lewis is taken from their interviews with the Works Progress Administration during the 1930s and genealogical research based largely on information recorded in the Dawes Rolls. Philip recalled living with his grandmother, Rachel, for much of his childhood. She was "the community humanitarian," as Philip put it. He recalled, "She always made a home for every orphan or destitute child in the country and reared many besides myself. During my years with her, I am sure there was never less than twenty such cases . . . including widows and orphans of both, Indians and Negroes."[13]

While living with his grandmother, Philip began his education at a school organized at the Fountain Church, which succeeded Ebenezer Mission. While the mission became defunct in the 1850s, the Creek Freedmen's Baptist Association organized a church and school on the grounds of the old mission. It appears that this school, opened by the freedmen, educated both black and nonblack Creek children, as Philip remembers attending "with the other children [Rachel] was caring for," which included both black and native children. According to one scholar, coeducation was the norm at Fountain Church, which was led by "an old Negro," Ketch Banard, "for many years." The Fountain Church School represents one of the many ways freedpeople organized for education in Indian Territory, despite their tenuous positions within their respective nations. As freedmen like Brashears and Ladd demanded equal citizenship, which included meaningful educational opportunity for black youth, Afro-Creek communities organized neighborhood schools using the insufficient educational funds allotted to them by the Creek council, while surely taxing themselves to make up the gap.[14]

Elzora Lewis does not relay any information about her early schooling experiences, if she had any. Her formal education likely began in her teenage years, in the 1880s. Indeed, the 1880s were a time when freedmen gained unprecedented educational resources that allowed them to envision, and build, a more expansive future in Indian Territory. This time of increased opportunities for the freedmen resulted from consistent political organizing and self-advocacy. During the 1880s, schools formed part of the heart of Afro-native communities, "allowing Indian freedpeople to create Black spaces within Indian nations."[15] However, the story of black education among the Five Tribes is not a singular one. Just as slavery existed on a sliding scale among the nations, so too did black access to educational opportunities as an entitlement of their newly won freedom and citizenship (for those tribes that granted them citizenship).

While formerly enslaved people among the Cherokee, Creek, and Seminole tribes achieved near-equal rights to native members of the tribes shortly after the Civil War, this was not the case for Choctaw and Chickasaw freedmen. Among the Cherokee, Creek, and Seminole tribes, formerly enslaved people were able to participate in elections and even served in various capacities as elected officials. In the Creek and Seminole nations, black people even rose to the rank of judges and members of the tribal supreme court in the decades following emancipation. However, nothing could be further from reality among the Choctaw and Chickasaw nations. Historian Alaina Roberts notes, "As non-tribal members, Chickasaw freedpeople could not serve on juries or vote and were vulnerable to racial violence and poverty." She also notes that the Choctaw and Chickasaw nations also "enacted legislation akin to the US 'Black Codes,'" which set certain wages for ex-slaves and attempted to force freedpeople to find employment under Indian tribal members.[16]

Such degrees of freedom and civic recognition had direct implications on the development of black education in Indian Territory during the decades following the Civil War. Consistent with the citizenship status of Chickasaw freedpeople after emancipation, the nation also refused to provide any financial support for black education. Dawes Academy, which was built in 1890, has been recognized by some as "the first Negro school in the Chickasaw Nation." Educational opportunities were better in the other four tribes, even as antiblackness conditioned such opportunities. Within the Choctaw nation, thirty-four freedmen's schools received funding, "but the disparities between their schools and those for Choctaw children were substantial." Of the fifty-nine schools in the Cherokee nation, three were devoted to the education of freedmen children. The disparity reflected in this small number of schools for black people, as a racially segregated group, persisted into the early twentieth century. As for the Creek and Seminole freedmen, Roberts explains, "The Creek and Seminole tribes provided for the education of their formerly enslaved people in a manner commensurate with that of Creek and Seminole children, with the Creek Nation funding eight neighborhood schools for Creek freedpeople."[17]

However, while some comparative numbers reflect the degrees of oppression black people experienced across the nations, the reality is that even in the best cases their status as citizens were often challenged and undermined. For instance, the Creek were known to have been some of the most accepting of their former slaves, but we also know that one of the most violent recorded attacks on black education took place in the Creek nation during the antebellum era, with the attack at Withington Station in 1828. What's more, Creek freedmen noted how their precarious status within the nation continued to be reflected in the material realities of their education during the Reconstruction Era and beyond. In 1876, several freedmen serving on the Creek National Council—including Simon Brown, whose advocacy for black education during the Civil War helped earn him a prominent role in the Afro-Creek community—presented evidence of chronic underinvestment in black education since the adoption of freedmen as citizens in 1866. Despite the funding of eight Afro-Creek day schools beginning in 1867, the freedmen argued, the council had not equitably funded schools. They showed that the council had systematically underfunded black education by a cumulative $3,000.[18]

Responding to the demands of Afro-Creek leaders, in 1876 the council agreed to apportion $3,000—the total sum of underinvestment—to a boarding school for the freedmen. It was intended that this school would match the prestige and political function of Creek national schools and Choctaw Academy. The payment of these funds was, however, delayed two years, with the funds eventually materializing when Afro-Creek voters were needed to block an emerging threat of US encroachment. In 1878, Brainerd alumnus Elias C. Boudinot convinced the Senate Committee on Territories to hold hearings in the Creek nation on the topic of dividing the nation into privately held land and extending US territorial governance over it. The council, understanding the importance of presenting a unified front against the proposed plan to effectively destroy Creek lifeways, finally completed the allocation of $3,000 for a freedmen's boarding school, which was understood to be a more academically advanced educational institution, a step above the neighborhood schools, which essentially functioned as primary schools. In exchange, black Creek leaders like Simon Brown and Sugar George testified against Boudinot's proposal. This political trend continued. Creek political leaders' investment in black education was a means by which they courted black support, which also displayed keen insights about the centrality of education to the political priorities of the freedmen.[19]

While the Creek nation funded eight day schools starting in 1867, the first freedmen boarding school opened in 1878. It was overseen by a nonblack Creek Baptist man, Robert Leslie, and his wife, Nellie Ann, a highly educated black woman. As an alumnus of Tullahassee, Robert subscribed to a liberal arts educational model for male students, which included history, geography, and philosophy, as well as "advanced reading, writing, and arithmetic." Nellie Ann had been born into slavery in Virginia and received education in Ohio before teaching for the Freedmen's Bureau in Louisiana and Mississippi, where she taught the girls "household arts" in addition to their academic training, which reflected broader trends pertaining to gender and curriculum in mission schools. They hosted the school at the Union Agency, a US Indian station that closed during the Civil War. Elzora Lewis recalled attending this school when it was run by the Leslies. In particular, she noted, Nellie Ann's "services were invaluable in the training of the students at the Evangel Mission, as the school was known."[20]

The Leslies and their Afro-Creek students were displaced after about a year when the federal government reclaimed the site of the school and allowed the Baptist Home Mission Society to open a traditional mission school there, serving largely nonblack Creek children. Attempting to keep their school going, Robert and Nellie Ann taught freedmen students from their home near Muskogee from 1879 to 1880, and they worked with the school's trustees—which included Afro-Creek Monday Durant, who helped establish a sabbath school for freedmen during the Civil War—to secure labor and materials to build an addition to their house to board the students. However, the school stopped after Leslie's favor and political influence with the African Creek community began to wane.[21]

TULLAHASSEE BECOMES A BOARDING SCHOOL FOR CREEK FREEDMEN

The Leslies' school closed. However, Creek freedmen's self-advocacy for education persisted. They continued to advocate for a boarding school, and Tullahassee was eventually repurposed for this reason in March 1881. This legacy of educational advocacy was deeply connected to the memory of the Leslies' work with Afro-Creek students, particularly the work of Nellie Ann. For instance, in 1891, when Tullahassee was transferred to black Creek supervision, an anonymous citizen wrote to the *Muskogee Phoenix* nominating Nellie Ann Leslie for the job of principal. Anticipating Elzora's praise for Nellie Ann, the writer explained, "She is a teacher of ability, experience, and success. . . . Educated and refined Mrs. Leslie is queen of her race, respected by Indians and Caucasian. She is the admiration of all Africans in the Territory, and fully competent to lead the daughters of her people through fields of success, to the home of religion." This writer, likely of Afro-Creek heritage, insisted that the school be placed under the leadership of a capable and well-regarded black teacher. Indeed, a teacher who was "a queen of her race" and "the admiration of all Africans in the Territory." Nellie Ann did return to run Tullahassee in January 1891 but by October had resigned to help her brother raise his daughters in Texas after the loss of his wife.[22]

Though black people would repurpose Tullahassee to serve their own visions of freedom, the series of events leading to it being designated a black school requires further unpacking. Tullahassee caught fire on December 19, 1880, because of a defective flue, which partially destroyed the main school building. Operations continued after the laundry facilities were converted into a dining room and the workshop and wagon sheds were used as classrooms and sleeping quarters. However, the converted facilities were unable to accommodate all the students. Alice Robertson—the white missionary who returned to run the school after the Civil War—got permission for twenty-five students to be moved to the historic Carlisle Indian Industrial School.[23] At the same time, the Creek Council "immediately" appropriated about $25,000 for the construction of a much larger building at Wealaka as a school for Creek children.[24] Then, in March 1881, the council apportioned $5,000 to repair Tullahassee. However, the reason for repairing the school was to repurpose it for educating Creek freedmen, with the Creek council promising $70 per pupil per year.[25] In April the council passed a resolution for the school's trustees to turn over the school and all materials for educational operations to "the Colored Peoples of the Nation" to be used as a boarding school for Creek freedmen.[26]

The Afro-Creek community opposed Tullahassee being the designated site for black education. They wanted a school closer to their own communities.[27] There was also the troubled history of Tullahassee—an institution that had long excluded them and where, in living memory, some of them like Simon Brown had worked as enslaved people. Using one of the common tools employed by black political organizers of the day, leaders in the Afro-Creek community held a convention at Simon

Brown's ferry and resolved to not accept the site. They preferred that the school continue to be located at the Union agency, where it had been held under Leslie's tenure.[28]

Despite freedmen's resistance, the last Creek students at Tullahassee were moved to Wealaka Mission under the care of Robert Loughridge in 1882, and in 1883 the school was turned over to the American Baptist Home Mission Society, which would help manage the newly converted institution.[29] Three prominent African Creek citizens were made the trustees of the new school: Sugar George (who had served as first sergeant, and effectively led Company H of the First Indian Home Guard), Henry C. Reed (the judge of Muskogee District), and Snow Sells (the chief of Arkansas Town).[30] The trustees had full control over which students were let into the school.[31] At the time, there were sixty acres of land under cultivation, and the Creek Council still made annual appropriations for each student in attendance.[32] Around this time, the Creek Council began sending three or four Afro-Creek students to the US for the educational equivalent to what one scholar referred to as "a modern high school or junior college." The council appropriated $250 for each student.[33]

After Tullahassee reopened as a freedmen's school in November 1883, it was placed under the leadership of Reverend J. P. Lawton as superintendent. Lawton was appointed by the Baptist Home Mission Society, which had full control over the curriculum, teacher and superintendent placements, and all remaining aspects of the educational program at Tullahassee. The school functioned on an industrial and manual labor training program for the fifty black students who initially enrolled.[34] After several tumultuous years of leadership change, E. H. Rishell was appointed as superintendent of the school in 1887. He would be the one to welcome a young Philip Lewis to Tullahassee as a student that same year.

Philip spent four years at Tullahassee, building off the education he received at the Old Fountain school. Under Rishell's leadership, Philip learned "rhetorical drills, object lessons, drawing, algebra, natural philosophy, physiology and hygiene, botany, and, most particularly, the principles and practice of teaching, because most students were expected to become teachers."[35] He would have witnessed the school's expansion in 1889 to accommodate fifty more sponsored students, and the decision to open admission for local students. These local students were likely black students from families who moved to Oklahoma Territory from the South and paid seven dollars a month for the chance to learn alongside the children of Creek freedmen. In 1890, Philip helped expand the school's farm, which grew to two hundred acres and included vegetable gardens, orchards with peach, cherry, and apple trees, livestock raising and slaughtering facilities, and root-vegetable fields.[36]

Following Rishell's prediction, Philip became an assistant teacher in 1891, a pivotal year for the school. As the 1891 elections approached, Legus C. Perryman, representing the Union Party, began campaigning to be reelected. During the Civil War, Perryman helped secure funding for black education behind Union lines, and he was likely of African descent himself. However, Perryman chose to "pass" as Creek while simultaneously relying on black citizens for political support. One of his strategies for gaining support from African Creek communities was by promising "to use the money from the sale of the Oklahoma lands to support more schools," as noted by historian Gary Zellar. Perryman made good on his promise. In the months leading up to the election, he and his allies on the Creek Council "approved the establishment of two more African Creek boarding schools, one at Pecan Creek and a Colored Orphan's school at the agency building west of Muskogee that had been the site of Ira Cain's Evangel School." What's more, the council seized control of the nation's boarding schools from missionary societies and turned this control over to the communities themselves. Thus in 1891 control of Tullahassee was taken away from Baptist missionaries and turned over to Afro-Creek leaders.[37]

Perryman's courting of the Afro-Creek vote resulted in more schools for black students, but more importantly, it was a critical step toward freedmen's control of their education. Nellie Ann Leslie, the well-respected "queen of her race," was appointed superintendent of the new community-controlled Tullahassee. Philip Lewis, by then a young adult, left the school just as Leslie took charge. He would return ten years later, filling the position she vacated.

Even as control of education was turned over to Creek citizens, these communities did not completely break ties with white missionaries involved in Creek education up to this point. By 1900, Alice Robertson—who was previously expelled from the nation during the Civil War—was still around. In fact, she was chosen to be the superintendent of Creek schools in 1900, where she served until 1904.[38] Robertson appointed Philip Lewis superintendent of Tullahassee in 1901, when he was thirty-four years old, and he served in this position until 1904.

In his first year as superintendent, Lewis was paid fifty dollars a month and oversaw an all-black staff composed of principal teacher Howard Jenkins, assistant teachers James Clark, Laura A. Jackson, and Maud L. Craw, matron Elzora Lewis (Philip's wife), cook Ellen Marshall, and laborer James Long. There were 38 boys and 54 girls enrolled that year, though average attendance was 67.[39] The next year, the staff remained the same but enrollment had increased to 116, with an average attendance of 71. This year, the average cost per pupil was the highest of any of the Creek boarding schools at $118.74.[40]

Afro-Creek students and teachers at Tullahassee Manual Labor School, 1891. Courtesy of the Oklahoma Historical Society.[41]

The story of Tullahassee evolving from a school built and sustained by enslaved labor while excluding freedmen, to a facility used as barracks for the Confederate army, to a school only for nonblack Creek students after the Civil War, to, finally, a segregated boarding school exclusively for the education of Afro-Creek students reflects key developments in racial formation in Indian Territory. It is a complicated story, one reflecting an ever-shifting racial landscape among the Five Tribes, in which schools and education played a pivotal role. As in the United States, schools and educational policies in Indian Territory—which were deeply shaped by US native policy and racial ideology—were key sites in the tug-of-war over race relations, functioning as a key stratifying agent in society. More than any other place, educational institutions continued to serve as the main physical place where race was made and remade through relational politics between native, white, and black people.

Tullahassee's transformation parallels the lived experiences of Philip, Elzora, and their ancestors. Their parents, grandparents, and great-grandparents labored as enslaved people owned by the wealthy Creek elite who sent their children to Tullahassee, envisioning a future of a unified, and "civilized," Creek nation built on black subjugation. King Kernel, Rachel Kernel, Charles Lewis, Rachel Lewis, Miley McIntosh, Sam Hawkins, Abram Lewis, Mary Ann Hawkins, Susie Bruner Scott, Elizabeth Scott Fulsom, Louis Fulsom, and Philip and Elzora Lewis each in their own way insisted on creating a space for themselves in Indian country based on alternative visions for the future. This family's multigenerational survival converged with decades of activism for black education among the Five Tribes when Philip became superintendent of Tullahassee in 1901. In previous generations, his ancestors' labor had been exploited to pay tuition for nonblack Creeks to be educated here. In 1901 he could walk the school grounds with the knowledge that this space now belonged to those black Creeks who, like his ancestors, persisted anyhow.

•••

THE LEGACY OF BLACK EDUCATION AND POLITICAL ADVOCACY AMONG THE FIVE TRIBES

In the years between Philip Lewis's graduation from Tullahassee in 1891 and his return as superintendent in 1901, the young man plunged himself into tribal politics. It was a crucial time for the Creek nation, which, through the political maneuverings mentioned earlier, had managed to present a unified front against the US government's ambitions to privatize Creek land and place the nation under direct territorial governance—a process eventually known as allotment. By the 1890s, this plan seemed more and more imminent. Creek people, including freedmen, were keenly aware that the nation was under pressure from private interests, encroachments—both US-sanctioned and nominally illegal—of white and black newcomers, as well as increasing political momentum in Washington around the cause of allotment.

The US government's role in manufacturing political conditions in Indian Territory during the 1890s is difficult to overstate. In 1877, as part of a political deal to be named president, Rutherford B. Hayes abruptly ended Reconstruction in the American South, almost overnight resigning black Americans to being governed by violent white supremacist regimes without the protection of federal troops or infrastructure. It is little wonder, then, that when the US government began opening lands in Oklahoma Territory (not yet a state) to US settlement—directly adjacent to the homelands of the Five Tribes—many African Americans looked west to imagine communities free of the state-sanctioned violence and economic depravity they faced in many Southern states.

Ida B. Wells, the famous antilynching crusader, was one such black American. Wells never personally fled to Oklahoma, but she visited the territory for three weeks in 1892 and wrote now-lost weekly reports in the Memphis *Free Speech*, in which she recalled "telling my readers exactly what I saw and of the chance they had of developing manhood and womanhood in this new territory."[42] Thousands of black citizens left Memphis for Oklahoma during the 1890s, in large part at Wells's urging.

The destruction of the *Free Speech* building and its issues means that almost all of Wells's trip to Oklahoma is lost to history. We cannot know, for example, whether she met William Sulcer and Jefferson Davis Randolph in Oklahoma City, two black teachers originally from Gallatin, Tennessee. What we do know, however, is that a year after Wells's time in Oklahoma, these men joined with about a dozen black educators and intellectuals to create the Ida M. Wells Teacher's Association (the *M.* is presumed to be a misnomer). Indeed, Wells herself was a public schoolteacher in Memphis and an active member of the black teachers association in her state.

Visions of more educational opportunity were also a key part of the black exodus to Oklahoma Territory. An 1898 column in the *Muskogee Phoenix* emphasizes this point, offering that all "Indications point to an influx of colored people, who will move to Muskogee to take advantage of the colored public schools. . . . The new colored school will be located on Baptist Hill and will contain four rooms, and two teachers will be employed."[43] The Ida M. Wells Teacher's Association endeavored to help meet the tremendous demand for education in Oklahoma, providing support for educators and advocating for causes like normal schools for black and white teachers in the territory.[44] The organization's name—in paying homage to Wells—highlights the close interconnections that black Oklahomans understood between emigration, freedom, and education.

The burgeoning activism for black education in Oklahoma paralleled, in many ways, longtime Afro-Creek activism for education in their nation. Indeed, it is possible that black newcomers living in the nearby Oklahoma territory enrolled their children in Tullahassee for the monthly fee of seven dollars beginning in 1889. However, even though black leaders in both contexts organized for education as part of their visions of freedom, there was considerable tension between "native" black people—those who had been enslaved among the Five Tribes—and the newcomers, most of whom had been enslaved in the American South. As Gary Zellar writes, "African creeks harbored considerable prejudice against state freed people, and those feelings grew as the number of black intruders increased." Surely a large part of this growing hostility was not simple xenophobia, but fear of what the growing presence of white and black settlers represented for the future of the Five Tribes. Once again it was the US government that structured the tension between Afro-native people and black newcomers, as federal actions (and inaction) must be accounted for in our assessment of the push and pull factors leading to black flight from Southern states.[45]

With the passage of the Dawes Act in 1887, Congress outlined a process whereby native nations would be broken up into privately held allotments. The Five Tribes, returning to their well-established strategies of civilization politics, successfully lobbied to be exempt from the Dawes Act. However, that did not stop the US government from trying to convince the nations to agree to allotment. In 1893, as William Sulcer and Jefferson Davis Randolph created their association for black educators in Oklahoma City, the Dawes Commission traveled to Okmulgee, one hundred miles east in the Creek nation, and at the same time, Afro-Creek leaders spoke against the aims of this commission. Indeed, the well-respected black town chief Paro Bruner warned his countrymen that "nothing good would come from division of property."[46]

It is unclear if Lewis heard Paro's warning, but he certainly agreed with the spirit of it. In 1895, as the Dawes Commission continued to make plans for allotting the Five Tribes, Philip Lewis ran for and was elected to the House of Warriors, the legislative branch of the Creek national government. He ran on a platform of Creek sovereignty, aiming to prevent the leasing of tribal lands to private cattle companies and the dismantling of illegally constructed fences. His campaign against cattle interests ultimately failed, but Lewis spent several years in the legislature, working to strengthen the nation's sovereignty in the face of private and federal pressure. Lewis's education and standing in the Afro-Creek community as a widely respected teacher certainly positioned him well for such positions of influence.[47]

Despite Philip Lewis's best efforts—and the efforts of black and native people across the Five Tribes—to forestall allotment, the Curtis Act of 1898 extended the Dawes process to include them. From this point forward, members of the Five Tribes were required to prove their ancestry within their respective nations to agents of the Dawes Commission in order to receive an allotment. The commission's "enrollment process" evaluated citizenship based upon blood quantum. Freedmen could also enroll, as long as they could prove that their ancestors were enslaved by members of the Five Tribes.

The Dawes Commission was stringent in judging citizenship. This was supposedly to protect against greedy settlers constantly seeking more land, but it seems more likely that such rigid standards were also motivated by a desire to dispossess *native* and *Afro-native* people of their land. Readers will, again, recall the story of Susan McCoy presented earlier. Tribal enrollment through the Dawes Commission was a cumbersome bureaucratic process that would allow for oversight, dismissal of claims on technicalities, and various other means of undermining the recognition of vulnerable people seeking to make claims on behalf of themselves and their people.[48]

As historian Kendra Field perceptively writes, "Acre by acre, the Dawes Act depleted the American Indian land base, forced American Indians into capitalist land markets, and, in turn, imposed patrilineal nuclear households in place of long-standing matrilineal societies."[49] Crucial community institutions, too, were shuttered through the allotment process. Tullahassee operated for about a decade following allotment, but it was closed in September 1913 and slated to be sold. Creek freedmen on the Creek Council attempted to organize a purchase of the school building so it could continue to serve their children; however, they were unable to raise sufficient funds. Though they could not purchase the school themselves, the Creek freedmen saw to it that the school was sold to a black organization: the African Methodist Episcopal Church purchased Tullahassee in 1916.[50]

The allotment process was devastating, but it also illuminated the strength of community ties in Indian country. In this history emerges people like Philip Lewis, who volunteered their services to work as advocates for their community during this process. The record also reveals the work of Afro-Creek Paro Bruner, the *micco*, or local leader, of an Afro-Creek community known as Canadian Colored Town. Paro helped shepherd his kin through the enrollment process, leveraging his knowledge and local power to ensure that the people with whom he shared relation were given adjacent allotments.[51] In fact, Paro had long been a community leader among the Afro-Creeks when it came to their educational strivings. He was one of the freedmen serving on the Creek National Council in 1876, when this cohort of representatives presented evidence documenting the Creek nation's underinvestment in black education. It was this advocacy that ultimately led to Tullahassee becoming a school for black citizens in the nation. Philip Lewis would be a beneficiary of this political advocacy on the part of Paro Bruner and the other freedmen on the council.

Philip Lewis also assumed a similar role as Bruner, as a leader and advocate in the Afro-Creek community. He too secured adjacent allotments for his daughters, Edna and Melvina, and he advocated for other freedmen as a volunteer and, eventually, as a federal agent. Lewis's recognition of literacy's role as an instrument of political advocacy and simultaneously as one that could be used to exploit an oppressed people is deeply reflective of black political orientations to education throughout the nineteenth century. In this moment, his education had a very practical use as Creek people navigated a deeply violent phase of US Indian policy. Paro and Philip would have visited the same office in Muskogee, as they supported freedmen during the enrollment process.[52]

What we learn from Lewis's work with the Dawes Commission amid this chaos of tribal enrollment and land allotment—after seeing no other viable choice but to do so—is that the freedmen, despite being segregated in education and subjected to increasing antiblackness, as race eclipsed nationality in the American West, understood themselves to be deeply implicated in the political future of the Five Tribes. Having long recognized education to be a critical site in their struggle for political life, the freedmen used their education to insist on a future of belonging, among themselves and within a world they were forced to help build, as it continued to evolve.

Philip Lewis's literacy was made possible by the self-funded and self-organized black day schools and later Tullahassee, a boarding school created as a result of advocacy among the Afro-Creek community. This very literacy would allow him to help secure the future prospects of

Creek people and especially freedmen and their descendants. While taken for granted in the twenty-first century, it is important to stress the significance of literacy in the nineteenth century as an important tool in the struggle for personhood and political organizing. It was (and still is) an educational resource inequitably distributed, even as it was heavily relied-on in political matters that affected the everyday life of all people. What's more, literacy was also about the struggle for recognition within the history-making process in a world of textual dominance, where the written word is the primary form of acceptable knowledge and the primary means for making political and economic claims against, and within, the settler nation. It was and continues to be a matter of survival—for all people, but especially those most vulnerable among us.

People like Philip Lewis, Paro Bruner, and so many unnamed and unheralded literate Afro-natives volunteered their time and leveraged their education to ensure that freedmen and their descendants received land to secure new futures within an ever-changing world. In doing so, they also made sure their names were written into the colonial archives of the settler state, indeed embedding a counternarrative in the transcripts of settler history, which makes the recovery of submerged histories possible—a kind of fugitive inscription. Such literacy acts carry multiple meanings, and they invite more than one way of reading. Some have called the Dawes Allotment era a time of "pencil genocide": a time when both native and Afro-native people were allowed to formally fall through the cracks of bureaucratic procedure; written out of tribal citizenship and, therefore, denied land and formal recognition of who they were. The decisions of committees appointed by the US government, and in particular the lines they drew on maps of indigenous lands, shrank nations, disenfranchised individuals, and foreclosed untold names from written history. Indeed, this chapter has noted people, like James Ladd and Ketch Banard, whose names never made it to the Dawes Rolls. However, it also notes those whom Philip Lewis and Paro Bruner helped, allowing them to escape, or at least mitigate damage caused by this "pencil genocide."[53]

Native nations use the Dawes Rolls to determine eligibility for tribal citizenship, even to this day. Lewis and Bruner may not have foreseen this, but their decision to fight for and claim citizenship as members of the freedmen community among the Five Tribes, and to help their kin and community members claim theirs, has had long-lasting implications for future generations. The insistence of black natives—like Philip, Elzora, and their parents, and so many more—to gain access to a meaningful education laid the groundwork for Afro-natives today to defend their claims to tribal citizenship, as they did in 2017's *Cherokee Nation v. Nash.*

Indeed, it is because of the nineteenth century struggle for black education in Indian country that Angela Walton-Raji, whose story appears in the beginning of Part III, was able to find her ancestors in the Freedmen Rolls as she searched for them in recent decades. Walton-Raji's research on the history of African–native American culture and genealogy is an extension of Lewis and Elzora's legacy.

The genuine pursuit of education is always, in some part, about the pursuit of self-knowledge. To seek understanding and knowledge about how to be in right relationship with (and in) the world, is always a search to encounter oneself and the relations that make us who we are in the world. Black people's particular struggle for education in Indian country was also about this universal quest in human experience.

PART IV

BOOKER T. WASHINGTON AND THE FOUNDING RACIAL TRIAD

13

BOOKER T. WASHINGTON: A MONUMENTAL AMERICAN LIFE

> In the fall of 1905 I spent a week in the Territories of Oklahoma and Indian Territory. During the course of my visit I had an opportunity for the first time to see the three races -the Negro, the Indian, and the white man -living side by side. . . . It was not my first acquaintance with the Indian. During the last years of my stay at Hampton Institute I had charge of the Indian students there, and had come to have a high respect both for their character and intelligence, so that I was particularly interested to see them in their own country, where they still preserve to some extent their native institutions.
>
> —Booker T. Washington (1908)

The final chapters of this book move from exploring the structural relations of black, native, and white education at a granular level to tracking this phenomenon in the intimate story of a single person. I can think of no better life to illuminate the centrality of slavery and settler colonialism in the development of the national educational landscape through the nineteenth century than that of Booker T. Washington, a formerly enslaved man who became one of the most recognizable education leaders in the United States by the turn of the century.

Washington is mostly associated with the story of African American education from the slavery era through Jim Crow, having been born enslaved in 1856, then educated through the Reconstruction period, before emerging as a key institution builder after graduating from Hampton Institute in 1875. However, Part IV takes the familiar life of Washington and reads it in an unfamiliar way, insisting that Washington's life offers a window to much more than a segregated perspective on American schooling. As demonstrated thus far, education for the founding racial triad was not altogether a separate reality; it was in fact fiscally, physically, and symbolically interconnected from the earliest years of US educational development. Therefore, I analyze key moments in Washington's educational journey that underscore how the relational formation of race was integral to the social foundations of American schooling. This offers a grounded narrative to reflect on key conceptual and historical arguments covered thus far.

I was prompted to think of Washington as a major figure in this narrative during my 2021 conversation with Afro-Choctaw scholar Angela Walton-Raji, as we discussed the subject of black education in Indian Territory. To emphasize the connection between this history and broader developments of black education in the US, Angela told a story passed down among Afro-native communities about Booker T. Washington's visit to Indian Territory and Oklahoma Territory in 1905. This was two years before Oklahoma statehood in 1907.

It was Washington's first visit to the territories, Angela explained. While touring, Washington asked to meet the "natives." However, each time he made this request the hosts introduced him to Creek freedmen—black people who descended from those formerly enslaved by the Creek nation, many of whom had Creek and African ancestry. Washington eventually made his request more specific. He wanted to meet natives that were Indian, not black. Angela shared this story to emphasize how strongly Indian freedmen identified as both black and native, but also to stress the connection between black education spanning Indian Territory and the broader United States. In the context of our conversation, Washington's visit and the Afro-native community's enthusiastic reception of him illustrated this point. It also emphasized the importance of Afro-native stories to black and indigenous histories.

I later found Washington's own discussion of his visit in a written account from 1908. He explained: "When I inquired, as I frequently did, for the 'natives,' it almost invariably happened that I was introduced, not to an Indian, but to a negro. During my visit to the city of Muskogee I stopped at the home of one of the prominent 'natives' of the Creek Nation, the Hon. C. W. Sango, Superintendent of the Tullahassee Mission. But he is a negro." Washington insisted "at length" on meeting "a genuine native Indian." This desire stemmed from Washington's previous experience teaching in the Indian Program at the Hampton Normal and Agricultural Institute between 1879 and 1881, where he also served as the dorm father for native American male students. Washington explained, "During the last years of my stay at Hampton Institute I had charge of the Indian students there, and had come to have a high respect both for their character and intelligence, so that I was particularly interested to see them in their own country, where they still preserve to some extent their native institutions."[1]

Washington visited various places in Indian Territory and Oklahoma Territory in the fall of 1905. The tour extended from his prominent standing in the United States, particularly as an influential voice in education. According to *The Muskogee Cimeter*, Washington's celebrity was widely known across the territories, especially when we account for the many African American Southerners who migrated west during the late nineteenth century, either to escape racial violence or to pursue landownership and a new life.[2] These people would have known of Washington's prominence from black newspapers and via word of mouth. *The Muskogee Cimeter* reported, "At each village and hamlet the people had gathered to see the Washington Special pass. The little school children had gathered at numerous places along the railroad with flags and waved as the train passed."[3]

Black people in and around Muskogee enthusiastically prepared for Washington's arrival. One can only imagine the abundance of stories circulating in classrooms and churches, and in passing chatter among the townsfolk. For indeed, there was much to discuss when it came to the life of Booker T. Washington—the man who was born a slave, worked in the salt mines after emancipation, then as a janitor to pay his way through Hampton Institute, only to go on and found the Tuskegee

Institute in Alabama, growing it into one of the largest and wealthiest educational institutions in the South. Black public school teachers, as well as those at the Pecan Mission and Tullahassee Mission schools, were well informed of Washington's accomplishments. Washington's educational leadership, particularly his founding of Tuskegee in 1881, likely resonated with black teachers working at Tullahassee's Mission School, given the institution's own history. Tullahassee students and those from surrounding schools were eager to lay eyes on Washington, perhaps even shake his hand. The train pulled into Muskogee at 4:47 p.m. on November 20, and as was the case in other towns, students "were in line and with the waving of flags . . . they bade welcome to the great race Leader who had journeyed so far to greet them." According to the local newspaper, Tuskegee's founder met an enthusiastic crowd of ten thousand people as he exited his train. The applause was deafening. *The Muskogee Cimeter* columnist explained, "for fully fifteen minutes it was impossible to get our distinguished visitor to the waiting carriage" due to the thunderous clapping and cheering among the jam-packed crowd. So extraordinary was the fanfare, the columnist declared: "The 20th of November will go down in the history of Muskogee as Booker Washington Day."[4]

THE STATURE OF BOOKER T. WASHINGTON

Jubilant celebrations of Booker T. Washington were not uncommon. Following the death of Frederick Douglass in February 1895 and Washington's historic speech at the Atlanta Cotton Exposition months later, the founder of Tuskegee quickly became the most prominent African American political leader. His ascent was partially due to his own commitment to black institution-building and the inspiring story of his personal and professional rise from the lowest rung of the social ladder. However, it was also due to the consolidated backing of wealthy white social reformers. White philanthropists and reformers preferred Washington's particular approach to racial uplift over other contemporary black political leaders, like W. E. B. Du Bois and Ida B. Wells-

Barnett. Washington avoided direct forms of political conflict with white Americans, instead strategizing around economic development in black communities and marketing such efforts as mutually beneficial to both groups living alongside one another in the racially volatile post-Reconstruction South.

Washington was widely respected among black communities for his institution-building, sincere commitment to the race, and concern about everyday black people, especially in the rural South. However, some among the black educated elite grew increasingly critical of the leader. They especially criticized the role of white philanthropists and social reformers selecting Washington as the spokesperson on all matters pertaining to "the Negro," which further undermined the power of an already disenfranchised people. Because of his backing by wealthy whites, Washington obtained an outsized influence over black politics and educational development. Wealthy reformers amplified and appropriated Washington's voice as a means of drowning out and suppressing others, making conscious decisions not to support African American leaders they deemed too radical.

Given the economic precarity among black communities, being one or two generations removed from slavery, they were forced to rely on private white capital to support their collective development, especially in light of the inequitable distribution of public resources and the curtailing of citizenship rights gained through emancipation. However, such support from white helping hands came with strings attached. Washington's silence on political affairs and endorsement of practical education (that is, industrial and agricultural training) as opposed to classical education (that is, the liberal arts) were the implied terms of an agreement between him and "the white architects of black education"—people like John D. Rockefeller, Andrew Carnegie, Thomas Jesse Jones, and Julius Rosenwald.[5] Washington's rise was accelerated by a group of well-coordinated white philanthropists and social reformers motivated by desires to reunite the North and the South in the wake of the Civil War, to keep racial tensions contained, and to increase the efficiency and expansion of corporate enterprises, all of which they understood to be in the best interest of the nation. For many in this group, the immediate political needs of black people were at best a secondary concern. While not minimizing Washington's contributions, and placing his personal intentions aside, it is important to name the manipulative functions of white private capital lurking in the background of Washington's story, which ultimately had a polarizing and divisive impact in black political life.

Black intellectuals and political figures such as Du Bois and Wells-Barnett critiqued Washington's approach to education and racial uplift, particularly his public eschewing of politics and protest. Though Washington secretly supported various political causes, which may or may not have been known to all his critics, many believed his public silence on things such as lynching, black disenfranchisement, and segregation helped perpetuate antiblackness, and they suggested he was too accepting of black people's status as second-class citizens. Professor Kelly Miller, dean of Howard University's College of Arts and Sciences beginning in 1907, made the following assessment of Washington's complex negotiation of race and power in America: "Mr. Washington's popularity and prominence depend largely upon the fact that his putative policy is acceptable to the Southern whites, because *he allows them to believe* that he accepts their estimate of the Negro's inferior place in the social scheme. . . . [E]ven when he protests against his [white Southerners'] practices the protestation is so palliatory that, like a good conscience, it is void of offense. Equality between the races, whether social, political, or civil, is an unsavory term to the white man's palate, and, therefore, Mr. Washington obliterates it from his vocabulary."[6]

As chairman of the Anti-Lynching League, Ida B. Wells-Barnett was one such critic of Washington's conspicuous silence. As a former public schoolteacher from Memphis, Tennessee, she was also extremely critical of Washington's narrow focus on practical education and heavy-handed criticism of liberal arts education for African Americans. In 1903 Wells-Barnett wrote the following: "That one of the most noted of their own race should join with the enemies to their highest progress in condemning the [classical/liberal arts] education they had received, has been to them a bitter pill" for educated African Americans. She insisted "this gospel of work" undergirding Washington's model of industrial education "is no new one for the Negro. It is the South's old slavery practice in a new dress."[7] Wells-Barnett was aware of Washington's response to his critics, that he did not oppose higher education outright, just simply advocated a different model for the masses of black people forced to make a living under the current agricultural economy in the South. Washington pointed to the faculty at Tuskegee, most of whom were educated at liberal arts colleges, as evidence that he was not dogmatic in his commitment to practical education. Such claims by Washington, however, failed to convince Wells-Barnett. "But the critics observe that nowhere does he speak for [higher education]," writes Wells-Barnett, "and they can remember dozens of instances when he has condemned every system of education save that which teaches the Negro how to work." She insisted that Washington's silence in one area and outspokenness in the other had the impact of threatening "the educational opportunities of the masses," which were "always limited enough." Wells-Barnett declared, "it is this feeling which prompts the criticism. They are beginning to feel that if they longer keep silent, Negro educational advantages will be even more restricted in all directions."[8]

Washington's most influential critic, however, was W. E. B. Du Bois. Du Bois was the first black person to earn a PhD from Harvard, in 1895—just one year before Harvard awarded Washington an honorary master's degree in 1896, and six years before Dartmouth conferred an honorary doctorate upon the Tuskegee founder in 1901, making Washington the only formerly enslaved person to hold a doctorate degree from an Ivy League institution. As readers may recall, both Harvard and Dartmouth are intimately connected to the exploitation of black enslaved labor and the dispossession of native people. Harvard's charter included in its mission the education of native people for settler-colonial objectives, while being economically developed and sustained by slave capital, and Dartmouth was founded as a school for "civilizing" native students while also relying on the physical labor of the enslaved people owned by its founder Eleazar Wheelock.[9] I emphasize the history of Du Bois and Washington in relation to such prominent white American institutions of higher education to stress their stature in the national educational landscape by the dawn of the twentieth century, just decades after the Civil War, but also to call attention to the presence of native dispossession in the trajectory of black education in Jim Crow America, even when individual native communities may not be immediately present in the stories.

In his most iconic book, *Souls of Black Folk*, Du Bois devoted an entire chapter to his criticisms of the Tuskegee founder, titled "On Booker T. Washington and Others."[10] In another instance, Du Bois succinctly asserts that while on one hand, Washington "was the greatest Negro leader since Frederick Douglass, and the most distinguished man, white or black, who came out of the South since the Civil War. . . . On the other hand, in stern justice, we must lay on the soul of this man, a heavy responsibility for the consummation of Negro disenfranchisement, the decline of the Negro college and public school, and the firmer establishment of color caste in this land."[11] Du Bois insisted that Washington allowed himself to be used as an instrument for the stripping away of political rights black Americans gained after emancipation by choosing to be publicly silent on matters of political urgency for fear of losing support from white funders. Du Bois held great influence among the black intellectual elite and the anti–Booker T. Washington faction of political leaders, which continued to grow after Washington's 1895 speech, which Du Bois later called "the Atlanta Compromise."

But what did Washington have to say on the matter? From Washington's perspective, protests and classical education could not meet the immediate needs of most black people, especially those living in the South in the wake of Reconstruction. He stressed the need to do "a real thing," as he often put it. Washington's emphasis on doing *a real thing* was his way of stressing the need to address the material conditions of black life and to engage in efforts that made "real" material impact in the day-to-day lives of African Americans. For Washington, this included things like creating more black businesses, increasing opportunities and training for black farmers, building modern school buildings for African American children, and ultimately expanding models of black capitalism, where black wealth could support the internal development of black communities in the absence of external support. Accomplishing these required resources from outside of African American communities. Therefore, Washington relied heavily on white philanthropists and reformers to raise funds and build institutions, while also encouraging in-kind services and donations from black communities as a way of cultivating self-help. As Washington explained at the Afro-American Council in July 1903: "We have a right in a conservative and sensible manner to enter our complaints, but we shall make a fatal error if we yield to the temptation of believing that mere opposition to our wrongs . . . will take the place of progressive, constructive action. . . . An inch of progress is worth more than a yard of complaint."[12]

Washington's approach was outlined in the 1895 Atlanta Exposition speech that catapulted him into the national spotlight. He made the following appeal to the majority-white audience, as black Americans sat in the balcony: "As we have proved our loyalty to you in the past, in nursing your children, watching by the sick-bed of your mothers and fathers, and often following them with tear-dimmed eyes to their graves, so in the future, in our humble way, we shall stand by you with a devotion that no foreigner can approach, ready to lay down our lives, if need be, in defense of yours, interlacing our industrial, commercial, civil, and religious life with yours in a way that shall make the interests of both races one." The heart of Washington's appeal is most immediately apparent in his assertion that, "In all things that are purely social we can be as separate as the fingers, yet one as the hand in all things essential to mutual progress."[13] This was a very distinct strategy of racial uplift—one that posed no immediate disruption to the social customs and hierarchy being enmeshed through law and policy during Jim Crow, but instead a strategy that attempted to work within its restraints. It was a strategy rooted in black capitalism and mutual economic progress between the races, all while forgoing demands for equal rights as citizens. In his message to white people, Washington insists that helping African Americans become more efficient laborers, by supporting projects like Tuskegee Institute, would serve the long-term interests of the Southern states and the nation. It was an appeal rooted in the logic of what present-day scholars have come to know as "interest convergence": Washington sought to advance the causes of black uplift by focusing on attainable goals that converged with the interests of whites, particularly those of white businessmen.[14]

While it seems obvious from our temporal vantage point why black American leaders organized against Washington's efforts, there were also some white Americans who found Washington's approach offensive. Notably, Washington's white critics were not only progressive white Americans who shared the concerns of Du Bois and Wells-Barnett. While a core group of wealthy white philanthropists and reformers preferred Washington to other black leaders, many white Southerners publicly expressed their distrust of Washington, even pointing to his public accommodationist politics as mere performance. Washington did not publicly insist on social equality; nevertheless, many white Southerners believed he was striving toward this goal in secret.

In 1904, the year before Washington's trip to Indian and Oklahoma Territories, Alabama Congressman James Thomas Heflin—also known as "Cotton Tom"—threatened to lynch the Tuskegee founder, insisting that he was sneaky and accusing Washington of pretending through his apolitical public posturing. Georgia Congressman Tom Watson not only accused the Tuskegee founder of teaching racial equality, but also insisted Washington preached that the Negro was superior to white people. This was not the only attack Washington received from white Southerners who questioned whether or not he knew his place.[15]

In August 1905, just months before Washington's visit to Indian Territory, the famous North Carolina writer Thomas Dixon wrote a pamphlet condemning Washington as a liar and conspirator, hoping to reveal what he understood to be the true mission of Tuskegee Institute. Screaming to white readers, hoping they would listen, Dixon asserted, "Tuskegee is not a servant training school!" The black leader had gotten along by telling Southerners his plan was not to educate African Americans in a manner that would take them away from the jobs available to them in the South—as domestics, agricultural laborers, and other roles that served white planters. However, Dixon insisted, Washington could not be trusted. It was all a lie. "Mr. Washington is not training Negroes to take their places in the industries of the South in which white men direct and control them. He is not training students to be servants and come at the beck and call of any man. He is training them to be masters of men, to be independent, to own and operate their own industries, plant their own field, buy and sell their own goods." Washington was tricking the public and needed to be held accountable for his deception. Dixon threatened that his next novel would be titled *The Downfall of Tuskegee.*[16] Indeed, this is what he hoped for, and so too did many other white Americans, especially in the South.

Despite the controversy Washington's name carried among the black intellectual elite, and especially among white Southerners, his success building Tuskegee Institute made him extremely popular among the masses of African American people. And for pragmatic reasons, many black leaders—especially business leaders—also held Washington in high esteem. The scale and scope of his influence led leading scholars of African American history to characterize the years between 1895 and 1915 as "the age of Booker T. Washington."[17] During this period, Washington had more influence in black social and political life—and arguably the Southern region—than any other single figure. Like his predecessor, Frederick Douglass, Washington even provided close consultation to US presidents. For instance, when discussing his African American appointees in 1903, Theodore Roosevelt explained all "were recommended to me by Booker T. Washington."[18] Simply put, the Tuskegee founder's celebrity and political influence was unprecedented among African Americans. This was the man traveling by train to meet black people and "genuine native Indians" out in Muskogee.

Muskogee's teachers and students likely learned about Washington from his widely celebrated book, *Up from Slavery*, published in 1901. They would have also heard stories in the black press, such as a recent controversy about President Theodore Roosevelt inviting the Tuskegee founder to dine at the White House that same year, making him the first African American to do so.

Up from Slavery was a postbellum slave narrative, detailing the story of Washington's rise from bondage, first through physical freedom occasioned by the Emancipation Proclamation, then through economic freedom that he obtained through a mixture of individual hard work, self-determination among poor black communities, and assistance from charitable white Americans willing to give a helping hand. The book was an early black iteration of the American dream. Though Washington's life is central to the text, the heart of the story is actually Tuskegee Institute—a school Washington founded while first teaching "in a stable and a hen house." In the book, Washington's rise is metaphorically represented by the rapid ascension of Tuskegee, which grew into one of the largest and most endowed educational institutions in the South by the early twentieth century. The epic story of this school and its founder gave hope to black people who still carried intimate memories of bondage. African Americans were still working to pull themselves up from slavery across the United States—even in Indian Territory. Black people looked to Washington's story hoping that his trajectory anticipated their collective ascent.

Even racist white Southerners admired the story of human striving and triumph displayed in Washington's book, though their commentary was couched in antiblack sentiments. North Carolina novelist Thomas Dixon Jr. wrote, "The story of this little ragged, barefooted pickaninny, who lifted his eyes from a cabin in the hills of Virginia, saw a vision and followed it, until at last he presides over the richest and most powerful institution in the South, and sits down with crowned heads and presidents, has no parallel even in the Tales of the Arabian Nights."[19] Such praise should not be misunderstood as wide-scale support by white Southerners, however. Dixon's reference to Washington sitting down with the US president was an event that inspired much ire among white Americans, especially white Southerners, though the event inspired pride among African Americans. A senator from South Carolina deemed the event unconscionable, insisting that "lynching a thousand niggers in the South" would be required to right this wrong, that this was the only way "they will learn their place again." White political leaders continued referencing this historic event as a disgrace. In 1903, Mississippi Governor James K. Vardaman insisted that the stench of Washington lingered in the White House. He complained that the place was "so saturated with the odor of the nigger that the rats have taken refuge in the stable."[20]

In contrast to such vile commentary among white Southern politicians, the story of Washington dining at the White House was cause for great excitement in African American communities, as the narrative traveled around the country. The event was awe-inspiring for a people constantly buked and scorned in the broader political sphere, as they continued fighting for equal opportunity and the rooting out of antiblackness in American society. One can imagine how teachers and community leaders might use such a historic narrative as a resource in their work of positive racial socialization with black youth in classrooms; how they may have used the story to cultivate the aspirations of black students, despite the barriers faced all around them. Washington sitting down and dining with the US president at the White House could have easily led some to interpret this as a first step toward imagining how someday a Negro might do more than just dine at the White House, but perhaps even become president. This would have been the substance of the stories circulating in classrooms, churches, and in the chatter among the townsfolk of Muskogee as they caught wind of Washington's visit. Perhaps some would have criticized such an aspiration, but either way, Washington's life offered teachable lessons that disrupted the status quo.

BOOKER T. WASHINGTON'S MONUMENTAL PRESENCE IN EDUCATIONAL HISTORY

I visited Tuskegee University to attend my sister's college graduation in 2022. This was exactly one year following my interview with Angela Walton-Raji. I recall thinking about the complexity of the school's legacy during the visit, holding the controversial memories associated with its founder in tension with the fact that Tuskegee continues to be an important site for black educational striving in the present moment. My own sister fell in love with "Mother Tuskegee" as a high school student while attending an HBCU tour, before enrolling in 2018. I remember her explaining why Tuskegee was the school for her. She wanted to be a nurse, and she wanted to attend an HBCU. Tuskegee was one of the few universities with a well-established undergraduate nursing program. She also loved the campus and the school's culture. A high school teacher she admired was a Tuskegee alumnus.

My sister's desire to go to Tuskegee was slightly ironic. At the time, I was writing a book about the history of black education, and I had published an academic article that was somewhat critical of Washington's legacy, thus adding my analysis to an expansive body of scholarly texts unpacking the conservative politics of the Tuskegee founder. My family was generally aware of my research on the history of black education, yet they were unaware of these particulars.

The graduation in 2022 was my second visit to Tuskegee's campus. My first trip was to help my sister move into her dormitory. On both occasions, I felt the weight of history. I felt it when interacting with the black students directing us around campus to various buildings, some of which I had seen in photographs being constructed by early members of the student body. However, witnessing the Booker T. Washington Monument (Figure 13.1) was the biggest reminder of history.

This towering bronze figure greets everyone who enters the campus through Tuskegee's main gates. I anticipated seeing the statue on both visits, having encountered the sight of it in archives on several occasions. I also recalled the memorable appearance of the monument in the novel of one of Tuskegee's most famous graduates: American writer and son of Oklahoma Ralph Ellison. Through the voice of Ellison's nameless narrator in *Invisible Man*, he writes: "And I stand in the circle where three roads converge near the statue. . . . I see the bronze statue of the college Founder, the cold Father symbol, his hands outstretched in the breathtaking gesture of lifting a veil that flutters in hard, metallic folds above the face of a kneeling slave." While recognizing the towering size of Washington's legacy, Ellison also points to the statue's ambiguity. Such uncertainty is quite fitting of Washington's legacy. He writes: "and I am standing puzzled, unable to decide whether the veil is really being lifted, or lowered more firmly in place; whether I am witnessing a revelation or a more efficient blinding."[21]

Finding myself at that very intersection, gazing up at this same statue, I too felt a sense of ambivalence regarding Washington's legacy.

13.1: Booker T. Washington Monument postcard.

My feelings, however, changed nothing of the fact that Washington is a towering figure in the history of American education. This statue was a physical reminder, as I witnessed families, individual students, and groups of friends stand in front of the monument in 2022—exactly one hundred years after it was first erected in 1922, just seven years after Washington's death, and having been paid for by the donations of ordinary black people around the country amounting to $25,000.[22]

As my own family gathered around my sister to take a photograph, I thought of the tens of thousands of people over the generations who passed this monument, as well as the dozens of photographs I had seen of historical leaders posing at the feet of the statue, becoming an extension of the unclothed black youth Washington unveils to the world, or—depending on how one reads the allegory—the youth to whom Washington is unveiling the world. The statue's placement as the focal point of the school's entryway positions it as a main attraction for group photos, even when visitors are unaware of the two men in the statue.

And just like that, Booker T. Washington is a permanent fixture in the background of one of the most important and intimate moments of my family's history (Figure 13.2). When I see Washington looming in the background of my family's photo, when I recall Ellison's iconic passage from *Invisible Man*, and when I hear stories like the one shared by Angela Walton-Raji, I am reminded of Washington's status as a monumental figure: a single individual whose life tells a national story.

I am also often reminded of Washington's prominence in unexpected ways, not the least of which are recurring appearances of the Booker T. Washington Monument in the archive. I recall searching the papers of educator Fannie C. Williams in New Orleans and stumbling upon a photo of her posing at the foot of the statue with a group of black women educational leaders in the 1930s, including Mary McLeod Bethune, standing in the center, wearing her iconic fur coat (Figure 13.3). Bethune appears in many photos in front of

13.2: Family photo at Alawna Sherouse's 2022 graduation from Tuskegee University.

Washington's statue. A similar photo from the 1920s can be found in Bethune's own papers. This earlier photo includes Bethune, Nannie Helen Burroughs, and Charlotte Hawkins Brown—all black women school founders in the early twentieth century—and it was likely taken at the ceremonies for the statue's unveiling (Figure 13.4). On a separate occasion, I came across a photo of Harper Councill Trenholm, a schoolteacher who eventually became president of Alabama's State College for Negros, appearing with two African American male educators, proudly standing in front of the statue during the 1920s (Figure 13.5). And again, a photograph of several hundred black educators of the American Teachers Association—formerly called the National Association of Teachers in Colored Schools—gathered in front of the Booker T. Washington Monument during their July 1938 annual meeting (Figure 13.6).

My favorite sighting of the monument, however, is a photograph depicting two African American men imitating the statue and its allegorical meaning. They stage a reenactment of Washington as "HE LIFTED THE VEIL OF IGNORANCE FROM HIS PEOPLE AND POINTED THE WAY TO PROGRESS THROUGH EDUCATION AND INDUSTRY," as the statue's inscription reads. One man kneels behind an old plow while holding an ax and a hoe as he looks out into the distance of what appears to be a farm in rural Alabama. The second man stands above him, pointing out into the distance as he lifts a veil—symbolically represented by a burlap sack—from the head of his kneeling companion (Figure 13.7).

This rehearsal of Washington's monumental stature best expresses the expansive nature of the educator's presence in history. Not just through the black–white binary usually offered to frame the black educational past, but indeed through the lens of the founding racial triad. The land depicted in the scenic photograph of these two educators posing as Washington and a black youth in transition to enlightenment and industriousness can be traced back to the longer story of Creek removal from what is currently known as the state of Alabama. Indeed, the same could be said for the very grounds on which the Booker T. Washington Monument stands.

13.3: Fannie Williams (far left), Charlotte Hawkins Brown (third from left), Mary McLeod Bethune (center). Fannie C. Williams Papers, Amistad Research Center.

13.4: School founders Nannie Hellen Burroughs, Charlotte Hawkins Brown, and Mary McLeod Bethune, ca. 1922.

13.5: Harper Councill Trenholm (far right), ca. 1922; Courtesy of the Harper Councill Trenholm Collection, Alabama State University Archives, Levi Watkins Learning Center.

13.6: Annual Meeting of American Teachers Association in 1938.

13.7: Two African American male educators posing as Booker T. Washington Monument in Alabama. Courtesy of the Harper Councill Trenholm Collection, Alabama State University Archives, Levi Watkins Learning Center.

Tuskegee Institute is named after the city in which it was founded. However, the name reveals more than a relationship between the school and the local municipality. Instead, it points to a relationality between native, white, and black Americans that is always already present in the history of the place commemorated by the monument. The city of Tuskegee was established in 1833, during the intense period of Indian Removal, and it takes its name from a Muskogee (Creek) word, *Taskeke*, which translates to "warriors." Taskeke was the name of a Creek settlement in Alabama prior to the tribe's forced displacement from their homelands in the Southeast. The Creek were one of several indigenous nations forced by the US government to leave the Southeast and re-establish their nations west of the Mississippi. This process of native dispossession is the very reason the city Booker T. Washington visits in the story told by Angela Walton-Raji is named "Muskogee." Creek people were forced out of their homelands, in and surrounding present-day Tuskegee, and forced to move to Indian Territory; making the same trek as Washington when his prominence as an educator pulled him to the territory nearly three-quarters of a century later.

Readers may also recall the story of Arbor (renamed Lee Compere) and William Barnard from 1827, two native youth adopted by Colonel Thomas McKenney, architect of the Civilization Fund Act. This captive adoption took place at the Creek Agency at Fort Mitchell, Alabama, just fifty miles west of Tuskegee's grounds. Such overlapping histories are not coincidental but instead reflect the structural realities of the national educational landscape, where native land loss and the exploitation of enslaved black labor were integral parts of the country's development and the construction of its ancillary institutions. The origin story of American schooling has always left its mark. Even as the schooling apparatus of the state evolved, took on new forms, and expanded into new places, its grammars persisted.

Booker T. Washington built Tuskegee Normal and Industrial School in 1881 with no apparent awareness of this local history of the city. However, he certainly carried some awareness of this past by the time he traveled to Muskogee in 1905, when he requested meetings with "a genuine native Indian." Washington expressed knowledge of the overlapping histories of African slavery in Indian country as well as the realities of native land dispossession in his written account of the Muskogee visit. He explained, "The negroes who are known in that locality as 'natives' are the descendants of slaves that the Indians brought with them from Alabama and Mississippi, when they migrated to this Territory, about the middle of the last century."[23] The irony of Washington's observation is that his travel from Tuskegee Institute to Muskogee, Oklahoma, literally retraced the journey made by the ancestors of Philip and Elzora Lewis, early Afro-Creek leaders at the Tullahassee

Mission School whose ancestors were forced to make the journey from old Creek Country when federal mandates forced their masters to remove. In more ways than one, the school Washington built was deeply connected—physically, fiscally, and symbolically—to this complicated history of native dispossession, African chattel slavery, and the expansion of a United States premised on white racial supremacy. The agro-capitalist economy of the South in which Washington found himself building a school for formerly enslaved people was structured by overlapping histories of conquest and captivity.

14

SLAVERY AND SETTLER COLONIALISM IN THE EDUCATIONAL WORLD OF BOOKER T. WASHINGTON, 1856–1872

Tucked away in Booker T. Washington's classic 1901 autobiography, *Up from Slavery*, is a chapter titled "Black Race and Red Race." The chapter points to a critical intersection in black and native American histories, though for many contemporary readers, it is experienced as a disorienting deviation of Washington's first-person account of his rise from an enslaved boy to becoming the successful leader of Tuskegee Institute. While seemingly out of place to eyes trained to see Washington merely as a historical figure relevant to black education, the chapter of Washington's life detailed in "Black Race and Red Race," recounting his time working in the Indian Program at Hampton Normal and Agricultural Institute, is a revelatory account of the more sprawling tale of race, education, and nation-building so central to the development of the schooling apparatus of the United States.

Hampton's Indian Program was the direct precursor to the infamous Carlisle Indian Industrial School in Carlisle, Pennsylvania—the notorious boarding school now known for its national influence, and its founder's philosophy of "Kill the Indian. Save the Man." Carlisle and its founder, General Richard Henry Pratt, set the tone for native education policies during the late nineteenth and early decades of the twentieth centuries.[1] While Washington himself does not name this institutional connection between Hampton and Carlisle in his narration of the story, I emphasize this point here because it is a period in Washington's life that has been significantly unappreciated.

Wedged between the chapter "The Reconstruction Period" and another titled "Early Days at Tuskegee," the chapter "Black Race and Red Race" details a period in Washington's life prior to his national recognition as the famous founder of Tuskegee Institute, and well before he is greeted by ten thousand people in Muskogee, Oklahoma, in 1905, as depicted in the previous chapter. It is a time when Washington, as a young teacher, was still being groomed as the poster child for, and eventual leader within, an education reform movement for black and native youth funded and controlled by leading white philanthropists and social reformers of the Progressive Era. Washington's experience with Hampton's Indian Program is an invitation to look more closely at the structural intimacies between native and black experiences in US schooling that have always existed. What's more, this relation can be traced throughout Washington's life, even during his time as an enslaved boy in Franklin County, Virginia.

Virginia is the first of the original American colonies, and it was also a place where the intersections of settler colonialism and chattel slavery shaped educational development from the very beginning. While the criminalization of black education can be traced back to Virginia's 1819 anti-literacy law and anti-assembly laws as early as 1804, the state's prioritization of settler schooling for native people can be traced to Virginia's colonial charter. The charter outlined instructions for the "propagating of *Christian* Religion to such People, as yet live in Darkness and miserable Ignorance of the true Knowledge and Worship of God, and may in timing bring the Infidels and Savages, living in those Parts, to human Civility, and to a settled and quiet Government."[2] The same is true of Virginia's first institution of higher education. According to the College of William and Mary's 1693 charter, which made it the second-oldest college in the United States, the school was established so that youth in the colony "may be piously educated in good letters and manners," and so "that the Christian faith may be propagated amongst the Western Indians."[3]

Such visions of European settlement and indigenous erasure through education developed in colonial America and they persisted after the founding of the United States. As *American Grammar* has shown, the political and economic motivations for criminalizing and suppressing black education while forcing settler schooling on indigenous people were distinct strategies of racial domination, all in service of a shared mission of national development for white benefit. These distinct racial projects in the schooling apparatus of the United States—one premised on native land dispossession, and the other on the superexploitation of black labor—and the relations between them conditioned key aspects of Booker T. Washington's early life.

Up from Slavery presents many sites of American schooling. In all of them, the intersection of slavery and settler colonialism form ornate details in the background. In pulling these details to the fore, I will show how such histories lying beneath the surface are relevant not only to black and native education, but also to the development of white education in the United States as well. Thus, while *Up from Slavery* presents the story of one man's life, it also reflects a national story. Washington's "Black Race and Red Race" invites readers to see the relational formation of race as an integral feature of the Indian Program at Hampton, but also as a central phenomenon in American education. Washington's story is a quintessential American one. It is a story where the founding racial triad is intimately bound up in the structural realities that conditioned Washington's life just as it is in the social foundations of American schooling.

MISS BURROUGH'S CLASSROOM ON THE HOLLAND PLANTATION

The education of white students in Franklin County, Virginia, was developed by slave labor and slave capital as well as the ongoing settlement of indigenous lands. Booker T. Washington's narrative provides a personal account of this historical reality. Washington's labor was exploited to support the education of local white children in Franklin County during his early life as an enslaved boy, and this structural relationship reflects broader patterns in the development of white education across the South.

Washington was born to an enslaved woman named Jane in 1856, and he never met his father, who was rumored to be a local white man.[4] Despite birth ties, Washington's family, consisting of his mother and two siblings, ultimately answered to the man and woman who owned them, Elizabeth and James Burrough. The Burroughs owned ten slaves at their plantation in the Hale's Ford community of Franklin County: two adult men, two adult women, and six children.[5] In 1860 there were around three thousand enslaved people in Franklin County, amounting to almost one-third of the population. Franklin County's cash crop was tobacco, and this was no different on the 107-acre Burrough plantation. In 1860, the Burrough plantation produced two thousand pounds of tobacco in addition to harvesting corn, wheat, potatoes, and other food-related crops.[6] Enslaved labor was primarily used in the tobacco field, and the enslaved were also tasked with chores related to the everyday maintenance of the estate and creating comfort for the Burrough family, which included fourteen children. Washington's mother was the cook for the Burrough family, and while small children were of little use in the tobacco field, the enslaved boy's labor could be used for various tasks on and off the plantation.

One use of Washington's labor was to complete errands for Laura Angeline Burrough in service of her work as a teacher on a nearby plantation. Laura was the daughter of Washington's owners. While most white women from slave-owning families did little work either in or outside the house of bondage, Laura began making a life for herself while still living in her parents' home. Born in 1842, Laura taught at a school built on the Holland Plantation in Franklin County. Booker T. Washington and his brother John were often assigned tasks that supported her work. They carried books and supplies to the schoolhouse, and they also traveled with Laura to and from the school each day—or at the beginning and end of each school week—before returning the Burroughs' family horse to the plantation for daily operations.

Common schools were not widely established in the South prior to the Reconstruction Era. However, they did exist in some places, even if they operated irregularly. Most schools operating in the South were privately run academies, some of which received support from state and local public funds. In 1860 more than two dozen schools were in operation across Franklin County, usually with one teacher and up to thirty students.[7] One can assume, given this number of schools in a county where nearly one-third of the population was enslaved, that many white school leaders relied on enslaved labor, requiring those in bondage to perform similar tasks demanded of Washington by his young mistress. The dozens of common schools in Franklin County, and the thousands across the antebellum South, relied on physical labor by enslaved people for their everyday operations, in addition to their funding streams being deeply tied to slave capital. Such economic links can be traced through contributions by individual slave owners to school construction efforts, and can also be traced to the public resources generated through property taxes that helped fund schools, because such property being taxed included enslaved people.

Washington was illiterate, and therefore unable to read or recall the titles of the books he carried for Laura Burrough. Nevertheless, one cannot help but wonder: What was the substance of these books carried by the enslaved boy for his white mistress that formed the foundation of the lessons taught to white students? Scholarship on antebellum children's literature and school textbooks provide a reliable basis for speculation.

As schooling became more widespread in the United States, particularly in the Northeast, efforts were made to establish curricular norms that supported the cultivation of a strong national identity among future citizens. Spellers and readers, which were used for teaching the fundamentals of literacy, laid the foundation; however, more complex texts such as geography, history, and math textbooks, as well as children's literature, made up the bulk of educational material used in common schooling once students achieved basic reading abilities. While these texts were used to instill widely accepted values associated with Protestantism, republicanism, and capitalism, as well as gender norms reflective of nineteenth-century America, these texts also had much to say about black and native people, both implicitly and explicitly.

Washington's mistress taught in Virginia, a state that required publicly supported schools to teach history beginning in 1849, following a precedent set by various New England states.[8] By the late 1840s, the textbook industry was rapidly growing, mirroring the increased number of common schools and private academies in the North and South. As one historian noted, "Between 1820 and 1849, sixty-nine different history textbooks appeared, and by 1859, 439 existed for all branches of history. By 1855 [the year of Washington's birth], spending on all textbooks had increased to over $5 million, outselling all other categories of books."[9] The market for textbooks expanded across regions, yet their production was overwhelmingly situated in the Northeast, where common schools were more widespread. Thus the textbooks used across the nation were in large part produced by publishing houses and writers in the Northeast. Despite this regional stronghold, core curricular materials being used in white schools, both in the North and South, during the antebellum era (and through the late nineteenth century) were generally the same, even as the classroom instruction of teachers likely emphasized certain lessons and interpretation of content based on local and regional interests.[10]

A history textbook was likely among the books Booker T. Washington was forced to carry by Laura Burrough. There were distinguishable patterns in history textbooks published during the antebellum era, especially as it related to race, and particularly when it came to representations of black and native people.

Northern textbook authors, many of whom personally condemned slavery, avoided direct discussions about the peculiar institutions by the 1840s. Some may have lacked knowledge or concern about the conditions of slavery, yet many avoided representing slavery because they feared it would limit the circulation of their texts in Southern markets. Slavery was, therefore, thinly discussed, if at all. For instance, a popular history textbook of the antebellum era was Charles Goodrich's *A Pictorial History of the United States*, which sold more than 500,000 copies between its original publication in 1843 and 1866. While the original edition reflected some of Goodrich's critiques of slavery, after its first year the textbook was "purged of any hostility to slavery" and generally included no discussion of African Americans or relevant topics such as abolition and colonization.[11]

While *A Pictorial History of the United States* included hundreds of images to accompany its narrative of the United States, not a single image depicted black people, enslaved or otherwise, in its five-hundred-plus pages. Black people occasionally appear in some narratives; however, illustrations were likely to incite controversy. This same textbook included dozens of portrayals of native people. In fact, the frontispiece of the book is an illustration of an indigenous man dressed in traditional attire, holding his bow, with a shield resting at his foot (Figure 14.1). The native elder is prominently featured at the front of the image, gazing into the distance; down the hill are key American monuments, which include an obelisk with a two-column listing of the thirty-five states that, at the time, comprised the United States. The image also includes the US Capitol at the center of the frame. The remaining images of native people throughout the book present similar conflicting yet stereotypical representations: some as "noble savages" willingly handing over land to white settlers for its proper development, while other images portrayed natives to be inherently violent and the primary aggressors when conflicts between settlers and native tribes are depicted in images accompanying the textbook's narrative. A small number of images depicting "civil" encounters between settlers and natives are also included in the textbook: scenes of treaty negotiations as well as illustrations of religious and educational instruction (Figures 14.2 and 14.3). One illustration even depicts the iconic story of rebel New Englanders dressed in Mohawk disguise tossing tea from the British East India Company into Boston Harbor (Figure 14.4). On this night in 1773, Goodrich writes, "three hundred and forty chests [of tea] were staved and emptied into the sea" by "seventeen sea captains, carpenters, etc., dressed and painted like Indians," out of protest to British colonization.[12]

Antebellum textbooks were noticeably silent on discussions of slavery while presenting a story of American independence and development predicated on a seamless handing over of land from native people to white settlers. Extravagant images of native people as something of the past and yet the people indigenous to the land were narratively used to construct a coherent story of a distinctly American identity over and against its British colonial past. This was on display with the actions of the Boston Tea Party in 1773, and such settler-colonial fantasies can be found across representations in antebellum narratives of US history offered to white students, in the North and South.[13]

14.1: Illustration of indigenous man sitting and gazing at historic sites in the United States. Frontispiece in *A Pictorial History of the United States*.

Textbook authors and publishers were intentional about what to include and what to exclude—or remove—based on the political interests of white families and leaders across the country. In making this observation, it is critical to emphasize that white students were educated not only through what was included in schoolbooks, but also through omission. As African American Studies scholar Sarah Lewis writes, "Racial domination became a process of conditioning, editing out what had to remain unseen." Ideas about race scripted onto the bodies of people and that informed the stratification of society were "not merely formed through racist caricature

14.2: "Eliot Preaching"

14.3: "Instructing the Indians"

14.4: "Throwing Over the Tea"

and distorting stereotypes. They are carved, formed through removals."[14] In her study of mapmaking and geography textbooks, Lewis "reveals a widespread tactic of omission" used to solidify white supremacy and the systems of domination that sustained this racial order. She documents how "an excision of details, ideas, and historical materials—a negative assembly—blocked scrutiny of the foundations of white racial supremacy and the legitimacy of the racial order it secured."[15] For instance, Lewis shows how geographers and mapmakers silently delinked references to "Caucasian" and the Caucasus Mountains from conceptions of whiteness as research exposed such long-standing associations to be extravagant myths, and as new findings by scholars had the potential to call white supremacy into question.

While some textbook authors included critical views on slavery in the 1830s, by the 1840s and '50s many of these same authors had removed such statements in later editions, responding to the demands of a growing Southern market.[16] Northern white authors and publishers understood their assignment to be the development of school resources to serve the unifying aims of education as a white good. Such a project had long been deemed central to the internal development of the nation. What's more, concessions made by authors and the textbook industry were also informed by marketplace logics, as publishing houses and writers made decisions that would lead to the greatest returns. For instance, prior to publishing *A Pictorial History*, Goodrich published *The First Book of History for Children and Youth*, with the first edition appearing in 1832. This book included discussions of slavery that many white Americans during the nineteenth century would have likely found to be balanced (though certainly problematic by nineteenth-century black and radical abolitionist perspectives), and yet the book would have still been deemed unacceptable by white Southerners during the same period. Goodrich declared to student readers that "slaves are generally well treated" and that "they have enough to eat, drink, and wear, and are not often required to labor beyond their strength."[17] In addition to Goodrich's description of slavery as a "generally" mild and tolerable experience for enslaved people, he also included an illustration of enslaved people working in a field with a white slave owner—stick in hand—delivering commands at the center of the scene (Figure 14.5). This image is accompanied by the author's structural criticism of slavery, as opposed to any hints of interpersonal violence or mistreatment. Goodrich described the power relations between masters and the enslaved. He notes that the latter have no education, liberty, or property and are often separated from their families when sold at auctions. Goodrich takes a clear abolitionist stance in the earlier work, even as his analysis is couched in a troubling paternalistic narrative that suggests slaves are generally well cared for. Yet no attempt at a balanced account would do. Such a text was likely to be unwelcomed in Miss Burrough's classroom in Franklin County, Virginia, and generally all classrooms across the South—a rapidly growing market for the textbook industry by the 1840s.

Direct discussions of slavery were conspicuously absent in popular history textbooks, yet ideas about black people were not completely absent in classrooms like Laura Burrough's in Franklin County. The concept or "science" of race was often discussed in geography textbooks. Students encountered direct comparisons of racial groups accompanied by illustrations, maps of the world, and other representations of the racial hierarchy sustained by white supremacist thought in nineteenth-century geography

14.5: "Negro Slaves at Work"

curriculum. In one of Goodrich's most common geography textbooks, for instance, he offered students "correct" views on racial difference. He presented narrow, stereotypical ideas about black people as slaves, and when discussing the people of the African continent, "he employed the words *ignorant*, *barbarous*, *uncivilized*, *indolent*, *weak*, and *degraded*," as one historian observes. According to Goodrich, black people on the African continent were "fond of dancing" and he declared, "When the sun goes down, dancing begins from one end of Africa to the other."[18]

Such stereotypical representations of black people were consistent across the nineteenth century. Representations of native people in history and geography textbooks, on the other hand, slightly shifted by the late nineteenth century, though all such representations bent in the direction of absolving settlers of any violence committed against indigenous nations. Scholars of nineteenth-century textbooks note that native people appear in the curriculum as uncivilized and hostile people who were racially inferior to white settlers. In the early nineteenth century, however, textbooks occasionally portrayed native people as "noble savages" who maintained more amicable relationships with settlers and willingly gave them land. These particular native peoples are presented as groups situated above more aggressive and violent natives in other locations, thus occupying a kind of romanticized position in the story of the nation's origins. Textbook authors generally described the procedures of settler colonialism and native land dispossession in sanitized terms. They appear as peaceful undertakings, implying that settlers inherited native land without much violence or force at all. By the late nineteenth century, however, textbooks overwhelmingly represented native people in much more narrow terms, as violent and uncivilized.[19]

Again, while this analysis is framed by Washington's experience as an enslaved boy in the South forced to support his white mistress in her duties as a teacher, the books most likely to be taught in this antebellum school on a Southern plantation were published in Northern states. Indeed, the top six best-selling authors of schoolbook histories from 1821 to 1861 were from New England. While white students in the North may not have attended schools on or near plantations, the same historical narratives and racist ideas about native and black people were used to construct a national white identity among students across regions.

Another source of curricular content used in antebellum schools was nineteenth-century children's fiction, though scholarship is unclear about how widely juvenile literature was used for classroom instruction. What is known, however, is that children's literature of the era reflected similar themes found in American history and geography schoolbooks. Regardless of where these authors stood on the question of slavery, they all seemingly agreed that black people were inferior, and they generally relied on minstrel figures to represent them in narratives they constructed for the literary world of white readers.[20] Representations of native people in popular juvenile literature, such as James Fenimore Cooper's *The Pioneers, or The Sources of the Susquehanna* (1823) and *The Last of the Mohicans: A Narrative of 1757* (1826), reflect similar themes as those appearing in textbooks. Indigenous people were generally cast as relevant only to the American past as an indistinguishable mass, presented as savages or in a romanticized view for their proximity to the land "discovered" by settlers. The violence of conquest is unaddressed. Instead, settler violence is elided by projections about the natural progression of history. Such literature rendered a story of progression that required the death of native people. A dismal reality that can be mourned, though not resisted. A settler future was inevitable, both in American history textbooks and young adult literature.[21]

Thus far I have painted a picture of how antiblackness and anti-indigeneity factored into the literary world of white youth during the antebellum era, both in formal curricula like history and geography textbooks, as well as less standardized curricular materials, like popular children's literature of the time. This is done to speculate about the content of the books Booker T. Washington likely carried for his mistress on her daily journeys to teach school on a plantation in Franklin County. However, ideas about race also appeared in seemingly objective school subjects, such as mathematics. It should be easy to imagine how the economic interests of white planters informed approaches to math instruction. Yet, even if we are limited in our imagination, one can look to arithmetic curricula of the day in our quest for answers.

Numeracy had long been intertwined with race in the United States, as the development of modernity required a rigorous accounting of slavery and settler colonialism, both the people who were turned into property and the land they were forced to cultivate. Such lessons would have been front and center in mathematics instruction for Laura Burrough's students. Matters of property management were deeply embedded in math education, and such mathematical concerns were directly informed by histories of race and domination.[22] Samuel Lander's *Our Own School Arithmetic* (1863) presented students with the following scenarios to apply their mathematical knowledge:

> A man owns $10,475 in real estate, $3,850 in slaves, $4,095 in good notes, and $1,415 in cash; what is the value of his whole estate?
>
> If 125 slaves sell for $75,125, what is their average value?
>
> A planter who worked 57 hands, raised 399 bales of cotton: how many bales did he raise to the hand?

> A planter who works 47 hands raises to each hand ten bales of cotton averaging 445lb.; how much does his cotton yield him at 9ct. per lb.?
>
> If 5 white men can do as much work as 7 negroes, how many days of 10hr. each will be required for 25 negroes to do a piece of work which 30 white men can do in 10 days of 9 hr. each?[23]

The pedagogy in white Southern classrooms (and beyond) was informed by racial logics, even—or especially—when it came to math. For while slavery was about power, it was also about numbers. So too was the buying, selling, and cultivation of land. The children in Laura Burrough's classroom needed to be skilled in arithmetic to manage the wealth they were to amass as future property owners. Therefore, it does not require much stretch of the imagination to consider how such a social context might have influenced classroom pedagogy in arithmetic. The math problems listed above provide clear examples of the relationship between race and math education in antebellum classrooms, reflecting what a culturally responsive education in arithmetic would have looked like in a white social world overwhelmingly built around the buying and selling of people and land, and the crops cultivated by those people who were property on that land.

Racial domination was not merely about hatred for black and native people. It was conditioned by a political economy formed through native land dispossession and the superexploitation of black labor, all situated within a rapidly expanding global economy. Miss Burrough's students learned this lesson in more than one way. It could be learned through their application of mathematical knowledge; however, it was also learned by studying the young Negro boy owned by their teacher's family. An enslaved boy whom they observed on a regular basis. Important lessons were communicated through the routines of enslaved people supporting the work of white teachers like Miss Burrough at school every day, by carrying her books and tending to her horse; these same enslaved people being legally forbidden to read, write, or to cross the threshold of the schoolhouse door. White students studied their books, and they also studied the people around them. Indeed, the white students in Burrough's classroom were taught to understand themselves as masters and mistresses in the making.

BLACK EDUCATIONAL STRIVING AMID PLANTATION FUTURES

Jane, Booker T. Washington's mother, gathered her three children and traveled by foot to Kanawha Salines, recently named Malden, in West Virginia, after the close of the Civil War in 1865. Booker was nine years old. Their family traveled to Malden in search of Jane's husband, a man named Wash Ferguson, who was enslaved on a neighboring plantation in Franklin County. Like many black people, Jane and her children set out to find loved ones, as they began experimenting with life as newly freed people. For the first time, Washington would have the opportunity to learn without the immediate threat of punishment. Like black people across the South, the African American community that formed near the salt mines in Malden immediately developed their own schools and educational opportunities.

What Washington witnessed was a sight unlike anything he'd ever seen or experienced: "It was a whole race trying to go to school. Few were too young, and none too old, to make the attempt to learn. As fast as any kind of teachers could be secured, not only were day-schools filled, but night-schools as well."[24] Tinkersville was the majority-black area of Malden, and it was in this community that African American families worked together to build their school. They did so without direction from white educators, funders, or any assistance from the Freedmen's Bureau. Rev. Lewis Rice, an illiterate man who held a deep regard for education, led the effort. He even opened the doors of his home as a site for the Tinkersville school until a building was constructed. It was at the Tinkersville school that Jane's son selected a last name for himself, where he first became "Booker Washington" (later adding Taliaferro as his middle name). In renaming himself, the young man engaged in a ritual of self-definition shared among many formerly enslaved people, where they chose names for themselves as opposed to adopting the name of their former owners.[25] This new educational journey was a critical juncture in Washington's coming of age. Yet while this period in his life was filled with such promise, according to Washington, it also "brought to [him] one of the keenest disappointments that [he] ever experienced."[26]

The economic situation of Washington's family reflected social conditions that carried over from the harsh realities of slavery—a period in their lives that was just days, weeks, and months in the past. To survive, black families were forced to rely on everyone's labor—children and adults. African American youth were a source of "free" wage laborers to be exploited by the same white elites who previously relied on enslaved labor for their capitalist pursuits on the plantations, but also in the mining industry, which was the primary source of employment in Kanawha Valley. Washington explained, "I had been working in a salt-furnace for several months, and my stepfather had discovered that I had a financial value and so, when the school opened, he decided that he could not spare me from my work."[27] Washington's work in the salt furnace severely limited his opportunities for study.

The challenges to Washington's educational pursuits were the result of newly formed structural arrangements that evolved from the antebellum plantation. As Black Studies scholar Katherine McKittrick has powerfully argued, the plantation "not only generated North Atlantic metropolitan wealth and exacerbated dispossession among the unfree and indentured, it also instituted an incongruous racialized economy that lingered long after emancipation." The racialized economy formed through structural arrangements and the ideology of slavery's capitalism continued to shape many aspects of black life after enslaved people were legally free. McKittrick notes "the idea of the plantation is migratory."[28] In fact, the plantation had long shaped operations in the salt-mining industry of the Kanawha Valley, even before the Civil War commenced. The link between the Kanawha salt industry and the plantations of Franklin County is likely the very thing that pulled Jane and her children to the town following emancipation.

Slave owners commonly hired out enslaved people across the South.

Enslaved black people functioned as laborers and capital in this way. As historian Jonathan Martin explains, "Southern slaveholders exploited both sides of slavery's intrinsic dualism. They expected . . . to see proceeds from the fruits of slave *labor*—among them, tobacco, cotton, wheat, sugar, and indigo—but they also expected returns on slave *capital*." By hiring out slaves, owners could hold on to their property during times when they had more enslaved people than needed on their plantations, yet still earning a profit from their labor by loaning them to other plantations or companies for a designated period of time.[29] Given the small number of enslaved people on the Burrough plantation, which included Washington and his family, it is likely that none of them were hired out. However, other slave owners in Franklin County hired out enslaved people to work in Kanawha Salines, leading Washington's biographer to suggest that the enslaved boy's stepfather was likely among them, prompting Washington's mother to travel there after emancipation.[30]

Before becoming a thriving salt-mining community in the early nineteenth century, however, the Kanawha Valley was "[f]irst known to the buffalo and other game which licked salt at the mouth of Campbell's Creek," as well as tribes indigenous to the region who relied on these animals. In the mid-eighteenth century, settlers learned of the salt in Kanawha Valley after the Shawnee used white captives to work "boiling brine dipped from the salt springs into dry salt, and one of the captives escaped." This led to a gradual increase in settler encroachment in the area, and by 1794 a man named Joseph Ruffner began systematically developing salt in the region.[31]

Joseph Ruffner was the grandfather of Lewis Ruffner, a former Union general who was also an owner of the Kanawha Salt Company, for which Booker T. Washington, his brother, and stepfather all worked. However, the Ruffner family was not only connected to Washington because of their ownership of the salt works company, which exploited his labor. Washington would eventually be hired by Lewis Ruffner's wife, Viola Ruffner, as a houseboy, for which he was paid five dollars a month.[32] Once more, Washington found himself under the supervision of a white woman teacher. Viola Ruffner was a former English teacher from Vermont. Unlike his time working for Laura Burrough, Washington was now legally free, though his life continued to be severely constrained by his economic status as an exploitable black child laborer in a racialized economy still conditioned by plantation logics.

Mrs. Ruffner was known for being very strict about manners, cleanliness, and grammar, having once been the head of a school's English Department. Washington initially despised working in the Ruffner home, at one point even running away, only to find limited opportunities available to him as a black teenager. After searching and finding no better option, Washington returned to the Ruffner home, more committed than ever to prove himself capable of the tasks placed before him. He hoped that proving himself a reliable worker in the Ruffner home might lead to more opportunities. Washington's biographer insists that Viola Ruffner "instilled in Booker the essence of what the German sociologist Max Weber later called the Protestant ethic, which taught that the values of industry, sobriety, thrift, self-reliance, and piety accounted for success in modern capitalist societies." It is likely that Viola also tutored Washington, helping him develop written and oral skills that would come in handy years later.[33]

14.6: "An Early Portrait of Booker T. Washington."

The teenage Washington worked for Viola Ruffner for less than two years before leaving in search of a school he learned about through word of mouth. He once heard two coal miners in town describe a school "more pretentious than the little coloured school" Washington had outgrown in Malden.[34] Seeking to move further up from slavery, Washington set out in search of Hampton Normal and Agricultural Institute in the fall of 1872, a school founded in 1868 on a former plantation and the unceded land of the Powhatan people.

15

"BLACK RACE AND RED RACE" AT HAMPTON INSTITUTE, 1872–1881

> I have often wondered if there was a white institution in this country whose students would have welcomed the incoming of more than a hundred companions of another race in the cordial way that these black students at Hampton welcomed the red ones.
>
> —Booker T. Washington, *Up from Slavery* (1901)

At sixteen years of age, Booker T. Washington arrived at Hampton Institute in the fall of 1872. Having no money for tuition, he accepted a janitorial position at Hampton to pay for his education. Labor was an integral part of Hampton's curriculum. In fact, students spent the bulk of their time working on the school's farm, helping construct buildings, and doing other tasks amounting to what the school's white founder, General Samuel Armstrong, understood to be a "practical education" for African Americans in the postbellum South. Under Armstrong's model, academic instruction was generally delayed to the evenings. Despite its curriculum, Hampton was primarily a normal school—an educational institution created for the specific purpose of training teachers. So, while a "practical education" reflected the school's ideology, its primary mission was to prepare teachers to work—not on farms or in white homes as domestics, but in the black schools being rapidly built across the Southern states. As historian James Anderson documented, "approximately 84 percent of the 723 graduates from

Hampton's first twenty classes became teachers."[1] Thus, from the school's founding well into the twentieth century, Hampton focused overwhelmingly on the training of teachers.

By emphasizing practical education, Hampton Institute "employed a unique manual labor routine and an ideology of 'self-help' as the practical and moral foundation of the teacher training process."[2] The school's curriculum required pre-service teachers to engage in manual labor for long periods of time with the objective of immersing them in the school's doctrine, hoping teachers thus trained would then cultivate an appreciation for domestic and agricultural labor as dignified work among their students. White educators leading Hampton insisted that a commitment to labor in the postwar South needed to be instilled in black students. They insisted this had to be done to thwart visions of education that presented schooling as a means of escaping labor in the South's agrocapitalist economy structured by the slave plantations of years past.

General Armstrong declared, "Let us make the teachers and we will make the people."[3] This was an articulation of education for racial domination—an effort to kill the drive for freedom and the cultural knowledge necessary for it as a means of saving some version of black subjects reminiscent of the slave past. White education reformers like Armstrong worked to socially control the newly freed people in a manner that would, once again, make them a kind of white possession. This was a parallel formation to the settler philosophy of "kill the Indian"—and particularly indigenous sovereignty and kinship with land—in order "to save the man." These two strategies of racial domination were interrelated and yet distinct. The similarity was not coincidental.

Armstrong had commanded colored troops during the Civil War and was the child of missionaries from Hawaii, where he was first exposed to a systematic schooling program employed by white settlers toward the domination of native Hawaiians. Armstrong's father, Richard Armstrong, was a leading figure in establishing colonial education in Hawaii and was the owner of a sugar plantation there.[4] As a teenager, Samuel Armstrong worked as his father's secretary, providing the future school founder with intimate instruction pertaining to the development and management of colonial education models meant to exploit the labor of racially oppressed people in service of the larger aims of expanding and sustaining a white supremacist racial order. He also learned that it was the right of white settlers to possess the lands of darker races who, according to Western knowledge, were naturally inferior. Building on his prior knowledge—and his learning by doing—Armstrong would formalize a model of black schooling in the former slave South that was a refined version of the colonial education models employed in earlier periods in places like Hawaii.

As several scholars have noted, Armstrong often made direct comparisons between black people and natives in Hawaii, recognizing them both to be inferior and childlike races.[5] His ideological approach to black education was also motivated by post–Civil War anxieties among white Americans about black indolence, as many white Americans believed the formerly enslaved people had proclivities to avoid labor. White Americans believed black people would be unreliable workers now that they were no longer compelled by the whip to do so. Armstrong offered his model of black education as a remedy: just enough academic training, while students focused most of their efforts on skills deemed appropriate for the roles white Americans imagined for African Americans as a permanent underclass of workers to be exploited for white benefit.

Like the majority of Hampton's students, Washington became a schoolteacher. He graduated in 1875 and returned to Malden, West Virginia, to teach in the community that became his home after emancipation. Washington quickly became the most prized alumnus of Hampton and a cherished mentee of the school's founder. This social standing led to an unexpected invitation in the summer of 1879. As Washington recalled, General Armstrong invited him "to return . . . partly as a teacher and partly to pursue some supplementary studies." This proposition later proved to be a major shift in Washington's trajectory as an educator. Describing Armstrong's proposal in more detail, Washington explained that his duties would largely entail working in Hampton's newly established Indian Program. In *Up from Slavery*, Washington wrote: "The special work which the General desired me to do was to be a sort of 'house father' to the Indian young men—that is, I was to live in the building with them and have the charge of their discipline, clothing, rooms, and so on."[6]

Building from the story of Washington's return to Hampton, this chapter reads the school's Indian Program as a critical node in the development of American education in the nineteenth century. To fully appreciate this point of historical convergence, however, requires that we also see it as more than an isolated story with implications for black and native histories, but instead see it for what it reveals about the schooling apparatus of the United States. Hampton's Indian Program is fundamentally a story about the entanglements of the founding racial triad in the national educational landscape and the political-economic factors that shaped this relational history of racial domination. As readers will see, Hampton's Indian Program, developed in 1879, was conditioned by long-standing relationships between slavery, settler colonialism, and the development of US education.

White education reformers like Armstrong insisted that native students also needed a practical education like the one Hampton offered to black students. Such an education would prepare them for broader incorporation into American society. Their rationale for this argument, however, was racially distinct. According to white reformers like Armstrong, as well as his accomplice in establishing Hampton's Indian Program, General Richard Henry Pratt, both black and native students needed practical education, yet they needed this education for different reasons. While black Americans were taught to labor, having been previously forced to work over centuries as enslaved people, these white reformers insisted that native people had no prior experience with labor. Pratt explained, while black Americans had now become citizens, "the fitness he had for that high place he had gained by training he was given during slavery, which made him *individual, English speaking, and capable industriously.* This was a lesson which in some way should be applied to the Indian."[7]

Looking past Pratt's twisted view of the moral and social benefits of slavery for African captives, the order of operation he implies when describing the educational program of Hampton is more complex, as

Armstrong's biography elucidates. Hampton's model of practical education was in fact a program imported from colonial education models used by white settlers to "civilize" native people long before it was systematically developed to educate formerly enslaved people in the South. Endemic to the Hampton model was an old strategy of conquest, where schooling had long been employed as an instrument of social control and racial domination, though Armstrong had now tailored it to be used toward distinct political and economic ends. So, while native students technically arrived at Hampton Institute in 1878, the native presence was there all along.

Hampton's "Indian Program" was just a year old when Armstrong invited Washington to join in this work. However, the native presence at Hampton can be traced back to the origins of the education model that informed the school's curriculum. This education model imposed on African Americans derived from methods previously imposed on native American populations. While it was used on the latter to disappear indigenous ways of life and clear a path for US land accumulation and national expansion, it was now appropriated to quell black demands for social equality and to continue the superexploitation of black laborers. In this way, Armstrong's vision was for an institution of social reproduction that would make freedpeople a permanent underclass of abject laborers now that they could no longer be legally owned as property. Hampton (and later Carlisle) was an institution built on white possessive logics structured by a racial capitalism derived from racial chattel slavery, in its obsession with "black labor," as well as settler colonialism, given that the "value" derived from the former slaves' labor was always tied to white Americans' continued settlement of and extraction from native land.[8]

Washington accepted Armstrong's invitation to work in Hampton's Indian Program. This decision placed him amid an important cross-current in black and native histories facilitated by white education reformers seeking to solve two enduring issues for a nation-state possessed by white Americans: "the Negro problem" and "the Indian problem." Yet the relationship between such distinct racial projects on display at Hampton reflected intersections that had always been present in the context of Washington's life. This relational formation of racial politics in US education expressed the national character of schooling, and it is a relational history of race and American education deeply ingrained in the very geography of Hampton, Virginia. To unearth such unseen truths, we need to look no further than the very land on which the Hampton Institute was built.

GEOGRAPHIES OF SLAVERY AND SETTLER COLONIALISM IN THE EDUCATIONAL CONTEXT OF HAMPTON, VIRGINIA

Hampton Institute was built in 1868 on an abandoned plantation. Like all plantations in the United States, the Little Scotland Plantation, and the land on which it stood in Hampton, Virginia, were at once a site of slavery and also of settlement, a site of black captivity and native land dispossession ordered by white possessive logics. The land carried a very old history in this regard; in fact, it is one of the oldest in Anglo-American history. Before it was the city of Hampton, the land was an important Powhatan settlement called Kecoughtan. English settlers attacked the Powhatan people in 1610 to forcibly remove them from their land. As Indigenous Studies scholar Bayley Marquez notes, Kecoughtan was "an Anglicized Indigenous word for the people who lived there on that part of the peninsula" and "when settlers decided that Kecoughtan was too heathen a name, the settlement was renamed Elizabeth City, and later renamed Hampton."[9]

Hampton, Virginia, is the longest continuously occupied English-speaking settlement in the United States. Jamestown was the first English settlement in 1607; however, it was abandoned by the mid-seventeenth century while Hampton has persisted to the present day since its origins in 1610. Settlers began forming the educational landscape of Hampton shortly after it was established, setting an important precedent in colonial America that would continue to structure the development of schooling through American independence.

America's first "free school" for white students was established in Hampton. Unsurprisingly, the school was developed from streams of funding directly related to the seizure of native land as well as the exploitation of enslaved black people. Just as there is no way to understand the early establishment of American colonies without accounting for the material realities of native land dispossession and the exploitation of black enslaved labor, the same must be said about the early development of education in the colonies that laid the foundation for early colonists'—and later "the founding fathers'"—visions of public education as the bedrock of American democracy and national expansion.

In 1619, an English ship carrying Angolan captives kidnapped from Portuguese slave traders arrived in Point Comfort, the tip of the Virginia Peninsula in Hampton, hoping to sell these African captives for food and supplies. These Angolans would be traded in Hampton and enslaved in Jamestown. On this ship were Anthony and Isabella Tucker, whose names were recorded in historical documents. This man and woman would later give birth to William Tucker, the first child of African descent born in colonial America.[10] As evidenced by this story, Hampton became an important port city, especially for exporting tobacco to England from the plantations along the James River.

RACIAL DOMINATION AND THE HISTORY OF AMERICA'S FIRST "FREE SCHOOL"

Hampton is a site of many beginnings in the history of American slavery, and the same can be said of its relationship to American schooling. Besides being the port of entry to slavery in English-speaking colonial America and the first continuous English settlement in the United States, Hampton is also home to the first educational institution established in the colonies, and it had an explicit public mission—though it was not technically a public school. Hampton Academy was founded in 1634, two years before the founding of Harvard College in colonial Massachusetts, the oldest institution of higher education in the United States. Just like its collegiate companion, Hampton Academy's legacy is one that cannot be understood apart from economic ties to black enslavement and native land dispossession, all toward the benefit of white settlement.[11]

4. Hampton Academy about 1855 showing in the background the new buildings erected by Col. Cary. Used by permission of the family of the late Hunter Booker.

15.1: Hampton Academy ca. 1855

Hampton Academy grew from the merging of Syms Academy and Eaton Academy, with the former being established in 1634. Virginia settlers founded this early institution after colonist Benjamin Syms gifted land, cattle, and tools for the creation of the first "free school" of the American colonies. Syms was considered a "free school" because education was offered to white children for free or reduced cost—and because it was privately managed, it would not qualify as a "public school" yet it was created to serve very clear public interests. In 1805, the original Syms school merged with another school built with a generous gift bequeathed by wealthy slave owner Thomas Eaton. In 1659, Eaton deeded a gift that included "Five Hundred acres of land whereon the s[ai]d Free School shall be kept . . . *Two negroes* . . . Twelve cows and two bulls, Twenty hogs, young and old, one bedstead, a table," and many more things included in his estate.[12] The records of these two institutions that became Hampton Academy—from their founding in the seventeenth century through the nineteenth century—reveal direct economic ties between the trafficking of enslaved African people, the settlement of indigenous land, and the growing number of prosperous plantations immediately surrounding the schools, as well as how all contributed to the fiscal and physical development of the institution.

When writing about Hampton Academy, one scholar described the range of "miscellaneous" funds provided by the two benefactors who established the two original school sites: "It will be found, on an inspection of Sym's and Eaton's donations, that the funds provided by them were of a very miscellaneous character, comprehending not only lands, but slaves, cattle, hogs, poultry, and various articles of household and kitchen furniture." When gifted, the land already had buildings upon it, possibly built by enslaved labor, and these buildings were designated "for the accommodation of the master and the pupils." Syms and Eaton made their gifts with the hopes that these schools would have staying power, one insisting "that the school master, residing on the land, should have the use and profits of the houses, as the means of enabling him to maintain his school."[13]

Slave labor and slave capital continued to play a role in Hampton Academy's development over the centuries, just as the land originally seized from the Powhatan people continued to be a site of continued extraction, all contributing toward the school's growing endowment. In 1692, the board of trustees required the outgoing schoolmaster of the Eaton School, Ebeneazer Taylor, to purchase clothing for an enslaved woman owned by the school within fourteen days. They insisted, "it is thought reasonable that a negroe Woman belonging to the s[ai]d schoole should be cloathed at the Charges of the Schoole master she being almost naked."[14] While the wealth of local white land and slave owners benefited Hampton Academy, the wealth amassed by the academy over centuries—through generous donations of local settlers along with the appreciation of the school's resources—also directly benefited local white Americans in the city. The school's records through the first half of the nineteenth century are "full of references to the borrowing of money from the school funds by the county people with lands, buildings, ships, slaves and furniture at various times given as security for these loans. Occasionally gentlemen obtained the release of slaves they had listed as security in order to sell them, replacing them with lands or buildings."[15] Hampton Academy's accumulated wealth and the business dealings of local property owners were deeply intertwined. It was an economic relationship forged first through the seizure of indigenous land and subsequently through the development of that land through the exploitation of enslaved African laborers and, until the late eighteenth century, European indentured servants as well.

It is important to note that Hampton Academy—the first free school in America—ultimately became absorbed into the city's modern-day public school system in 1852, when it became the city's first public high school. When this transition occurred, the wealth amassed by the academy flowed directly into Hampton City Schools. This school district persists in the twenty-first century.

Long before the Hampton Normal and Industrial Institute was founded in 1868 for former slaves, or before the Hampton Indian Program was established to "civilize" native youth, Hampton Academy operated as a site where American education was developed and maintained as a white good—an educational project where the interests of white people were served at the expense of black and native peoples. The geography of Hampton carried a long memory of racial domination and educational development. Such relations continued to animate the schooling apparatus of the United States even in the late-nineteenth-century context when Hampton's Indian Program was established, though the terms of black and native incorporation in the national educational landscape had evolved. Just as race and racial ideology evolve and transform over time, black and native peoples' relationships to the schooling apparatus within the local context of Hampton also shifted. Such shifts were not only local but also national in scope.

"FREEDOM'S FORTRESS" AND BLACK EDUCATION IN HAMPTON BEFORE GENERAL ARMSTRONG'S ARRIVAL

The city of Hampton became a critical site during the Civil War. It was the first place where enslaved people, upon fleeing plantations, could be protected by the Union army. After turning away several waves of runaways who arrived at Hampton's Fort Monroe, Major General Benjamin Butler made a decision on May 24, 1861, that created a historic opportunity for the enslaved to participate in the war against the Confederacy. While previously abiding by the Fugitive Slave Act of 1850, which required that runaways be returned to their owners, Butler changed his position as a military strategy. "The Fugitive Slave Act did not affect a foreign country, which Virginia claimed to be" as part of the Confederate States of America, he declared. He also reasoned that since the enslaved people were otherwise used by their legal owners to fight against the Union, "it would seem to be a measure of necessity to deprive their masters of their service."[16] By Butler's command, enslaved men, women, and children fleeing from their masters were to be seized as "contraband of war."

Word spread of Butler's "contraband order" and thousands of enslaved people fled to Fort Monroe. They stopped work on plantations as well as other sites where their labor was used in service of the Confederacy, and they fled to what became known as "Freedom's Fortress"—a name that must be remembered with an asterisk, in that the runaways were deemed "contraband" and therefore still recognized as property. The name also elides the fact that the United States built Monroe as a coastal fortification using enslaved labor and then military convicts following the War of 1812. Yet, despite the history of Hampton's Fort Monroe, the enslaved sought out Freedom's Fortress, hoping to remake their lives as a free and self-determined people.

Union camps became contraband camps. They were sites of embattled freedom for the runaways who found themselves somewhere between captive and self-emancipated persons. Across the South, nearly 500,000 people waged a general strike by running away from plantations to seek protection from the Union army.[17] The enslaved came not only in search of protection, but also with intention for action. As memorialized by nineteenth-century poet Paul Laurence Dunbar, many of "those noble sons of Ham" were now "The gallant colored soldiers / Who fought for Uncle Sam!"[18] The runaways physically fought in the war to help bring about slavery's demise. However, they also did much more. These people, deemed "contraband of war" by the federal government, began dreaming and experimenting with building up a new world. Education would be a key strategy employed by the fugitives. In contraband camps, black people expanded on educational activities in which they previously engaged subversively. Places like Freedom's Fortress became primary sites for "the general strike" waged by enslaved people, both in their running away, but also in their efforts to create schools and opportunities to learn as a critique of the conditions of slavery; conditions that had long included the criminalization of black education. It was here, in places like Freedom's Fortress, that these fugitive slaves began to work, out in the open, to implement strategies to manifest their dreams of freedom.[19]

Importantly, Fort Monroe and Hampton do not represent an isolated incident. Just as Booker T. Washington recalled the community-led educational efforts he witnessed upon his arrival in Malden, West Virginia, after the Civil War, the black people of Hampton shared a similar story. African Americans in Hampton were self-taught well before General Samuel Armstrong founded Hampton Institute on an abandoned plantation in 1868 with funding from the American Missionary Association and support from the Freedmen's Bureau. Many learned from a free black woman named Mary Peake, who taught black students in Hampton since 1847 in defiance of Virginia's anti-literacy law. Peake was educated in Washington, DC, only returning to Virginia, according to her own account, after black education became criminalized in the nation's capital too.[20] As more and more black people fled to Freedom's Fortress, the number of students Peake taught out of her home continued to increase. She taught fifty-three during the day, and twenty in the evening.[21]

Prior to Samuel Armstrong's work, the land of Hampton, Virginia, had been marked by a long legacy of race, education, and nation-building. It was a story of racial domination, and it was also a place marked by legacies of resistance. This tension would persist.

•••

15.2: Portrait of Mary S. Peake, "First Teacher of the Freed People at Fortress Monroe, Va."

BUILDING HAMPTON'S INDIAN PROGRAM AMID SHIFTS IN US RACIAL POLITICS AND POLICIES

Hampton's Indian Program began as a partnership between two white military officials. In April 1878, General Samuel Armstrong welcomed General Richard Henry Pratt along with sixty-two native men from various tribes to Hampton Institute. Pratt's experiment with native education began in 1875, when he was placed in charge of native prisoners at Fort Marion, in St. Augustine, Florida. After receiving national recognition for his work "civilizing" native American prisoners of war, Pratt decided to build out his educational methods. Pratt's model of settler schooling built on pedagogical methods long imposed on native people, including three distinctive features: His program relied on extreme distance between students and their families, therefore minimizing the prospect of runaways; it included native people from different tribes, helping to disrupt cultural coherence in hopes of shattering tribal identities; and Pratt developed an infamous "outing program," where native learners worked in white communities or the homes of white families. The outing system hired out native students to earn wages while stressing the importance of saving, all toward the goal of immersing native learners into Western ideals of individual property and wage labor.[22] Teaching native students to own property, and especially individual plots of land, was always a key strategy for disrupting tribal claims to lands, thus creating fewer barriers to opening paths for increased white possessions.

Armstrong was a likely collaborator for Pratt. As readers will recall, before his time commanding black soldiers or educating formerly enslaved students at Hampton, Armstrong was the child of white missionaries who engaged in settler-schooling projects among native Hawaiians. To say the least, he took a personal interest in Pratt's effort.

At the time of Armstrong's and Pratt's collaboration, political realities for black and native peoples were at critical junctures, though for distinct reasons. The Reconstruction Era abruptly ended through political agreements formed between white politicians in the North and the South, eventually leading to the rise of Jim Crow, and after the Civil War, federal policies toward native people shifted toward strategies to incorporate indigenous people more aggressively into the American citizenry, and in the process directly trampled on the sovereignty of native nations. Hampton Institute and its Indian Program were both deeply informed by such shifts in the national political landscape regarding race and American society. Thus, to appreciate the convergence of black and native histories at Hampton requires astute reading across multiple timelines. Such an analysis also requires that we abandon linear approaches to historical narratives when seeking deeper conceptual understandings of said experiences.

The Indian Program was formed one year after the Compromise of 1877, whereby Southern Democrats and supporters of Republican candidate Rutherford B. Hayes settled their dispute surrounding the outcome of the 1876 presidential election through an informal agreement. The opposing political camps agreed to seat Hayes as president and immediately withdraw federal troops from the South. The Compromise of 1877 ended Reconstruction and ushered in the era of Redemption: a time "when the gains of Reconstruction were systematically erased and the country witnessed the rise of a white supremacist ideology" that animated Jim Crow laws and customs, prompting large numbers of black people to flee the South, which in turn led to increased white anxieties and resistance to the black presence in the North.[23] During the Redemption period, which continued well into the twentieth century, white Southerners worked to "rescue" the former Confederate states from strict federal control while seeking to establish racial hierarchies reminiscent of the slavery era. Education became a key battleground in this tug of war over US race relations.

A new phase in US policies toward native Americans was already in motion by the end of the Reconstruction Era. The Indian assimilation period gradually developed in the wake of the Civil War. During this period, US leaders placed greater emphasis on breaking up native tribal governments and absorbing native peoples into white American society.[24] During his presidency, Ulysses S. Grant declared an end to wars with native nations, insisting there was a need for more "peaceful" policies. Grant leaned heavily on religious organizations to act on behalf of the government in facilitating this new "peaceful" relationship with native people. The greatest shift to occur under Grant's Peace Policy was the end of treaty-making between the United States and indigenous nations. For instance, the Indian Appropriation Act, passed in 1871, declared: "That hereafter no Indian nation or tribe within the territory of the United States shall be acknowledged or recognized as an independent nation, tribe, or power with whom the United States may contract by treaty."[25] This legislative turn carried devastating consequences for native people. Since the Colonial Era, America entered legal agreements with native nations. To be clear, such legal recognitions of native sovereignty existed even as settlers coerced native nations to enter such agreements and often violated them. Nevertheless, through this legal procedure, which ended treaty-making, the federal government effectively rooted out any formal recognition of native sovereignty.

The legislative campaign that led to the end of treaty-making with native nations reflected a widely shared political goal among American politicians during the postbellum era: the decimation of tribal governments and the absorption of native people into the United States as wards of the government, and eventually individual property-owning citizens, thus doing away with tribal identity and collective claims on land altogether.[26] In short, policies set by white government actors in the decades following the Civil War initiated important shifts in the political economy of race, as adjustments in race relations via specific political actions directly influenced the social and material realities of particular black and native communities. Such shifts in national policies also had direct implications for the education of these racialized groups.

At the same time, settler-schooling projects imposed on native students increased and reached an intensified level of coordination. As with many Progressive Era reform movements, white education reformers worked to increase the efficiency of their efforts and create more centralized educational programs, striving to create the "one best system" for each of the nation's problem populations: the Indian and the Negro. Since the Colonial Era, settlers used education to systematically alienate indigenous students from their natal communities—violating kinship networks, condemning traditional native ways of life, and particularly targeting indigenous heritage claims and traditional relations to land. Yet settler schooling for native students took on a more distinctive political goal during the last decades of the nineteenth century, as native sovereignty became formally denied by the United States government. Native schooling was appropriated toward the national goal of dismantling the organization of tribal governments, an achievement that would form an even clearer path toward continued seizure of native land. The highly coordinated federal boarding school system of the late nineteenth century, championed most forcefully by Richard Henry Pratt, was an institutional formation conditioned by such major shifts in the national character of US Indian policies of the day.

White reformers were concerned with using education to prepare native and black students to be Americans. However, they did so while demanding that these groups "incorporate their American identities at various degrees of inclusion, depending on their race and gender," to borrow from historian Kim Warren.[27] Thus, even in the context of a single school like Hampton Institute, distinct racial projects were at play. As the history outlined throughout *American Grammar* has demonstrated, despite distinction, such racial educational projects formed and evolved in relation to one another, and they constitute central components in the story of the nation's development, even when they were not housed in a single location.

A NATIONAL AFFAIR: BOOKER T. WASHINGTON'S ADDRESS AT HAMPTON'S 1879 COMMENCEMENT

Booker T. Washington's first encounter with the Hampton Indian Program occurred when he attended its 1879 commencement as an alumni speaker, marking the first full year of the school's program for native education. The historical significance of Hampton's 1879 commencement could not be more potent, as it was a striking expression of American schooling. Assembled in the audience were approximately three hundred black and native students, and more than six hundred black, native, and white American guests. The event took place in the main auditorium of Hampton's Virginia Hall, a building that stood as a testament to the promise of the school's curriculum centered on teaching students the value of labor, having been constructed in 1874 with the assistance of student workers.[28] The list of dignitaries seated in Virginia Hall signals the importance this event carried in the world of white educational reformers as well as the federal government. Among them were several high-ranking governmental officials, including Secretary of the Interior Carl Schurz and Secretary of War George W. McCreary, as well as two commissioners of Indian affairs and a long list of state actors and prominent education reformers.[29]

The intimacy between education and warfare when it came to "the Indian problem" was top of mind for many of the federal officials sitting in Virginia Hall. Schurz once declared, "It cost nearly a million dollars to kill an Indian in warfare, whereas it cost only $1,200 to give an Indian child eight years of schooling."[30] The same year he attended the Hampton commencement, Schurz pressured Congress to support native boarding schools as opposed to day schools on reservations, insisting the former was more effective in disrupting the ties between native students and their natal communities. He stated, "It is the experience of the department [Interior] that mere day schools, however well conducted, do not withdraw the children sufficiently from the influences, habits, and traditions of their home life." Educating native students in close proximity to their tribal communities, by his assessment, had only a "limited effect."[31] What Schurz witnessed at Hampton convinced him that Pratt's method was the way forward.

The ideas informing Hampton's Indian Program were new articulations of an old praxis. Likewise, Schurz's vision of native education might have taken on more distinct institutional characteristics in the late nineteenth century, however the ideology he expressed, like Hampton's Indian Program, was conditioned by a racial grammar that had long

THE HAMPTON INSTITUTE—THE NEW BUILDING, VIRGINIA HALL.

15.3: Illustration of Virginia Hall, location of 1879 Hampton Commencement.

shaped the form and function of American schooling. Very little was novel. However, the Indian Program's establishment at this historically black college exposed what was often hidden—a deep-seated structural relationship between these two racial projects in American schooling.

Also in attendance at the 1879 commencement was a small delegation of tribal leaders and relatives of some of the Cheyenne prisoners who were "students" in the Indian Program. According to Hampton's newspaper, *The Southern Workman*, "A very striking addition to the distinguished guests were six tall Indian braves in blankets and feathers; a delegation of Northern Cheyennes from Indian Territory who have been consulting with the 'Great Father' in Washington, and came down to Hampton under escort of Capt. Pratt and Agent Miles to see the young men of their tribe here at school, to some of whom they are related." The delegation included: "Anchi Vib, Little Chief, chief of their band, High Wolf, Porcupine, Black Wolf, Eagle Feather, and Little Wolf, all leading braves." These men were reportedly suspicious of the activities they observed while touring Hampton's campus, when they visited classes and observed artifacts in the Academic Hall, including agricultural tools, sewing machines, and "Indian art." Hampton representatives also gifted the Northern Cheyenne leaders "[p]hotographs of all the Indian students, in their student uniform and neat dresses, at study and work, and of the school grounds and buildings." They also gave samples of students' work to share back on the reservation, in hopes that doing so would be "in the interest of peace and civilization."[32]

Commencement exercises consisted of musical performances by Hampton's band, reading selections from books, and several original essays by students. Speech topics ranged from "The Uses of Time" and "Our Government" to student reflections on the "Duty of the Government to Educate the Indian," "Should the Negro Emigrate?," and "What We Should Do for Africa." One native student was listed on the program. A twenty-three-year-old Kiowa student, Etahdleuh Doanmoe (Boy Hunting), appeared as the ninth student speaker on the program.

Etahdleuh's essay was titled "My Home in Indian Territory," a speech he reportedly sketched out on his own. He wrote parts of it, while also orally communicating ideas to his teachers, who then wrote down his narrative and helped him memorize the words for the ceremony. According to *The Southern Workman*, Etahdleuh's speech was "accompanied by a running translation into the Indian sign language, a very graceful system of natural gestures common to all the tribes from the Gulf to the lakes." The paper described the young man as "a fine representative of his race and its possibilities." Etahdleuh was likely nervous standing before such a large crowd, which approached one thousand people in total, even as his Hampton teachers surely prepared him for the occasion, requiring him to recite his speech repeatedly in the days leading to the event. Hampton's staff knew the young man's speech would not only be a representation of him alone. It would also be used to assess the degree to which they were successful in "civilizing" Indians.

Etahdleuh was a new speaker of English and his speech consisted of short declarative sentences. This string of assertions rendered details about Etahdleuh's life, though framed through the settler gaze of Pratt and his followers. Etahdleuh begins with a simple introduction: "I am a Kiowa Indian boy twenty-three years old. My home is in Indian Territory." The narrative then pivots to a racial assessment of his origins: "My people are not much civilized. They live in houses made of skins of the buffalo. They like to hunt and fight." Etahdleuh speaks of battles between the Kiowa and neighboring tribes, and "scalps of white men and women, as well as Indian men and women." He talks of big dances among the Kiowa. With heavy-handed assistance from his teachers, Etahdleuh paints a stereotypical picture of native life, reducing it to flattened narratives of violence and childlike disputes and desires. Compelled to condemn his Kiowa past, Etahdleuh confesses, "This was all I heard and all I saw, and I thought it was good."[33] Striking the chord of a newly converted Christian, Etahdleuh describes his personal transformation under the tutelage of General Pratt.

Nothing is said of US military aggression. No words of the prison-turned-school at Fort Marion. Hampton's teachers assisted Etahdleuh in constructing a narrative where native people were the singular cause of their own devastation. Pratt—and now Hampton Institute—were the sources of his rescue.

Etahdleuh spoke these words. However, the words were not his alone. They were rehearsed lines. A force-fed testimony. The young man's educational journey is revelatory: first, in a prison-turned-school in the state of Florida, now in an experimental Indian Program at a school founded for ex-slaves on a former plantation, and soon in a native boarding school established in former military barracks—all under complete control of white military officials working in the capacity of education reformers.

Booker T. Washington was the fourteenth and final speaker on the program. The 1879 graduation was a meaningful occasion for Washington. His brother John was among the graduates. "The Force That Wins" was the subject of Washington's speech, where he offered a strong endorsement of Hampton's practical approach to education, using his years as a young teacher to reflect on the lessons he took from the school. Speaking from his "humble experience, as a teacher in the South for the last four years," Washington declared, "there is a force with which we can labor and succeed. . . ." This force that wins "requires not the wise gentleman whose store of knowledge consists, merely, in what he memorized from books," Washington insisted, for "it requires not mere education, but wisdom and common sense, a heart set on the right and a trust in God."

Knowing that most Hampton's graduates would go on as teachers, just as he had done, Washington tailored his comments for this specific vocation. "As a teacher," the force that wins "requires him who can exchange the teacher's desk for the plow or shovel, not him whose heart is set on his salary and not the results of his labor. He who remains in the school-room six hours simply because the law demands it, has not a force that will win." The task of a teacher, and that of their students, must be about more than sitting behind a desk and reading from books, Washington insisted. They must also be willing to roll up their sleeves, to work on the land. Teachers must model the lesson for their students: that there is dignity in toil.

Washington would only lightly broach the large elephant in Virginia Hall. Looking out at the black and native students in the audience and on the stage, Washington spoke to the plight they shared as members of racially dominated groups. His mention of the subject, however, is more tactful and subdued, less direct: Slavery. The Ku Klux Klan. Indian Wars. Such specific language would be deemed impolite by the white spectators making up a large section of the audience, especially the most esteemed guests of the school's leader. Instead, Washington spoke of "misfortune," "discouragement," and "the color of our skins." The fact that black people had been enslaved for generations, that native nations had been and were continuing to be violently displaced and killed on the American frontier (and in native schools), and that these things were being orchestrated by several people sitting in the room was beyond the scope of his commencement address. It is also possible that in this moment, such a structural perspective was beyond what Washington's eyes could see from his teaching post in a small black mining community in Appalachia.

Nevertheless, history was in the room. Hampton was established on a former plantation, in a city that emerged from one of the earliest sites of English settlement in the American colonies, and on grounds where slavery was first introduced as an indispensable part of the United States. Instead of acknowledging this past, Washington encouraged students to look ahead—to *work* toward better days—to "Let no misfortune, no discouragement cause us to think that there is not work to be performed by each of us." Speaking to the black and native students before him,

Washington professed: "Our beginning in life may have been cloudy and crowded by disadvantages, but there is a work for the weakest as well as the strongest, and if performed well, in the end it is as honorable as that performed by the greatest. . . . No matter what the disadvantages may be, no matter what the color of our skins, no matter whether he is rich or poor, a life begun and ended upon this foundation will be a success and will be crowned with that honor which shall be eternal. May it ever be our aim through life to build ourselves and those whom we teach firmly upon this foundation, for it is more priceless than wealth, will do far more for us than any legislation, and will win when other forces fail. . . ."

Washington's speech served its purpose. White spectators experienced this son of Hampton's "earnest and sympathetic delivery" as a grand display of the school's success in transforming the youth of America's two problem populations into tolerable subjects. Washington's speech was followed only by General Armstrong's presentation of the diplomas and closing musical performances by students. This final act included "Plantation songs and glees" as well as "a War Song from the Kiowas, and a simple hymn or two by the Indian students, rather shyly sung."[34]

A FORMER SLAVE BECOMES A DORM FATHER TO NATIVE STUDENTS

Washington's commencement speech was a job talk. Shortly after returning home to Malden, as Washington prepared for his fifth year as a teacher, he received General Armstrong's invitation to work in Hampton's Indian Program. He recalled, "General Armstrong was anxious to try the experiment systematically on a large scale," to increase the number of native students enrolled in the program.[35] The successful commencement ceremonies helped secure funding for this expansion. Following the event, Secretary of the Interior Carl Schurz agreed to provide Hampton with additional funding for educating native students. He committed $167 in federal funding per student for up to 120 native students annually. Twenty thousand dollars a year was no small amount for a growing institution constantly in need of more resources, and Hampton certainly fell in this category.[36]

Washington moved back to Hampton and became the house father of "the Wigwam"—the new dormitory built for native male students—where he supervised the young men. Washington worked in the Indian Program while also serving in other capacities at the school, until 1881, when he left to found Tuskegee. This new role at Hampton required Washington to support native youth as they became socialized into the new geographic and cultural environment. Washington explained, "I was to live in the building with them and have the charge of their discipline, clothing, rooms, and so on." He reflected positively on his experience with the students. This feeling, he believed to be mutual. Washington wrote, "It was not long before I had the complete confidence of the Indians, and not only this, but I think I am safe in saying that I had their love and respect. I found that they were about like any other human beings; that they responded to kind treatment and resented ill-treatment."[37] Washington recalled acts of gratitude and affec-

15.4: Louis Firetail (Sioux, Crow Creek), wearing tribal clothing, in American history class, Hampton Institute, Hampton, Virginia. Photograph by Frances Benjamin Johnston, Library of Congress.

tion he received from the native students, noting "they were continually planning to do something that would add to my happiness and comfort." While the students took well to Washington's kindness toward them, they resented school policies that violated their cultural norms and identities.

"The things that they disliked most," writes Washington, "were to have their long hair cut, to give up wearing their blankets, and to cease smoking." By Washington's characterization, such schooling practices meant to force native students to shed their cultural identities reflected a universal experience of racially dominated groups at the hands of white supremacy. Exposing a sense of solidarity with native students, Washington declared, "No white American ever thinks that any other race is wholly civilized until he wears the white man's clothes, eats the white man's food, speaks the white man's language, and professes the white man's religion."[38]

In a way, Washington's experience working in the Indian Program became an opportunity to sharpen his understanding of racial ideology. It made him more attentive to the racial logics shaping social relations between black, native, and white people in American social institutions like education, but also in the public sphere. I say this because in "Black Race and Red Race," Washington offers some of his more elaborate assessments of racism enacted by white Americans in comparison to other sections of his autobiography. While black students at Hampton were decidedly welcoming to native students, in that they willingly mixed and mingled despite divisive structures imposed on them both, Washington cast doubt as to whether the same would occur at a white institution: "I have often wondered if there was a white institution in this country whose students would have welcomed the incoming of more than a hundred companions of another race in the cordial way that these black students at Hampton welcomed the red ones."[39] Washington's speculation exposes his belief that white Americans were the primary culprits of racial hostilities, and that they were interested in maintaining mainstream American educational institutions exclusively for the benefit of white students. Such indictments are rare in Washington's public writings.

The seemingly egalitarian social interactions of black and native students at Hampton—albeit by Washington's account—in contrast to their experiences when they traveled outside the institution, also led Washington to gain a deeper understanding of race as a relational phenomenon. Washington notes the differential treatment experienced by him and native students when navigating the white supremacist world beyond Hampton. After a student became sick, Washington was charged with escorting him to the secretary of the interior's office, where the student would then be sent to his family out west. The black educator and native student traveled by steamboat and were instructed to stay at a hotel the evening they arrived in the capital. When it became time for dinner on the steamboat, Washington waited for most of the white passengers to finish eating, then proceeded to enter the dining hall, only to be refused. He recalled, "The man in charge politely informed me that the Indian could be served, but that I could not." Washington experienced the same thing when arriving at the hotel, writing, "the clerk stated that he would be glad to receive the Indian into the house, but said that he could not accommodate me."[40]

While such relative privilege may have been experienced by native students in the public sphere, it was a shallow form of inclusion, and always predatory in nature. This was a lesson native students would learn time and time again as they left schools like Hampton and Carlisle, and the many boarding schools that proliferated in the late nineteenth century.

16

A SIOUX STUDENT, A BLACK PRINCIPAL, AND THE US PRESIDENT

During the early stages of research for *American Grammar*, I wrote to historian David Wallace Adams inquiring about relevant books and primary sources to advance my thinking about the intersections of black and native schooling, and especially their relationship to the national development of US education. Adams's book *Education for Extinction* had a major influence on my understanding of native educational history; therefore I was curious about his perspective on these questions. He expressed support for the project, pointing to "a quote by President Garfield when he spoke at Hampton in which he compares the educational needs of both Blacks and Indians."[1] According to Adams, Garfield's 1881 address was worth revisiting. After pulling the transcript of Garfield's speech, and sitting with the weight of the president's words, I immediately began working on this book in earnest.

Garfield described the aims of American education to be a racial project, reflecting the reality that black and native education were not merely about exclusion from the democratic project of American schooling offered to white citizens, but instead revealing these two distinct racial trajectories in American schooling to be integral to the national educational landscape. He speaks of American education as a relational project of racial formation and, simultaneously, as central to the national-building project—particularly gesturing toward needs for rebuilding the country in the postwar period. The president's concern with the education of native and black people clarifies that they were always included—albeit via force and violence—within the schooling apparatus of the United States, even if to varying degrees, and even if their inclusion was on predatory terms—in service of extracting value from their land and labor for the ultimate benefit of white Americans. These key themes in *American Grammar* all appear in Garfield's message to Hampton's black and native students in 1881.

In the audience for the president's address was likely a twenty-five-year-old Booker T. Washington. At the time, the young teacher was still at Hampton completing his final days working in the Indian Program while preparing to travel south in just a couple of weeks to begin building Tuskegee Institute as its founder and principal. Thus, consistent with the history outlined in previous chapters, the occasion of President Garfield's visit is yet another episode in Washington's life where long-standing ties between the founding racial triad in American schooling are on full display. Another likely attendee was a Sioux student named Dawée (David Simmons). Readers may recall Dawée as the brother of Yankton-Sioux activist and writer Zitkala-Ša (Gertrude Simmons), discussed in Part II. Dawée lived in the "Wigwam" at Hampton during Washington's time as the dorm father to native male students. Like Washington, Dawée was also preparing to depart Hampton to begin educational work. Dawée returned home that summer of 1881, eventually became a teacher and later a clerk in the Indian Service at the Yankton Agency. Both Washington and Dawée were likely present for the president's speech, and if they were not physically in attendance, they certainly heard about it from their peers and colleagues or through the school's paper.

THE PRESIDENT'S ADDRESS TO BLACK AND NATIVE STUDENTS

President James A. Garfield visited Hampton Institute on June 5, 1881. It was a Sunday morning, and he arrived just in time to catch the last fifteen minutes of the chaplain's sermon at Bethesda Chapel. According to the president's diary, the chaplain's message was "vigorous and sensible."[2] Accompanying the president was his daughter, Mary, and one of his two eldest sons, either Harry or James, as well as several dignitaries, including Secretary of the Navy William Henry Hunt.

The school community felt honored. It was not every day that the president of the United States visited campus. Yet, while this was indeed a special occasion, President Garfield was no stranger to Hampton. He had "so long been a friend" of the school, according to its newspaper, *The Southern Workman*. In fact, Garfield was a former trustee of Hampton. This appointment likely developed through the educational ties between Garfield and Hampton's founder, General Samuel Chapman Armstrong.[3] Both men were graduates of Williams College, and Garfield's early relationship to Hampton likely formed through this connection.[4] However, Garfield's interest in the institute also extended from his decades of work in education, both before and during his career in politics.

As previously mentioned, the president's visit overlapped with Washington's time at Hampton, as well as that of Dawée. Garfield had distinct messages for Washington and Dawée, though the lessons for both had to do with "the labor problem," as he framed it. While the problem of labor was the central educational concern for black and native students, his message on this subject for African Americans like Washington deviated from his message to native students like Dawée. Garfield insisted both needed an education that cultivated an appreciation for labor as central to the development and maintenance of human civilization. Yet according to Garfield, black people's "labor problem," as he referred to it, extended from their recent history as enslaved people, where they were forced to labor under the lash. On the other hand, native people's "labor problem" was that they had no history of labor at all. According to Garfield, this was evidenced by the fact that indigenous lands were undeveloped prior to European settlement. Garfield stressed these were racially distinct problems and thus called for distinct philosophical approaches to black and native education. He argued that the appropriate methods were important if these two inferior groups were to be productive citizens of the nation.

Garfield began his remarks by honoring the dead veterans buried in the National Cemetery, just outside Bethesda Chapel. As he explored the grounds of the cemetery earlier that day, Garfield was "impressed with the thought that [he] was between the representatives of the past and the future."[5] The deceased Union and Confederate soldiers represented men of the past who fought valiantly to preserve their competing visions of freedom in the United States. The students before him represented the future, as schools like Hampton worked to incorporate them more fully in the national polity, to varying degrees, as citizens. This was "a future made possible by the past, by the graves around us," Garfield imparted. According to the president, the children of freedmen and women, as well as the children of native peoples thousands of miles west, were indebted to these brave soldiers laid to rest just outside the chapel. Black and native students were the beneficiaries of white sacrifice. It was the blood of white soldiers that made their present and futures possible.[6]

Following his reflections on the historic nature of the grounds surrounding the chapel, Garfield turned his attention to the aims of education for black and native students. He stated, "Two phases of the future strike me as I look over this assemblage. For I see another race here; a race from the far west," speaking to the recent presence of native students enrolled at Hampton through its "Indian Program," which began in 1878. The president's geographic orientation—in addressing native students as "a race from the far west"—reveals the settler-colonial gaze framing his conception of black and native schooling. The settler gaze in the US had long been west facing. It began at the eastern shores of North America. Hampton, Virginia, was a point of origin for this gaze inherited by Garfield. It was a place representing the beginning of English-speaking colonial America. This gaze moved farther and farther west as settler-colonial time progressed, with white Americans staring down at native nations along the frontier, where indigenous resistance to the settler state persisted.

The president continued, "These two classes of people [referring to natives and blacks] are approaching the great problem of humanity, which is Labor, from different sides." As Garfield constructed it, the "Labor problem" for black and native students had to be framed from two "different sides" because the importation of enslaved African people from east of the Americas—via the trans-Atlantic trade—

posed different challenges than indigenous youth from the West. In the post–Civil War era, Southern planters and Northern industrialists were both concerned with questions of labor, especially as it pertained to the formerly enslaved, who comprised a large segment of the Southern workforce. Such concerns were national in scope, because the Southern agricultural economy supplied vital materials that fed Northern industries. Though native labor was not vital to the nation's economy, many settlers believed that teaching them to labor was about character-building and fitting them to be industrious as *individual* citizens, an intentional disruption of tribal identities. More importantly, their lessons in labor—that is, socializing native people into becoming workers in a free wage economy as well as property owners and farmers—was about unmaking traditional indigenous relations to land, which directly served the interests of national expansion. Appreciating this context helps underscore how Garfield's lecture on the vitality of labor was informed by specific political and economic motivations—namely continued dispossession of native peoples as well as ongoing extraction of surplus value from black labor, all toward the expansion of American empire.

President Garfield addressed native students first on this subject of "the Labor problem." He explained, "I would put that problem into four words: *Labor must be free.* And for those of you from the far west, I would omit the last word in order to enforce the first lesson. To you I would say: *labor must be!*—for you, for all.—Without it there can be no civilization."[7] Garfield insisted that a civilized society must be predicated on the ability of individual people having the freedom to exchange their labor and skills for wages, to allow them to function in a capitalist society. In short, the function of settler schooling for native youth was to teach students to become "buying workers, and working buyers," to borrow from the late Toni Morrison's assessment of capitalist schooling.[8] Continuing his message to native students—though the audience was multiracial, including the black Hampton students as well as Garfield's two school-aged white children—the president explained, "The white race has learned that truth. They came here as pioneers, felled the forests and swept away all obstacles before them by labor." Here Garfield's racialized vision of native education is conceptualized relationally. It is defined over and against his construction of whiteness in the United States. European colonists' appreciation for labor stood in stark contrast to the lack of appreciation for labor on the part of indigenous peoples. The president then summed up the past and present of native people using the following anti-indigenous interpretation of history: "You come from a people who have been taught to destroy;—to fight but not to labor." Such an assessment led Garfield to the following lesson for the students sitting before him: "[T]o you I would say that without labor you can be nothing. The first text in your civilization is; Labor must be!"

Importantly, Garfield's message on labor, for native people, was in fact always about land. Native students came from a people who roamed the wilderness prior to European colonialism, he declared. They did nothing "productive" with the land. His aim for native schooling was fundamentally about natal alienation, a disruption of traditional indigenous relations with the earth. He insisted that native youth of the future might be more industrious in their use of the land, as laborers and landowners. Simply put, the labor problem in the native context—as articulated by white settlers, including the US president—was always also a land problem.

Education reformers like Hampton's founder, Samuel Armstrong, agreed with Garfield's formulation of the essential lesson for native students: that they must learn to appreciate and internalize labor as the foundation of civilized life. To make this point, Armstrong often made comparisons between black and native histories. According to the Hampton founder, one of slavery's benefits was that it offered black people a valuable education that settlers never extended to native peoples, at least not nearly to the same extent. In an essay on "Indian Education in the East" published in 1880, Armstrong framed slavery as an educational institution that offered important lessons for teaching native students. He explained, "While we all rejoice in the fact that slavery is a thing of the past . . . I firmly believe that under the most favorable conditions it was *a much more successful school for training of a barbarous race than is the reservation*. Slavery brought the colored men into close contact with his white brother, training him in habits of work."[9] Such assessments led white reformers like Armstrong and his colleague Richard Henry Pratt, founder of the Carlisle Indian Industrial School, to critique the organization of native reservations because it prevented closer contact between native people and white settlers. These white reformers argued that native Americans suffered because they were not offered the privilege of greater proximity to white Americans. Such proximity, in their view, benefited black Americans during slavery. In this line of argumentation, black Americans also came from a barbarous race of natives in Africa—a people who lacked industriousness and an appreciation for labor and civilized life. Yet African Americans became civilized through their enslavement and tutelage by white owners. They became a kind of "model minority" over the centuries, with lessons they could now teach others—indeed, this is how some white reformers justified the Indian Program at Hampton.[10] It was implied that black people's proximity to whiteness during slavery taught them the essential lessons in labor. Yet, as Garfield goes on to outline, and to which Armstrong agreed, black Americans had to learn and relearn this lesson.

Garfield turned his attention to the black students in the audience. He explained, "You of the African race have learned this text," referring to the centrality of labor to civilization, "*but you learned it under the lash*. Slavery taught you that labor must be. The mighty voice of war spoke out to you, and to us all, that Labor must be forever free. The basis of all civilization is that Labor must be. The basis of everything great in civilization, the glory of our civilization, is that Labor must be free!" Garfield believed black people carried a negative association with labor because of their history as enslaved people. Therefore they needed to relearn lessons of labor: that one could labor with dignity; that they must labor even when they are not coerced by the whip. Garfield declared black people's education needed to prepare them for their lives as free wage earners, insisting this was essential to good citizenship. What he did not say, however, is that black labor was first and foremost good for the agrocapitalist economy of the South and that this was essential to key industries driving the national economy.[11]

The president's concerns about formerly enslaved people's potential aversion toward labor echoed widespread anxieties about black indolence among white Americans after emancipation. Observing this phenomenon in the political discourse, Black Studies scholar Saidiya Hartman noted, "From the vantage point of abolitionists, policy makers, Freedmen's Bureau officials, and Northern entrepreneurs, the formerly enslaved needed to be trained as free laborers since they had never worked under condition of consent and contract and were ignorant of the principles of self-discipline and restraint." Therefore, many white education reformers, like General Samuel Armstrong, but also President Garfield, looked to education as a means of securing "the productivity of black labor." It was an education meant to "replace the love of leisure with the love of gain."[12] Never mind the spiritual work of education, and what it was to do for a people who for centuries were reduced to fungible laborers and forced to work through violent means. This was to be an afterthought. As articulated by white education reformers both from the North and the South, the primary concern in educating the freedpeople was that they continue to work in the absence of the whip; better yet, that they internalize the whip, and willingly submit to the persistent labor demands placed on their bodies.

Black labor did indeed decrease in the postbellum context. Some historians point to a drop between 28 and 37 percent among rural African Americans. However, this is to be expected. One has to note the absurdity of the idea that black people would choose to work at the same or even nearly the same levels as they were forced to labor under the institution of chattel slavery. Yet it appeared that some white people expected this very thing. From the perspective of white Americans—and motivated by white possessive logics—what other purpose could the Negro serve? For so long, they had only been recognized as *valuable* for the labor extracted from their bodies and wealth stored in them as property, having been deemed generally *worthless* and expendable in all other regards—socially, culturally, and spiritually.[13] In exploring the economic consequences of black emancipation, economic historians Roger Ransom and Richard Sutch explained that "emancipation gave the ex-slave the freedom to lighten his burden." Given the chance to do so, the formerly enslaved now found ways to "reserve a portion of his time for himself." Having been worked to exhaustion for generations, the enslaved "quite naturally chose to work less."[14]

Such actions on the part of black people were cause for concern for white Northerners and Southerners alike. Observing this dynamic among late-nineteenth-century school reformers and politicians, Ethnic Studies scholar Sarah Fong writes, "For Southern planters, freed peoples' enactments of freedom and the withdrawal of labor appeared as a labor shortage" and "for Northerners, they portended troubling signs of idleness unfitting of workers in a free labor society."[15] To address this problem Garfield declared to black students that the key lesson in their education centered on the centrality of labor to their future in American civilization. More specifically, he emphasized that such labor must be uncoerced and without force. But this was a misnomer, since coercion persisted, and education—as Garfield and Armstrong imagined it—would serve as a key instrument of domination, for administering the whip, even if not in physical form. As the decades following the Civil War revealed, coercion of black laborers was a social force not only facilitated by the lash, as other mechanisms were also developed to curtail black freedom for the purposes of extracting value from African Americans as exploitable laborers. This included oppressive mechanisms such as black codes, debt peonage, and vagrancy laws, but it also included the strategic underdevelopment of black education by imposing an educational ideology that encouraged African Americans to be content as low-wage agricultural and domestic workers, while eschewing pressing political concerns.

The president did not address the subject of white education directly in his Hampton address. However, white students formed an invisible comparand in Garfield's formulation of black and native students as problems within the schooling apparatus of the United States. Native learners needed to understand the centrality of labor to civilization, and this required adopting possessive logics in relation to land. Black students needed to learn that there could be dignity in toil, that labor was not only about subjugation; that they must continue working in the agrocapitalist economy of the South to earn their rightful place as citizens. By implication, the president's message also asserted that white students came from communities that had already grasped such fundamental lessons in civilization. Such lessons were passed down to them from their predecessors, a heritage distinct from black and native students. According to President Garfield, white students came from a race of people who understood the importance of labor, as their ancestors "came here as pioneers" who developed lands which were so long neglected by its original inhabitants. The president insisted that, while native people simply roamed the lands, it was white settlers who "felled the forests and swept away all obstacles before them by labor." While the president's comments directly addressed the matter of black and native education, these racial projects were also narratively linked to the invisible presence of white education—an educational project represented not only through Garfield's own trajectory and that of his children in the audience, but also the entire "Continent of Anglo-Saxon civilization," as referenced in the president's remarks.

It is worth noting that Garfield's eldest son, Harry Garfield, became the president of Williams College, and the second eldest, James R. Garfield, was secretary of the interior from 1907 to 1909. One can only wonder how their father's views on race and education may have informed their own work as educational leaders—one directly responsible for the administration of native schooling, and the other the president of a highly influential historically white college.[16] As Garfield's children sat in the audience, they too received lessons about the racial grammars of American schooling, all of which were shaped by their father's educational journey as a white student, then educator, and ultimately president of the United States.

THE EDUCATIONAL JOURNEY OF PRESIDENT GARFIELD

While the previous event in 1881 may seem like an unlikely convergence between the lives of Washington, Dawée, and Garfield, the reality is that the relationship between these historical actors was always deeply intertwined. In fact, James Garfield's educational journey and life in public service reveals such structural entanglements. Thus, to further contextualize the president's address to black and native students, I deem it appropriate to shed light on the president's own history with race and education. For indeed, his own educational journey informed the content of his remarks about race, education, and the ongoing project of building the United States.

Garfield was a longtime teacher and school administrator before his successful career in politics, having served in positions on the local level in Ohio and in the federal government. Garfield served as a teacher and principal at his alma mater, Western Reserve Eclectic Institute (later called Hiram College) in Hiram, Ohio, where he attended school from 1851 to 1854 before enrolling at Williams College. As a congressman he led the charge to establish the US Department of Education in 1866 and Garfield fought tooth and nail to maintain this federal agency for the remainder of his life. As a testament to his professional experience and political advocacy for education, Garfield is remembered by many as "the Education President."[17]

However, it is the substance of Garfield's education that I want to emphasize here. Like many white students throughout the nineteenth century, Garfield learned explicit ideas about race in relation to his own position as a young white male American citizen, and these ideas found expression in his actions as a political leader.[18] In his diary, Garfield described encountering ideas about black and native people on several occasions as a student. We learn, for instance, that when he was seventeen years old, Garfield was president of the Philomathean Society at Eclectic Institute in Ohio, where during one meeting he and his classmates debated whether or not "the African race have suffered greater injustice from the whites than the Indians."[19] That this is a topic for discussion among this all-white student group is indicative of racial discourse in the educational lives of students, not only in textbooks, but also in peer-to-peer relationships. Garfield also notes in his diary on August 31, 1849, that he and his classmates in the Zetelethian debate society at Geauga Seminary took the following question as the basis for their debate: "Are the negroes naturally inferior to the whites?"[20] The young Garfield recorded his position on the subject: he "voted in the aff[irmative]." Then, less than a year later, these same students encountered a fugitive who gave a lecture about slavery. According to Garfield, the experience was memorable. He recalled, "The Darkey had some funny remarks and witty too." At the time, Garfield was still exploring his personal position on the matter of slavery. He was especially concerned with whether owning people stood at odds with Christianity. After studying the subject of slavery and its treatment in the Bible, the young scholar concluded that "the simple relation of master and slave is NOT UNCHRISTIAN."[21]

As a young boy, Garfield was also interested in aspects of native American history. According to Garfield's close cousin, Henry Boynton, the future president was so fascinated with native history that he named the trees in his family's orchard after different chiefs.[22] Such fetishization of native people has always been integral to the construction of white American identity, even as settlers continued to advocate for the erasure of indigenous people. It was one of the many illogical dimensions of racism and racial ideology. In the fall of 1851, Garfield and his classmates also had explicit discussions of US land-based expansion, and therefore native land dispossession. According to Garfield, he and his peers had a "warm time" discussing whether "we would hail with joy the day when . . . the American Union should encircle the whole American continent." The following spring, the young white students in their late teens discussed the following resolution: "Resolved, that the discovery of the gold mines in California are, and will be, a benefit to the United States." While such debates and discussions about American expansion were just theoretical at the time, given that these were teenage white boys engaging in discussion with no immediate influence on matters of US policy, we must consider that these same young men would later be in positions of great influence. Therefore, such theoretical debates and intellectual exercises among white teenagers should be appreciated for the practical implications they would later have when applied in the real world. Indeed, in this instance, one of the students would literally become the president of the United States.[23]

And indeed, Garfield did apply the lessons he learned about race and American society at various moments in his political career, well before his address to black and native students at Hampton. One of the most historic events took place twenty years after his debates about the "discovery" of gold in California and the benefits this resource would have to the nation's development. In 1872, President Ulysess Grant tasked the then-Congressman Garfield with settling a conflict between white settlers and Salish natives in the Bitterroot Valley of Montana. This event would require a practical application of the early lessons of settler colonialism internalized by Garfield. As the *Helena Weekly Herald* explained, "Hon. James A. Garfield arrived at Helena on Sunday and left this morning for the Bitterroot Valley, to remove the Flathead Indians to their new reservation."[24] The assignment ended in Garfield, at the time chair of Appropriations, ordering the Salish people to leave their ancestral lands, having falsely reported that their chief, Charlo, had signed a treaty.[25] As the president's biographer explained, "An ugly scene awaited Garfield. . . . The Bitterroot Salish people ('Flathead' was an unfortunate, erroneous misnomer) were facing down hordes of white settlers in their ancestral lands, while the president—drawing on a prior treaty made under duress, that his government had not honored anyway—was ordering the tribe to vacate." Despite Garfield's falsified treaty, the Salish people continued to resist removal. But US Army troops eventually forced them to leave their homeland. [26]

Just as Garfield encountered ideas about native people in school, before enacting policy and governing in ways that had material implications on native people's survival, he also made decisions when dealing with African Americans based on internalized ideas about black inferiority. This ranged from his stance on the Fugitive Slave Act, which he continued debating, even during his first run for the Ohio senate in 1859, to his personal dealings with black people in his everyday life.[27] For instance, when searching for a permanent residence for his family in Washington, Garfield took care to find a place with a comfortable distance from the large black population in the nation's capital. When purchasing his townhome in 1868, the future president was sure to find a neighborhood that was not "infested with Negroes."[28]

• • •

I usually resist top-down narratives of history, preferring instead to center the voices and actions of people furthest from the levers of power. This feels important to say, because my attention to Garfield's words and actions—as well as other white government actors, like Thomas McKenney—is in some ways a deviation from this commitment. In this book I have been intentional to emphasize structure, and particularly the role of state actors in forging the grammar of the nation's schooling apparatus. Doing so has allowed me to expose the role of government officials in shaping the relational educational experiences of black, native, and white Americans during the country's first full century, thus, demonstrating—in their own words—how highly race-conscious these powerful white political actors were in their educational practices, policies, and ideologies.

My turn to Garfield also stems from an awareness that *American Grammar* has mostly focused on unveiling little-known yet deeply entrenched structural ties between black and native schooling and their centrality to the national story of educational development. My focus on the two persecuted groups within the founding racial triad has been intentional—an emphasis on elements of the national story that have been studiously carved out or, at best, designated sidelines to "the main script" in American educational history. However, I also want to emphasize the realities of white racial socialization in American education, because that too has often gone unnamed—though whiteness is indeed a racial category just the same; a racial category that also formed and evolved relationally. Thus my focus on Garfield's educational journey and his ties to Hampton sheds light on the black and native presence in the white educational imagination. And what better way to expose these relations than the educational journey, ideas, and actions of America's "education president"?

Education's function as a racial project, and simultaneously as an instrument of nation-building, was of deep concern for the man looking down from the highest office of the American empire. Garfield's speech was addressed to students at Hampton, but it was a more expansive vision denoting the racial grammars of the national educational landscape. His words clarified how the inner workings of Hampton—as one particular institution in Virginia—were fitted to what he understood to be more general aims of schooling in the United States when it came to developing descendants of formerly enslaved black people and the children of indigenous nations. These racial projects—the education of black and native people—were not political concerns beyond the purview of the president's office. They were of central concern to white education reformers developing the schooling apparatus of the United States, and this also included President Garfield.

Black and native education were not outside of the schooling apparatus of the state. They were always central to its development. This is reflected in Garfield's educational vision as framed through the lens of the founding racial triad, but it is also reflected in his own educational journey. For even as black and native students were not physically present in the Ohio classrooms of Garfield's youth, ideas about black and native people were integral to the formulation of his own racialized identity as a white student, and eventually teacher, then political leader.

Turning our collective attention to the black and native presence, alongside the white presence, in the stories we tell ourselves of US educational beginnings, helps us to see the entire story anew. It renders a more expansive history, where multiple claims about what happened and the implications of such historical developments are allowed to feature in the frame, where they can all be studied and analyzed for their relationships to one another; indeed, where they can all be accounted for given their essential role as racial projects helping to drive the development of the United States. As *American Grammar* has shown, the history of US education must always be framed by the colorful conflicts of conquest and captivity that conditioned the melding together of the founding racial triad, because the history of US education, as it developed within this relation, is fundamentally a story that begins in red, black, and white. This is the origin story of American education. Like all origin stories, it continues to inform our collective educational lives.

CONCLUSION: THE PRESENCE OF HISTORY IN THE FUTURE(S) OF AMERICAN EDUCATION

Apaches and Tar-babes are mascots for the two rival high schools in my hometown of Compton, California. The former refers to the Apache tribe of native Americans, and while the latter refers to the Tartars, which were Turkic warriors, one cannot help but hear historic references to black children as "tar babies" in the name. Centennial High School and Compton High School were established when Compton was predominantly white, prior to the deindustrialization and white flight that marked the city I encountered in the 1990s. My most prominent memories of the schools and their mascots involve the annual Compton Christmas Parade: black and brown students of Compton High's drill team and band, marching and performing in their powder blue uniforms; Centennial's drill team, mostly composed of African American girls sporting two braids, one on either side of their heads, faux-animal skin costumes, red accessories, and headbands with a single feather. I participated in the parade as a member of my elementary and middle school drum squad. We younger students always circled back to stand near the judges' booth to see the high school performances. Their bands and dance teams were always the parade's main attraction, because their sound and routines were the most sophisticated and high-energy. It was like watching a music video, live and in color. I never questioned their mascots or costumes, nor the histories they referenced and flattened. They seemed to have always been there, part of the backdrop of the city.

The schools' official colors intensified their rivalry: Compton High's blue and Centennial's red coincidentally mapped onto the colors associated with Crips and Bloods—two organizing branches of dominant gangs in the city. However, the mascots expressed a more insidious and deep-seated violence than gang wars and cultural appropriation. In hindsight, it is hard to miss the specter of America's violent racial past looming over my childhood and education, where APACHE LAND was written in big, bold red letters across the front façade of Centennial's building, accompanied by a giant image of an Apache warrior's head in profile. I saw this figure daily when I glanced over my right shoulder while heading north on Central Avenue during my ride to King/Drew Magnet High School in Watts, between 2002 and 2006. Though I did not attend Centennial or Compton High, their symbols are forever etched in my mind. They were central to the educational landscape of the city: allusions to the intertwined experiences of black, native, and white Americans, a much longer story of education and racial domination hiding in plain sight.

As symbolically reflected in the educational landscape of my childhood, the consequences of the past are omnipresent. Such consequences are also reflected in the social realities of American education in the contemporary moment, as black and native students continue to experience the most alienation in US schools. They experience the harshest forms of school discipline at disproportionate rates. They are the two racial groups most overrepresented in the bottom percentiles of school achievement measures in English, math, and other standardized assessments, and they are consistently the least likely to persist through college.[1] And while these things are well documented, the American public and scholars alike have limited context for thinking about the longer history that has led to such strained relationships between these communities and American education.

The past is critical for interrogating present conditions in education, because the consequences of past racial projects are cumulative and they structure our present realities. Yet, as I have demonstrated in *American Grammar*, a rigorous reckoning with this history requires that we move beyond the language of exclusion that for so long has characterized narratives of educational injustice. By focusing on the ways black and native people were "left out" of particular educational opportunities, we elide the structural realities of race that conditioned American schooling from its beginnings—structural realities that expose how black and native people were always present in the story.

More critical engagements with the past require that we account for the centrality of antiblackness and anti-indigeneity in the social foundations of American schooling, how they were central to the political and economic development of the national educational landscape.

The choices we make about how to remember the past has political implications for the present. Therefore I employed a lens of racial domination to demonstrate how at every turn—from the Colonial Era, and especially through the nineteenth century—black and native people were present in US education, even when they were not physically present in most American classrooms, even during moments of racialized exclusion. For indeed, the fiscal and physical development of US education, even when exclusively intended for white benefit, was built through the subjugation of black and native peoples.

To account for the structural realities of racial domination in early US schooling, I emphasized the relational formation of race in American education—tracking how racial ideas and practices targeting one particular group in education were defined over and against the racialized experiences of others. Using the lives of familiar and unfamiliar characters in US educational history—including native students like James McDonald and Zitkala-Ša, formerly enslaved people like Susan McCoy and Booker T. Washington, and white political actors like Colonel Thomas McKenney and President James Garfield—I revealed not only how race was relationally formed through American schooling, but also how central education, as a racial project, was to the building of the nation itself. At every turn, the story of educational development was conditioned by the exploitation of black labor and native land dispossession toward the larger aims of expanding the United States as a white possession. Such relations, rooted in conquest and captivity, reflect the habitus of American schooling. These individual yet intertwining stories of educational formation were not scattered, unrelated phenomenon, but are instead expressions of the national character.

And yet, while the founding racial triad is essential for understanding the beginnings of US education, I am also aware that the racial projects facilitated by the schooling apparatus of the United States expanded and became more diverse by the dawn of the twentieth century. For instance, while President Garfield conceptualized American education as a racial project through a relational assessment of black, native, and white learners in his 1881 speech recounted in the previous chapter, the reality is that the racial configuration of the United States population grew increasingly more complex by the late nineteenth century. The enlistment of Asian and Latin American peoples into the US political context in increasing numbers gradually reshaped the racial landscape of the nation. The racialized experiences of these groups were distinct, since their relationship to the mode of production in the United States, and the racial ideas ascribed to them, made for particular methods of inclusion and distinct experiences of racial oppression. While a deep dive into this history unfolding by the turn of the century is beyond the scope of *American Grammar*, I will say that the incorporation of these groups into the schooling apparatus was framed in relation to the existing strategies of racialized schooling imposed on black, native, and white Americans. Indeed, ghosts from the educational past continued to haunt schooling in the present. Therefore, gaining clarity on the structural relations within US education as it pertains to the founding racial triad is essential context for understanding the relational projects of schooling imposed on other racial and ethnic groups into the twentieth and twenty-first centuries.

The racial grammars of American education were formalized within the landlocked context of North America; however, they also informed technologies of schooling exported to other contexts. This phenomenon grew with American imperialism, a process conditioning the push-and-pull factors leading to many racial and ethnic groups migrating to the United States. For instance, after the US defeated Spain in 1898, the country took control of Cuba, Puerto Rico, Guam, and the Philippines. The US then immediately worked to establish education systems in these territories, building directly on strategies of educational domination imposed on black and native people. When setting up schools in the Philippines, for instance, representatives of the US government looked to Hampton, Tuskegee, and Carlisle for inspiration. Fred Atkinson, the first general superintendent of education in the Philippines, visited these schools for native and black students to prepare for his work in the newly acquired US territory. He was impressed by the educational models of these schools, and he became committed to not "overdoing the matter of higher education and unfitting the Filipino for practical work." The model of education Atkinson desired for the Filipino natives was "an agricultural and industrial one, after the pattern of our Tuskegee institute at home," he explained.[2]

The similarity in the tools of domination applied at home and abroad led some black Americans like T. Thomas Fortune, owner of a black newspaper called the *New York Age*, to declare in 1903 that black Americans and Filipinos were political companions. "For it is construed that we stand largely where they stand," Fortune argued, "outside of the American Constitution, but under the American flag. The hazards of war make strange bedfellows, but none stranger than this of the Afro-American and Filipino peoples." As Indigenous Studies scholar Bayley Marquez explained, schooling was a primary weapon employed in the expansion of American empire. She notes how distinct technologies of schooling were transported internationally, all toward furthering "currents of colonialism" across lands and waters.[3]

Such currents of educational domination flowed not only to territories in the Pacific and Latin America but also to Africa. Racialized ideas about "the Negro" informed colonial education as it expanded on the continent, as European and American powers scrambled for control of its people, land, and natural resources. Collaborations between US and European-based education reformers and missionary associations illustrate this point. These groups worked collaboratively to systematize and exchange best practices for educating African natives in a manner that aligned with the aims of "those who are concerned with the development of Africa," to quote from Thomas Jesse Jones, a leading white American reformer who directed educational efforts funded by powerful white philanthropists in the early twentieth century.[4]

This transnational collaboration among white reformers would appropriate the life of Booker T. Washington in their efforts to expand antiblack models of schooling on the African continent. Leading white philanthropists and missionaries involved in the development of colonial education in Africa drew direct connections between the racialized education of black people in the United States and those across "West, South, and Equatorial Africa." On the occasion of the Booker T. Washington Monument's 1922 unveiling at Tuskegee Institute, leading white reformers made these connections explicit. In advocating for industrial education for African natives in a 1922 report entitled *Education in Africa*, Thomas Jesse Jones turned to the story of Hampton's most famous alumnus and founder of Tuskegee Institute. Jones was chairman of the African Education Commission at the time, which was formed under the direction of the US-based Phelps-Stokes Fund and Foreign Missions Societies of North America and Europe. However, it is important to stress that such trans-Atlantic ties were not novel. They were merely an expansion of earlier efforts, where the subjugation of racially marginalized peoples was enacted by allied groups comprised of American and European colonial forces—collaborations shaped by white possessive logics that harken to the trans-Atlantic slave trade and settler-colonial procedures, to be clear. For instance, as early as 1901 German colonial authorities looked to Tuskegee Institute, as an all-black school focused on industrial education to introduce a similar educational program in the German colony of Togo, West Africa, having found this educational program suitable to Germany's imperialist visions—particularly its interest in making headway in the global cotton industry.[5] As time progressed, educational strategies conditioned by racial ideologies continued to be exported from the United States in service of imperial interests abroad.[6]

In his report, Jones declared that if one needed evidence of "the working of these essentials of education in moulding the life of individuals and communities"—referring to US style industrial education in the South—"we can turn to a demonstration successfully made by a man of African origin." Jones pointed readers to "a recent occasion when a monument was unveiled to commemorate the work of Dr. Washington."[7] Jones described the statue in the following terms:

"This monument presents *Booker Washington lifting the veil of ignorance from the brow of an African youth*, and revealing to him not only the lessons of the printed page, but the Divine gifts that come through cooperation with God in the use of the plow and the anvil."[8] That the youth in Jones's description is "African" speaks to the bidirectional racialization of native Africans and black people in the United States, where difference is conveniently collapsed and a singular notion of blackness (which is always tethered to Africanness) is read onto the monument erected on the grounds of the school Washington founded forty years earlier, in Tuskegee, Alabama—a monument built on the former homelands of the Creek nation.

Jones insisted that Washington's life presented a model for what could be done with all of the African continent. His life "reveal[ed] the possibilities of men of African blood, the qualities of mind and soul they may attain, and the peculiar value of their contribution to human welfare." Simply put, Jones's interpretation of "Booker Washington's life and work" led him to believe Washington "personif[ied] the methods, the principles, and the ideals necessary for those who would work for and with Africans." However, Jones continued, "the Africans themselves [must] be guided and inspired by these ideals if they would participate in the salvation of their great continent."[9]

...

Education, more than anything else, has been the underside of American empire. The imperialist aims of education manifested through scattered racial projects serving as building blocks for a larger schooling apparatus of the United States, one where distinct educational initiatives and institutions interacted with one another toward a singular goal: national expansion based on the subjugation of some to the benefit of others, all structured by a deep investment in a culture of white supremacy and the racial order it structured. The educational landscape that developed internally within the United States, then gradually beyond its borders, has been deeply intertwined with the relational formation of race. Indeed, schools—more than any other space—have been a key physical site in which this social phenomenon of racial formation has taken place. As shown over the course of this book, such alignment manifested through the financing, physical construction, as well as the curricular, social, and legal foundations of education.

Many have described public education as the bedrock of American democracy.[10] To some degree this is true. The conception of universal schooling as a hallmark of democracy was a relatively great achievement in America—a vision of education based on a kind of egalitarianism unmatched by any country around the world in the nineteenth century. However, it was a costly endeavor. Such duality illuminates a major lesson expressed by philosopher Walter Benjamin when he professed, "There is no document of civilization which is not at the same time a document of barbarism."[11] While public education emerged as an impressive achievement in American civilization, where education was based on a virtuous idea of democratic possibility, it was at once forged through barbarous methods, and from its inception, this democratic vision of schooling was predicated on savage inequalities.

By retracing the origin story of American education, I hope to have clarified its racial grammar, demonstrating how such embedded ideological structures have long been conditioned by political and economic forces. The goal of such conceptual clarity is that we might see and speak such origins with more collective awareness and intentionality. By noticing the intimacy between early US schooling, chattel slavery, and native dispossession—as well as derivative forms of antiblackness and anti-indigeneity in policies and laws through the nineteenth century—we achieve a new starting place for tracing a set of relations that have reverberated over the lifespan of the nation and its apparatus of schooling.

Seeing this origin story, these beginnings, with a fresh perspective has allowed me to analyze how racial domination conditioned a kind of internal coherence within US education—a national system made up of a diverse set of institutions, policies, and peoples—to be clear—yet all formed in clear political-economic relation with one another. Such clarity is important because the stratifying function of

American schooling has persisted—especially along the lines of race. For indeed, American education continues to function as a racial project, stratifying society along various lines of difference, such as class, citizenship, gender, sexuality, and disability—all of these being social locations of difference constituting modalities through which race is lived and experienced.

Given the diverse experiences of racial domination in US schooling and society, aggrieved parties have long identified schools as key sites of racial suffering.[12] Operationalizing such educational criticism, persecuted groups also work to appropriate educational institutions, seeking to use them toward emancipatory ends—working to root out injustice that has been symbolically and materially constructed. Indeed, oppressed communities have engaged education as a battleground to fight against inequities formed through various strategies of narrative condemnation and structural exclusion. This too is part of the origin story of American education. Recognizing education as an organizing institution of US society, and one that functions as a key site for the consolidation and curtailing of power, those on the receiving end of racial domination have also appropriated education as a site for protesting, mitigating, and undoing their oppression.

And yet, strategies to achieve educational justice have not looked the same. The distinct forms of racial domination experienced by various groups—particularly black and native Americans—have led to distinct strategies for negotiating power and seeking social transformation through US education. It has also led to distinct conceptualizations of justice, at times even competing visions of what justice can and should look like.[13] In more than one way, the question of what constitutes repair and meaningful racial justice in education continues to be unsettled.

I believe that studying such foundational relations of race and power in American education is a necessary step as we search for meaningful intervention and models of reconstruction. For indeed, how we understand our beginnings as a multiracial society has direct implications for how we interpret our present and how we imagine our futures, because whether we are conscious of it or not, in the words of James

Baldwin, "it is to history that we owe our frames of reference, our identities, and our aspirations."

To be concerned with injustice in schools requires that we also concern ourselves with the history of that injustice. That we study it and name it, to then hold it accountable. The story of race and power in American education is not static. It is something that we all experience and must reckon with. Again, from Baldwin: "The great force of history comes from the fact that we carry it within us, are unconsciously controlled by it in many ways, and history is literally present in all that we do."[14] The roots of racial domination, which fed the United States education system since its creation, continue to have lived consequences. We must all sharpen our view of America's educational past, so that we might reckon with how it acts upon us and through us today.

ACKNOWLEDGMENTS

I began conceptualizing this book during a course I taught in the spring of 2019, The American School and Racial Formation. My discussions with students over that semester convinced me that there was a need for a book to help education scholars, historians, and the general public make sense of the structural connections between black, native, and white education, and that such a work would help retool our understanding of the critical role schools played in shaping the American social order. Therefore, my first expression of gratitude goes to my students. Thank you for being my earliest thought partners on this project. I began working on the book in earnest after teaching my course, eventually presenting a book proposal at a Wine & Wisdom faculty colloquium at the Harvard Graduate School of Education in December 2019. The feedback I received at this event gave me confidence to move forward with my research and writing. Thanks go to Ebony Bridwell-Mitchell for organizing the event, and to all my colleagues who attended this session. I am particularly grateful to Howard Gardner, Jal Mehta, Allison Pingree, and Julie Reuben. Thank you for your hard questions, encouragement, and deep engagement during Wine & Wisdom and the days that followed.

So many colleagues and friends pushed my thinking in important ways. Some introduced me to new readings that helped refine arguments and my analysis of the historical record, and others provided feedback on parts of the manuscript at key stages. Joshua Bennett, Mahasan Chaney, Philip Deloria, Kendra Field, Sarah Fong, Sande Grande, Adrian Hernandez-Acosta, Jennifer Lynn Johnson, Khalil Johnson, Sarah Lewis, Carla Lillvik, Bayley Marquez, DeRay McKesson, Mary McNeil, Roshad Meeks, Ernest Mitchell, Timothy Pantoja, Imani Perry, Therí Pickens, Julie Reuben, Alaina Roberts, and Brandon Terry, I am deeply grateful to each of you for supporting me through this process. Thank you for taking my ideas seriously, and for telling me when I needed to go back to the drawing board.

My development of *American Grammar* benefited greatly from various student research assistants between 2020 and 2025. Thanks to the Research Partners Program at the Radcliffe Institute for Advanced Study, I had the honor of working with Farah Afify, Anna Kate Cannon, Anna Farronay, Samantha Gamble, Abbe Goldstein, Keanu Gorman, Grey Johnson, and William Sutton. No matter how much you contributed during our group discussions or how many reports by Commissioners of Indian Affairs you combed through, I am tremendously grateful for your support as I followed hunches and arbitrary leads in historical collections. During this process Ashley Ison, at the time an HGSE doctoral candidate, was of great support, as she helped keep our research team organized. I owe a huge debt to Ashley, as well as Will, Anna Kate, and more recently, Chloe Becker, who were more than just research assistants, but also thought partners at critical phases in my process of writing this book. I appreciate your contributions and for taking the questions at the heart of this work seriously.

I also workshopped pieces of *American Grammar* in an ongoing research seminar with my PhD advisees. They offered extremely valuable feedback on early drafts of various chapters. Rebecca Horwitz-Willis, Zenzile Riddick, Christian Walkes, Kemeyawi Wahpepah, Ivelisse Ramos, Cassondra Hannah, Darien Dey, Esther Anfo-Whyte, and Jordan Jackson-Collins, thank you for "returning the favor" and taking me to task when necessary. Our work is stronger because of the intellectual community we continue to build, where we maintain a commitment to critiquing and refining the things that we value because we want them to be better, and because we have our own standards of rigor that are responsive to the communities most important to who we are and what we do.

Thank you to Nate Muscato for helping me find a publishing home for this book; to Gail Winston for bringing *American Grammar* to Harper; and a huge note of gratitude to Adenike Olanrewaju for picking up the baton mid-race as my editor and helping me cross the finish line. I appreciate your patience as this project grew, unexpectedly, from five to sixteen chapters, and for your sharp editorial eye when it came time to let some things go. Adenike and Nate, I appreciate your partnership in this work.

I am also grateful to my cousins Duke Givens, in Long Beach, California, and Jarita Givens, in Chickasha, Oklahoma. Thank you for helping me think through the family connection in this work via text messages and phone conversations. In a similar vein, I would like to acknowledge genealogists Angela Walton-Raji and Simon Ligon for their decades-long work to elevate the stories of Choctaw freedmen and for making time to talk with me about this unexpected line of research. Your contributions ignited a different kind of motivation for completing this book. You all reminded me to take seriously the ancestral presence despite disciplinary conventions in history and academia that downplay the power of such connections to the past.

When I set out to write this book, I had no idea how central my family's story would be in clarifying the stakes of my arguments and the history I unveiled. Thus, my final offering of gratitude is to my ancestors who cleared a path for me to do this work; those whose names I have always known, those whom I encountered while writing *American Grammar,* as well as the many I have yet to encounter but who offered me covering in ways that I may never know.

NOTES

INTRODUCTION

1. United States Department of the Interior and Sixty-Second Congress, *Five Civilized Tribes in Oklahoma: Reports of the Department of the Interior and Evidentiary Papers in Support of S. 7625: A Bill for the Relief of Certain Members of the Five Civilized Tribes in Oklahoma* (Washington, DC: US Government Printing Office, 1913), 651.
2. Susan [McCoy] Brashears Petition filed on January 15, 1906, pp. 8–9 of hearing transcript, in Commissioner to the Five Civilized Tribes Department of the Interior, "Joe and Dillard Perry Case Number F-005: Petition of Susan [McCoy] Brashears Submitted by Attorney Albert J. Lee," January 15, 1906, Page/Document 10, Record Groups 75: Records of the Bureau of Indian Affairs, Applications to Change from Freedmen to Citizens by Blood, 1905–1907, National Archives at Fort Worth, https://catalog.archives.gov/id/1225129.
3. Choctaw nation, *The Constitution and Laws of the Choctaw Nation* (Park Hill, Cherokee Nation: Mission Press, 1847), 20.
4. Jarvis R. Givens, "Black Education as the General Strike: The Radical Origins of African American Teaching and Learning," *Journal of African American History* 109, no. 2 (March 2024): 231–59.
5. "Letter of the Choctaw Mission," in *The Missionary Herald, Containing the Proceedings of the American Board of Commissioners for Foreign Missions*, vol. 44 (Boston: T. R. Marvin, 1848), 355–58.
6. Joel H. Spring, *The Cultural Transformation of a Native American Family and Its Tribe, 1763–1995: A Basket of Apples, Sociocultural, Political, and Historical Studies in Education* (Mahwah, NJ: Lawrence Erlbaum, 1996), 157; Ruby Wile, "'Yakni Achukma, the School with a Soul': A History of the Goodland Indian Orphanage," https://gateway.okhistory.org/ark:/67531/metadc2016873/m1/8/ .
7. Nick Estes, "The World of Paper, Restoring Relations, and the Lower Brule Sioux Tribe," in *Allotment Stories: Indigenous Land Relations under Settler Siege*, ed. Jean M. O'Brien and Daniel Heath Justice (Minneapolis: University of Minnesota Press, 2022), 49.
8. The issue of indigenous peoples' kinship with land had been perpetually identified by American leaders. As President Thomas Jefferson explained in 1803, native people through education were "learning to do better with less land." This same ideological sentiment informed the words of President Theodore Roosevelt in 1901, during the allotment era, when he declared, "The General Allotment Act is a mighty pulverizing engine to break up the tribal mass. It acts directly upon the family and the individual. . . . The Indian should be treated as an individual—like the white man." Jefferson to Benjamin Hawkins, February 18, 1803, in *Writings*, ed. Merrill D. Peterson (New York: Library of America, 1984), 1115; Theodore Roosevelt, First Annual Message to Congress, December 3, 1901.
9. Angela Y. Walton-Raji, *Oklahoma Freedmen of the Five Tribes* (Charleston, SC: Arcadia, 2023), 13; Barbara Krauthamer, "In Their 'Native Country': Freedpeople's Understandings of Culture and Citizenship in the Choctaw and Chickasaw Nations," in *Crossing Waters, Crossing Worlds: The African Diaspora in Indian Country*, ed. Sharon Patricia Holland and Tiya Miles (Durham, NC: Duke University Press, 2006), 100–20; Kevin Mulroy, *The Seminole Freedmen: A History* (Norman: University of Oklahoma Press,

2007); Alaina E. Roberts, *I've Been Here All the While: Black Freedom on Native Land* (Philadelphia: University of Pennsylvania Press, 2021).

10. Francis Paul Prucha, *The Great Father: The United States Government and the American Indians*, abridged ed. (Lincoln: University of Nebraska Press, 2014), 260.
11. Estes, "The World of Paper," 47.
12. Terry Ligon, "Isaac Alexander, 'Negro Blood Denied,'" *Bettie's List* (blog), April 7, 2024, https://bettieslist.blogspot.com/2024/04/isaac-alexander-negro-blood-denied.html; Terry Ligon, "Bettie's List ~ Julia Jackson," *Bettie's List* (blog), December 14, 2011, https://bettieslist.blogspot.com/2011/12/betties-list-julia-jackson.html.
13. Susan [McCoy] Brashears Petition.
14. Sworn statements were submitted by Charles Cohee, Ellis Williams, Solomon Gilbert, W. L. Bennett, and Thomas Norman during Susan's 1906 hearing in which they detailed these actions by the Dawes Commission. See *Five Civilized Tribes in Oklahoma: Reports of the Department of the Interior and Evidentiary Papers in Support of S. 7625: A Bill for the Relief of Certain Members of the Five Civilized Tribes in Oklahoma*, 651.
15. Susan [McCoy] Brashears Petition, 9.
16. Phrase used by Richard Wilcox, interviewed in the film *Black Indians: An American Story* (Rich-Heape Films, 2000): "There was a lot of people that was using what we call pencil genocide. In other words, they were changing documents in the town halls, and this and that, and unless you had some questions about it, you didn't even know it" (27:55).
17. For "narratively condemned," see Sylvia Wynter, "No Humans Involved: An Open Letter to My Colleagues," *Forum N.H.I. Knowledge for the 21st Century* 1, no. 1 (Fall 1994): 42–73.
18. See "Affidavit of Susan Brashears" in Petition of Susan [McCoy] Brashears, 21.
19. Thavolia Glymph, "Paper Tracings in the Spectacularly Boisterous Archive of Slavery," *The American Historical Review* 130, no. 1 (March 1, 2025): 2.
20. Ibid., 6.
21. On "racial projects" see Michael Omi and Howard Winant, *Racial Formation in the United States: From the 1960s to the 1990s* (New York: Psychology Press, 1994).
22. Daniel Martinez HoSang and Natalia Molina, eds., "Introduction: Toward a Relational Consciousness of Race," in *Relational Formations of Race: Theory, Method, and Practice* (Oakland: University of California Press, 2019), 1–18.
23. As constitutional law scholar Derek Black (2020) has argued, "the nation's commitment to public education predates the Constitution." Like previous scholars, Black rightfully points to the Ordinances of 1785 and 1787, principally constructed by future presidents John Adams and Thomas Jefferson (12–13) as the earliest expressions of public education being a fundamental expression of the US as a constitutional democracy. He demonstrates how "[o]ur founding fathers were deeply concerned with common people's access to public education" and that their concern "has stuck with our nation ever since. At the nation's two most pivotal periods—Independence and the Civil War—the nation embedded education in our constitutional democracy" (51–52). These early shapers of the republic "believed that if this experiment had any chance of standing the test of time, the nation needed to ensure everyday citizens had access to learning opportunities that prepared them for self-government" (54). Derek W. Black, *Schoolhouse Burning: Public Education and the Assault on American Democracy* (New York: PublicAffairs, 2020); David B. Tyack, Thomas James, and Aaron Benavot, *Law and the Shaping of Public Education, 1785–1954* (Madison: University of Wisconsin Press, 1987); Carl Kaestle, *Pillars of the Republic: Common Schools and American Society, 1780–1860* (New York: Hill & Wang, 1983).
24. Toni Morrison, "Unspeakable Things Unspoken: The Afro-American Presence in American Literature (1988)," in *The Source of Self-Regard: Selected Essays, Speeches, and Meditations* (New York: Knopf, 2019), 172–73.

25. Michel-Rolph Trouillot, *Silencing the Past: Power and the Production of History* (Boston: Beacon Press, 1997).
26. For instance, in *Pillars of the Republic: Common Schools and American Society: 1780–1860*, which is rightfully a foundational and widely taught text on the subject, historian Carl Kaestle notes, "Because state policies about common schooling had little impact on Native and Hispanic Americans in the pre–Civil War East, these groups play no part in my analysis." African Americans appear in Kaestle's narrative; however, their presence is merely to document their experience of exclusion from white schools. He writes, "Because they were excluded from most northern common-school systems, blacks were faced with a strategic dilemma, whether to make the best of separate-and-unequal black schools or to press for integration into white schools." His narrative implies that even as America continued to be settled on indigenous land and through the superexploitation of black captive labor, black and native peoples were beyond the bounds of citizenship and generally excluded from common schools. It leads one to assume that these groups play little or no part in the story of American school beginnings. In a broad stroke, Kaestle's framing is consistent with dominant narratives about early American education in public memory and in academic assessments. However, some scholars have offered alternative framings. The greatest example is the work of James D. Anderson, who argues that "within American democracy there have been classes of oppressed people and . . . there have been essential relationships between popular education and the politics of oppression. Both schooling for democratic citizenship and schooling for second-class citizenship have been basic traditions in American education." Anderson underscores the relationality between education for citizenship and education for domination, outlining how "These opposing traditions were not, as some would explain, the difference between the mainstream of American education and some aberrations or isolated alternatives. Rather, both were fundamental American conceptions of society and progress, occupied the same time and space, were fostered by the same governments, and usually were embraced by the same leaders." When writing of Thomas Jefferson's 1787 proposal for tax-supported schooling in Virginia, Andersons asks: "But what of the enslaved children who constituted about 40 percent of the total number of Virginia's children and who along with the enslaved adults formed the basis of wealth for Jefferson, as well as for the state of Virginia?" The astute historian recognizes that, for white architects of American schooling, like Jefferson, "It was believed that Virginia's peace, prosperity, and 'civilization' depended as much, if not more, on the containment and repression of literate culture among its enslaved populations as it did on the diffusion of literate culture among its free population." Though writing about the history of African American education, specifically, Anderson points to a key structural dynamic in the racial life of American schooling more generally, thus clarifying how the underdevelopment of educational opportunity in one area has always been inextricably linked to the development of educational opportunity in another. *American Grammar* is an elaboration on Anderson's incisive social analysis of education in the United States. Kaestle, *Pillars of the Republic*, xii, 172; James Anderson, *The Education of Blacks in the South, 1860–1935* (Chapel Hill: University of North Carolina Press, 1988), 1.
27. Danielle S. Allen, "Invisible Citizens: On Exclusion and Domination in Ralph Ellison and Hannah Arendt," in *Nomos XLVI: Political Exclusion and Domination* (New York: New York University Press, 2004), 30–31.
28. My conception of the "schooling apparatus of the United States" is informed by Althusser's conception of the Ideological State Apparatus (ISA) and its close ties with the Repressive State Apparatus (RSA). It also extends from Williams J. Novak's conceptualization of "the well-regulated society," where he employs a nimble conceptualization of governance that disrupts myths about the American nation-state in the

nineteenth century as primarily defined by its absence or a lack of influence from centralized federal power. Employing nuanced conceptions of everyday governance, Novak disrupts the myth of a nineteenth-century America "as a lagging mercantilist stage of development," a tale in which well-established regulatory practices in the first century are nearly erased for the purposes of advancing patriotic narratives about liberal individualism and America's distinctiveness from its European predecessors. Louis Althusser, *Lenin and Philosophy, and Other Essays* (Chicago: Monthly Review Press, 1972); William J. Novak, *The People's Welfare: Law and Regulation in Nineteenth-Century America* (Durham, NC: Duke University Press, 1996), 7–9.

American Grammar renders a new history of education that accounts for what I refer to as the founding racial triad—what Alexis de Tocqueville in 1835 described as the "Three Races That Inhabit the Territory of the United States" in his critical treatise *Democracy in America*, and what Tiffany King, a scholar of Black Studies and Native Studies, has formulated as an "Indian-European-Negro or Red-White-Black" triadic formulation for thinking about race, power, and human experience in the early United States. Alexis de Tocqueville, *Democracy in America*, trans. Arthur Goldhammer (New York: Library of America, 2004), 336; Tiffany Lethabo King, *The Black Shoals: Offshore Formations of Black and Native Studies* (Durham, NC: Duke University Press, 2019), 18.

29. Aileen Moreton-Robinson argues that racism in the United States "is predicated on the logic of possession," particularly possessions by white people. She explores how the United States and its national identity is "built on the disavowal of Indigenous sovereignty because the nation is socially and culturally constructed as a white possession," and this argument also extends to the bodies of African captives subjected to racial chattel slavery. Aileen Moreton-Robinson, *The White Possessive: Property, Power, and Indigenous Sovereignty* (Minneapolis: University of Minnesota Press, 2015), xiii–xiv.
30. Robin Mitchell, "Bringing Ourselves Along with Us: The Realities of Historical Writing," *Women's History Network* (blog), June 28, 2021, https://womenshistorynetwork.org/bringing-ourselves-along-with-us-the-realities-of-historical-writing/.
31. Saidiya Hartman, *Lose Your Mother: A Journey Along the Atlantic Slave Route* (New York: Farrar, Straus & Giroux, 2008), 18.

1: A CROSSROADS IN EARLY US EDUCATION

1. From Kathryn L. MacKay's analysis of US Census data from 1820, see "Statistics on Slavery," https://faculty.weber.edu/kmackay/statistics_on_slavery.htm.
2. William H. Gaines, *Thomas Mann Randolph: Thomas Jefferson's Son-in-Law* (Baton Rouge: Louisiana State University Press, 1966), 77.
3. The House of Delegates first proposed revising and consolidating the state's black codes in 1816. See *Journal of the House of Delegates of the Commonwealth of Virginia* (Richmond, VA: Thomas Ritchie, 1816), 107.
4. *The Revised Code of the Laws of Virginia: Being a Collection of All Such Acts of the General Assembly, of a Public and Permanent Nature, as are Now in Force*, vol. 1, ed. Benjamin Watkins Leigh (Richmond, VA: Thomas Ritchie, 1819), 424.
5. Ibid., 421.
6. Ibid., 424.
7. Acts of the Fifteenth Congress of the United States, Chapter 85, 15th Congress, 2nd Session, November 16, 1818–March 3, 1819.
8. Ibid.
9. Zitkala- Ša, "Impression of an Indian Childhood" (1900), in *American Indian Stories* (Washington, DC: Hayworth, 1921).

10. See Angela Valenzuela, *Subtractive Schooling: U.S.-Mexican Youth and the Politics of Caring* (Albany: State University of New York Press, 1999).
11. Leilani Sabzalian, *Indigenous Children's Survivance in Public Schools* (New York: Routledge, 2019).
12. *Journal of the House of Delegates of the Commonwealth of Virginia* (Richmond, VA: Thomas Ritchie, 1820), 7.
13. *Journal of the House of Delegates of the Commonwealth of Virginia*, 1810, chapter 14, p. 15.
14. Greg Crawford, "Virginia Untold: Joe of Nottoway County—The UncommonWealth," accessed July 23, 2024, https://uncommonwealth.virginiamemory.com/blog/2021/01/27/virginia-untold-joe-of-nottoway-county/.
15. Jill Lepore, *A Is for American: Letters and Other Characters in the Newly United States* (New York: Knopf, 2003); Kaestle, *Pillars of the Republic*; Benjamin Justice, "Schooling as a White Good," *History of Education Quarterly* 63, no. 2 (May 2023): 154–78.
16. Ibid.; for final quote, Leigh's *The Revised Code of the Laws of Virginia*, 424.
17. *Journal of the House of Delegates of the Commonwealth of Virginia* (Richmond, VA: Thomas Ritchie, 1820), 7.
18. Kaestle, *Pillars of the Republic*; Tyack, *The One Best System*. For more on the limitations of dominant historical framings, see Jarvis R. Givens and Ashley Ison, "Toward New Beginnings: A Review of Native, White, and Black American Education Through the 19th Century," *Review of Educational Research* 93, no. 3 (June 1, 2023): 319–52.
19. "Jefferson to Benjamin Hawkins, February 18, 1803," in *Writings*, 1115.

2: FEDERAL FUNDING FOR NATIVE SCHOOLING IN THE EARLY NINETEENTH CENTURY

1. Typescript copy of Cyrus Kingsbury's 1869 autobiography, 6, original in Sue L. McBeth papers at the Oklahoma Historical Society, copied March 1957. Papers of Frances Hope Kerr Holway, 1871–1962, A-59, 5, Box 1, Schlesinger Library, Radcliffe Institute.
2. Ibid.
3. Francis Paul Prucha, *The Great Father: The United States Government and the American Indians*, vol. 1 (Lincoln: University of Nebraska Press, 1984), 81–83.
4. Claudio Saunt, *A New Order of Things: Property, Power, and the Transformation of the Creek Indians, 1733–1816* (Cambridge: Cambridge University Press, 1999), 249–72.
5. Prucha, *The Great Father*, 81–83.
6. Ibid., 86.
7. See Matthew J. Clavin, *The Battle of Negro Fort: The Rise and Fall of a Fugitive Slave Community* (New York: New York University Press, 2019).
8. Prucha, *The Great Father*, 88.
9. *American State Papers: Indian Affairs 2, 1815–1827* (Washington, DC: Library of Congress), 478.
10. Ibid., 477.
11. Ibid.
12. Ibid., 478.
13. Ibid.
14. Ibid.
15. Ibid. (emphasis added).
16. Ibid.
17. Ibid. (emphasis added).
18. Such a sentiment appears in Jacqueline Fear-Segal, *White Man's Club: Schools, Race, and the Struggle of Indian Acculturation* (Lincoln: University of Nebraska Press, 2007), 73, and Prucha, *The Great Father*, 687. For similar critique, see Rowan Faye Steinker, "'Fully

Equal to That of Any Children': Experimental Creek Education in the Antebellum Era," *History of Education Quarterly* 56, no. 2 (2016): 273–300.

19. *The Papers of Thomas Jefferson, Retirement Series*, vol. 12, September 1, 1817–April 21, 1818, ed. J. Jefferson Looney (Princeton, NJ: Princeton University Press, 2014), 114–27.
20. *American State Papers: Indian Affairs 2, 1815–1827* (Washington, DC: Library of Congress), 478.
21. Cyrus Kingsbury's 1869 autobiography, 6; for the treaty, see Charles Keppler, ed., *Indian Affairs: Laws and Treaties* (Washington, DC: US Government Printing Office, 1904), 141.
22. Cyrus Kingsbury's 1869 autobiography, 6.
23. *The Papers of John C. Calhoun*, ed. W. Edwin Hemphill, vol. 2 (Columbia: University of South Carolina Press, 1963), 142.
24. Ibid., vol. 3 (Columbia: University of South Carolina Press, 1963), 227.
25. Ibid.
26. Ibid.; Thomas Lorainne McKenney, *Memoirs, Official and Personal: With Sketches of Travels Among the Northern and Southern Indians; Embracing a War Excursion, and Descriptions of Scenes Along the Western Borders* (New York: Paine & Burgess, 1846), 109.
27. McKenney, *Memoirs*, 109.
28. Quoted in Herman J. Viola, *Thomas L. McKenney: Architect of America's Early Indian Policy, 1816–1830* (Chicago: Sage Books, 1974), 40 (emphasis added).
29. Frederick E. Hoxie, *This Indian Country: American Indian Activists and the Place They Made* (New York: Penguin Press, 2012), 71.
30. W. Stitt Robinson, "Indian Education and Missions in Colonial Virginia," *Journal of Southern History* 18, no. 2 (1952): 152–68, https://doi.org/10.2307/2954270; Margaret C. Szasz, *Indian Education in the American Colonies, 1607–1783* (Albuquerque: University of New Mexico Press, 1988).
31. Francis Paul Prucha, *The Great Father: The United States Government and the American Indians*, vol. 1 (Lincoln: University of Nebraska Press, 1995), 141.
32. Ibid., 146.
33. Ibid., 115–34.
34. *The Papers of Thomas Jefferson*, vol. 39, November 13, 1802–March 3, 1803, ed. Barbara B. Oberg (Princeton, NJ: Princeton University Press, 2012), 350–54 (emphasis added).
35. "Message of January 18, 1803," in James D. Richardson, comp., *A Compilation of Messages and Papers of the Presidents*, vol. 1, 340–41.
36. Prucha, *The Great Father.*
37. James Madison, "Eighth Annual Message," speech, Washington, DC, December 3, 1816, American Presidency Project, https://www.presidency.ucsb.edu/documents/eighth-annual-message-0.
38. *American State Papers: Indian Affairs 2, 1815–1827* (Washington, DC: Library of Congress), 151.
39. Ibid.
40. Herman J. Viola, *Thomas L. McKenney: Architect of America's Early Indian Policy, 1816–1830* (Chicago: Sage Books, 1974), 42.
41. *American State Papers: Indian Affairs 2, 1815–1827* (Washington, DC: Library of Congress), 671.
42. Ibid., 201.
43. Ibid., 272.
44. Ibid.
45. Ibid., 275.
46. Ibid., 459.
47. Viola, *Thomas L. McKenney*, 93.
48. Ibid., 94.

49. Ibid.
50. "Religious Intelligence: The American Indians," *Connecticut Courant* (1791–1837), May 20, 1817.
51. *The Brainerd Journal: A Mission to the Cherokees, 1817–1823*, ed. Joyce B. Phillips and Paul Gary Phillips (Lincoln: University of Nebraska Press, 1998), 379.
52. *American State Papers: Indian Affairs 2, 1815–1827* (Washington, DC: Library of Congress), 273.
53. Prucha, *The Great Father.*
54. *Report of the American Board of Commissioners for Foreign Missions; Compiled from Documents Laid Before the Board at the Thirteenth Annual Meeting, which was Held at New Haven, Con., Sept 12, & 13, 1822* (Boston: Crocker & Brewster, 1822), 64.
55. *Register of Debates in Congress, Comprising the Leading Debates and Incidents of the Second Session of the Eighteenth Congress*, vol. 1 (Washington, DC: Gales & Seaton, 1825), 639.

3: ANTI-LITERACY LAWS AND THE ROOTS OF ANTIBLACK EDUCATION POLICY

1. Edward R. Laurens, "An Address Delivered before the Agricultural Society of South-Carolina, September 18th, 1832," *Southern Agriculturist and Register of Rural Affairs* 5, no. 11 (November 1832): 565.
2. John W. Blassingame, ed., *Slave Testimony: Two Centuries of Letters, Speeches, Interviews, and Autobiographies*, annotated ed. (Baton Rouge: Louisiana State University Press, 1977), 465.
3. Heather Williams, *Self-Taught: African American Education in Slavery and Freedom* (Chapel Hill: University of North Carolina Press, 2007), 208.
4. *Acts Passed at a General Assembly of the Commonwealth of Virginia, Begun and Held at the Capitol, in the City of Richmond, Monday, the Sixth Day of December, in the Year of Our Lord, One Thousand Eight Hundred and Thirty, and of the Commonwealth the Fifty-Fifth* (Richmond, VA: Thomas Ritchie, 1831).
5. Jarvis R. Givens, "Black Education as the General Strike: The Radical Origins of African American Teaching and Learning," *Journal of African American History* 109, no. 2 (2024): 231–59.
6. Ibid.
7. Janet Cornelius, "'We Slipped and Learned to Read': Slave Accounts of the Literacy Process, 1830–1865," *Phylon* 44, no. 3 (1983): 174.
8. "Ben Brown, Federal Writers' Project: Slave Narrative Project, Vol. 12, Ohio, Anderson-Williams," June 9, 1937, 13, in *Born in Slavery: Slave Narratives from the Federal Writers' Project, 1936 to 1938* (603), Library of Congress.
9. "Minnie Davis, Federal Writers' Project: Slave Narrative Project, Vol. 4, Georgia, Part 1, Adams-Furr," August 29, 1938, 257, in *Born in Slavery.*
10. "'Douglas Dorsey,' in Federal Writers' Project: Slave Narrative Project, Vol. 3, Florida, Anderson-Wilson (with Combined Interviews of Others)," January 11, 1937, 95–96, in *Born in Slavery.*
11. Similar account found in Henry Bibb. *The Life and Adventures of Henry Bibb, An American Slave* (Madison: University of Wisconsin Press, 2001), 22.
12. Jarvis R. Givens, "Reading in the Dark: Becoming Black Literate Subjects," in *School Clothes: A Collective Memoir of Black Student Witness* (Boston: Beacon Press, 2023).
13. Cornelius, "'We Slipped and Learned to Read.'"
14. Richard Fuller and Francis Wayland, *Domestic Slavery Considered as a Scriptural Institution* (New York, 1845), 159.
15. *The Statutes at Large of South Carolina*, ed. David J. McCord, vol. 7 (Columbia, SC:

A. S. Johnston, 1840), 397; *Georgia: Colonial Laws, 17th. February 1755–10th. May 1770* (1770, reprint, Washington, DC: Statute Law Book Company, 1932), 514; *The Revised Code of the Laws of Virginia: Being a Collection of All Such Acts of the General Assembly, of a Public and Permanent Nature, as are Now in Force*, vol. 1, ed. Benjamin Watkins Leigh (Richmond, VA: Thomas Ritchie, 1819), 425; *The Revised Code of Mississippi, in which are Comprised all such Acts of the General Assembly, of a Public Nature, as were in Force at the End of the Year 1823* (Natchez, MS: Francis Baker, 1824), 390.

16. See James Breeden, *Advice Among Masters: The Ideal in Slave Management in the Old South* (Westport, CT: Greenwood Press, 1980).
17. Bibb, *The Life and Adventures of Henry Bibb*, 32.
18. Edward L. Ayers, *Vengeance and Justice: Crime and Punishment in the 19th Century American South* (Oxford: Oxford University Press, 1984), 62; Estelle B. Freedman, *Their Sisters' Keepers: Women's Prison Reform in America, 1830–1930* (Ann Arbor: University of Michigan Press, 1984).
19. "Commonwealth of Virginia vs. Margaret Douglass," *Independent* 6, no. 273 (February 23, 1854): 64.
20. Margaret Douglass, *Educational Laws of Virginia: The Personal Narrative of Mrs. Margaret Douglass, a Southern Woman, who was Imprisoned for One Month in the Common Jail of Norfolk, under the Laws of Virginia, for the Crime of Teaching Free Colored Children to Read* (Boston: John P. Jewett, 1854), 4.
21. Angela Y. Davis, *Women, Race, & Class* (New York: Vintage, 1983); Stephanie E. Jones-Rogers, *They Were Her Property: White Women as Slave Owners in the American South* (New Haven, CT: Yale University Press, 2020); Thavolia Glymph, *Out of the House of Bondage: The Transformation of the Plantation Household* (Cambridge: Cambridge University Press, 2008).
22. Douglass, *Educational Laws of Virginia: The Personal Narrative of Mrs. Margaret Douglass*, 12, 9.
23. Ibid., 14.
24. Ibid., 15.
25. Ibid.
26. Ibid., 18, 19.
27. John D. Lawson, ed., *American State Trials*, vol. 7 (St. Louis: F. H. Thomas, 1917), 53, 56, 64.
28. "Commonwealth of Virginia vs. Margaret Douglass," 64.
29. *The Statutes at Large of South Carolina*, ed. David J. McCord, vol. 7 (Columbia, SC: A. S. Johnston, 1840), 397.
30. Ibid.
31. Alexis de Tocqueville, *Democracy in America*, trans. Arthur Goldhammer (New York: Library of America, 2004), 393.
32. Ibid.
33. Heather Williams, *Self-Taught: African American Education in Slavery and Freedom* (Chapel Hill: UNC Press, 2005), 7.
34. Ibid.
35. William Whewell, *The Elements of Morality: Including Polity*, vol 1. (London: J. W. Parker, 1845), 350.
36. Fuller and Wayland, *Domestic Slavery Considered as a Scriptural Institution*, 114.
37. Julius S. Scott, *The Common Wind: Afro-American Currents in the Age of the Haitian Revolution* (London: Verso, 2018).
38. Edward R. Laurens, "An Address delivered before the Agricultural Society of South-Carolina, September 18th, 1832," *Southern Agriculturist and Register of Rural Affairs* 5, no. 11 (Nov. 1832): 565.

39. Eric Williams Rose, "The Charleston 'School of Slavery': Race, Religion, and Community in the Capital of Southern Civilization," (PhD diss., University of South Carolina, 2014), 179.
40. John Belton O'Neall, *The Negro Law of South Carolina* (Columbia, SC: John G. Bowman, 1848), 23.
41. Rose, "The Charleston 'School of Slavery,'" 180.
42. "Commonwealth of Virginia vs. Margaret Douglass," 64.
43. Levine, *Black Culture and Black Consciousness.*
44. David Walker, *David Walker's Appeal to the Coloured Citizens of the World* (Boston, 1830).
45. Rita Dover, "David Walker (1785–1830)," in *The Yellow House on the Corner* (Pittsburgh: Carnegie Mellon University Press, 1980).
46. Scott, *The Common Wind*, 210.
47. Kenyon Gradert, "The Book That Spooked the South," *Smithsonian*, February 8, 2018, https://www.smithsonianmag.com/history/book-spooked-south-180968101.
48. Charles Colcock Jones, *The Religious Instruction of the Negroes in the United States*, ATLA Monograph Preservation Program ATLA Fiche 1988–3246 (Savannah, 1842), 12–13; Leslie M. Harris, *In the Shadow of Slavery: African Americans in New York City, 1626–1863* (Chicago: University of Chicago Press, 2004), 34, 40.
49. "Negro College—City Meeting," *Columbian Register*, September 13, 1831; "Southampton Affair," *Columbian Register*, September 13, 1831; "From the Albany Evening Journal: Gabriel's Defeat," *Columbian Register*, September 13, 1831.
50. Hilary J. Moss, *Schooling Citizens: The Struggle for African American Education in Antebellum America* (Chicago: University of Chicago Press, 2009), 18–20.
51. "Commonwealth of Virginia vs. Margaret Douglass," 64.
52. Ibid.
53. Ibid.
54. Douglass, *Educational Laws of Virginia*, 22.
55. Ibid., 50.
56. "Interview of Miss Mary Jane Wilson, Portsmouth Virginia by Thelma Dunston," in Federal Writers' Project, *Slave Narrative Project*, vol. 17, Virginia, Berry-Wilson, 1936, 55, https://www.loc.gov/item/mesn170/.
57. Tera Hunter, *Bound in Wedlock: Slave and Free Black Marriage in the Nineteenth Century* (Cambridge, MA: Harvard University Press, 2017), 6.
58. "Interview of Miss Mary Jane Wilson," 56.
59. Ibid.
60. Ibid.
61. Ibid.
62. Ibid.
63. "Emanuel A.M.E. Church," Historical Marker Database, retrieved May 10, 2023.

4: NATIVE LAND, BLACK LABOR, AND THE DEVELOPMENT OF SCHOOLING AS A WHITE GOOD

1. Benjamin Justice, "Schooling as a White Good," *History of Education Quarterly* 63, no. 2 (May 2023): 154–78.
2. David B. Tyack, Thomas James, and Aaron Benavot, *Law and the Shaping of Public Education, 1785–1954* (Madison: University of Wisconsin Press, 1987), 21.
3. Carl Kaestle, *Pillars of the Republic: Common Schools and American Society, 1780–1860* (New York: Hill & Wang, 1983).
4. Tyack, James, and Benavot, *Law and the Shaping of Public Education, 1785–1954*, 14. A

similar argument can be found in Derek W. Black, *Schoolhouse Burning: Public Education and the Assault on American Democracy* (New York: PublicAffairs, 2020), 62–65.

5. Justice, "Schooling as a White Good."
6. Tyack, James, and Benavot, *Law and the Shaping of Public Education, 1785–1954*, 32. For more relevant discussion on Land Ordinances of 1785 and 1787, see Nancy Beadie, *Education and the Creation of Capital in the Early American Republic* (Cambridge: Cambridge University Press, 2010), 325; Nancy Beadie, "Resource Extraction and Education Funding: Nature and Political Economies of State Formation in the United States," *Paedagogica Historica* 56, no. 1–2 (March 3, 2020): 150–70; Black, *Schoolhouse Burning*, 62–65.
7. Joyce B. Phillips and Paul Gary Phillips, ed., *The Brainerd Journal: A Mission to the Cherokees, 1817–1823* (Lincoln: University of Nebraska Press, 1998), 31. Similar references in *First Ten Annual Reports of the American Board of Commissioners for Foreign Missions, with Other Documents of the Board* (Boston: Crocker & Brewster, 1834), 197; *Brainerd Journal*, 105.
8. Justice, "Schooling as a White Good," 167.
9. Nancy Beadie's work is a notable exception. When writing about the history of resource extraction, capital development, and early public-school funding, Beadie observes, "state funding of education has always been tied to resource extraction." More specifically, she declares, "It began with appropriation of land itself. In the 1780s, Congress directed that portions of all newly appropriated lands be set aside to support schools, a tradition that continued in subsequent acts. This tradition of tying state school funding to land acquisition, exploitation, and/or sale had a number of major historical consequences for the politics and political economy of education in the US." However, as Beadie observes, these relationships "are seldom recognized or commented upon by US historians or historians of education." Beadie, "Resource Extraction and Education Funding," 151; Beadie, *Education and the Creation of Capital in the Early American Republic*, 325.
10. Tyack, James, and Benavot, *Law and the Shaping of Public Education, 1785–1954*, 20.
11. Justice, "Schooling as a White Good," 166.
12. United States Continental Congress, Rufus King, William Samuel Johnson, and Continental Congress Broadside Collection, "An ordinance for ascertaining the mode of disposing of lands in the Western Territory: Be it ordained by the United States in Congress assembled, that the territory ceded by individual states to the United States, which has been purchased of the Indian inhabitants, shall be disposed of in the following manner" [New York: s.n., 1785], https://www.loc.gov/item/90898224/.
13. J. S. Higgins, *Subdivisions of the Public Lands, Described and Illustrated with Diagrams and Maps* (St. Louis: Higgins, 1887).
14. "Resolution and memorial of Ohio on the subject of school lands in that State," in *American State Papers: Public Land 4*, 1823–27 (Washington, DC: Library of Congress), 47.
15. Alexandra Usher, "Public Schools and the Original Federal Land Grant Program," Center for Educational Policy, 2011, 12.
16. Ibid., 21–25.
17. Ibid.
18. "FY21 Member State Data," National Association of State Trust Lands, 2022, statetrustlands.org.
19. J. Hammond Trumbull, *The Public Records of the Colony of Connecticut Prior to the Union with New Haven Colony, May, 1665* (Hartford: Brown & Parsons, 1850), 554–55. This mandate came between the Pequot (1636–38) and Metacomet's (1675–78) Wars, effectively wars of conquest that established Connecticut's dominance over native nations' claims, demonstrating how closely schooling followed/accompanied conquest.

20. Many states surrendered their claims to the federal government in exchange for cancellation of their war debts. See Harriet Taylor Upton, *History of the Western Reserve* (Chicago: Lewis, 1910), 9.
21. Bernard C. Steiner, *The History of Education in Connecticut* (Washington, DC: US Government Printing Office, 1893), 39.
22. John Eaton, *Report of the Commissioner of Education for the Year 1876* (Washington, DC: US Government Printing Office, 1878), 44; Steiner, *The History of Education in Connecticut*, 40.
23. *Indian Affairs: Laws and Treaties 2*, ed. Charles J. Kapper (Washington, DC: US Government Printing Office, 1904), 39.
24. Steiner, *The History of Education in Connecticut*, 39.
25. *Indian Affairs: Laws and Treaties 2*, 77.
26. Ibid., 77.
27. Robert Nichols, *Theft Is Property! Dispossession and Critical Theory* (Durham, NC: Duke University Press, 2019), 8.
28. Jack Campisi, "New York-Oneida Treaty of 1795: A Finding of Fact," *American Indian Law Review* 4, no. 1 (1976): 75.
29. Ibid., 78.
30. Alan Taylor, *The Divided Ground: Indians, Settlers, and the Northern Borderlands of the American Revolution* (New York: Knopf, 2006), 143, 201.
31. New York Comptroller's Office, Albany 25th, January. "Sir. I have the honor to enclose herein the annual report, directed to be exhibited to the Legislature, in and by the act, entitled. 'An act relative to the office and duties of the Comptroller o.'" Albany, 1805. https://www.loc.gov/item/2020771338/.
32. Ibid., 186.
33. *Journals of the Senate and House of Commons of the General Assembly of the State of North Carolina, at the Session of 1834–35* (Raleigh, NC: Philo White, 1835), 116.
34. *Documents Printed by Order of the General Assembly of North Carolina, at its Session of 1842–43* (Raleigh, NC: Weston R. Gales, 1843), 124, https://digital.ncdcr.gov/digital/collection/p249901coll22/id/85808/.
35. Peter Wallenstein, *From Slave South to New South: Public Policy in Nineteenth-Century Georgia* (Chapel Hill: University of North Carolina Press, 1987), 27.
36. Ibid., 27.
37. "An Act Establishing Schools in the County of Mobile," in *Acts Passed at the Seventh Annual Session of the General Assembly of the State of Alabama* (Cahawba, AL: William B. Allen, 1826), 18; "An Act Concerning the Revenue of Mobile County," in *Acts Passed at the Sixth Annual Session of the General Assembly of the State of Alabama* (Cahawba, AL: William B. Allen, 1825), 84; Stephen B. Weeks, *History of Public School Education in Alabama* (Washington, DC: US Government Printing Office, 1915), 43.
38. "An Act to extend and improve the system of Public Education in the state of Louisiana, Approved February 16, 1821," in *General Digest of the Acts of the Legislature of Louisiana* (New Orleans: Benjamin Levy, 1828), 257.
39. Kevin Outterson, "Slave Taxes," in *Studies in the History of Tax Law*, ed. John Tiley (London: Hart, 2004), 269.
40. Ibid.; Wallenstein, *From Slave South to New South*, 40.
41. Carole E. Scott, "The Troubled World of Antebellum Banking in Georgia," 2016, 9, https://www.westga.edu/~bquest/2000/antebellumGAbanks.pdf.
42. "An Act to further increase the common School Fund," in *Laws of the State of New York*, vol. 5 (Albany, NY: Webster & Skinner, 1809), 40–41.
43. *Journal of the Senate of the State of New York, at their Thirty-Sixth Session* (Albany, NY: Southwick, 1813), 172.

44. *Journal of the Senate of the State of New York, at their Forty-Second Session* (Albany, NY: Buel, 1819), 69.
45. Joshua D. Rothman, *The Ledger and the Chain: How Domestic Slave Traders Shaped America* (New York: Basic Books, 2021), chap. 4.
46. Helen Jones Campbell, "The Syms and Eaton Schools and Their Successor," *William and Mary College Quarterly Historical Magazine* 20, no. 1 (1940): 2–61.
47. Charles L. Coon, *The Beginnings of Public Education in North Carolina: A Documentary History, 1790–1840*, vol. 1 (Raleigh, NC: Edwards & Broughton, 1908), 95.
48. Ibid., 96.
49. Ibid.
50. Ibid., 97. More on "Dickson Charity Fund" at https://us4.courthousecomputersystems .com/duplinncnw/application.asp.
51. Leon H. Sikes, "Warsaw, N.C.: Historical Briefs," Duplin County Historical Society, July 2005, http://duplinhistory.org/?p=Duplin%20Towns.
52. Sylviane A. Diofe, *Slavery's Exiles: The Story of the American Maroons* (New York: New York University Press, 2014), 266–76.
53. 1850 US Census, Slave Schedule.
54. South Carolina had anti-literacy language on the books starting in 1740; Virginia's first explicit anti-literacy legislation passed in 1819.
55. Williams, *Self-Taught*, Appendix.
56. See, for example, the WPA testimony of formerly enslaved George Rogers, quoted in Carl Kaestle, *Pillars of the Republic: Common Schools and American Society, 1780–1860* (New York: Hill & Wang, 1983), 197. See also Janet Cornelius, "*'When I Can Read My Title Clear': Literacy, Slavery, and Religion in the Antebellum South* (Columbia: University of South Carolina Press, 1991), 64–65.
57. "An Act requiring to be paid into the School Fund money derived from the sale of Slaves under the Act of November 22, 1829," in *Acts and Resolutions of the General Assembly of the State of Florida, Passed at its Fifth Session* (Tallahassee: Office of the Floridian and Journal, 1851), 103.
58. Alan Arellano, "'. . . to the Encouragement of Learning': Virginia's Literary Fund—The UncommonWealth," accessed July 23, 2024, https://uncommonwealth.virginiamemory .com/blog/2022/11/23/to-the-encouragement-of-learning-virginias-literary-fund/.
59. Sarah Hyde, *Schooling in the Antebellum South: The Rise of Public and Private Education in Louisiana, Mississippi, and Alabama* (Baton Rouge: Louisiana State University Press, 2016).
60. Renee K. Harrison, *Black Hands, White House: Slave Labor and the Making of America* (Minneapolis: Fortress Press, 2022); White House Historical Association, "Slavery and the White House," https://www.whitehousehistory.org/press-room/press-backgrounders /slavery-and-the-white-house.
61. Brown University Steering Committee on Slavery and Justice, *Slavery and Justice*, 2006; UNC Libraries, "Slaves and the University Buildings," *Slavery and the Making of the University*, 2005, https://exhibits.lib.unc.edu/exhibits/show/slavery/university _buildings.
62. Presidential Committee on Harvard and the Legacy of Slavery, *Harvard & the Legacy of Slavery* (Cambridge, MA: Harvard University, 2022), 11.
63. Daina R. Berry, "The Ubiquitous Nature of Slave Capital," in H. Boushey, J. Bradford DeLong, and M. Steinbaum, eds., *After Piketty: The Agenda for Economics and Inequality* (Cambridge, MA: Harvard University Press, 2017), 126–49.
64. Harrison, *Black Hands, White House*, 10.
65. Margaret Chapman, B. R. Taylor, and Madie Smith, "Rock Church School District," in *History of Bell County Public Schools, 1854–1976* (Bell County, TX: Temple-Bell Retired Teachers Association, 1976), 343; Thad Sitton and Milam Rowold, *Ringing the Children*

In: Texas Country Schools (College Station: Texas A&M University Press, 1987), https://www.familysearch.org/library/books/viewer/89302/?offset=0#page=348&viewer=picture&o=search&n=0&q=slav.

66. Christina Snyder, *Great Crossings: Indians, Settlers, and Slaves in the Age of Jackson* (New York: Oxford University Press, 2017). On use of enslaved labor by missionaries, see *The Brainerd Journal: A Mission to the Cherokees, 1817–1823*, ed. Joyce B. Phillips and Paul Gary Phillips (Lincoln: University of Nebraska Press, 1998), 162, 176, 254, 276.
67. "Viney Baker," Federal Writers' Project: Slave Narrative Project, vol. 11, *North Carolina*, Part 1, "Adams-Hunter" (1936), 69, https://www.loc.gov/item/mesn111/.
68. Ibid., 67.
69. James Anthony Owen, "The Peachtree Valley and Valley Town Mission: A Baptist Recategorization of a Cherokee Landscape" (MA thesis, Western Carolina University, 2012). Around the same time the 1819 treaty between the US government and the Cherokee nation was being signed, the lead missionary from Valley Town was reportedly in DC to solicit funds from the newly passed Civilization Fund Act. See Robert Fleming, *Sketch of the Life of Humphrey Posey* (Georgia, Western Baptist Association, 1852), 58. Disbursements from the Civilization Fund are recorded in *American State Papers: Indian Affairs 2, 1815–1827* (Washington, DC: Library of Congress), 272.

5: THE AIMS OF NATIVE SCHOOLING FOR AN EXPANDING SETTLER NATION

1. Winona LaDuke, *Last Standing Woman* (Stillwater, MN: Voyageur Press, 1999).
2. Quoted in Herman J. Viola, *Thomas L. McKenney: Architect of America's Early Indian Policy, 1816–1830* (Chicago: Sage Books, 1974), 40.
3. *The Papers of John C. Calhoun*, ed. W. Edwin Hemphill, vol. 3 (Columbia: University of South Carolina Press, 1963), 227 (hereafter *John C. Calhoun Papers*, vol. 3).
4. David Wallace Adams, *Education for Extinction: American Indians and the Boarding School Experience, 1875–1928* (Lawrence: University Press of Kansas, 1995), 54, 156.
5. Thomas L. McKenney, *Memoirs, Official and Personal: With Sketches of Travels Among the Northern and Southern Indians; Embracing a War Excursion, and Descriptions of Scenes Along the Western Borders* (New York: Paine & Burgess, 1846), 111.
6. In reference to McKenney's slaves: Federal Population Census, District of Columbia, 1820, Records of the Bureau of the Census.
7. McKenney, *Memoirs, Official and Personal*, 111.
8. *John C. Calhoun Papers*, vol. 3, 230.
9. Quoted in Viola, *Thomas L. McKenney*, 43.
10. American State Papers, 559 (No. 220).
11. McKenney, *Memoirs, Official and Personal*, 116.
12. Ibid.
13. Ibid., 114.
14. Ibid.
15. Frederick Hoxie, "The First Indian Lawyer: James McDonald, Choctaw," in *This Indian Country: American Indian Activists and the Place They Made* (New York: Penguin Books, 2012), 92.
16. My conceptualization builds on the work of Orlando Patterson, *Slavery and Social Death: A Comparative Study*, 2nd ed. (Cambridge, MA: Harvard University Press, 2018), 5.
17. K. Tsianina Lomawaima, "The Mutuality of Citizenship and Self-Determination: Proposing Alternatives to Adversarial Binarism in United States/Native American Relations," in *The Settler Complex: Recuperating Binarism in Colonial Studies*, ed. Patrick Wolfe (Los Angeles: American Indian Studies Center, UCLA, 2016), 85.

18. Philip J. Deloria, *Playing Indian* (New Haven, CT: Yale University Press, 1999); Shari M. Huhndorf, *Going Native: Indians in the American Cultural Imagination* (Ithaca, NY: Cornell University Press, 2015); Hayden White, "The Noble Savage Theme as Fetish," in *Tropics of Discourse: Essays in Cultural Criticism* (Baltimore: Johns Hopkins University Press, 1978), 183–96.
19. On "domestication" of native cultures see K. Tsianina Lomawaima and Teresa L. McCarty, *"To Remain an Indian": Lessons in Democracy from a Century of Native American Education* (New York: Teachers College Press, 2006), 43–66.
20. Ibid., 6.
21. Thomas S. Williamson letter to Commissioner of Indian Affairs, in Orlando Brown, *Annual Report of the Commissioner of Indian Affairs* (Washington, DC: Gideon, 1850), 124–25.
22. Letter from E. C. Chirouse, 1861, in *Annual Report of the Commissioner of Indian Affairs—1861–1862* (Washington, DC: Office of Indian Affairs, 1862), 406 (emphasis added).
23. Patterson, *Slavery and Social Death*, 5.
24. Daniel Martinez HoSang and Natalia Molina, eds., "Introduction: Toward a Relational Consciousness of Race," in *Relational Formations of Race: Theory, Method, and Practice* (Oakland: University of California Press, 2019), 1–18; Givens and Ison, "Toward New Beginnings."
25. Patterson, *Slavery and Social Death*, 5–6 (emphasis added).
26. Saidiya Hartman, *Scenes of Subjection: Terror, Slavery, and Self-Making in Nineteenth-Century America* (New York: Oxford University Press, 1997), 40.
27. "Condition of the Several Indian Tribes" (No. 182), Report of Secretary of War Calhoun, February 11, 1822, *American State Papers: Indian Affairs 2, 1815–1827* (Washington, DC: Library of Congress), 275.
28. General Calvin Jones, "Education: Accounts of the Cherokee Schools," *Nashville Whig and Tennessee Advertiser*, October 3, 1818, 2.
29. This account is dated September 28, 1818. See *The Brainerd Journal*, 83 (emphasis added).
30. For more details about this student's story, see Brent Gary Bergherm, "The Little Osage Captive: The Tragic Saga of Lydia Carter," *Arkansas Historical Quarterly* 62, no. 2 (2003): 123–52.
31. *Brainerd Journal*, 83.
32. "Indian Missions," *The Guardian, or Youth's Religious Instructor* 6, no. 9 (September 1, 1824): 317.
33. Margaret D. Jacobs, *White Mother to a Dark Race: Settler Colonialism, Maternalism, and the Removal of Indigenous Children in the American West and Australia, 1880–1940* (Lincoln: University of Nebraska Press, 2011).
34. Elizabeth Taylor, "Letter to Miss Abigail Parker," in Theda Perdue, *The Cherokee Removal: A Brief History with Documents* (Boston: St. Matrtin's, 2016), 47.
35. American Board of Commissioners for Foreign Missions (ABCFM) Papers, 18.3.1 v. 2, item 432.

6: SETTLER SCHOOLING AS AN ACT OF WAR

1. Francis Paul Prucha, *The Great Father: The United States Government and the American Indians* (Lincoln: University of Nebraska Press, 1986), 38–40, 54–57.
2. Herman J. Viola, *Thomas McKenney: Architect of America's Early Indian Policy, 1816–1830* (Chicago: Sage Books, 1974), 22–24.
3. Prucha, *The Great Father*, 58–59.
4. Bryan Newland, "Federal Indian Boarding School Initiative Investigative Report,"

US Department of the Interior, May 2022, 31, 30, 28–31, https://www.bia.gov/sites/default/files/dup/inline-files/bsi_investigative_report_may_2022_508.pdf.

5. John C. Calhoun, “Report of the Secretary of War, March 29, 1824,” in *American State Papers: Indian Affairs 2, 1815–1827* (Washington, DC: Library of Congress), 461–62.
6. *American State Papers: Indian Affairs 2, 1815–1827*, 460–78, “Extinguishment of Indian Title to Lands in Georgia” (No. 204), April 2, 1824, documents compiled by James Monroe.
7. Report of Secretary of War John C. Calhoun, “Progress Made in Civilizing the Indians” (No. 162), January 15, 1820, *American State Papers: Indian Affairs 2, 1815–1827*, 200–201.
8. Ibid.
9. Report of Secretary of War John C. Calhoun, “Condition of the Several Indian Tribes (No. 182),” February 11, 1822, *American State Papers: Indian Affairs 2, 1815–1827*, 276.
10. Nancy Reece, “Letter to Reverend Daniel Campbell,” in Perdue, *The Cherokee Removal*, 49–50.
11. Jon Reyhner and Jeanne Eder, *American Indian Education*, 2nd ed. (Norman: University of Oklahoma Press, 2017), 51; David Wallace Adams, *Education for Extinction: American Indians and the Boarding School Experience, 1875–1928* (Lawrence: University Press of Kansas, 1995), 27.
12. Ngũgĩ wa Thiong'o, *Decolonising the Mind: The Politics of Language in African Literature* (Portsmouth, NH: Heinemann, 1986).
13. “Thomas Crawford: Commissioner of Indian Affairs (October 22, 1839–October 29, 1845),” in David H. Dejong, *From Paternalism to Partnership: The Administration of Indian Affairs, 1786–2021* (Lincoln: University of Nebraska Press, 2021), 62–63; Crawford quote on 67.
14. Adams, *Education for Extinction*, 31.
15. *Annual Report of the Commissioner of Indian Affairs for 1891*, 1144.
16. *American State Papers: Indian Affairs 2*, 478.
17. Carl Schurz, “Present Aspects of the Indian Problem (July 1881),” *North American Review* 258, no. 4 (1973): 45–54.
18. “Army Charges Answered: The Indian Service Upheld by Mr. Schurz,” *New York Times*, December 7, 1878.
19. Adams, *Education for Extinction*, 43, 46–48.

7: “BOARDING SCHOOL IS NOW THE ANCESTOR”

1. We find one such case with Thomas H. Crawford, the Commissioner of Indian Affairs from 1838 to 1845, having been appointed by President Martin Van Buren. Crawford is reported to have informally adopted four native boys. Indian Agent Thomas S. Williamson referenced above, for his advocacy to “[separate native students] from their people young,” provides another case of such captive adoptions. See Reyhner and Eder, American Indian Education, 2nd ed., 46; letter submitted by Thomas S. Williamson to Major N. McLean, Indian Agent, in *Annual Report of the Commissioner of Indian Affairs to the Secretary of the Interior 1850–1851*, 174–75.
2. *Annual Report of the Commissioner of Indian Affairs*, 1827, Doc. No. 2, Sig. 26, 144–45; Tiya Miles, “The Lost Letter of Mary Ann Battis: A Troubling Case of Gender and Race in Creek Country,” *NAIS* 1, no. 1 (2014): 91.
3. Thomas L. McKenney, *Memoirs, Official and Personal: With Sketches of Travels among the Northern and Southern Indians, Embracing a War Excursion, and Descriptions of Scenes along the Western Borders* (New York: Paine & Burgess, 1846), 187–88.
4. Francis Paul Prucha, *The Great Father: The United States Government and the American Indians*, abridged ed. (Lincoln: University of Nebraska Press, 1986), 59.

5. *Annual Report of the Commissioner of Indian Affairs*, 1827, Doc. No. 2, Sig. 26, 144–45. For more on Asbury Mission School, see Miles, "The Lost Letter of Mary Ann Battis," 91.
6. McKenney, *Memoirs, Official and Personal*, 188.
7. Ibid.
8. Adams, *Education for Extinction*, 224.
9. McKenney, *Memoirs, Official and Personal*, 188.
10. Sari Horwitz et al., "'In the Name of God': Native American Children Endured Years of Sexual Abuse at Boarding Schools," *Washington Post*, May 29, 2024; Chris Finley and Camilla Townsend, "'All He Had Told Them . . . Was True': Native American History and the Witnessing of Abuse in the Archive," *Native American and Indigenous Studies* 9, no. 2 (2022): 95–123.
11. McKenney, *Memoirs, Official and Personal*, 189.
12. Ibid.
13. Thomas S. Williamson letter to Commissioner of Indian Affairs, in *Annual Report of the Commissioner of Indian Affairs* (Washington, DC: Gideon, 1850), 124–25.
14. Writing three years later, in August 1851, Williamson spelled the matter out in clearer terms. He complained of the slow progress made by Dakota students being taught by his sister, Jane Williamson: "we have never succeeded in teaching any to understand or speak much of it, until they have resided for some time in a family where it is the spoken language. Hence appears the importance of placing as many of the children as possible in such families; for in this way alone are they likely to acquire any useful knowledge of our language, which our Government regards so important that they should learn. In this way, also, they may best acquire the habits, and learn something of the economy, of civilized life—a kind of knowledge not less necessary than that of letters and our language—to enable them to sustain themselves in the reservation to which it is expected they will be confirmed in a few years." Letter submitted by Thomas S. Williamson to Major N. McLean, Indian Agent, in *Annual Report of the Commissioner of Indian Affairs to the Secretary of the Interior 1850–1851*, 174–75.
15. Report of Fletcher J. Cowart, US Indian Agent, in *Annual Report of the Commissioner of Indian Affairs*, 1886, 202.
16. Adams, *Education for Extinction*, 263.
17. Child, "The Boarding School as Metaphor," 38.
18. Adams, *Education for Extinction*, 16.
19. Reyhner and Eder, *American Indian Education*, 2nd ed., 51; Adams, *Education for Extinction*, 27.
20. Thomas S. Williamson letter to Commissioner of Indian Affairs, in Orlando Brown, *Annual Report of the Commissioner of Indian Affairs* (Washington, DC: Gideon, 1850), 124–25.
21. "September 28, 1818," in *The Brainerd Journal: A Mission to the Cherokees, 1817–1823*, ed. Joyce B. Phillips and Paul Gary Phillips (Lincoln: University of Nebraska Press, 1998), 83.
22. "November 21, 1823," in *The Brainerd Journal*, 379.
23. Robin Bernstein, *Racial Innocence: Performing American Childhood from Slavery to Civil Rights* (New York: New York University Press, 2011), 8–13.
24. General Calvin Jones, "Education: Accounts of the Cherokee Schools," *Nashville Whig and Tennessee Advertiser*, October 3, 1818, 1.
25. Letter from Jeremiah Evarts, Treasurer of the American Board of Commissioners for Foreign Missions, reprinted in Rufus Anderson, *Memoir of Catharine Brown: A Christian Indian of the Cherokee Nation* (Crocker & Brewster, 1825), 26–30.
26. Abel Bingham, "Indian School at Tonawanda," *Columbia Star*, June 26, 1824, 403.

27. John H. Oberly, "Report of the Indian School Superintendent," in John DeWitt Clinton Atkins, *Annual Report of the Commissioner of Indian Affairs to the Secretary of the Interior for the Year 1885* (Washington, DC: US Government Printing Office, 1885), 111–12 (emphasis added).
28. Helen Sekaquaptewa, *Me and Mine: The Life Story of Helen Sekaquaptewa* (Tucson: University of Arizona Press, 1969), 31–32.
29. Ibid.
30. Letter from S. M. McCowan to Sukulai Homar, January 22, 1900, in Lorraine M. Sherer, "Great Chieftains of the Mojave Indians," *Southern California Quarterly* 48, no. 1 (1966): 18 (emphasis added).
31. Tadeusz Lewandowski, *Red Bird, Red Power: The Life and Legacy of Zitkala-Ša* (Norman: University of Oklahoma Press, 2016), 19–20.
32. Zitkala-Ša, "The School Days of an Indian Girl," in *American Indian Stories* (Washington, DC: Hayworth, 1921), 54–56.
33. Letter from S. M. McCowan to Sukulai Homar, January 22, 1900 (emphasis added).
34. Patterson, *Slavery and Social Death*, 5–6.
35. Letter from S. M. McCowan to Sukulai Homar, January 22, 1900.
36. Margaret Connell Szasz, *Indian Education in the American Colonies, 1607–1783* (Lincoln: University of Nebraska Press, 2007), 5–6.
37. Adams, *Education for Extinction*, 47; more discussion of before and after photos, 275; for images, see 104–6, 252–55.
38. Lee D. Baker, *Anthropology and the Racial Politics of Culture* (Durham, NC: Duke University Press, 2010), 5, 41.
39. On "curricular standpoint" see Leilani Sabzalian, *Indigenous Children's Survivance in Public Schools* (New York: Routledge, 2019), 53.
40. Tina M. Campt, *Listening to Images* (Durham, NC: Duke University Press, 2017).

8: NATIVE STUDENT RESISTANCE AND THE ROOTS OF NATIVE AMERICAN LITERATURE

1. Joyce B. Phillips and Paul Gary Phillips, ed., *The Brainerd Journal: A Mission to the Cherokees, 1817–1823* (Lincoln: University of Nebraska Press, 1998), 285.
2. Ibid.
3. Ibid., 351.
4. Brenda J. Child, "The Boarding School as Metaphor," *Journal of American Indian Education* 57, no. 1 (2018): 53. See also the historic example recorded in Richard Henry Pratt, *Battlefield and Classroom: Four Decades with the American Indian, 1867–1904* (Norman: University of Oklahoma Press, 2003), 266.
5. Ruth Spack, *America's Second Tongue: American Indian Education and the Ownership of English, 1860–1900* (Lincoln: University of Nebraska Press, 2002), 11.
6. Ibid.
7. Frederick E. Hoxie, "Exploring a Cultural Borderland: Native American Journeys of Discovery in the Early Twentieth Century," *Journal of American History* 79, no. 3 (1992): 989.
8. Frederick E. Hoxie, *This Indian Country: American Indian Activists and the Place They Made* (New York: Penguin Press, 2012), 4.
9. John C. Calhoun, "No. 219-Treaty with the Choctaws, Communicated to the Senate, on the 27th January, 1825," in *American State Papers: Documents, Legislative and Executive, of the Congress of the United States . . . , by United States Congress* (Washington, DC: Gales & Seaton, 1834), 549–58.
10. Hoxie, *This Indian Country*, 50–51.

11. James L. McDonald, "No. 220-An Application of the Choctaw Tribe for Aid from the United States in Improving Their Condition, Communicated to the Senate, February 21, 1825," in *American State Papers*, 558–59.
12. McDonald cited in Hoxie, *This Indian Country*, 49–50.
13. Amelia V. Katanski, *Learning to Write "Indian": The Boarding School Experience and American Indian Literature* (Norman: University of Oklahoma Press, 2007), 7, 6.
14. Arnold Krupat, *From the Boarding Schools: Apache Indian Students Speak* (Lincoln: University of Nebraska Press, 2023); Arnold Krupat, *Boarding School Voices: Carlisle Indian School Students Speak* (Lincoln: University of Nebraska Press, 2021); Spack, *America's Second Tongue*; Paula Gunn Allen, *Voice of the Turtle: American Indian Literature, 1900–1970* (New York: Ballantine Books, 1994); Lawana Trout, *Native American Literature: An Anthology* (Lincolnwood, IL: McGraw-Hill, 1998); Katanski, *Learning to Write "Indian."*
15. Katanski, *Learning to Write "Indian,"* 18.
16. Gunn Allen, *Voice of the Turtle*, 12–13 (emphasis added).
17. Trout, *Native American Literature*, xix.
18. Ibid., xxi.
19. Ibid., xxii; Katanski, *Learning to Write "Indian."*
20. Allen, *Voice of the Turtle*, 12–13.
21. Francis La Flesche and David A. Baerreis, *The Middle Five: Indian Schoolboys of the Omaha Tribe* (Lincoln: University of Nebraska Press, 1978), 96–103.
22. Zitkala-Ša, "An Indian Teacher among Indians," in *American Indian Stories* (Washington, DC: Hayworth, 1921), 98.
23. La Flesche and Baerreis, *The Middle Five*, 96–103.
24. Ibid., 3, 128.
25. Spack, *America's Second Tongue*, 4.
26. Ibid., 14.
27. David Wallace Adams, *Education for Extinction: American Indians and the Boarding School Experience, 1875–1928* (Lawrence: University Press of Kansas, 1995), 224.
28. Ibid.
29. La Flesche and Baerreis, *The Middle Five*, 118.
30. See, for instance, *Annual Report of the Commissioner of Indian Affairs*, 1886, 195: "for the first offense, unless a serious one, a reprimand before the school is far better than a dozen whippings, because one can teach the whole schools that the offender has done something that is wrong, and they all know it and will remember it, while it is humiliating to the offender and answers better than whipping."
31. La Flesche and Baerreis, *The Middle Five*, 118, 111–12, 122.
32. Spack, *America's Second Tongue*, 13.
33. Lewandowski, *Red Bird, Red Power*, 63.
34. Ibid., 17–18.
35. Ibid., 55.
36. Zitkala-Ša, "The School Days of an Indian Girl," 54–56.
37. J. F. Kinney, "Reports of Agents in Dakota, Yankton Agency Dakota, August 24, 1885," in John DeWitt Clinton Atkins, *Annual Report of the Commissioner of Indian Affairs to the Secretary of the Interior for the Year 1885* (Washington, DC: US Government Printing Office, 1885), 58.
38. Zitkala-Ša, "The School Days of an Indian Girl," 75.
39. Zitkala-Ša, "An Indian Teacher among Indians," *American Indian Stories*, 81, 83, 85.
40. Ibid., 90.
41. Ibid., 98.
42. Lewandowski, *Red Bird, Red Power*, 33.
43. Ibid.

44. Gertrude Simmons, "Side by Side [Awarded Second Place at State Oratorical Contest]," *Earlhamite*, March 16, 1896, 178.
45. Ibid.
46. Zitkala-Ša, "The School Days of an Indian Girl," 79–80.
47. Zitkala-Ša, "An Indian Teacher among Indians," 95–96.
48. Ibid., 97–98.
49. Katanski, *Learning to Write "Indian,"* 98.
50. Ibid., 94.
51. Quoted in Lewandowski, *Red Bird, Red Power*, 46, 52 (emphasis added).

9: RACE, SLAVERY, AND EDUCATION AMONG THE FIVE "CIVILIZED" TRIBES

1. Angela Walton-Raji, Zoom interview by Anna Kate Cannon and Jarvis R. Givens, April 29, 2021.
2. Heather Andrea Williams, *Help Me to Find My People: The African American Search for Family Lost in Slavery* (Chapel Hill: University of North Carolina Press, 2012).
3. Angela Walton-Raji interview.
4. Ibid. The Carlisle Indian School Digital Resource Center maintains a collection of documents related to this case, which can be accessed at "Question Regarding Eligibility of Students with Black Heritage," September 25, 1912–December 13, 1912, Carlisle Indian School Digital Resource Center, https://Carlisleindian.dickinson.edu/documents/question-regarding-eligibility-students-black-heritage.
5. Herbert H. Smith Student Information Card, a member of the Shinnecock nation, who entered the school on September 4, 1892, and departed on September 8, 1892, National Archives and Records Administration, RG 75, Series 1329, box 14, https://Carlisleindian.dickinson.edu/student_files/herbert-h-smith-student-information-card.
6. Tiya Miles, "Preface: Eating Out of the Same Pot?," in Tiya Miles and Sharon Patricia Holland, eds., *Crossing Waters, Crossing Worlds: The African Diaspora in Indian Country* (Durham, NC: Duke University Press Books, 2006), xvii.
7. Tiya Miles, "The Lost Letter of Mary Ann Battis: A Troubling Case of Gender and Race in Creek Country," *NAIS* 1, no. 1 (2014): 88–98; Tiya Miles, *Ties That Bind: The Story of an Afro-Cherokee Family in Slavery and Freedom*, 2nd ed. (Oakland: University of California Press, 2015); Christina Snyder, *Great Crossings: Indians, Settlers, and Slaves in the Age of Jackson* (Oxford: Oxford University Press, 2017); Alaina E. Roberts, *I've Been Here All the While: Black Freedom on Native Land* (Philadelphia: University of Pennsylvania Press, 2021); Tiffany Lethabo King, *The Black Shoals: Offshore Formations of Black and Native Studies* (Durham, NC: Duke University Press, 2019); Miles and Holland, *Crossing Waters, Crossing Worlds*; Kyle T. Mays, *An Afro-Indigenous History of the United States* (Boston: Beacon Press, 2021); Christina Dickerson-Cousin, *Black Indians and Freedmen: The African Methodist Episcopal Church and Indigenous Americans, 1816–1916* (Urbana: University of Illinois Press, 2021).
8. Angela Walton-Raji to Anna Kate Cannon and Jarvis R. Givens, email correspondence, April 15, 2021.
9. The story of Philip and Elzora comes from three oral interviews conducted for the Pioneer Papers, a project of the Oklahoma Historical Society in collaboration with the Works Progress Administration: Elzora L. Lewis, interview by Jas. S. Buchanan, Works Progress Administration Indian-Pioneer History Project (June 29, 1937): 342–44; Philip A. Lewis, interviewed by Jas. S. Buchannan, Works Progress Administration Indian-Pioneer History Project for Oklahoma (May 4, 1937): 391–404; Philip A. Lewis, interviewed by Jas. S. Buchannan, Second Interview, Works Progress Administration Indian-Pioneer History Project for Oklahoma (June 29, 1937): 406–13. Hereafter,

these interviews will be referred to as "Elzora Lewis Interview," "Philip Lewis Interview Part 1," and "Philip Lewis Interview Part 2," respectively.

10. Elzora Lewis Interview; Philip Lewis Interview Part 1.
11. David Chang, *The Color of the Land* (Chapel Hill: University of North Carolina Press, 2010), 12; Rowan Faye Steineker, "The Struggle for Schools: Education, Race, and Sovereignty in the Creek Nation, 1820–1907," (PhD diss., University of Oklahoma, 2016), 128, 131.
12. Barbara Krauthamer, "In Their 'Native' Country: Freedpeople's Understandings of Culture and Citizenship in the Choctaw and Chickasaw Nations," in *Crossing Waters, Crossing Worlds*, ed. Tiya Miles and Sharon P. Holland (Durham, NC: Duke University Press, 2006), 100.
13. Philip Lewis Interview Part 1, 399–400.
14. Ibid.
15. Ibid.
16. *Niles Weekly Register* 27, no. 3 (1825): 224–25.
17. Christina Snyder, *Slavery in Indian Country: The Changing Face of Captivity in Early America* (Cambridge, MA: Harvard University Press, 2010), 5; Roberts, *I've Been Here All the While*, 23.
18. Snyder, *Slavery in Indian Country*, 6.
19. Ibid., 160.
20. Kendra Field, *Growing Up with the Country* (New Haven, CT: Yale University Press, 2018), 35.
21. Roberts, *I've Been Here All the While*, 27.
22. Snyder, *Slavery in Indian Country*, 201, 203.
23. Field, *Growing up with the Country*, 50.
24. Elzora Lewis Interview.
25. Jedidiah Morse, *A Report to the Secretary of War of the United States on Indian Affairs* (New Haven, CT: Converse, 1822), 310.
26. *Brainerd Journal*, 193, 67.
27. *Brainerd Journal*, 77; Snyder, *Slavery in Indian Country*, 199; *Brainerd Journal*, 93.
28. Joseph Tracey, "History of the Board of Commissioners for Foreign Missions," in *History of American Missions to the Heathen* (Worcester, MA: Spooner & Howland, 1840; reprint 1970), 149.
29. *Brainerd Journal*, 254, 276.
30. "Letter of the Choctaw Mission," in *The Missionary Herald, Containing the Proceedings of the American Board of Commissioners for Foreign Missions*, vol. 44 (Boston: T. R. Marvin, 1848), 355–56.
31. Snyder, *Slavery in Indian Country*, 205.
32. Ibid.; Tiya Miles, "The Lost Letter of Mary Ann Battis: A Troubling Case of Gender and Race in Creek Country," *Native American and Indigenous Studies* 1, no. 1 (Spring 2014): 88–98.
33. Lee Compere, "Letter from Lee Compere," *American Baptist Magazine* 7 (Boston: Lincoln & Edmunds, 1827), 87.
34. Adam Hodgson, *Remarks during a Journey through North America in the Years 1819, 1820, and 1821* (New York: Samuel Whiting, 1823), 287.
35. Quoted in Miles, "Lost Letter of Mary Ann Battis," 90.
36. Craig Steven Wilder, *Ebony and Ivy: Race, Slavery, and the Troubled History of America's Universities* (New York: Bloomsbury Press, 2013), 114.
37. Snyder, *Slavery in Indian Country*, 199. Details of the attack are quoted in Steineker, "The Struggle for Schools," 43, original citation: Lee Compere to Thomas McKenney, May 20, 1828, Letters Received by the Commissioner of Indian Affairs, Creek Agency, 1824–1876, microcopy, M234, roll 221, slide 703.

38. Steineker, "The Struggle for Schools," 45.
39. Ibid., 44.
40. Tiya Miles, "Preface: Eating Out of the Same Pot?," in Tiya Miles and Sharon Patricia Holland, eds., *Crossing Waters, Crossing Worlds: The African Diaspora in Indian Country* (Durham, NC: Duke University Press Books, 2006), xvii.
41. Susannah Compere, "Extract of a Letter from S. Compere, Withington Station, April 4, 1829," *American Baptist Magazine* 9 (1829), 247.
42. Opthleyehola's role in ordering the attack appears in Miles, "The Lost Letter of Mary Ann Battis," 95, and Zellar, *Africans and Creeks*, 45.
43. Elzora Lewis Interview; Philip Lewis Interview Part 1; Field, *Growing Up with the Country*, 35.
44. Diane Miller, "Wyandots, Shawnee, and African American Resistance to Slavery in Ohio and Kansas" (PhD diss., University of Nebraska–Lincoln, 2019), 90–92; Joseph Mitchell, *The Missionary Pioneer: A Brief Memoir of James Stewart* (New York: J. C. Tottes, 1827), 68; American State Papers (ASP), *Indian Affairs* 2, 459.

10: BLACK EDUCATION IN THE POST-REMOVAL CHAOS OF INDIAN TERRITORY

1. Barbara Krauthamer, "Slavery," *Encyclopedia of Oklahoma History and Culture,* Oklahoma Historical Society, https://www.okhistory.org/publications/enc/entry?entry=SL003.
2. Francis Paul Prucha, *The Great Father: The United States Government and the American Indians* (Lincoln: University of Nebraska Press, 1995), 236–37.
3. Philip Lewis Interview Part 1.
4. "The Articles of Agreement and Cession," April 24, 1802, in *American State Papers, Public Lands* (Washington, 1834), vol. 1, 125–26.
5. Tiya Miles, *Ties That Bind: The Story of an Afro-Creek Family in Slavery and Freedom* (Berkeley: University of California Press, 2005), 155; Roberts, *I've Been Here All the While*, 22, 24.
6. Snyder, *Slavery in Indian Country*, 210.
7. Roberts, *I've Been Here All the While*, 25.
8. Theda Perdue, *Slavery and the Evolution of Cherokee Society, 1540–1866* (Knoxville: University of Tennessee Press, 1979), 70.
9. "Indigenous Resistance Is Post-Apocalyptic, with Nick Estes," *Dissent Magazine* (blog), accessed May 8, 2024, https://www.dissentmagazine.org/online_articles/booked-indigenous-resistance-is-post-apocalyptic-with-nick-estes/.
10. Choctaw nation, *The Constitution and Laws of the Choctaw Nation* (Park Hill, Cherokee Nation: Mission Press, 1847), 20, 35–36.
11. Ibid., 61.
12. Cherokee nation, *The Constitution and Laws of the Cherokee Nation: Passed at Tahlequah, Cherokee Nation, 1839–51* (Tahlequah, Cherokee Nation, 1852), 55, 173, 71.
13. Quoted in Steineker, "The Struggle for Schools," 54.
14. This was the case at the Choctaw Academy in Kentucky. Julia Chin was the enslaved mistress of Richard Mentor Johnson, the white schoolmaster, who also relied on Julia to run the operations for this school. Christina Snyder, *Great Crossings: Indians, Settlers and Slaves in the Age of Jackson* (New York: Oxford University Press, 2017), 41–69.
15. T. Lindsay Baker and Julie P. Baker, eds., *The WPA Oklahoma Slave Narratives* (Norman: University of Oklahoma Press, 1996).
16. On "culture of dissemblance," see Darlene Clark Hine, "Rape and the Inner Lives of Black Women in the Middle West," *Signs* 14, no. 4 (1989): 912–20.
17. Baker and Baker, *The WPA Oklahoma Slave Narratives*, 497; Albert J. Raboteau, *Slave*

Religion: The "Invisible Institution" in the Antebellum South (Oxford: Oxford University Press, 2004).

18. Raboteau, *Slave Religion*; Janet D. Cornelius, *"When I Can Read My Title Clear": Literacy, Slavery and Religion in the Antebellum South* (Columbia: University of South Carolina Press, 1992).
19. Alaina Roberts, *I've Been Here All the While*, 23, quote on 21.
20. Christina Snyder, *Slavery in Indian Country: The Changing Face of Captivity in Early America* (Cambridge, MA: Harvard University Press, 2012), 210.
21. *Annual Report of the Commissioner of Indian Affairs–1842/1843* (Washington, DC: Office of Indian Affairs, 1843), 165–66 (emphasis added).
22. Claudio Saunt, *A New Order of Things: Property, Power and the Transformation of the Creek Indians, 1733–1816* (Cambridge: Cambridge University Press, 1999), 188, 189.
23. Angie Debo, *The Road to Disappearance* (Norman: University of Oklahoma Press, 1941), 120; Saunt, *A New Order of Things*, 188, 189; Philip Lewis Interview Part 1.
24. Virginia E. Lauderdale, "Tullahassee Mission," *Chronicles of Oklahoma* 26, no. 3 (1948): 287; "Treaty with the Creeks and Seminoles, 1845," in *Indian Affairs: Laws and Treaties*, vol. 2, ed. Charles Kappler (Washington, DC: US Government Printing Office, 1904), 550.
25. Rowan Faye Steineker, "'Fully Equal to That of Any Children': Experimental Creek Education in the Antebellum Era," *History of Education Quarterly* 56, no. 2 (May 2016): 294; Zellar, *African Creeks*, 25.
26. Debo, *The Road to Disappearance*, 120, 121.
27. Lilah Denton Lindsey, interviewed by Effie S. Jackson, Works Progress Administration Indian-Pioneer History Project, March 15–16, 1938, 195–96.
28. Lindsey WPA interview, 192, 194, 195–96.
29. Zellar, *African Creeks*, 46; Steineker, "Fully Equal," 294; Lauderdale, "Tullahassee Mission," 287.
30. Typescript copy of congregational missionary Cyrus Kingsbury's 1869 autobiography (original in Sue L. McBeth papers at the Oklahoma Historical Society), copied March 1957, Papers of Frances Hope Kerr Holway, 1871–1962, A-59, 5, Box 1, Schlesinger Library, Radcliffe Institute, 4.
31. Charles King Whipple, *Slavery and the American Board of Commissioners for Foreign Missions* (New York: American Anti-Slavery Society, 1859), 2–3; "Letter of the Cherokee Mission" in *The Missionary Herald, Containing the Proceedings of the American Board of Commissioners for Foreign Missions*, vol. 44 (Boston: T. R. Marvin, 1848), 352–55; "Letter of the Choctaw Mission," in *The Missionary Herald*, vol. 44., 355–58.
32. William G. McLaughlin, "Indian Slaveholders and Presbyterian Missionaries, 1837–1861," *Church History* 42, no. 4 (December 1873): 535.
33. Jerry L. Faught II, "John Davis and Joseph Islands: Indigenous Missionaries among the Creeks in Indian Territory," *Baptist History and Heritage* 43, no. 2 (2008): 33–34.
34. Davis is quoted in E. C. Routh, *The Story of Oklahoma Baptists* (Baptist General Convention, 1932), 27; Faught, "John Davis," 36.
35. Quoted in Faught, "John Davis," 36; Faught, "John Davis," 27.
36. E. C. Routh, *The Story of Oklahoma Baptists* (Baptist General Convention, 1932), 27; Philip Lewis Interview Part 1.
37. Barbara Krauthamer, "Blacks on the Borders: African-Americans' Transition from Slavery to Freedom in Texas and the Indian Territory, 1836–1907" (PhD diss., Princeton University, 2000), 185.
38. Quoted in Daniel Littlefield, *Africans and Creeks: From the Colonial Period to the Civil War* (Westport, CT: Greenwood Press, 1979), 141.
39. Henry Bibb, *The Life and Adventures of Henry Bibb, An American Slave* (Madison: University of Wisconsin Press, 2001), 152–59. For more on connection between

black people in the US and among the Five Tribes, see Saunt, *A New Order of Things*, 122–23.

40. Littlefield, *Africans and Creeks*, 141–42.
41. Baker and Baker, *The WPA Oklahoma Slave Narratives*, 421.
42. Miles, *Ties That Bind*, 169–71, 170; Celia Naylor-Ojurongbe, "'More at Home with the Indians': African-American Slaves and Freedpeople in the Cherokee Nation, Indian Territory, 1838–1907" (PhD diss., Duke University, 2001), 81.
43. Miles, *Ties That Bind*, 171, 172.
44. Ibid., 170; Baker and Baker, *The WPA Oklahoma Slave Narratives*, 314.
45. Naylor-Ojurongbe, "More at Home with the Indians," 87.
46. John Ross, "Killed," *Cherokee Advocate*, December 17, 1846.
47. Ibid.
48. Ibid.
49. Ibid.

11: A CREEK SCHOOL BECOMES BARRACKS FOR THE CONFEDERATE ARMY

1. Virginia E. Lauderdale, "Tullahassee Mission," *Chronicles of Oklahoma* 26, no. 3 (1948): 292.
2. Rowan Faye Steineker, "'Fully Equal to That of Any Children': Experimental Creek Education in the Antebellum Era," *History of Education Quarterly* 56, no. 2 (May 2016): 283.
3. Lauderdale, "Tullahassee Mission," 292.
4. Gary Zellar, *African Creeks: Estevelte and the Creek Nation* (Norman: University of Oklahoma Press, 2007), 46.
5. Ibid., 42–43.
6. United States War Department, *The War of Rebellion: A Compilation of Official Records of the Union and Confederate Armies* (Washington, DC: US Government Printing Office, 1880–1900), Series 1, vol. 3, 585–86.
7. Angie Debo, *The Road to Disappearance* (Norman: University of Oklahoma Press, 1941), 144 (emphasis added).
8. Ibid. For discussion of the internal debates in the Cherokee nation, see Bryan Pollard, "How the U.S. Civil War Divided Indian Nations," History.com, November 23, 2020; Charles Minges, *Slavery in the Cherokee Nation: The Keetowah Society and the Defining of a People, 1855–1867* (New York: Routledge, 2003).
9. Congress of the Confederate States of America, "Treaty with the Creek Nation, July 10, 1861"; Zellar, *African Creeks*, 43.
10. Debo, *The Road to Disappearance*, 144. Congress of the Confederate States of America, "Treaty with the Creek Nation, July 10, 1861."
11. Lauderdale, "Tullahassee Mission," 292; Ely S. Parker, *Report of the Commissioner of Indian Affairs made to the Secretary of the Interior for the Year 1868/69* (Washington, DC: US Government Printing Office, 1870), 451.
12. Parker, *Report of the Commissioner of Indian Affairs*, 451; Dennis B. Miles, "'Educate or We Perish': Armstrong Academy's History as Part of the Choctaw Educational System," *Chronicles of Oklahoma* 89 (Fall 2011); Zellar, *Africans and Creeks*, 75.
13. Francis Paul Prucha, *The Great Father* (Lincoln: University of Nebraska Press, 1995), 419–23.
14. James Franklin Tindle, "'Peace and Perpetual Friendship': The Cherokee-Confederate Coalition in the American Civil War" (PhD diss., Kansas State University, 2019), 110–14.
15. Ibid., 96, 98.
16. Zellar, *African Creeks*, 43.

17. Ibid., 69.
18. Tindle, "'Peace and Perpetual Friendship,'" 96; Zellar, *African Creeks*, 48–52.
19. Zellar, 46, 47.
20. Ibid., 60.
21. Jarvis R. Givens, "Black Education as the General Strike: The Radical Origins of African American Teaching and Learning," *Journal of African American History* 109, no. 2 (March 2024): 231–59.
22. Zellar, *African Creeks*, 60.
23. Ibid., 53.
24. Zellar, "First Indian Home Guard," *Chronicles of Oklahoma* 76, no. 1 (Spring 1998): 65.
25. Zellar, *African Creeks*, 74.
26. "Ratified Treaty 353: Seminole—Washington, D.C., March 21, 1866," Indian Treaties, National Archives; L. C. Perryman, ed., *Constitution and Laws of the Muskogee Nation* (Muskogee, Indian Territory: Phoenix, 1890), 224; Zellar, 92.
27. "Ratified Treaty 358: Cherokee—Washington, D.C., July 19, 1866" (Indian Treaties, National Archives).
28. Baker and Baker, *The WPA Oklahoma Slave Narratives*, 176.
29. Barbara Krauthamer, "In Their 'Native' Country: Freedpeople's Understandings of Culture and Citizenship in the Choctaw and Chickasaw Nations," in *Crossing Waters, Crossing Worlds*, ed. Tiya Miles and Sharon P. Holland (Durham, NC: Duke University Press, 2006), 107.
30. Krauthamer, "In their 'Native' Country," 115, 116.
31. Hiram Price, "Report of the Commissioner," in *Annual Report of the Commissioner of Indian Affairs, for the Year 1883* (Washington, DC: US Government Printing Office, 1883), lii–liii.
32. Roberts, *I've Been Here All the While*, 7–8.
33. Zellar, *African Creeks*, 74.
34. Parker, *Annual Report of 1868*, 451.
35. Ely S. Parker, *Annual Report of 1868*, 451; Steineker, "The Struggle for Schools," 118; Parker, *Annual Report of 1868*, 415–16; Jacqueline Fear-Segal, *White Man's Club: Schools, Race, and the Struggle of Indian Acculturation* (Lincoln: University of Nebraska Press, 2007): 143.
36. Parker, *Annual Report of 1868*, 415–16.

12: EDUCATION AND FREEDMEN FUTURITY AMONG THE FIVE TRIBES

1. Alaina E. Roberts, *I've Been Here All the While: Black Freedom on Native Land* (Philadelphia: University of Pennsylvania Press, 2021), 9–11.
2. Philip Lewis Interview Part 1; Tera W. Hunter, *Bound in Wedlock: Slave and Free Black Marriage in the Nineteenth Century* (Cambridge, MA: Belknap Press, 2017).
3. Historian Eric Foner writes of the US political consensus around some version of allotment in the years immediately following the Civil War. See *Reconstruction: America's Unfinished Revolution* (New York: Harper & Row, 1988), 462.
4. Brian Klopotek, "Of Shadows and Doubts: Race, Indignity, and White Supremacy" in *inDivisible: African-Native Lives in the Americas*, ed. Gabrielle Tayac (Washington, DC: Smithsonian National Museum of the American Indian, 2009), 86.
5. US Congress, 1870, *Memorial of a Committee on Behalf of the Colored People of the Choctaw and Chickasaw Tribes of Indians* (41st Cong., 2nd sess., S. Misc. Doc. 106.), 5.
6. United States, *Five Civilized Tribes in Oklahoma: Reports of the Department of the Interior and Evidentiary Papers in Support of S. 7625, a Bill for the Relief of Certain Members*

of the Five Civilized Tribes in Oklahoma (Washington, DC: US Government Printing Office, 1913), 318.

7. US Congress, *Memorial of a Committee on Behalf of the Colored People*, 5.
8. P. Gabrielle Foreman, "Black Organizing, Print Advocacy, and Collective Authorship," in *The Colored Conventions Movement* (Chapel Hill: University of North Carolina Press, 2021), 30, 31.
9. US Congress, *Memorial of a Committee on Behalf of the Colored People*, 5.
10. A. B. Greenwood, *Annual Report of the Commissioner of Indian Affairs, 1859/1860* (Washington, DC: Office of Indian Affairs, 1860), 141 (emphasis added).
11. Dennis B. Miles, "'Educate or We Perish': Armstrong Academy's History as Part of the Choctaw Educational System," *Chronicles of Oklahoma* 89 (Fall 2011): 319–20; US Congress, *Memorial of a Committee on Behalf of the Colored People*, 4.
12. Philip Lewis Interview Part 1; Elzora Lewis Interview.
13. Philip Lewis Interview Part 1, 6.
14. Jerry L. Faught II, "John Davis and Joseph Islands: Indigenous Missionaries among the Creeks in Indian Territory," *Baptist History and Heritage* 43, no. 2 (2008): 38; J. M. Gaskin, "Fountain Baptist Church," *Oklahoma Baptist Chronicle* 4, no. 1 (1961): 20; Philip Lewis Interview Part 1, 6.
15. Alaina Roberts, *I've Been Here All the While*, 62.
16. Ibid., 47.
17. Ibid., 60–61.
18. Zellar, *African Creeks*, 110.
19. Ibid., 115–16.
20. Zellar, *African Creeks*, 120; L. A. Scruggs, *Women of Distinction* (Raleigh, NC: L. A. Scruggs, 1893), 248; Elzora Lewis Interview, 3.
21. Zellar, *African Creeks*, 121.
22. *Muskogee Phoenix*, June 18, 1891; Zellar, *African Creeks*, 188.
23. Lauderdale, "Tullahassee Mission," 297.
24. Hiram Price, *Annual Report of the Commissioner of Indian Affairs to the Secretary of the Interior—1881/82* (Washington, DC: US Government Printing Office, 1882), 104.
25. L. C. Perryman, ed., *Constitution and Laws of the Muskogee Nation* (Muskogee, Indian Territory: Phoenix, March 1, 1890), 55, sec. 10.
26. Zellar, *African Creeks*, 135.
27. Ibid.
28. Ibid.
29. "Presbyterian Missions," Works Progress Administration Indian-Pioneer History Project, April 17, 1937, 365; "The Educational Work of the American Baptist Home Mission Society," 42.
30. Debo, *The Road to Disappearance*, 249.
31. Steineker, "The Struggle for Schools," 90.
32. "Educational Work," 42.
33. Debo, *The Road to Disappearance*, 250.
34. Zellar, *African Creeks*, 177.
35. Ibid., 179.
36. Ibid., 180; E. H. Rishell, interviewed by Amelia Harris, Works Progress Administration Indian-Pioneer History Project for Oklahoma (June 1937).
37. Zellar, *African Creeks*, 188.
38. Bob Burke, "Robertson, Alice Mary," *The Encyclopedia of Oklahoma History and Culture*, https://www.okhistory.org/publications/enc/entry.php?entry=RO004.
39. William Arthur Jones, *Annual Reports of the Department of the Interior for the Fiscal Year 1900/1* (Washington, DC: US Government Printing Office, 1902), 317.

40. Williams Jones, *Annual Reports of the Department of the Interior for the Fiscal Year 1901/2* (Washington, DC: US Government Printing Office, 1901), 127.
41. http://african-nativeamerican.blogspot.com/2010/05/remembering-tullahassee-manual-school.html?m=1.
42. Ida B. Wells, *Crusade for Justice: The Autobiography of Ida B. Wells* (Chicago: University of Chicago Press, 1970), 51.
43. Evelyn Richardson Strong, "Historical Development of the Oklahoma Association of Negro Teachers: A Study of Social Change, 1893–1958" (PhD diss., University of Oklahoma, 1961), 45–49; *Muskogee Phoenix*, September 1, 1898.
44. Strong, "Historical Development of the Oklahoma Association of Negro Teachers," 48.
45. Zellar, *African Creeks*, 190.
46. Ibid., 198–99.
47. Ibid., 202.
48. Alaina Roberts, *I've Been Here All the While*, 43, 63–64.
49. Kendra Field, *Growing Up with the Country* (New Haven, CT: Yale University Press, 2018), 38.
50. Acting Commissioner to Cato Sells, January 10, 1913, in ProQuest Indian Claims Insight; Gabe Parker to Cato Sells, November 17, 1916, in ProQuest Indian Claims Insight; Henry M. Tidwell and G. W. Grayson to Dana H. Kelsey, September 17, 1914, in ProQuest Indian Claims Insight; Creek Freedman Council, through Gabe E. Parker, to Franklin Knight Lane, January 9, 1915, in ProQuest Indian Claims Insight; Gabe Parker to Cato Sells, November 17, 1916, in ProQuest Indian Claims Insight.
51. Field, *Growing Up with the Country*, 40–48.
52. Ibid., 40.
53. Phrase used by Richard Wilcox, interviewed in the film *Black Indians: An American Story* (Rich-Heape Films, 2000).

13: BOOKER T. WASHINGTON: A MONUMENTAL AMERICAN LIFE

1. Booker T. Washington, "Boley, A Negro Town in the West," *The Outlook*, January 4, 1908, 28–31.
2. Field, *Growing Up with the Country*.
3. W. H. Twine, "Booker T. Washington Royally Received in Muskogee," *Muskogee Cimeter*, November 23, 1905.
4. Twine, "Booker T. Washington Royally Received in Muskogee."
5. William Watkins, *The White Architects of Black Education: Ideology and Power in America, 1865–1954* (New York: Teachers College Press, 2001).
6. Kelly Miller, "Radicals and Conservatives," in *Race Adjustment: Essays on the Negro in America* (New York: Neale, 1909), 23 (emphasis added).
7. Ida B. Wells-Barnett, "Booker T. Washington and His Critics," in *The Negro Problem from the Negro Point of View*, 519.
8. Ibid., 520.
9. Tomiko Brown-Nagin et al., "Harvard and the Legacy of Slavery," President and Fellows of Harvard College, 2022; Deborah King and Peter Carini, "Dartmouth and Slavery Project," Dartmouth College, 2023.
10. W. E. B. Du Bois, *The Souls of Black Folk* (Chicago: McClurg, 1903).
11. W. E. B. Du Bois, "The Late Booker T. Washington," *The Crisis* 11 (December 1915): 82.
12. Quoted in August Meier, *Negro Thought in America, 1880–1915: Racial Ideologies in the Age of Booker T. Washington* (Ann Arbor: University of Michigan Press, 1988), 107.
13. Booker T. Washington, *Up from Slavery* (New York: Doubleday, 1901), 221–22.
14. On "interest convergence," see Derrick Bell, *Silent Covenants: Brown v. Board of Edu-*

cation and the Unfulfilled Hopes for Racial Reform (New York: Oxford University Press, 2005).

15. Robert J. Norrell, *Up from History: The Life of Booker T. Washington* (Cambridge, MA: Belknap Press, 2011), 5.
16. Thomas Dixon Jr., "Booker T. Washington and the Negro," *Saturday Evening Post*, August 19, 1905, 1–2.
17. John Hope Franklin, *From Slavery to Freedom: A History of American Negroes* (New York: Vintage Books, 1969), 397; Meier, *Negro Thought in America*.
18. Meier, *Negro Thought in America*, 112.
19. Dixon, "Booker T. Washington and the Negro," 1–2.
20. Norrell, *Up from History*, 4.
21. Ralph Ellison, *Invisible Man* (New York: Random House, 1952), 35–36.
22. Ellen Daugherty, "Negotiating the Veil: Tuskegee's Booker T. Washington Monument," *American Art* 24, no. 3 (2010): 52–77.
23. Washington, *Boley, A Negro Town in the West*, 2.

14: SLAVERY AND SETTLER COLONIALISM IN THE EDUCATIONAL WORLD OF BOOKER T. WASHINGTON, 1856–1872

1. David Wallace Adams, *Education for Extinction: American Indians and the Boarding School Experience, 1875–1928* (Lawrence: University Press of Kansas, 1995).
2. W. Stitt Robinson, "Indian Education and Missions in Colonial Virginia," *Journal of Southern History* 18, no. 2 (1952): 153.
3. Ibid., 162.
4. Washington, *Up from Slavery*, 2, 229.
5. Norrell, *Up from History*, 19.
6. United States Department, Interior National Park Service, *The Hales Ford Community: 1856–1865*, by Barry Mackintosh, Booker T. Washington National Monument, 1968, 2, 4.
7. Ibid., 12.
8. Donald Yacovone, *Teaching White Supremacy: America's Democratic Ordeal and the Forging of Our National Identity* (New York: Pantheon Books, 2022), 84.
9. Ibid., 84.
10. Ibid., xiii.
11. Ibid., 92.
12. Samuel G. Goodrich, *A Pictorial History of the United States: With Notices of Other Portions of America, North and South* (Philadelphia: E. H. Butler, 1866), 180.
13. Ibid.
14. Sarah Lewis, *The Unseen Truth: When Race Changed Sight in America* (Cambridge, MA: Harvard University Press, 2024), 3.
15. Ibid., 138.
16. Yacovone, *Teaching White Supremacy*, 89.
17. Samuel G. Goodrich, *The First Book of History, for Children and Youth* (Philadelphia: Key, Meilke, & Biddle, 1832), 81.
18. Yacovone, *Teaching White Supremacy*, 93.
19. Mindy Spearman, "Race in Elementary Geography Textbooks: Examples from South Carolina, 1890–1927," in *Histories of Social Studies and Race* (New York: Palgrave Macmillan, 2012), 72.
20. Paula T. Connolly, *Slavery in American Children's Literature, 1790–2010* (Iowa City: University of Iowa Press, 2013), 55; Donnarae MacCann, *White Supremacy in Children's Literature* (New York: Routledge, 2001), 12.

21. Susan Scheckel, *The Insistence of the Indian: Race and Nationalism in Nineteenth-Century American Culture* (Princeton, NJ: Princeton University Press, 1998), 19; Gina Ocasion, *Imagining Futures: Margaret Fuller and Nathaniel Hawthorne on Women, Children and History* (Oxford: Oxbow Books, 2018), 57–58.
22. Caitlin Rosenthal, *Accounting for Slavery: Masters and Management* (Cambridge, MA: Harvard University Press, 2019).
23. Rev. Samuel Lander, *Our Own School Arithmetic* (Greensboro, NC: Sterling, Campbell & Albright, 1863), 135, 136, 140, 157, 171.
24. Washington, *Up from Slavery*, 30.
25. Louis Harlan, "Booker T. Washington in Biographical Perspective" in *Booker T. Washington in Perspective: Essays of Louis R. Harlan*, ed. Raymond Smock (Jackson: University Press of Mississippi, 2012), 31.
26. Washington, *Up from Slavery*, 31.
27. Ibid.
28. Katherine McKittrick, "Plantation Futures," *Small Axe* 17, no. 3 (2013): 3.
29. Jonathan D. Martin, *Divided Mastery: Slave Hiring in the American South* (Cambridge, MA: Harvard University Press, 2004), 18–19.
30. Harlan, "Booker T. Washington in Biographical Perspective," 28.
31. Ibid., 27.
32. Washington, *Up from Slavery*, 43.
33. Harlan, "Booker T. Washington in Biographical Perspective," 26–27.
34. Ibid., 42.

15: "BLACK RACE AND RED RACE" AT HAMPTON INSTITUTE, 1872–1881

1. James Anderson, *The Education of Blacks in the South, 1860–1935* (Chapel Hill: University of North Carolina Press, 1988), 34.
2. Ibid.
3. Ibid., 45.
4. Bayley Marquez, *Plantation Pedagogy: The Violence of Schooling across Black and Indigenous Space* (Berkeley: University of California Press, 2024), 87.
5. Ibid., 82; Jacqueline Fear-Segal, *White Man's Club Schools, Race, and the Struggle of Indian Acculturation* (Lincoln: University of Nebraska Press, 2007), 108.
6. Washington, *Up from Slavery*, 96–97.
7. Richard Henry Pratt, *Battlefield and Classroom: Four Decades with the American Indian, 1867–1904* (Norman: University of Oklahoma Press, 2004), 214 (emphasis added).
8. Aileen Moreton-Robinson, *The White Possessive: Property, Power, and Indigenous Sovereignty* (Minneapolis: University of Minnesota Press, 2015).
9. Marquez, *Plantation Pedagogy*, 29.
10. "History of Hampton and America's Story," Hampton.gov, Civic Plus, accessed 2024, https://hampton.gov/91/History-of-City.
11. Presidential Committee on the Legacy of Slavery, *The Legacy of Slavery at Harvard: Report and Recommendations of the Presidential Committee* (Cambridge, MA: Harvard University Press, 2022).
12. Helen Jones Campbell, "The Syms and Eaton Schools and Their Successor," *William and Mary College Quarterly* 20, no. 1 (1940): 23–24 (emphasis added).
13. Ibid., 40.
14. Ibid., 6.
15. Ibid., 14.
16. Amy Taylor, *Embattled Freedom: Journeys through the Civil War's Slave Refugee Camps* (Chapel Hill: University of North Carolina Press, 2018), 3.

17. Ibid., 5.
18. Paul Laurence Dunbar, "The Colored Soldiers," in *Majors and Minors* (Toledo, OH: Hadley & Hadley, 1895).
19. W. E. B. Du Bois, *Black Reconstruction in America 1860–1880* (New York: Free Press, 1935); Jarvis R. Givens, "Black Education as the General Strike: The Radical Origins of African American Teaching and Learning," *Journal of African American History* 109, no. 2 (March 2024): 231–59.
20. Heather Williams, *Self-Taught: African American Education in Slavery and Freedom* (Chapel Hill: University of North Carolina Press, 2007), 18.
21. Ibid., 38.
22. David Adams, *Education for Extinction: American Indians and the Boarding School Experience, 1875–1928* (Lawrence: University Press of Kansas, 2020), 174–75.
23. Henry Louis Gates Jr., *Stony the Road: Reconstruction, White Supremacy, and the Rise of Jim Crow* (New York: Penguin Press, 2019), xv.
24. Kim Cary Warren, *The Quest for Citizenship: African American and Native American Education in Kansas, 1880–1935* (Chapel Hill: University of North Carolina Press, 2010), 7.
25. Francis Paul Prucha, *The Great Father: The United States Government and the American Indians*, abridged ed. (Lincoln: University of Nebraska Press, 1986), 165.
26. Ibid.
27. Warren, *The Quest for Citizenship*, 7.
28. M. F. Armstrong and Helen Ludlow, *Hampton and Its Students, by Two of Its Teachers* (1874), 63, 127, 125, 35.
29. "Anniversary Exercises at Hampton Institute," *Southern Workman* 8, no. 6 (June 1, 1879): 71.
30. Adams, *Education for Extinction*, 20.
31. Ibid., 30.
32. "Anniversary Exercises at Hampton Institute."
33. Ibid.
34. Ibid.
35. Washington, *Up from Slavery*, 97.
36. Fear-Segal, *White Man's Club Schools*, 107.
37. Washington, *Up from Slavery*, 97.
38. Ibid., 98.
39. Ibid., 99.
40. Ibid., 102.

16: A SIOUX STUDENT, A BLACK PRINCIPAL, AND THE US PRESIDENT

1. David Wallace Adams, "Education in Hues: Red and Black at Hampton Institute, 1878–1893," *South Atlantic Quarterly* 76 (1977): 159–76.
2. James A. Garfield Papers: Series 1, Diaries; vols. 1–12, 1848–1881, November 9, 1849, Manuscript/Mixed Material, Library of Congress (hereafter "Garfield Diaries"), June 5, 1881.
3. "A Visit from the President," *Southern Workman* 10, no. 7 (July 1, 1881): 74.
4. Ibid.; Robert Francis Engs, *Educating the Disfranchised and Disinherited: Samuel Chapman Armstrong and Hampton Institute, 1839–1893* (Knoxville: University of Tennessee Press, 1999), xii.
5. Garfield Diaries, June 5, 1881.
6. Though two black Union soldiers are buried in the cemetery, it is overwhelmingly white Union and Confederate soldiers buried there, according to reports by the

National Park Service. "Hampton National Cemetery," National Register of Historic Places registration form (Washington, DC: US Department of the Interior, National Parks Service, January 6, 1996).

7. "A Visit from the President," 74 (emphasis added).
8. Toni Morrison, "Toni Morrison Address to the Second Chicago Humanities Festival," 1991, https://www.youtube.com/watch?v=KxqQhkMKlC0.
9. Samuel Armstrong, "Indian Education in the East," *Southern Workman* 9, no. 6 (November 1, 1880): 114 (emphasis added).
10. Bayley J. Marquez, "The Black Model Minority: Slavery, Settlement, and the Genealogy of the Model Minority," *Du Bois Review* 19, no. 1 (March 2022): 129–45.
11. Sven Beckert and Seth Rockman, eds., *Slavery's Capitalism: A New History of American Economic Development*, Early American Studies (Philadelphia: University of Pennsylvania Press, 2016); Walter Johnson, *River of Dark Dreams: Slavery and Empire in the Cotton Kingdom* (Cambridge, MA: Belknap Press, 2017).
12. Saidiya Hartman, *Scenes of Subjection: Terror, Slavery, and Self-Making in Nineteenth-Century America* (New York: Norton, 2022), 225.
13. This distinction between "value" and "worth" extends from Charisse Burden-Stelly, "Modern U.S. Racial Capitalism: Some Theoretical Insights," *Monthly Review*, July 1, 2020, https://monthlyreview.org/2020/07/01/modern-u-s-racial-capitalism/.
14. Roger L. Ransom and Richard Sutch, *One Kind of Freedom: The Economic Consequences of Emancipation* (Cambridge: Cambridge University Press, 2001), 44–46.
15. Sarah Fond, *The Character of Capitalism*, forthcoming.
16. "Meet the Children of President and Mrs. Garfield (U.S. National Park Service)," accessed October 3, 2024, https://www.nps.gov/jaga/meet-the-children-of-president-and-mrs-garfield.htm.
17. Burke Aaron Hinsdale, *President Garfield and Education: Hiram College Memorial* (Boston: Osgood, 1882); C. W. Goodyear, *President Garfield: From Radical to Unifier* (New York: Simon & Schuster, 2023); "Education Congressman, Education President (Part I) (U.S. National Park Service)," accessed September 16, 2024, https://www.nps.gov/articles/000/education-congressman-education-president-part-i.htm.
18. Donald Yacovone, *Teaching White Supremacy: America's Democratic Ordeal and the Forging of Our National Identity* (New York: Pantheon, 2022).
19. Garfield Diaries, https://www.loc.gov/item/mss219560001/; Jerry Bryant Rushford, "Political Disciple: The Relationship Between James A. Garfield and the Disciples of Christ," University of California, Santa Barbara, 1977, 27, 30.
20. Garfield Diaries, August 31, 1849, entry states: "Studying attended Lyceum evenng / Question Are the negroes naturaly inferior to the whites. voted in the aff. I J Fitzgerald enraged and left society."
21. Goodyear, *President Garfield*, 38, 42.
22. Horatio Alger, *From Canal Boy to President: The Boyhood and Manhood of James A. Garfield* (New York: John R. Anderson, 1881), 87, 89.
23. Goodyear, *President Garfield*, 48.
24. "Hon. James A. Garfield," *Helena Weekly Herald*, August 22, 1872, https://www.loc.gov/item/sn84036143/1872-08-22/ed-1/.
25. Department of the Interior, Office of Indian Affairs, letter from the Secretary of the Interior, transmitting draught of a bill for the sale, etc., of lands of the Flathead Indians in Montana, August 22, 1890, 33.
26. Nora Mabie, "Missoula Se Lis Trail of Tears in Bridge Dedication," *TCA Regional News*, October 10, 2022; Alyssa Kelly, "Pieces of History Come Home," *Char-Koosta News*, November 29, 2018; Marie Torosian, "Chief Charlo, SLMXE Q OXQEYS (Small Grizzly Bear Claws)," *Char-Koosta News*, February 11, 1994.
27. Leading up to the Civil War, Garfield generally played the middle on matters per-

taining to slavery. One paper, the *Anti-Slavery Bugle*, summarized his position on the subject of the Fugitive Slave Law as follows in 1859: "He believes the Fugitive Slave Law of 1850 unconstitutional but holds that the master has a constitutional right to reclaim his slaves." "Communications," *Anti-Slavery Bugle*, October 15, 1859.

28. Goodyear, *President Garfield*, 71, 206.

CONCLUSION

1. Gloria Ladson-Billings, "From the Achievement Gap to the Education Debt: Understanding Achievement in U.S. Schools," *Educational Researcher* 35, no. 7 (October 1, 2006): 3–12; Bryan McKinley Jones Brayboy and K. Tsianina Lomawaima, "Why Don't More Indians Do Better in School? The Battle between U.S. Schooling & American Indian/Alaska Native Education," *Daedalus* 147, no. 2 (March 1, 2018): 82–94; Michael J. Dumas, "'Losing an Arm': Schooling as a Site of Black Suffering," *Race Ethnicity and Education* 17, no. 1 (January 1, 2014): 1–29; K. Tsianina Lomawaima and Tėresa L. McCarty, "'To Remain an Indian': Lessons in Democracy from a Century of Native American Education (New York: Teachers College Press, 2006).
2. Clif Stratton, *Education for Empire: American Schools, Race, and the Paths of Good Citizenship* (Oakland: University of California Press, 2016), 2; Sarah Steinbock-Pratt, *Educating the Empire: American Teachers and Contested Colonization in the Philippines* (Cambridge: Cambridge University Press, 2019), Atkinson quote cited on 17.
3. Fortune quoted in Roland Sintos Coloma, "'Destiny Has Thrown the Negro and the Filipino Under the Tutelage of America': Race and Curriculum in the Age of Empire," *Curriculum Inquiry* 39, no. 4 (2009): 504; Bayley J. Marquez, *Plantation Pedagogy: The Violence of Schooling across Black and Indigenous Space* (Berkeley: University of California Press, 2024).
4. Phelps-Stokes Fund African Education Commission (1920–21) and Thomas Jesse Jones, *Education in Africa: A Study of West, South, and Equatorial Africa by the African Education Commission, Under the Auspices of the Phelps-Stokes Fund and Foreign Mission Societies of North America and Europe* (Phelps-Stokes Fund, 1922), 13.
5. Andrew Zimmerman, *Alabama in Africa: Booker T. Washington, the German Empire, and the Globalization of the New South* (Princeton, NJ: Princeton University Press, 2010).
6. William H. Watkins, "Pan-Africanism and the Politics of Education: Toward a New Understanding," in *Imagining Home: Class, Culture, and Nationalism in the African Diaspora*, ed. Sidney Lemelle and Robin D. G. Kelley (New York and London: Verso, 1994), 222–42; Mahasan Offutt-Chaney, "'Black Crisis' and the 'Likely' Privatization of Public Education in New Orleans and Liberia," *Critical Studies in Education* 63, no. 2 (March 15, 2022): 180–95; Jarvis R. Givens, "'A Grammar for Black Education beyond Borders': Exploring Technologies of Schooling in the African Diaspora," *Race, Ethnicity and Education* 19, no. 6 (2016): 1288–1302.
7. Jones, *Education in Africa*, 13.
8. Ibid., 13–14.
9. Ibid., 15.
10. Claudia Goldin and Lawrence F. Katz, "The 'Virtues' of the Past: Education in the First Hundred Years of the New Republic," NBER Working Paper Series, 2003, 9958, https://doi.org/10.3386/w9958; Derek W. Black, *Schoolhouse Burning: Public Education and the Assault on American Democracy* (New York: PublicAffairs, 2020); David B. Tyack, Thomas James, and Aaron Benavot, *Law and the Shaping of Public Education, 1785–1954* (Madison: University of Wisconsin Press, 1987); Carl Kaestle, *Pillars of the Republic: Common Schools and American Society, 1780–1860* (New York: Hill & Wang, 1983).

11. Walter Benjamin, "Theses on the Philosophy of History," in *Illuminations*, trans. Harry Zohn (New York: Schocken Books, 2007), 256.
12. Michael J. Dumas, "'Losing an Arm': Schooling as a Site of Black Suffering," *Race, Ethnicity and Education* 17, no. 1 (January 1, 2014): 1–29; Carter G. Woodson and Jarvis R. Givens, *The Mis-Education of the Negro*, ed. Henry Louis Gates (New York: Penguin Classics, 2023); Renato Constantino, "The Miseducation of the Filipino," *Journal of Contemporary Asia* 1, no. 1 (1970); W. E. B. Du Bois, "Does the Negro Need Separate Schools?," *Journal of Negro Education* 4, no. 3 (1935): 328–35; Zitkala-Ša, *American Indian Stories* (Washington, DC: Hayworth, 1921); Brenda J. Child, "The Boarding School as Metaphor," *Journal of American Indian Education* 57, no. 1 (2018): 37–57.
13. Eve Tuck and K. Wayne Yang, eds., *Toward What Justice? Describing Diverse Dreams of Justice in Education* (New York: Routledge, 2018).
14. James Baldwin, "The White Man's Guilt," *Ebony*, August 1965, in James Baldwin, *Collected Essays*, ed. Toni Morrison (New York: Library of America, 1998), 722–23.

INDEX

Page numbers of photographs appear in italics.

ABOUT THE AUTHOR

JARVIS R. GIVENS is a professor of education and of African and African American Studies at Harvard University. He is also a Leverhulme Visiting Professor at University College London's Institute of the Americas. Givens is the author of two books: *Fugitive Pedagogy: Carter G. Woodson and the Art of Black Teaching* and *School Clothes: A Collective Memoir of Black Student Witness.* He is also the cofounding faculty director of the Black Teacher Archive at Harvard. Givens is originally from Compton, California, and lives in Roxbury, Massachusetts.